Perspectives of Dissociative Identity Response:

Ethical, Historical, and Cultural Issues

Perspectives of Dissociative Identity Response:

Ethical, Historical, and Cultural Issues

Emily Christensen, PhD (Ed.)

2022

First Printing: 2022

ISBN-13: 978-1-948088-00-8
HWC Press, LLC
PO Box 3792
Bartlesville, OK 74006
emmasunshaw@gmail.com
www.SystemSpeak.org
Special discounts are available on quantity purchases by organizations, associations, educators, and others. For details, contact the publisher at the above listed address.

U.S. trade bookstores and wholesalers:
Please contact HWC Press.

Cover photo by Jason Leung on Unsplash

Typeface is "Octarine" by Alex Slobzheninov

Table of Contents

Foreword

by Laura S Brown, PhD, ABPP

One of the many joys and privileges of being asked to write a Foreward to a volume is that one gets a first look at what are often exciting, provocative, and important new contributions to a field of study. When Emily Christensen first asked me to contribute to this book at a time when I was not in a position to write an entire chapter, I asked her if, instead, I could do this job. I'm thrilled that she said yes, as reading the chapters that follow has precisely been that exciting, provocative, and important experience for which I had hoped when I took on this assignment.

I'll start with my positionalities in relationship to this book's topic, which I believe to be important here, as they are for anyone attempting to practice in a decolonial, liberatory, and culturally responsive manner, which was my own over-arching goal as a psychologist. In the course of more than forty years I have had the privilege to sit across the room from people who self-identified with various of the terms used in this book – some as people living with dissociation, some as having DID, some with complex trauma, some as Plural, some as systems, and one as "it's not *borderline* personality disorder, you idiot" (the idiot in question being yours truly, at the very beginning of four decades of stumbling through this work).

I have sat with people whose pain and confusion over how their lives were, and mostly were not, working. I have sat with people who were just fine with who and how they were, the rest of us be damned, and I have been in the presence of almost every position in between. My goal was always one of finding ways to invite people to change experiences of disempowerment into those of personal power, capacity, and self-knowledge, with little allegiance to any particular methodology for achieving those ends. I have always been more interested in finding pathology in structural forms of oppression than I have been in structures of how people are organized. Thus, I find the various models that have informed our field interesting, and I have been mostly curious about which one felt most right to whomever I was working with that particular hour (I have had several people who pledged allegiance to structural dissociation). I have no particular loyalty to the rightness of any of the various models that my colleagues have developed, although I see value in many of the paradigms for how people come to live as "there's more to me than meets the eye," to quote the favorite t-shirt of the first person I worked with who I knew *a priori* to be dissociative in how they were organized.

I was also, always, interested in people living through and coming out the other side of the debris of what had been heaped on them. The majority of the suffering people who sat across the room from me had had horror shows in their childhoods, and I was interested in not allowing the hands of those who had harmed them to pull a trigger or knot a noose in the here and now. A therapist, in short. Some of the people I have worked with are alive to tell the tale. Some are furious at me, which is not, in my lights, a bad outcome; others, not so much. None are dead at their own hands.

I know that some people who dissociate suffer from their dissociation, and some people have come to dissociation as a means of surviving intolerable suffering. I am among those who are not willing to call that suffering a disorder. I do not think that we need to pathologize people to offer them healing. As Christensen's lucid discussion of the history of how dissociation has been coded throughout time makes abundantly clear, Western culture has chosen to put dissociative suffering in the camp of pathology; she also makes clear that this is not, and has not always been, the only direction that a discussion of dissociation, and even its suffering, needs to go.

So what I know is that at the end of time, I, as a person who dissociates (not very effectively) from her painful emotions through vigorous applications of reading fiction, but who has little native skill at other forms of dissociation, has come to the task of reading this book and writing this forward with the same curious and humble spirit and very open mind that I hope I brought to my healing work. It should surprise no one who knows me, then, that the piece that leapt out at me most forcefully, and which I wish every person working in any way with anyone dissociative to read is Jamie Marich's *Cultural Humility* chapter.

I read it, I applauded, I cried, I realized that I had been among those who had perpetrated ignorance and distancing, and I sit here in deep gratitude for her/their clarity and honesty about what the "field" of dissociation "treatment" has done to harm people whose inner experiences we little understand. I bow in honor to her/their willingness to be out, and to claim the deepened expertise that can only emerge from lived experience, to place it on equal footing with whatever new alphabet soup of "evidence-based" therapies might be in a clinician's quiver.

I was poignantly reminded by that chapter of what it was like, as a young lesbian in psychology fifty years ago, being told that my being out about my identity would somehow detract from my credibility, as if lived experience were a so much lesser form of data than that allegedly "objectively" derived through the distant gaze of someone vaguely disapproving and uncomfortable with the human specimen under their microscope.

If there had no other chapters in this book it would have been worth the read. Yet, there are many other, and equally in their own ways, powerful, provocative, and important chapters in this book. In the interest of time, and my own well-being, I will mention only a few, hoping that no author will feel slighted if not mentioned; everything in this book is excellent, and some of it is more interesting to the person I am than are others. So here goes...

One of the take-home messages of this volume that I believe to be foundational, and to make this a book that all of us should be reading, is that *to be a person who is dissociative is to also be a person who has a wide range of other intersectional identities, which inform the experiences of dissociation, inform its visibility to others, and inform access to support in whatever form that person wants or needs it, be it therapeutic or otherwise*. One thing that I do think is true is that it is impossible to know a person without having a deep dive into their intersectional identities occur during the course of the relationship, be it therapy, friendship, marriage, you name it. I also know that there are aspects of intersectionality that are easy to see, and thus make misinformed assumptions about, while others are invisible, and on whose emotional toes we can tread, sometimes repeatedly and painfully, and even others with aspects of identities that are still invisible to the person who keeps wondering why their soul aches. This book does a stellar job of pointing the reader at various of the threads of intersectionality, and it reminds the reader that no one book can encompass all of them.

For instance, as this book helps us to see, it is one thing to be a cisgender woman with dissociative ego states, which is an collection of intersectionalities that falls squarely into both lay and "mental health" stereotypes about dissociative people, and another to be a trans woman who is dissociative, and who may encounter stigma and marginalizing in both trans and dissociative communities, and extreme skepticism on the part of the mental health "experts" from whom she is seeking support. As someone herself who has had to disrupt a narrative about whether a particular person with dissociative ego states was "really trans" on more than one occasion, I found the chapter on working with LGBTQ+ folks who are living with dissociation to be particularly relevant and thought-provoking. Since many people have dissociative ego states, including some of which are not the gender of the sex assigned at birth, and also have a gender orientation that is not in general congruence with the sex assigned at birth, being able to think in a more informed and sophisticated manner about the intersection of these experiences will liberate people who live in those intersections from having their lived experiences disbelieved due to not fitting into a clinician's pre-existing cognitive frameworks.

Even technology plays a role in how a person who contains multitudes comes to define themselves, or is defined by those around them. As Emily Christensen's chapter on the Plural community implies, to be a part of that community almost requires access to the internet; in parts of the world where getting online is dicey at best, a person's dissociative phenomenology may not be read as psychopathology, but that person may not have the chance to find people who identify as Plural.

I was also particularly intrigued by the chapter on Autism and dissociation. Being late-diagnosed with autism, especially in people assigned female at birth, is distressingly common. The stories of late-in-life-diagnosed autistic women and the stories of people living with dissociation that was well-hidden both from themselves and others both parallel and overlap. This chapter makes clear that each of these forms of neurodiversity – for is not the talent to dissociate, akin to the talent for perfect pitch, a kind of neurodiversity, just as is autism – can interact with one another, and that to accompany those in one group well we must consider how to accompany those in the other.

I could say more, and that would delay you, the reader, from entering into the company of a collection of brilliant, analytic minds that have synthesized so many topics into the central theme of dissociation. I applaud Emily Christensen for taking on what is a difficult task of editing a book (also known among my friends and colleagues as herding feral cats with the Microsoft Track Changes tool), and producing a volume that is coherent, comprehensive, and indispensable.

Cultural Humility in the Treatment and Healing of Dissociation

by Jamie Marich, Ph.D., LPCC-S, LICDC-CS, REAT, RYT-500

Who We Are

I/we am/are a woman/system in long-term recovery from an addictive and a dissociative disorder. And we cannot stand to hear most *experts* in the field of trauma and dissociative disorders speak, nor can we tolerate reading much of their work. Quite frankly it feels ugly, as though they are talking or writing about us without ever having really gotten to know us. There have been certain experiences at mainstream conferences where it feels like a proverbial *mean girl*, mansplainer, or person in authority of any gender is up on the stage talking down *at* the people they are claiming to serve. They impart, either implicitly or explicitly, that because of things like poor boundaries, intensity, and constant switching, that we cannot be trusted in our own healing. They suggest safeguards in working with us (like endless clinical inventories) that are inherently demeaning to minds like ours, minds that are anything but linear. They convey this tone of, "I know these people are damaged and you want to help them but be careful about getting too close." And some supposed experts have even suggested that people with Dissociative Identity Disorder can never really get better. But what I receive as most insulting are when some experts are up there on the stage clearly conveying knowledge about dissociation from their own lived experience, but they will not claim it as their own. They mask it as a "case."

For many years as my reputation grew in the field of EMDR therapy and traumatic stress studies, many of my EMDR colleagues asked me when I was going to develop a course on dissociation. I was very dissatisfied with what was available on the market and at conferences, yet I stopped short. I knew that I could not teach on dissociation until I was fully ready to be "out" about my own disorder and treatment, and I could teach from that place of candidness and transparency. Like many *comings out*, the process was gradual. I dipped my toe into the waters back in 2011 in my first book, *EMDR Made Simple,* mentioning that significant dissociation was part of my trauma profile when I presented for my own EMDR therapy. As my confidence grew in offering trainings over the next several years, I began to speak about it more boldly where appropriate, even naming that I carried a formal diagnosis.

After one presentation, a fellow professional approached me and said, with a mixture of gratitude and horror, "I cannot believe that a speaker was that open about her own experiences with dissociation."

The conversation that followed, coupled with my continually mounting experiences of uneasiness at conferences, further confirmed that I had to come out about the way that my mind works, fully and unapologetically. After my separation and eventual divorce in 2017, when my now ex-husband tried to use my dissociation against me, I knew the time was right. He tried and he failed, and I finally knew that, in the words of the late poet and activist Audre Lorde, my silence was not protecting me. So, in 2018 I published my official coming out article and began offering courses on how I believe dissociation ought to be trained based on my lived experience—in a qualitative, process-oriented manner.

Since coming out and continuing to speak out more boldly, I have received so much appreciation from other professionals who have felt more emboldened to come out themselves, or to at least practice from a place of trust in their own experience. I believe it will take more active participation in a cultural shift towards authentic openness for us to truly find each other. Within the EMDR community specifically, many of my senior colleagues have offered tremendous words of affirmation and support for my decision and my advocacy. As expected, others chose not to address it with me, and several have done it in a snide manner. I know there is a fear that I "share too much," as revealed to me in an email from one of the established names in trauma and dissociation treatment. Yet even when I read this email, it felt like I was reading a reflection of her discomfort with vulnerability. Every step of my coming out has been guided by my own fabulous therapist who has my own interests at heart, and we constantly evaluate that delicate dance between boundaries and vulnerability, and between transparency and privacy. Anything I share has been thoroughly worked through in therapy, and I do not mind it being out there in the public forum, especially if there is a chance someone else can benefit from my being so "out."

This leader's email also imparted a fearful tone that by overpowering my teaching with lived experience, I was downplaying the scientific power of what I can offer. I have heard this criticism from others too—that by underemphasizing the gains that she and others had made to regard dissociative disorders legitimately in the scientific community at large, I was getting in the way of progress. I have heard and can even accept that in the early days of dissociation studies, too much phenomenology (the study of lived experience that rejects any scientific notions that the lived experience can be quantified) made dissociation doubters question the veracity of dissociation and the legitimacy of dissociative disorders. The science and peer-reviewed research was needed to legitimize what we *do* in naming and treating dissociation and putting an end to the so-called "Memory Wars" and debates about the authenticity of dissociated memories.

I am not a doubter of science and agree that these more empirical measures facilitated people like me being taken more seriously by the mental health establishment. Yet as I continuously state in interviews and throughout my teaching, we have put so much emphasis on the science that the soul has gone missing. We forget that mental health is not a pure "science," and ought not be considered as such. There is an art to interacting with human beings, and that is best informed by embracing the principles of phenomenology (lived experience) and cultural humility.

What is Cultural Humility?

There is a construct in multi-cultural counseling and in the widening fields of diversity that we as professionals working with dissociation must heed—cultural humility. Most, if not all of us as clinicians, took some type of course in *cultural competency* during our graduate studies, or at least read a book or took a continuing education workshop. Tervalon and Murray-Garcia (1998) coined an alternative term to cultural competence in the nineties, arguing that *competence* suggests you have reached some kind of benchmark - even that you can stop learning because you've mastered what you need to know.

On the contrary, *cultural humility* suggests that we must adopt an attitude of constantly being willing to learn, especially from individuals whose experiences are different from our own. Tervalon and Murray-Garcia (1998) define cultural humility "not as a discrete end point but as a lifelong commitment to self-evaluation and critique to address redressing power imbalances and to developing mutual beneficial and non-paternalistic partnerships with communities on behalf of individuals and defined populations" (p. 123). If you are white person or a member of a dominant culture, for instance, practicing cultural humility involves really listening to those oppressed populations. This listening must include an openness to receiving what they say that they need to bring about change without being steamrolled by what you, especially if you are in a position of authority, thinks is a good idea. Cultural humility also requires that we go beyond just doing a few nice things as a token. Rather, cultural humility challenges us a step farther and asks, how do we work to actively dismantle oppressive systems?

There are a few other insights on cultural humility that we can further examine as a context for unpacking how a greater sense of humility can be practiced in working with people who dissociate. The National Institute of Health (NIH) defines cultural humility, adopted from Tervalon and Murray-Garcia, as "a life-long process of self-reflection and self-critique whereby the individual not only learns about another's culture, but one starts with an examination of their own cultural identities." The Hogg Foundation for Mental Health (Sufrin, 2019), in discussing cultural humility, rightly reminds us that being humble is a state of being free from pride or arrogance. And there is a growing body of literature that demonstrates the impact of cultural humility practices in improving healthcare practices, namely in increasing trustworthiness of the practitioner as rated by consumers (Yaeger & Bauer-Wu, 2013), and reducing LGBTQ+ health disparities in end-of-life care (Spirk & Gentile, 2020).

Listening to Those with Dissociative Disorders as an Act of Cultural Humility

While there is much more to mine in the literature on cultural humility, there are several key points that we can take from these summaries that can inform the path forward for how we practice a greater sense of humility as therapists, helpers, and healers in working with people who dissociate. The greatest message is that if we are competent in working with dissociation, or even specialize in it, we must never stop learning, especially from those we most need to learn from—the people we serve. While it is important that we never treat our clients as our sole educators about dissociative disorders (just as we must never treat clients of other cultures as sole informants about their culture), we must regard them as experts on their own lives. Keeping this open mind and heart, in addition to absorbing the necessary training and reading that we need, can promote a higher degree of collaborative care.

Secondly, we as professionals (even if we are a professional with dissociative disorders ourselves) must engage in active listening with our clients. While we can facilitate the process of helping a client better understand their system (where applicable), always keep in mind that they are the ones living with their system. The expert-patient paradigm simply must be replaced with one of greater collaboration, even with clients whose behaviors may cause us alarm or even a sense of fear. In my vast experience offering EMDR therapy consultation to blooming EMDR clinicians, I can identify this fear factor as a tremendous barrier.

Clinicians may fear what their client will do or how they may act out if they rapidly switch. There is a great deal of fear that they will not be able to get the client "back" if they totally dissociate to the point of collapse. Thus, it can become tempting to over plan to assure that these demonstrations of dissociation will not happen, or to have a perfect plan in place if they do. Part of this fear is why, I believe, there is such an emphasis in certain circles on evaluating for dissociation utilizing testing tools to guide the treatment. Yet, as me or anyone else with a system like mine will tell you, asking us to take that dense of an inventory is re-traumatizing, *and* part of having a dissociative mind is needing a great deal of flexibility from your provider, even if it is flexibility within the structure.

The answer, for me, rests in another concept from cultural humility—doing your own work to evaluate your biases and to know yourself and your own blocks in relationship to the material. I continue to be amazed at how many clinicians I consult with who operate from biases or downright misinformation about dissociation and dissociative disorders. Within the EMDR community especially you will hear this idea that if a person has a certain score on the Dissociative Experiences Scale (DES) or the MID, then they are not appropriate for EMDR. My feeling on this has always been that people with high scores on either are usually the ones who can benefit most from EMDR therapy *if* the clinician offering the EMDR therapy is not afraid of dissociation *and* is willing to consult as needed and not operate from biases.

My skin also crawled when learning about another trainer in the EMDR community who seemed to teach that you have to intervene immediately at the first signs of dissociation to shut down the reprocessing of the trauma using insensitive methods to "bring a person back" (i.e., clicking fingers in the face, saying things like "You are safe now...look at me, look into my eyes."). In reality, dissociation is much more nuanced than that. Many people can, and do, reprocess in a light degree of dissociation—for many of us, it is the only way we can go further into the work. There can be this sense imparted that dissociation is automatically bad and somehow a dirty word that must be avoided for good work to be done. Yet what if clinicians can learn to pivot and realize that dissociative processes have kept people like me alive and even thriving in many instances up until the point we came into your offices. So why wouldn't we continue to work with the tool of dissociation to further help us/our system reach our goals? We are just yearning for clinicians who will dance this dance with us instead of being afraid of us or constantly "othering" us.

The primary thesis of my clinical training on dissociation is recent years is that for clinicians to be more effective in working with dissociation, we must eliminate the "us vs. them" barrier that even many *experts* in the field of dissociation studies have helped to create. To do this, we must identify and name the ways that we dissociate in our own lives—even if you do not have a disorder, you dissociate in some way, more regularly than you think. And, if you do not have a dissociative disorder, there are still likely parts or aspects of yourselves that interplay with each other on a regular basis.

Understanding all these interworking for yourself, perhaps guided by your own therapist, can assist greatly in eliminating your fear around working with dissociative clients. They may be displaying more extreme tendencies than you, yet it is all part of the same pattern. As expressed by Elizabeth Howell (2008), "In my view, DID is simply an extreme version of the dissociative structure of the psyche that characterizes us all" (p. ix).

Perhaps notice what it feels like to read a statement like Howell's. Does it resonate for you, or do you feel challenged or maybe even offended in some way that you too, dissociate? I do not judge you if it is the latter because so much of the conventional training in our field literally teaches you to dissociate from your humanity as a way to survive in this field. Yet, you are a being who dissociates just like your clients—dissociation is a normal part of the human experience. Learning to embrace it and dance with it can be critical not just in helping you be more effective for your clients, but also in helping you live a more present and fuller life for yourself. You can refer to the resources list at the end of this chapter to reference my original coming out article, which includes more information about beginning to work with your dissociative profile.

Lastly, we as clinicians who work with dissociation must ask what we are doing to dismantle these power imbalances in the mental health professions and in society at large; power imbalances that inevitably harm those with dissociative disorders. For me, writing a chapter of this nature is only a part of the larger work. Speaking out against conferences and organizations that do not include consumers (i.e., clients, especially clients who are not clinicians themselves) in their proceedings or in their decision-making is another practice in which I engage. Or you are answering the call to be more vocal within your professional organization about including voices of people who are out and open about their dissociative disorders and other mental health issues.

For those of you with a heart for social justice, you also know that there is bigger work ahead. For instance, it is common practice in American mental health for the best, most trained clinicians to go into private practice because they become overburdened and frustrated with how they are treated (and paid) in the agency system. While clinicians have a right to do what is best for them, what ends up happening is that people with dissociative disorders who tend to need the most high-quality care cannot afford it, especially if they are uninsured. And so many talented private practitioners, frustrated with the ever-harrowing bureaucracy and unfairness of working with managed care end up setting up their practices as self-pay only. While many can afford this and it can certainly make life less stressful for clinicians (and we deserve less stress, to be clear), the people most in need of the best care often cannot access it.

I will speak plainly: I do not have an easy answer for how we dismantle the current mental health system and build one that is newer, more trauma-informed, more dissociation-competent, and ultimately more effective. Yet I do know that the system is a big part of the problem in what is keeping people stuck, especially in my home country of the United States of America. Improving access to basic needs and other necessary social services is also an imperative for more trauma-focused care, and people in my profession often fail to see the connection.

I know it can feel frustrating to tackle all of this and I continue to work with the dilemma of how to do my part in bringing about a change in our systems while still needing to work within what already exists. For me this has meant using my privilege, especially as an established person, to speak out when I am invited to chapters like these. Not to mention bending the proverbial ear of elected officials and using my social media platform to inspire people to take control of their own health and healing as much as possible. This can also mean donating money, if you are able, to causes you support that are doing much of the heavy advocacy lifting on a policy level, especially those organizations that regularly involve consumers and clients. The work of An Infinite Mind, sponsor of the Healing Together Conference on dissociation that actively brings together scholars, clinicians, clients, and the general public is an action-based organization that is near and dear to my heart.

In the words of my collaborator Dr. Kellie Kirksey, a brilliant African American educator on issues of social justice and mental health, "What is your action?" I like to ask this question of myself regularly, as a form of inventory—what action am I taking to bring about the world I want to see for people like me on a daily basis? And I would ask you to adopt the same question into your daily practice as an ultimate practice in cultural humility.

Concluding Thoughts

I am currently in the process of writing my own book on navigating the dance of dissociation as part of my "Made Simple" series which started with *EMDR Made Simple* back in 2011. With a working title of *Dissociation Made Simple* (North Atlantic Books, 2023), my book project encouraged me to dust off my cap as a phenomenological researcher (the primary method practiced during my doctoral studies). In this book project I interviewed over fifty individuals who responded to my call for participation. Numerous insights will be relayed in the final work on just how many different ways there are for a person with dissociative conditions to heal and to thrive in life. Many of the participants speak openly and candidly about what they want the mental health and medical establishment to know about people like them. A common theme is that they wish their providers would listen more...

While many of the participants who came forward are people who I did not know, I also invited several people who I know and respect in the field of dissociation studies to be interviewed for the work.

One of those participants was Dr. Curtis Rounazoin, a Southern California-based psychologist and EMDR therapy trainer with over forty years of experience in the field. I remember him first catching my attention when he trained one of my friends in EMDR therapy. She returned from her training reporting such refreshingly candid thoughts on how to approach dissociation, I knew I liked him, solely from her report! As I came of age as a leader in my own right in the EMDR community, I got to know Curt even better. He was truly one of the most supportive and affirming figures to me when I came out about my own diagnosis and treatment, and my system has always regarded him as a very safe person for us.

Like many clinicians of his generation, Curt did not have a great deal of information about how to work with dissociation and dissociative identity disorder when he first entered the field. Though he eventually obtained the training he needed, he has always readily identified his own clients as his greatest educators.

Says Rounazoin, “Most of the stuff I’ve learned how to do I’ve learned from my patients. I tell my colleagues all the time, find a dissociative client and really listen to them, that will make you a good therapist.”

When Curt said this during his interview for the project, my draw dropped, and chills overcame my body. I wish more therapists would approach us like this, even the experts who may have become so caught up in their models and ways of operating, they have forgotten to really listen to the client who is in front of them. Even as someone with a dissociative mind and diagnosis, I can admit my guilt in this area and embracing an attitude of cultural humility asks me to constantly look at myself and do better.

What is your action? This action can be something as simple as listening to their request for a modification or a different approach when they are not feeling right about the skill or the direction of treatment. This action can be attending to the therapeutic relationship above all else, knowing that boundaries and transparency about what your role is (a therapist) and isn’t (a replacement parent) creates a safe enough space for your client. Your action can be knowing when you can share knowledge you have learned about certain models or approaches with a client and maybe even use some of them, but also knowing when a greater degree of flexibility and humanity is required in how you deliver them. Your action can be intentionally listening instead of leaning constantly into what you know—recognizing that this leaning in might be an expression of your own insecurity to do good work with the client. Speaking for myself, this can be the greatest barrier to me being a good listener.

What keeps you from really listening to and learning from your clients? As a major step in your own development as a culturally humble therapist in delivering services to people who dissociate, I ask you to engage in this inventory with an open mind and heart. Put your ego aside as much as possible and write or reflect honestly. Just as we ask our clients to do, see your own therapist, or visit with a colleague for support, if you find yourself getting stuck.

REFERENCES

Howell, E. 2008. The dissociative mind. New York: Routledge.

Spirk, P., & Gentile, D. 2020. Cultural humility: A way to reduce LGBTQ health disparities at the end of life. *American Journal of Hospice and Palliative Medicine, 37*(6), 404-408.

Sufrin, J. 2019. Cultural humility: 3 things to know [blog]. *Hogg Foundation for Mental Health*. Accessed 18 October, 2021, from https://hogg.utexas.edu/3-things-to-know-cultural-humility

Tervalon, M. & Murray Garcia, J. 1998. Cultural humility versus cultural competence: A critical distinction in defining physician training outcomes in multicultural education. *Journal of Health Care for the Poor and Underserved, 9*(2), 117-25.

Yeager, K. & Bauer-Wu, S. 2013. Cultural humility: Essential foundations for clinical researchers. *Applied Nursing Research, 26*(4), doi: 10.1016/j.apnr.2013.06.008

RESOURCES

Trauma Made Simple (Web-Based Resources for Clinicians and Clients)

www.traumamadesimple.com

Dissociation and Addiction Resources (from The Institute for Creative Mindfulness)

www.instituteforcreativemindfulness.com/dissociation-addiction-resources/

Dr. Jamie's "Coming Out Article:" A Personal and Professional Take on Dissociative Disorders (The Mighty, 2018)

https://themighty.com/2018/12/dissociative-disorders-professional-personal-perspective/

Historical Context of Dissociative Disorders

by Emily Christensen, PhD, LCPC, S

The history of Dissociative Identity Disorder (DID) goes back at least 4,000 years (Robertson, 2019). Ancient cultures describe many cases of dissociative identity disorder through their stories and art. Many of these are reframed as "demonic possession" or misrepresented through Westernized and Christianized documents. Some cultures still view their healers and shamans as multiple, without it even having any negative connotation, until they were persecuted through genocide by Western religions such as three hundred years of Inquisition. For the focus of this chapter, we will focus on more recent history and the Western medicine perspective.

Both Elizabeth Howell (2011) and Judith Herman (2015) give beautiful histories of the treatment of hysteria – and later dissociation. They explore the medical writers of the early 1900's, which led to the identification of post-war "moral invalids" (Leri, 1919). They discuss World War I British Psychologist Charles Myers identifying "shell shock" as a clear trauma response after the war (Myers, 1940). Myers was also the first to use the term *emotional personalities*, referring to behavior during flashbacks and trauma-related nightmares, and *apparently normal personalities* who are detached from the experiences of reliving trauma. However, Barach (2019) clarified that while these terms were later adopted by Structural

Dissociation Theory, Myers himself did not use them in reference to multiplicity:

> "I think he used the term "personality" in a much looser sense than we think of parts or alters, [as] we use in DID. He was not talking about survivors of childhood trauma. Myers was not talking about parts or alters with different names and ages. He was talking about veterans. An example of this is a veteran with PTSD working as an auto mechanic who hits the ground when there is a loud noise at work, such as a tire popping suddenly off its rim. This is an automatic response without thinking or planning, then leaves the veteran feeling embarrassed."

The first group therapy and peer support groups for veterans developed as "rap groups" following the war in Vietnam (Herman, 2015; Norman, 1989). It was women themselves, then, who had not been to war but recognized war in their own domestic lives, and women themselves, then, who began to organize their own peer support and clinical support teams that later developed into the first rape crisis centers (Herman, 2015). Judith Herman wrote, "The pioneering research on the psychological effects of victimization was carried by women who saw themselves as active and committed participants in the movement."

What is missing in the literature is a simple documentation of the unfolding history of the actual diagnostic categories. This is primarily because much of it has happened so recently that most clinicians lived it. New generations of clinicians and physicians, however, are not taught this history nor are they given the psychodynamic foundation to understand these diagnoses in context – which begins with lived experience.

History of Lived Experience

Jeanne Féry (1584) was one of the first women to document her own her own multiple personalities (Van der Hart, O., Lierens, R. & Goodwin, J. 1996). Her symptoms correlate with the modern diagnosis of Multiple Personality Disorder (MPD), now renamed DID, in her reported experience of multiple alters with names and different identities. She listed their features, gave descriptions of their roles and ages and behaviors, and demonstrated different knowledges, capacities and skill sets depending on which identity was presenting. She experienced different voices in her own head and spoke in different voices when these identities presented. She herself documented that they resulted from childhood abuse.

Ten years after Jeanne Fery, Theophrastes Paracelsus grew up to be a Swiss physician, alchemist, and astrologer of the German Renaissance. He was a pioneer in several aspects of the "medical revolution" of the Renaissance and lectured at the University of Basel. One of the cases he reportedly spoke and published about was a woman who had amnesia about an alternate personality who stole her own money (Bliss, 1980).

In 1623, the story of Sister Benedetta was published. Sister Benedetta was a woman who was supposedly possessed by three angelic boys who would beat her to cause chronic pain. When they took control of her body, each would speak with a different dialect and tone of voice while using different facial expressions. Benedetta had amnesia for some of their actions, including a sexual relationship that they had initiated. Like Jeanne Fery, Sister Benedetta suffered from self harm and disordered eating. Her parents had also shown signs of dissociation and had been rumored to be possessed, and one of the “angels” was frozen at age 9, the same age at which Sister Benedetta's father had died. Her symptoms had become uncontrollable, and she had been sent to the convent (van der Hart, Lierens, Goodwin, 1996).

In 1791, Eberhardt Gemelin published the first known detailed case study of multiple personality, which he called “exchanged personality” in reference to the switching between two or more personalities (Putnam, 1989). The 20-year-old German woman could speak perfect French and speak German with a French accent when she was “the French Woman”, but only knew German when she was “the German Woman”. The French Woman knew everything the German woman did, but the German Woman didn’t know what happened to her while the French Woman was out. Eventually these two could switch intentionally when prompted by him, but only after some time working together - they could not do so early in their discovery.

Benjamin Rush is known as the “Father of American Psychiatry” and was the only signer of both the *Declaration of Independence* and the *Constitution*. He was the chief surgeon of the continental army and worked with many children and adults who suffered trauma because of the war. In 1809, he published a four-volume set of books about treating mind disorders, called “Medical Inquiries and Observations of the Mind”. In these essays, Dr. Rush included the concept of multiple personalities, which he referred to as a “doubling of consciousness”. He reasoned that the cause of this happening in trauma patients was a “disconnection between the two hemispheres of the brain”. This was the first sign of hope for survivors, that the shame of the impact of DID was not entirely theirs to carry, and the first validation received of the neurobiological impact of trauma.

In 1811, Samuel Mitchel identified both Mary Reynolds and Rachel Baker as multiple personality patients (Putnam, 1989). The most famous was Mary, whom he first wrote about in 1816, with a description of Mary's symptoms as "preaching in her sleep, as well as writing poetry and music." While none of those activities are in and of themselves signs of mental illness, these were unusual behaviors for her and activities she was otherwise unable to do.

Dr. Mitchel expanded on this account in 1860, in an article entitled "The Strange Case of Mary Reynolds" in *Harper's New Monthly Magazine*. In this account, he reported that Mary was born to a devout family in England in 1785. The family later moved to Pennsylvania, and she grew up as a "reserved and quiet and melancholy child". Then, inexplicably, she became blind and deaf for six weeks at age 19. Three months following this, she "suddenly forgot things she had learned", even having to re-learn how to read and write. No longer a reserved and melancholy child, Dr. Mitchel described her now as "buoyant, witty, fond of company, and a lover of nature." Then, just as inexplicably, she reverted back to her quiet and melancholy self, without memory of either of the other two incidents. Dr. Mitchell reported that Mary Reynolds seemed to alternate these three identities, with no memory shared between them, for the next sixteen years. She then maintained her "more excited" state until her death at age 61, but still without recall of what she experienced during the other two states of consciousness. This was the first case study that described some of the more functional aspects of multiplicity, that many of the separately developed talents and skills are just as valid and not unusual or maladaptive in and of themselves.

In 1840, Antoine Despine published a monograph that documented the story of an 11-year-old Swiss girl, Estelle, who initially presented with paralysis and sensitivity to touch. She later displayed another personality who was quite different, could walk, liked to play, and could not tolerate her mother's presence. Despine documented his treatment course, which he reported cured the child, and many of which are recognized as valid still today. This was the early description of our body memories, of our differing abilities based on the trauma response in the brain and which parts are active, and the connection between the severity of the impact of Adverse Childhood Experiences and chronic pain illness and autoimmune disorders.

Eugene Azam, a professor of neurology with a large interest in hypnosis, published the most detailed account of multiple personality in the 1800's. The woman, Felida X, had three different personalities and he detailed what they acted like, who they were, and what caused them to appear.

Felida X was born in 1843, lost her father in infancy and had a difficult childhood. She exhibited three different personalities, each considering itself to be Felida's normal state and the others to be abnormal. The second personality state first manifested when Felida was 13 years old and suffered none of the physical illnesses that the first personality suffered. Initially, switching was reported to happen almost every day after a pain in the temple and a profound sleep for two to three minutes but the frequency of switching decreased over time to the point that it would happen only every 25 to 30 days and last only a few hours at a time. The third personality, which appeared only on occasion, suffered from anxiety attacks and hallucinations. At one point, the first personality was pregnant without explanation and the second personality emerged and took responsibility for the pregnancy.

Still, even after a great deal of research into the idea of multiple personalities, people who had symptoms like those of dissociative identity disorder were either seen as having epileptic fits or being possessed. He followed the case for 35 years and published his book about "alternating personalities" in the "double consciousness" in 1887.

This is the early documentation as alters not just presenting as real, but perceiving themselves as real within their own awareness and consciousness. It is documentation of interactions that hint at an inner world with rules and codes and dynamics by which they lived and took turns, whether that was revealed or known or not. It tells the story of explicit switching and passive influence and natural consequences for a shared body.

In 1882, the first person officially diagnosed with Multiple Personality Disorder, instead of the previously French diagnosis of "double personality" was Louis Auguste Vivet. He had been physically abused and neglected as a child and had frequent "attacks of hysteria." One such these occurred when he was 17 and bitten by a snake. He lost use of his legs for almost one year, and when the use returned after a 50 hour attack, he didn't remember any of the physicians who had been treating him in an asylum for the last month or any of his fellow patients. His manner, morals, and appetite were different as well. Following additional attacks, the next year, his character would change from impulsive and dangerous to calm and gentle. In 1884, he had another attack that left him gentle of manner but unable to walk, and yet another attack returned the use of his legs but left him quarrelsome and inclined to steal as he had done as a child in order to survive. Amnesia for intervals spanning episodes was noted. By 1888, he had been recorded as having 10 personality states, each of which were different in character, memory, and somatic symptoms (Faure, Kersten, Koopman, & Van der Hart, 1997).

This case study tells the story of individual alters, followed and observed over long periods of time, detailing their individuality, their reality, and even their humanity. This was not the delusion of one dominant personality creating a bunch of lesser ones. This was a group of distinct insiders sharing a body, taking distinct turns fronting. This case was also significant because it was a *male patient*, which meant the disorder could not be blamed on the uterus.

Development of Diagnoses

Prior to this case, these people were not diagnosed as either MPD or DID. If anything, they would have gotten – and some of them did receive - a label of *hysteria*, common since Ancient Egypt characterized the syndrome two thousand years before. Hysteria was described as a manifestation of multiple physical and behavioral dysfunctions (North,

2010 and 2005). This diagnostic label was assigned to women all the way until 1951, when it was renamed "Briquet's Syndrome" (see below).

It was Dr. Thomas Sydenham (England) who declared in 1697 that hysteria was not just a physical disorder (Gomes and Engelhardt, 2014). He classified it as an *emotional disorder*, specifically. He also is the one who clarified hysteria's source was actually in the central nervous system, rather than the uterus.

19th Century France gave us Paul Briquet. He was considered an expert in hysteria, having treated 430 cases over ten years of his career. In 1859, he announced that the physical symptoms of hysteria could not be medically explained (Purtell, Robins, & Cohen, 1951). It was his *Traité de l'Hystérie* that agreed with Sydenham in that hysteria had nothing to do with the reproductive system or genitalia at all, and Briquet confirmed the root of the disorder as being brain-based (Mai and Merskey, 1981).

At the time, however, his work was temporarily drowned out by the development of the psychoanalytic movement. We often think of Freud's contributions to this bit of history, but he was a "struggling 29-year-old Viennese physician" when he "received a traveling fellowship to study in Paris with Europe's most renowned neurologist, Jean Martin Charcot. Freud was later to remember the 4½-month stay... as catalytic in turning him toward the practice of medical psychopathology and away from a less financially promising career in research neurology" (Aguayo, 1986). It was Charcot who held court in society with his demonstrations of women fainting from hysteria – and his public use of hypnosis to treat them. This is a piece we will come back to in a later chapter, but that being said, it was still Freud who distinguished psychoanalysis as its own treatment approach apart from the famed hypnosis treatment (Baker & Nash, 2008).

Psychoanalytic history deserves more attention to it than can be included in this chapter, but what we must include is this psychodynamic process.

> "According to Freud's theory, therapists were stand-ins. The feelings directed at them unresolved remnants of their client's most profound and unresolved feelings from infancy and childhood. People had a tendency to unconsciously create and then globally apply these templates, which had been forged in early childhood relationships. These internal models shaped people's perceptions and expectations and all the significant relationships that came afterward… In short, these templates provided the emotional rules for how to function in relationships" (Lott, 1999).

That leads us to the famous case of another woman, *Anna O*. We told a small part of this story on the *System Speak* podcast in 2021:

> "Anna O is a famous case going all the way back to the time of Freud. But it wasn't Freud that saw her, it was Dr. Breuer that saw her. She was a young Jewish woman who still lived with her family because she wasn't married. Her father was very sick and in the process of dying. It was her role as the oldest daughter of the family to sit up with him during the night. So this is how it began.

"And as his illness continued, and she began to feel more and more helpless. She had been very close to her father, by all accounts that we know. But there's not a great deal that she shared, that remains of her own words about what happened. The longer she had to nurse him overnight, and the sicker he got, over this, these period of weeks that he was very ill and dying, she became more distraught about not just his condition, but her helplessness in not being able to save him or to help him.

"She started having some hallucinations. She started having some symptoms in her body where her body literally couldn't move. But notably, these symptoms matched what she experienced.

"So, for example, there was a time when her father asked her what time it was, but she was crying because he was so sick and dying. She didn't want her father to know she was crying. She also she couldn't see the hands on her watch because of the tears in her eyes. And when that happened, she started having episodes where she couldn't see at all.

"There was another time where she couldn't hand him something that he needed, and so then she couldn't feel her hand anymore.

"She started having these physical symptoms that matched emotional experiences that happened to her, and things escalated until she was basically not functioning anymore.

> "So, her family called Dr. Breuer, and Dr. Breuer came out to meet with her. He ended up doing analysis with her. But this was back in the days where there were zero boundaries at all. So he would sit with her for hours and hours just letting her share anything she wanted to share, listening to her talk. They would go for carriage rides, he would help her to eat, and he was very attentive to her. She basically transferred her feelings of love for her father to loving Dr. Breuer.
>
> "Anna O had a lot of very dissociative symptoms. Her case is mentioned in the context of the book *In Session* (Ibid) because it's really one of the first times we have documented about the therapeutic relationship and what it is that's curing her. Is it actually the talking that is helping people feel better? Or is it the relationship that helps people feel better?"

This therapeutic relationship is critical in treating trauma disorders, which we will explore in later chapters.

In 1918, multiple personalities were first acknowledged in the predecessor of the DSM under Hysterical Psychoneuroses, a subgroup of Psychoneuroses and Neuroses that included alternate states of consciousness acting on normally unknown desires, amnesia, and sensory and motor disturbances ("Statistical Manual for the use of Institutions for the Insane," 1918).

In 1919, Pierre Janet published his work, *Les Médications Psychologiques*, which included several detailed accounts of multiple personalities. One was the story of Leonie, a poor and "mundane" woman trapped in married life. When Janet began hypnotic regression, she underwent an unprecedented metamorphosis into a lively, boisterous, and sarcastic woman who emphatically repudiated all associations with the 'normative' stream of consciousness. As if having escaped her prison, the second personality evoked her quick-wittedness and intellectual superiority in claimed biological and psychological independence from the first; her argument rested on the internal perspective that the cerebral chasm separating the two was far too great to assume that they were one and the same person. She even said that her children belonged to her but that the husband was a complete stranger. In time, a third personality materialized, and she was far more narcissistic and pejorative, even referring to the first personality as "a good and stupid woman, but not me" and the second as "a crazy creature". After seven months of working with her, Janet realized that the fragmented personality system resembled an actualization hierarchy: the third alter knew about the second and the first; the second only about the first; and the first was completely oblivious of the existence of the others.

Leonie appeared to have three or more personality states including a child alter named Nichette, a childhood name. In the case of Lucie, who also reportedly had three personality states, there was an alter personality named Adrienne who would seem to experience flashbacks of a traumatic childhood event. In the case of Rose, she would suffer from a variety of somnambulistic states. In some, she was paralyzed and in others she was able to walk.

Janet wrote extensively about traumatic memories (*primary idées fixes*), and how these memories could be subdivided and so cause functional loss, but also cause sensorimotor and perceptual changes ("mental accidents"). From these changes in sensory experiences, functioning, and perception, he proposed that the mind could then present alternate personalities that were secondary to the first - much like dreams might replay themes from throughout the day. He documented how, in several cases, some "subpersonalities" shared memories and experiences, while others did not. He was also the first to explore which personalities got to "drive" the body (fronting), and why. He was also the first to propose that the severity of fragmentation depended upon the depth of traumatization, an idea which prevails still today.

In 1906, Mortin Prince published the Christine Beauchamp case in "The Dissociation of a Personality". Beauchamp allegedly had three personality states including one calling herself Sally who was childlike. Sally differed greatly from a very regressed alter called Idiot. Prince wrote about the case in paper of *The Journal of Abnormal Psychology* which "was the most quoted reference in the history of the illness". After this documentation, however, no further mention of multiple personalities was mentioned in the journal until Prince's published famous account of Christine Costner Sizemore. In 1957, the case was made into a film starring Joanne Woodward playing the title role in *The Three Faces of Eve*.

It wasn't until Ferenczi's "Confusion of Tongues" paper in 1932 that dissociation and subsequent splitting of the personality were explicitly linked to childhood abuse. However, at the time, any theory involving the subconscious mind was unpopular, and few paid attention to what Ferenczi had discovered - and what Jeanne Fery herself had written in 1584.

There is an unusual gap in the literature, then, following Stengel's famous statement in 1943 that the condition was "extinct". This statement is often used to explain the gap in literature, and the poor presentation of the article and misapplication of the conclusion confused many who then misunderstood the article to mean that the condition is no longer studied or believed to happen as previously documented for over four hundred years. This is entirely false, however.

It is true that the article was published during the transition between French-speaking psychiatry and German-speaking psychiatry and the development of English-speaking psychiatry as its own field. But also, when Stengel wrote about dissociation, he was referring to the external version (fugues) and the internal version (multiple personality) (Stengel, 1943). Then, in the 1970's, H. Ellenberger published a paper entitled "The Discovery of the Unconscious: The History and Evolution of Dynamic Psychiatry" focused on multiple personality disorder. Many clinicians continued to collaborate and work toward establishing official diagnostic criteria for the disorder. Margareta Bowers along with six other contributors published "Therapy of Multiple Personality" in 1971, which included outlines and rules for treatment.

Further, the 1970's also offered the first workshops and trainings for how to treat multiple personalities. Pioneers in the field, such as Dr. Wilbur (of Sybil fame), Ralph B. Allison, and David Caul, M.D. developed programs and treatment workshops to teach other clinicians how to recognize, diagnose, and treat the condition - which naturally led to an increase in the number of cases diagnosed and reported, once treatment for it became available.

The stigma of "hysteria" was not acknowledged until 1951, where there was an attempt to rename it "Briquet's Syndrome". It was classified as a syndrome because there were so many different symptoms possible, but only included 25 of the original 59 symptoms on the diagnostic checklist for the disorder (Purtell, Robins, and Cohen, 1951). Thus, the use of "hysteria" was paused in 1952, with the publication of the first *Diagnostic and Statistical Manual* (DSM), until 1968 "when the American Psychiatric Association (APA) and World Health Organization (WHO) put out identical nosologies under different names: DSM-II and ICD-8" (O'Neil, 2021).

The DSM-First Edition in 1952 included: Psychoneurotic Reactions, Anxiety Reaction, Dissociative Reaction, Conversion Reaction, Phobic Reaction, Obsessive-Compulsive Reaction, Depressive Reaction, and Psychoneurotic Reaction. As mentioned, the DSM-II and ICD-8 both came out in 1968 and were identical – including the re-emergence of "hysteria" in the diagnosis of "Hysterical Neurosis" that encompassed both Conversion and Dissociation (Conversion Type and Dissociative Type). "In order to preserve the DSM-I distinction between dissociative and conversion reactions, DSM-II recommended specifying Conversion or Dissociative Type in making the diagnosis" (Ibid). Other diagnoses included Depersonalization Neurosis (its own neurosis) and Hypochondriacal Neurosis.

The ICD-9 was released in 1977, three years before the DSM-III (1980). ICD-9 shifted focus to "Neurotic Disorders", which included Hysteria again. However, "it dropped the conversion/dissociative types in favor of a grab-bag" (O'Neil, 2021). Conversion-type items now included Astasia-abasia,

Hysterical, and Conversion Hysteria/Reaction. Dissociative-type items included: Dissociative Reaction/State, Ganser Syndrome, with "Multiple Personality" last on the list. Other diagnoses included: Compensation Neurosis, which "later became factitious disorder ± malingering" (Ibid) and Hysteria, not otherwise specific (NOS). Depersonalization Syndrome was still its own neurosis, and it included derealization. Hypochondriasis became its own diagnosis. Briquet's Disorder was included as a neurotic disorder, but now with only 25 of the 59 symptoms on the checklist.

The DSM-III was released in 1980, and it included ICD-9 reprinted as Appendix D (pp. 399-457). This, for the first time, created a separate category with the term "dissociative" being introduced as its own class of disorders. It also officially set forth the criteria for a diagnosis of Multiple Personality Disorder. Other diagnoses included: Psychogenic Amnesia, Psychogenic Fugue, and Atypical Dissociative Disorder – which was "anticipating DDNOS with the three examples of Trance-Like States, Derealization Without Depersonalization, and Brainwashing Victims" (O'Neil, 2021). Depersonalization was also considered dissociative for the first time and did not include a memory disturbance.

When the DSM-III-R was released, the essential feature of dissociative disorders was officially "a disturbance in the normally integrative functions of identity, memory, or consciousness . . ." This "ended the psychodynamic assumption of etiology as the process of distinguishing dissociation, conversion, and somatization... [and] shifted to "measurable" and "quantifiable" symptoms and symptom durations, separating diagnosis from theory for the first time (Reynolds, 2012). The "only remaining thread of theory was phenomenological, which streamlined a simplified Briquet's

Syndrome, now renamed as "Somatization Disorder" and only requiring 14 of the original 59 observed symptoms on the checklist" (North, 2015).

Landmark publications quickly followed, including the study of fourteen patients by Bliss (1985), the Coons writing on the systematic treatment of making a diagnosis (1992), and Braun's treatment recommendations (1986). Frank W. Putnam, of the National Institute of Mental Health (NIMH), published the classic *Diagnosis and Treatment of Multiple Personality Disorder* (1989), which was quickly followed the same year by the research of Colin Ross in *Multiple Personality Disorder: Diagnosis, Clinical Features, and Treatment*.

Then, in 1991, came Peter Barach's breakthrough article considering multiple personality disorder as an attachment disorder. He did *not* mean that disorganized attachment caused dissociation. Barach (2021) was following "the observations of Bowlby and others:

> When parents fail to respond to the distress signals of infants, infants will detach or dissociate from their emotional and physical pain. This forms the basis for dissociative detachment in response to continued abuse. But when these people grow up and come to therapy with a responsive therapist, their attachment behaviors are reactivated, which some therapists view as dependent behavior and manufactured crisis calls and then back away from them [just when] the hard-wired attachment system has been reactivated, which is actually a healthy thing!"

This, along with the earlier mentioned pieces of transference, will be discussed later.

The ICD-10 was released in 1992 and abolished 'NOS'. There was a "new supergrouping" (O'Neil, 2021). Neurotic, stress-related and somatoform disorder included Obsessive-Compulsive Disorder, extracted from Anxiety Disorders and promoted to its own group, with subdiagnoses; Reaction to Severe Stress, and Adjustment Disorders; Acute Stress Reaction and PTSD extracted from Anxiety Disorders; and Adjustment Disorders, demoted from being their own group to becoming a subgroup. Another change was that Hysterical Neurosis became Dissociative [Conversion] Disorders (D[C]Ds), which was a title that kept "dissociation and conversion together, with dissociation now taking first place" (Ibid). Somatoform Disorders were similar to the DSM-III, but without Conversion (which remains with D[C]Ds). Other Neurotic Disorders included Depersonalization-Derealization syndrome, which still kept it separate from Dissociative Disorders generally.

In 1994, the DSM-IV was released, officially changing the name of Multiple Personality Disorder to Dissociative Identity Disorder (DID). This set the stage for confusion between models of multiplicity (multiple personalities, consciousnesses, etc.) and models of divisibility (division of consciousness, personality, into mere parts – as in the *Theory of Structural Dissociation of the Personality*), which will be discussed later. The criteria for DID was now:

- The presence of two or more distinct identities or personality states (each with its own relatively enduring pattern of perceiving, relating to, and thinking about the environment and self);
- At least two of these identities or personality states recurrently take control of the person's behavior;
- Inability to recall important personal information that is too extensive to be explained by ordinary forgetfulness; and
- The disturbance is not due to the direct physiological effects of a substance (e.g., blackouts or chaotic behavior during Alcohol Intoxication) or a general medical condition (e.g., complex partial seizures). Note: In children, the symptoms are not attributable to imaginary playmates or other fantasy play.

Other Dissociative Disorder renamings included "Psychogenic Amnesia, which became Dissociative Amnesia; Psychogenic Fugue, which became Dissociative Fugue; and Atypical Dissociative Disorder, which became Dissociative Disorder Not Otherwise Specified (DDNOS) with six examples (up from three): 'Subthreshold' DID (two kinds); Derealization without depersonalization (borrowed from DSM-III); Victims of brainwashing (borrowed from DSM-III); Dissociative trance disorder (borrowed from DSM-III); Loss of consciousness, stupor, coma without medical explanation (should have been moved to Conversion Disorders); and Ganser Syndrome - so rare it would be dropped by DSM-5" (O'Neil, 2021).

This was a profound year for the field. Besides the renaming of MPD to DID, the International Society for the Study of Dissociation (ISSTD) released their 100-page document "Guidelines for Treating Dissociative Identity

Disorder in Adults". Screening instruments, structured interviews and assessments, and specialized mental status examinations quickly followed. In addition, this was the same year that the Polyvagal Theory was introduced by Porges in the Presidential Address for the Society for Psychophysiological Research.

Then, in 2006, the Structural Dissociation Theory was published in *The Haunted Self: Structural Dissociation and the Treatment of Chronic Traumatization* by Onno van der Hart, Ellert Nijenhuis, and Kathy Steele. The theory essentially proposed that all children are born with an identity or personality that is structured with separate states and that it is through attunement and caregiving and being raised in a healthy and safe environment by positive caregivers with good attachment that these states are integrated into one person in "normal" development. However, with abuse and neglect or other severe misattunement experiences, these states do not get to integrate into one "personality" during development, and instead they remain dissociated (or separated) from each other. This was a significant shift from the dissociation theory of the 80's and 90's that viewed the separate personality states, or alters, as having "split off" from a core personality and needing to be integrated back into that core. This also results in the assumption of one personality, which dismisses four millennia of more-than-one personality understanding, ultimately shifting the concept from "multiplicity" to "divided" in only two decades. This will be examined further in a later chapter.

The DSM-5 was released in 2013, maintaining the previous renamings. Differential diagnosis paragraphs were added to each diagnosis, providing alternatives to consider in the diagnostic process. In the *Dissociative*

Disorders chapters, the following are referenced as possible *Differential Diagnoses*: Psychotic Disorders, Catatonic Stupor, Bipolar Disorders, Major Depressive Disorder, Anxiety Disorders, OCD, PTSD, Conversion Disorder, Factitious Disorder, Malingering, Substance/medication-Induced Disorders, Personality Disorders, Neurocognitive Disorders. However, "the only disorders that reciprocally mention *Dissociative Disorder* in their various *Differential Diagnosis* sections are PTSD, ASD, and Conversion Disorder" (O'Neil, 2021). This means that if a clinician has a patient with Psychotic Disorders, Catatonic Stupor, Bipolar Disorders, Major Depressive Disorder, Anxiety Disorders, OCD, Factitious Disorder, Malingering, Substance/medication-Induced Disorders, Personality Disorders, or Neurocognitive Disorders, the DSM-5 *fails* to alert them to considering that this may be a case of Dissociative Disorder! It is "as if, outside of Dissociative Disorders and ASD/PTSD & Conversion Disorder, Dissociative Disorders don't exist" (Ibid). O'Neil also points out that especially *glaring* omissions include Personality Disorders (especially Borderline Personality Disorder, as its Criterion 9 even mentions 'dissociative episode'); Bipolar Disorders (global mood swings); Schizophrenia (voice hearing); and Gender Dysphoria (cross-gender alters).

This is significant because there are concerns from survivors themselves that this may result in a higher prevalence of misdiagnoses, lack of study, poor clinical discernment, and inadequate education. That, then, becomes passed down from clinician to clinician, creating historical trauma for the dissociative patient through misdiagnoses and improper treatment. It also leaves dissociative disorders included but isolated in the diagnostic manual, in a way that seems to re-enact the abuse dynamic even in diagnosis. Further, no other diagnosis has to "go in knowing" (since it is not referenced in differential diagnoses), even though by its very nature this is a "not-knowing" diagnosis.

Recent Discussion

In 2020, research began to shift back to prevalence, validity, and the process of dissociative disorders. Kate, Hopwood, and Jamieson (2019) released a large meta-analysis on the prevalence of dissociation in college students. Jepson pointed out that the Emotional Personality (or Part, EP) are where the "stuff" goes when Apparently Normal Personality (or Part, ANP) dissociates from it. This author (2020) recommended adding functional multiplicity (first described as "functional cooperation" by Steinberg and Schnall in 2001) to increase safety and improve functioning during treatment, much like the earlier shift from abreaction-focused therapy to safety and stabilization.

Finally, the ICD-11 (2022) officially confirms "Complex Post Traumatic Stress Disorder" (CPTSD) as a broader understanding of complex trauma (Voorendonk, De Jongh, Rozendaal, and Van Minnen, 2020). It is differentiated from PTSD by alterations in affect and behavioral regulation; interpersonal problems; dissociative symptoms; and somatizations (Herman, 1992; Salter and Hall, 2021). CPTSD is "linked to concepts of developmental and attachment trauma... and associated disruptions in the child-caregiver bond" (Farina, Liotti, & Imperatori, 2019).

There were also significant shifts in some of the leaders of field in 2021 and 2022. Kathy Steele moved away from ANP/EP language back to Ego

State language (2021). Van der Hart shifted his stance, stating he was changing "levels" of dissociation to "degrees", as awell as acknowledging the broader understanding of dis-association while emphasizing "*multiplicity in division of actions (unique to DID*)" (emphasis added) (2021). He also stated that using the terminology of "ego states" is "not enough" (ibid). He wrote that "dissociative parts of the personality may comprise any number of psychobiological states, which implies that *labeling them ego-states or self-states is giving them a too low degree of reality*" (ibid, emphasis added). These subtle shifts increase the dignity of those with Dissociative Identity Response, the term published by this author in the lived experience workbook (2021). As Ken Benau said, "I am determined to replace 'shame' with 'understanding' of all human behavior, and therefore to assume natural capacities of the mind/body can sometimes serve us or harm us, depending upon the intra-relational and inter-relational contexts from which they originated and now 'reside'..."

Conclusion

In conclusion, Pete Walker's 2014 book, *Complex PTSD: From Surviving to Thriving* delves into this from the perspectives of both clinical expertise (classifying trauma responses neurologically) and lived experience (addressing relational trauma and focusing on recovery), bringing the diagnostic history of trauma full circle. Most recently, Coy (2020) and Salter and Hall (2021) called for the de-pathologizing of trauma, exploring how to include cultural humility as part of treatment serving patient dignity. Similarly, the Blue Knot Foundation released the updated treatment guidelines in 2020, taking more sensitive approach to clinical treatment. They and more recent papers have also included emphasis on the impact of historical, racial, and social trauma (Gomez, 2021, 2019; Christensen, 2021; Masiero, Mazzocco, Harnois, Cropley, and Pravettoni, 2020; Yellowhorse-Braveheart, 2016). These issues, along with relevant research into the neurobiological impact of trauma, appear to be upcoming foci of research across fields (Roydeva and Reinders, 2021; Salami, Andreu-Perez, and Gillmeister, 2020; Howard, 2019; Ortega-Williams, Crutchfield, Hall, 2019; O'Neil, Fraser, Kitchenham, and McDonald, 2018).

This brings back relational trauma to the forefront, including the psychodynamic process in treatment itself (Osher, Cantor, Berg, Steyer, and Rose, 2020; Sedighimornani, Rimes, and Verplanken, 2020). This is confirmed by the most recent research of Simone Reinders (2020; 2021) and others, who have confirmed with brain imaging studies that DID is a distinct diagnosis, traumagenic, and relational in nature.

REFERENCES

Aguayo, J. 1986. Charcot and Freud: Some Implications of Late 19th Century French Psychiatry and Politics for the Origins of Psychoanalysis. *Psychoanalysis and Contemporary Thought*, 9(2):223-260.

American Psychiatric Association. 1952. *Diagnostic and Statistical Manual: Mental Disorders*. 1st ed. American Psychiatric Association; Washington, DC, USA.

American Psychiatric Association. 1968. Diagnostic and Statistical Manual of Mental Disorders. 2nd ed. American Psychiatric Association; Washington, D.C., USA.

American Psychiatric Association. 1980. Diagnostic and Statistical Manual of Mental Disorders. 3rd ed. American Psychiatric Association; Washington, DC, USA.

American Psychiatric Association. 1987. Diagnostic and Statistical Manual of Mental Disorders. 3rd Revised ed. American Psychiatric Association; Washington, DC, USA.

American Psychiatric Association. 1994. Diagnostic and Statistical Manual of Mental Disorders. 4th ed. American Psychiatric Association Press; Washington, DC, USA: 1994.

American Psychiatric Association. 2000. Diagnostic and Statistical Manual of Mental Disorders. 4th ed. American Psychiatric Association; Washington, DC, USA. Text Revision.

American Psychiatric Association. 2013. Diagnostic and Statistical Manual for Mental Disorders. 5th ed. American Psychiatric Association; Washington, DC, USA.

Babcock Fenerci, R.L., and DePrince, A.P. 2018. Shame and alienation related to child maltreatment: Links to symptoms across generations. Psychologicaly Trauma: Theory, Research, Practice, and Policy, 10(4), 419-426.

Baldwin JR, Reuben A, Newbury JB, Danese A. 2019. Agreement between prospective and retrospective measures of childhood maltreatment: a systematic review and meta-analysis. *JAMA Psychiatry*, 76(6):584–93. doi: 10.1001/jamapsychiatry.2019.0097

Barach, P. 1991. Multiple Personality disorder as an attachment disorder. Dissociation, 4(3), 117-123.

Barach, P. 2021. Personal Communication and Podcast Interviews.

Berrios GE, Sierra M (June 1997). "Depersonalization: a conceptual history". *Hist Psychiatry*. **8** (30 Pt 2): 213–29.

Bliss, E. L. 1980. Multiple Personalities: A Report of 14 Cases With Implications for Schizophrenia and Hysteria. *Arch Gen Psychiatry*, 37(12):1388–1397.

Bliss, E. L., and Jeppsen, E. A. (1985). Prevalence of multiple personality among inpatients and outpatients. *American Journal of Psychiatry*, 142, 250–251.

Blue Knot Foundation (2020) *Practice Guidelines for Identifying and Treating Complex Trauma-Related Dissociation Authors*: Kezelman C.A. Stavropoulos P.A.

Boon, S., Steele, K., van der Hart, O. 2011. *Coping with Trauma-Related Dissociation: Skills Training for Therapists and Patients*. New York: W. W. Norton & Company.

Bowers, M. K., Brecher-marer, S., Newton, B. N., Piotrowski, Z., Spyer, T.C., Taylor, W. S., & Watkins, J. G. (1971) Therapy of multiple personality, *International Journal of Clinical and Experimental Hypnosis*, 19:2, 57-65

Brewin, C. R., Cloitre, M., Hyland, P., Shevlin, M., Maercker, A., Bryant, R.A., Humayun, A., Jones, L.M., Kagee, A., and Rousseau, C. 2017. A review of current evidence regarding the ICD-11 proposals for diagnosing PTSD and complext PTSD. Clinical Psychology Review, 58, 1-15.

Briquet P. 1859. *Traité clinique et thérapeutique â l'hystére*. Parise, France: J-B Bailliére & Fils. Bromberg, P. M. (2003). One need not be a house to be haunted: on enactment, dissociation, and the dread of "Not-me". Psychoanalytic Dialogues, 13(5), 689-710.

Cannon WB. 1914. The interrelations of emotions as suggested by recent physiological researches. *Am J Psychol* 25(2):256–82. doi: 10.2307/1413414

Christensen, E. 2019. System Speak Podcast. Online.

Clayton, E., Jones, C., Brown, J., and Taylor, J. 2018. The aetiology of child sexual abuse: a critical review of the empirical evidence. Child Abuse Review, 27(30), 181-197.

Corrigan, P., Rüsch, N., Scior, K. (2018). Adapting disclosure programs to reduce the public stigma of mental illness. *Psychiatric Services*. On-line early.

Courtois, C.A. 2020. Updates on Complex Trauma. Presentation.

Courtois, C.A. and Ford, J.D. 2013. *Treatment of Complex Trauma: A Sequenced, Relationship-Based Approach*. New York, New York: The Guilford Press.

Courtois, C.A. and Ford, J.D., (eds). 2009. *Treating Complex Traumatic Stress Disorders*. New York, New York: The Guilford Press.

Coy, M. 2020. List-Serv email and personal communication 29 December 2020.

Despine, C. H. A. 1840. De l'emploi du magnetisme animal et des eaux minerales dans le traitement des maladies nerveuses, suivi d'une observation tres curieuse de guerison de nevropathie. Germer Baillière, Librairie-éditeur, rue de l'École de médecine, 17.

Dorahy, M.J., and van der Hart, O. 2015. DSM-5's posttraumatic stress disorder with dissociative symptoms: Challenges and future directions. Journal of Trauma and Dissociation, 16(1), 7-28.

Ellenberger, H. F. 1970. *The Discovery of the Unconscious: The History and Evolution of Dynamic Psychiatry*. New York: Basic Books.

Farina, B, Liotti, M., and Imperatori, C. 2019. The role of attachment trauma and disintegrative pathogenic processes in the traumatic-dissociative dimension. *Frontiers in Psychology*, 10, 933, 1-18.

Friedan, B. 1963. *The Feminine Mystique*. New York: Dell.

Friedman MJ, Kilpatrick DG, Schnurr PP, Weathers FW. 2016. Correcting misconceptions about the diagnostic criteria for posttraumatic stress disorder in DSM-5. *JAMA Psychiatry,* 73(7):753–4. doi: 10.1001/jamapsychiatry.2016.0745

Fussell, P. (ed). 1983. *Siegfried Sassoon's Long Journey: Selections from the Sherston Memoirs*. New York: Oxford University Press, xiv.

Gomes, M., and Engelhardt, E. 2014. A neurological bias in the history of hysteria: from the womb to the nervous system and Charcot. *Arq Neuropsiquiatr. 2014 Dec; 72(12):972-5.*

Gomez, J. M. 2021. Presentation at ISSTD Conference (virtual).

Gomez, J.M. 2019. What's the harm? Internalized prejudice and cultural betrayal trauma in ethnic minorities. *American Journal of Orthopsychiatry*, 89(2), 237-247.

Gomez, J.M. and Freyd, J.J. 2019. Betrayal trauma. In Ponzetti, J.J. (Ed.), *Macmillan Encyclopedia of Intimate and Family Relationships: An Interdisciplinary Approach* (pp. 79-82). Boston, MA: Cengage Learning Inc.

Goodman, Rachael. (2013). The transgenerational trauma and resilience genogram. *Counselling Psychology Quarterly*. 26. 10.1080/09515070.2013.820172.

Hart, O. & Lierens, R. & Goodwin, J. 1996. *Jeanne Fery: A sixteenth-century case of dissociative identity disorder*. The Journal of psychohistory. 24. 18-35.

Herman, J. 2015. *Trauma and Recovery: The Aftermath of violence – from domestic abuse to political terror*. New York: Basic Books.

Howard, J.A. 2019. A systemic framework for trauma-informed schooling: complex but necessary! *Journal of Aggression, Maltreatment & Trauma*, 28(5), 545-565.

Howell, E. F. 2011. Understanding and Treating Dissociative Identity Disorder: A Relational Approach. New York: Routledge.

Janet, P. (1889). *L'Automatisme psychologique*. Paris: Félix Alcan.

Janet, P. (1894). *Histoire d'une idée fixe*. Revue Philosophique, 37, 121-163.

Janet, P. (1904). L'amnésie et la dissociation des souvenirs par l'émotion. *Journal de Psychologie*, 1, 417-453.

Janet, P. (1907). The major symptoms of hysteria. London & New York: Macmillan.

Janet, P. (1909). *Les névroses*. Paris: E. Flammarion.

Janet, P. (1911). *L'Etat mental des hystériques* (Reprint: Lafitte Reprints, Marseilles, 1983 ed.). Paris: Felix Alcan.

Janet, P. (1919). Les médications psychologiques. Paris: Félix Alcan. English edition : Psychological healing. New York: Macmillan, 1925.

Janet, P. (1928). *L'évolution de la mémoire et de la notion du temps*. Paris: A Chahine.

Jepsen, E. 2020. Approach Dissociative Disorder Patient Difficulties. Presentation at ISSTD Virtual Conference on the Impact of Societal Trauma on Marginalized Communities.

Kardiner, A. and Spiegel, H. 1947. *War, Stress, and Neurotic Illness* (rev. ed. *The Traumatic Neuroses of War.* New York: Hoeber.

Kate, M.A., Hopwood, T., and Jamieson, G. 2019. The prevalence of dissociative disorders and dissociative experiences in college populations: a meta-analysis of 98 studies. *Journal of Trauma & Dissociation*, 1-46.

Kezelman C.A. & Stavropoulos P.A. (2012) *Practice Guidelines for Treatment of Complex Trauma and Trauma Informed Care and Service Delivery.* Blue Knot Foundation.

Kezelman C.A. & Stavropoulos P.A. (2019) *Practice Guidelines for Clinical Treatment of Complex Trauma*. Blue Knot Foundation

Kezelman C.A. & Stavropoulos P.A. (2019) *Complementary Guidelines to Practice Guidelines for Clinical Treatment of Complex Trauma.* Blue Knot Foundation

Kigar SL, Chang L, Guerrero CR, Sehring JR, Cuarenta A, Parker LL, et al. 2017. N(6)-methyladenine is an epigenetic marker of mammalian early life stress. *Sci Rep*, 7(1):18078. doi: 10.1038/s41598-017-18414-7

Kluft, R.P. (1986). High-functioning multiple personality patients: Three cases. *Journal of Nervous and Mental Disease*, 174, 722-726.

Kluft, R.P. (1991). Multiple personality disorder. In A. Tasman & S.M. Goldfinger (Eds.), *American psychiatric press review of psychiatry* (Vol. 10, pp. 161-188). Washington, DC: American Psychiatric Press.

Kluft, R. P. (2006). Dealing with alters: a pragmatic clinical perspective. *Psychiatric Clinics of North America*, 29, 281-304.

Kluft, R. P. 2020. Podcast Interview. System Speak: A Podcast About Dissociative Identity Disorder. Airdate pending for Fall 2021.

Leri, A. 1919. *Shell Shock: Commotional and Emotional Aspects*. London: University of London Press, 118.

Ludwig AM, Brandsma JM, Wilbur CB, Bendfeldt F, Jameson DH. The Objective Study of a Multiple Personality: Or, Are Four Heads Better Than One? *Archives of General Psychiatry*. 1972;26(4):298–310. doi:10.1001/archpsyc.1972.01750220008002.

Mai FM, Merskey H. Briquet's Concept of Hysteria: An Historical Perspective. *The Canadian Journal of Psychiatry*. 1981;26(1):57-63.

Masiero, M., Mazzocco, C., Harnois, C., Cropley, M., & Pravettoni, G. 12 July 2020. From Individual To Social Trauma: Sources of Everyday Trauma in Italy, The US, and UK

During the Covid-19 Pandemic. *Journal of Trauma and Dissociation*, 21(5):513-519.

Myers, C. S. 1940. *Shell Shock in France*. Cambridge: Cambridge University Press.

Norman, M. 1989. *These Good Men: Friendships Forged From War*. New York: Crown, p. 139, 141.

North C. S. 2015. The Classification of Hysteria and Related Disorders: Historical and Phenomenological Considerations. *Behavioral sciences (Basel, Switzerland)*, *5*(4), 496–517.

North C.S. Somatoform disorders. In: Rubin E.H., Zorumski C.F., editors. *Adult Psychiatry*. 2nd ed.

Blackwell; Malden, MA, USA: 2005. pp. 261–274.

North C.S., Yutzy S.H. Goodwin and Guze's Psychiatric Diagnosis. 6th ed. Oxford University Press; New York, NY, USA: 2010. Somatization disorder (hysteria) pp. 207–226.

O'Neil, J. 2021. Personal Communication and Podcast Interview. System Speak: A Podcast About Dissociative Identity Disorder.

O'Neill L, Fraser T, Kitchenham A, McDonald V (June 2018). "Hidden Burdens: a Review of Intergenerational, Historical and Complex Trauma, Implications for Indigenous Families". Journal of Child & Adolescent *Trauma*. **11** (2): 173–186

Ortega-Williams, A., Crutchfield, J., Hall, J.C.,2019. The colorist-historical trauma framework: Implications for culturally responsive practice with African Americans. *Journal of Social Work*, https://journals.sagepub.com/doi/abs/10.1177/1468017319890083.

Osher, D., Cantor, P., Berg, J., Steyer, L., and Rose, T. 2020. Drivers of human development: How relationships and context shape learning and development. *Applied Developmental Science*, 24(1), 6-36.

Porges, S.W., 1994. Orienting in a defensive world: A poly-vagal theory of our evolutionary heritage. Presidential Address. Society for Psychophysiological Research.

Purtell, J.J., Robins, E., and Cohen, M. E. 1951. *Observations on clinical aspects of hysteria; a quantitative study of 50 hysteria patients and 156 control subjec*ts. J Am Med Assoc. 1951 Jul 7; 146(10):902-9.

Putnam, F. 1989. *Diagnosis and Treatment of Multiple Personality Disorder*. New York: Guilford Press.

Reinders, S. 2020. *The Aetiology and Neurobiology of Dissociative Identity Disorder*. Presented at ISSTD Annual Conference.

Reynolds, E.H. 2012. Hysteria, conversion and functional disorders: a neurological contribution to classification issues. *Br J Psychiatry. 2012 Oct; 201(4):253-4.*

Robertson, Rachel. (2019). The History of Dissociative Identity Disorder. Retrieved via ResearchGate 03/19/19.

Ross, C. A. (1989). Multiple personality disorder. Diagnosis, clinical features, and treatment. New York: John Wiley and Sons.

Roydeva, M. I. and Reinders, A.T.S. April 2021. Biomarkers of Pathological Dissociation: A Systematic Review, *Neuroscience & Biobehavioral* Reviews, 123: 120-202. https://doi.org/10.1016/j.neubiorev.2020.11.019. (https://www.sciencedirect.com/science/article/pii/S0149763420306485)

Salami, A.; Andreu-Perez, J.; Gillmeister, H. (1 November 2020). "Symptoms of depersonalisation/derealisation disorder as measured by brain electrical activity: A systematic review". *Neuroscience & Biobehavioral Reviews*. **118**: 524–537.

Salter, M. and Hall, H. 2021. *Reducing Shame, Promoting Dignity: A Model for the Primary Prevention of Complex Post-Traumatic Stress Disorder, Trauma Violence Abuse*, forthcoming.

Sar, V. 2011. Epidemiology of dissociative disorders: An overview. *Epidemiology Research International*, 2011, 1-8.

Sarachild, K. 1975. "Consciousness-Raising: A Radical Weapon," in *Feminist Revolution*, ed. K.

Sarahchild (New York: Random House, 1978), 145. (Orig. ed. *New York Redstockings*, 1975).

Saraiya, T. and Lopez-Castro, T. 2016. Ashamed and afraid: a scoping review of the role of shame in post-traumatic stress disorder (PTSD). *Journal of Clinical Medicine*, 5(11), 94-115.

Sedighimornani, N., Rimes, K., and Verplanken, B. 2020. Factors contributing to the experience of shame and shame management: Adverse childhood experiences, peer acceptance, and attachment styles. *Journal of Social Psychology*, forthcoming.

Sierra, M; Nestler, S; Jay, E; Ecker, Christine; Feng, Yue; David, Anthony S. (30 October 2014). "A structural MRI study of cortical thickness in depersonalisation disorder". *Psychiatry Research*. **224** (1): 1–7.

Steele K, van der Hart O, Nijenhuis ER. 2005. Phase-oriented treatment of structural dissociation in complex traumatization: overcoming trauma-related phobias. *Journal of Trauma & Dissociation*, 6(3):11-53.

Steele, K., van der Hart, O., & Nijenhuis, E. R. S. (2009). The theory of trauma-related structural dissociation of the personality. In P. F. Dell & J. A. O'Neil (Eds.), *Dissociation and the dissociative disorders: DSM-V and beyond* (pp. 239–258). Routledge/Taylor & Francis Group.

Steele, K. 11 February 2021. *Things I Wish I Had Been Told About Working With Complex Trauma and Dissociation.* Webinar Presentation for International Society of the Study of Trauma and Dissociation.

Steele, K. 20 February 2021. *Calming the Inner Critic: Working with Punitive Introjects, Ego States, and Dissociative Parts.* Envision Webinar. Online.

Steinberg, M. and Schnall, M. 2001. *The Stranger in the Mirror: Dissociation – The Hidden Epidemic.* New York: Harper.

Stengel, E. (1943). Further Studies on Pathological Wandering (Fugues with the Impulse to Wander). *Journal of Mental Science,* 89(375), 224-241. doi:10.1192/bjp.89.375.224

van der Hart, O., & Dorahy, M. J. (2009). *History of the concept of dissociation.* In P. F. Dell & J. A. O'Neil (Eds.), *Dissociation and the dissociative disorders: DSM-V and beyond* (p. 3–26). Routledge/Taylor & Francis Group.

van der Hart, O., Nijenhuis, E., and Steele, K. 2004. Trauma-related structural dissociation of the personality. Trauma information pages website. Retrieved 11 November 2020.

van der Hart, O., Brown, P., & Graafland, M. (1999). Trauma-induced dissociative amnesia in World War I combat soldiers. *Australian and New Zealand Journal of Psychiatry,* 33, 37-46.

van der Hart, O., & Nijenhuis, E. (1995). Amnesia for traumatic experiences. *Hypnos,* 222, 73-86.

van der Hart, O., & Nijenhuis, E.R.S. (1998). Recovered memories of abuse and dissociative identity disorder. *British Journal of Psychiatry,* 173, 537-538.

van der Hart, O. & Nijenhuis, E.R.S.. (2001). Loss and recovery of different memory types in generalized dissociative amnesia. *Australian and New Zealand Journal of Psychiatry,* 35 (5), 589-600.

van der Hart, O., & Op den Velde, W. (1995). Posttraumatische stoornisssen [Posttraumatic disorders]. In O. Van der Hart (Ed.), Trauma, dissociatie en hypnose [Trauma, dissociation and hypnosis] (pp. 103-145). Lisse: Swets & Zeitlinger.

van der Hart, O., & Steele, K. (1997). Time distortions in dissociative identity disorder: Janetian concepts and treatment. *Dissociation,* 10, 91-103.

van der Hart, O., & Steele, K. (1999). Relieving or reliving childhood trauma? A commentary on Miltenburg and Singer (1997). *Theory and Psychology,* 9, 533-540.

van der Hart, O., Steele, K., Boon, S., & Brown, P. (1993). The treatment of traumatic memory: synthesis, realization, integration. *Dissociation,* 6, 162-180.

van der Hart, O., Van der Kolk, B.A., & Boon, S. (1998). Treatment of dissociative disorders. In J.D. Bremner & C.R. Marmar (Eds.), *Trauma, memory, and dissociation* (pp. 253-283). Washington, DC: American Psychiatric Press.

van der Hart, O., Van Dijke, A., Van Son, M., & Steele, K. (2000). Somatoform dissociation in traumatized World War I combat soldiers: A neglected clinical heritage. *Journal of Trauma and Dissociation,* 1(4), 33-66.

van der Hart, O. 2021. Trauma-related dissociation: An analysis of two conflicting models, *European Journal of Trauma & Dissociation,* Volume 5, Issue 4.

van Honk, J., Nijenhuis, E.R.S., & Van der Hart, O. (1999). Identity-dependent psychophysiological responses to subliminal threat cues in DID patients. Paper presented at the 15th Annual Meeting of the International Society for Traumatic Stress Studies, Miami, FL.

Van IJzendoorn, M.H., Schuengel, C., & J., Bakersman-Kranenberg, M. (1999). Disorganized attachment in early childhood: Meta-analysis of precursors, concomitants, and sequelae. *Development & Psychopathology*, 11, 225-249.

van der Kolk, B.A. (1994). The body keeps the score: memory and the evolving psychobiology of posttraumatic stress. *Harvard Review of Psychiatry*, 1, 253-265.

van der Kolk, B.A., & Fisler, R. (1995). Dissociation and the fragmentary nature of traumatic memories: Overview and exploratory study. *Journal of Traumatic Stress*, 8, 505-525.

van der Kolk, B.A., & Van der Hart, O. (1991). The intrusive past: The flexibility of memory and the engraving of trauma. *American Imago*, 48, 425-454.

van der Kolk, B. 1997. *Traumatic memories.* In P. S. Appelbaum, L. A. Uyehara, & M. R. Elin (Eds.), *Trauma and memory: Clinical and legal controversies* (p. 243–260). Oxford University Press. (Portions are reprinted from "Journal of Traumatic Stress," 7, 1995, pp. 505–526)

van der Kolk BA, Roth S, Pelcovitz D, Sunday S, Spinazzola J. 2005. Disorders of extreme stress: The empirical foundation of a complex adaptation to trauma. *J Trauma Stress,* 18(5):389–99. doi: 10.1002/jts.20047

van der Kolk BA, Courtois CA. 2005. Editorial comments: complex developmental trauma. *J Trauma Stress,* 18(5):385–8. doi: 10.1002/jts.20046

Voorendonk, E. M., De Jongh, A., Rozendaal, L., and Van Minnen, A. 2020. Trauma-focused treatment outcome for complex PTSD patients: results of an intensive treatment programme, *European Journal of Psychotraumatology*, 11:1, 1783955, DOI: 10.1080/20008198.2020.1783955

Walker, P., & Walker, P. (2013). *Complex PTSD: From surviving to thriving*.

Walusinski, O. 2014. *The girls of La Salpêtrière*. Front Neurol Neurosci. 2014; 35():65-77.

Way, K. G. (2006). How metaphors shape the concept and treatment of dissociation. In R. A. Chefetz (Ed.), *Dissociative disorders: An expanding window into the psychobiology of the mind* (Vol. 29:1, pp. 27-43). Philadelphia: Elsevier

Wilbur, C.B., 1984. Treatment of Multiple Personality Disorder. *Psychiatric Annals*, 14(1):27ff.

Wilbur, C.B., 1986. Psychoanalysis and multiple personality disorder. *Treatment of multiple personality disorder*, pp.133-142.

World Health Organization. 1977. The ICD-9 Classification of Mental and Behavioural Disorders: Clinical Descriptions and Diagnostic Guidelines. 9th ed. World Health Organization; Geneva, Country.

World Health Organization. 1992. The ICD-10 Classification of Mental and Behavioral Disorders: Clinical Descriptions and Diagnostic Guidelines. 10th ed. World Health Organization; Geneva, Switzerland.

Yellowhorse-Braveheart, M. 2016. *Intergenerational / Historical Trauma*. Targeted Resources for Tribal Welfare. Capacity Building Center for Tribes. Retrieved Online 19 December 2020. https://tribalinformationexchange.org/files/products/HistoricalTraumaResourceGuide.pdf

Therapeutic Presence and the Therapeutic Relationship as Both Trigger and Container to Healing

by Jillian Hosey, MSW, RSW

> "The relationship is the heart of healing trauma. Relational damage is the core of trauma" (Norcoss and Wampold, 2019, p. 393).

It has taken time to find just the right way to open this chapter, a chapter that explores the often-implicit relational work of psychotherapy with persons living with complex trauma and dissociated identities. How do you find words to explain work that is often wordless, and unfolds within the unique relationship we know as the 'therapeutic relationship?' This unique relationship, unlike many others, offers a container for healing and meaning making of the atrocities of human experience, often times at the hands of another. In the treatment of complex trauma and dissociated identities, relational models of psychotherapy have been developed through an abundance of research and practice, that elucidate the role of a close, bonded therapeutic relationship as what enables healing, possibly an even greater predictor in treatment success than the specific modality or method (Norcross & Wampold, 2019; Courtois & Ford, 2016; Howell, 2011; APA Presidential Task Force on Evidence-Based Practice, 2006; Dalenberg, 2004, 2000; Fosha, 2000). Through this therapeutic connection and bond, it is proposed that the psychic phobia connected to being in relationship to another may be counteracted (Courtois & Ford, 2013), attachment circuitry can be reactivated to optimize change via neuroplastic processes (Cozolino, 2006, 2014), and complex trauma symptoms may be explored and worked through to resolution (Ellis et al., 2018). With complex trauma having such deleterious effects on the experience of being in connection to another, the therapeutic relationship is spoken of as offering a space of repair to explore and experiment with new ways of relating to the self, others, and the world. However, this relationship is not one that forms expeditiously or without challenges and is the basis of this chapter.

According to Herman (1997, 2015), relational trauma, by definition, involves loss. Like all traumatic events, relational trauma "overwhelm[s] the ordinary systems of care that give people a sense of control, connection, and meaning" (p. 33; Schore, 2003a & 2003b). Such loss, the loss of relationship as safe, connected, and meaningful, has profound impacts on the formation of the therapeutic relationship. As a result, clinicians working with clients with histories of complex relational trauma and dissociated identities may experience struggles with client engagement and dyadic collaboration, which often manifest in paradoxical and perplexing reactions in the client. When such reactions become observable through process within the therapeutic relationship, clinicians may notice clients disengage through silence, loss of eye contact, loss of speech and language, avoidance of content or connection (as a defensive adaptation), change in posturing and body language (through the body's motor movement), and switching of dissociated identities to manage the overwhelm that closeness brings. For some clients, this may be their observed baseline presentation when in proximity. As these reactions emerge in relation to being in proximity to another, clinicians may experience or interpret them as qualitative impediments to developing the very relationship that heals, or more simply, as resistance to therapy.

In having a more humane of way of understanding these reactions and *why* clients may present as deeply guarded from the therapeutic relationship, a different conceptual lens is offered that considers the intricate role of our neurophysiology as mediator of distress in the face of perceived danger – the danger of being close to another. Considerations like this allow for a more mindful stepping into the therapy space, and while grossly simplistic for a more complex interactional pattern, this chapter offers a place to start, a springboard of sorts from which we can explore more complex theories of mind, conceptual aetiologies, and particular treatment methodologies. The purpose in offering a baseline method of understanding is in the service of offering a greater ability to predict therapeutic ruptures in psychotherapy, build and maintain empathic attunement and resonance, and even mitigate client re-traumatization and premature therapy terminations. While in stark contrast to briefer models of psychotherapy, Chefetz (2022) reminds us that "in the practice of psychotherapy, there is no "fast food," no short-cut to relatedness, no hyper-link to the creation of intimacy with people who may only have experienced a relationship as a source of pain" (p. 60). With reflection, how much sense it makes that it takes time to build the ability to connect and be in connection, when so much time has passed, and survival has been achieved through disconnection from self and other.

As such, the focus of this chapter is to offer therapists with a conceptual framework to make meaning of why clients may present with obscure and paradoxical reactions to therapy, the therapist, and the therapist's proposed therapeutic interventions in the treatment of complex trauma and dissociation. Honoring the ways in which the mind and body steps in to defend, The Polyvagal Theory (PVT) is proposed as said conceptualization. PVT illustrates a neurophysiological process that emerges in the therapy room as the therapist inadvertently sets off cues of danger through a process called neuroception. The work of attachment theory and epistemic trust will also be utilized to promote an understanding of the underpinnings for such triggers, as a guide to expect such responses in therapy and to enhance empathic understanding and corresponding responses in therapists. Lastly, this chapter will explore the use of a more finely calibrated attunement to client's cues of danger and their corresponding defensive adaptations in response to proximity to the therapist, alongside the ways in which the often-wordless experience of inner safety may be conveyed through the intentional use of aligned verbal and non-verbal language. Such considerations flow from a therapeutic stance that is aligned with a philosophy of deep respect, collaboration, and humility in the treatment of complex trauma and dissociation, and places value on process, rather than technique or modality. These considerations also deeply support the scaffolding of a new experience of inner safety when in relationship to another, in a layered, ongoing manner. In doing so, therapists are offered increased opportunities of *being with* their clients in process and developing comfort in the uncertainty of a therapeutic grey space – a space that recognizes the therapist as both trigger and solution and honors the unique pacing and distance each unique human being needs within their therapeutic healing journey's.

Polyvagal Theory

As human beings, we have an exquisite ability to sense the presence of another, a sensing that occurs within the relationship between the mind, body, and world external to it. In his text, *Feeling & Knowing: Making Minds Conscious*, Damasio (2021), speaks to this direct and abundant interaction between the body and brain, allowing for communications to occur via our nervous system based on what is happening in the external world. According to Dr. Stephen Porges (2009), "the human nervous system, similar to that of other mammals, evolved not solely to survive in safe environments but also to promote survival in dangerous and life-threatening contexts" (p. S88). With the autonomic nervous system also responsible for regulating our visceral organs (stomach, lungs, heart etc.), PVT (Porges, 2003, 2009, 2011, 2017, 2018, 2021) offers a greater understanding of the mind-body connection with respect to our emotional state, a felt sense of safety, responding efficaciously to a real or perceived lack of safety, and overall well-being. This regulation happens automatically and outside of our conscious awareness. With respect to complex relational trauma and dissociation, when the trauma is over or when we have shifted into a space and place where we are safe, the overriding physiological reaction to cues of danger may become mistimed or mismatched. As the past gets triggered by the cues that became linked to the trauma(s), and as the past floods into the present, our nervous system steps in to promote survival.

Honoring this delicate and intricate interplay between the mind and body, Porges (2003, 2009, 2011, 2017, 2018, 2021) details that the Autonomic Nervous System, as influenced by the Central Nervous System, responds to cues from the external world and has evolved to become functionally and behaviorally adaptive to respond to safe, dangerous, and threatening life events, people, situations, and contexts. These responses have been linked to the evolving circuity of the Vagus Nerve, or the tenth cranial nerve, which provides neural regulation of our physiological and emotional states in response to what is sensed, both externally and internally, and influences heart rate variability. These vagal circuits, or systems, are understood to dynamically mediate "...social communication (e.g,, facial expression, vocalization, listening), defensive mobilization (e.g,, fight–flight behaviors), and defensive immobilization (e.g,, feigning death, vasovagal syncope, and behavioral shutdown)" (Porges, 2009, p. S87). As part of the Autonomic Nervous System, social communication and engagement is mediated via the evolutionally refined ventral vagal parasympathetic system, which offers an option to modulate and regulate internal states by way of a vagal brake that suppresses heart rate. In other words, the vagal brake regulates the ability to move fluidly through engagement and disengagement, or connection and disconnection, "...with objects and other individuals and to promote self-soothing behaviors and calm states" (Porges, 2007, p. 9; Dana, 2018, 2020). When we are within our social engagement system, we are able to be within connection to another, think and feel simultaneously, and move with greater ease through different emotional states according to context, accessing energy by way of the ventral vagal system as needed to appropriately respond. Alternatively, mobilization, or the ability to act and move to protect, is mediated by the sympathetic system and immobilization, or the ability to slow down into a stillness as a last resort to ensure survival, is mediated via the parasympathetic dorsal vagal system, which are greatly needed capacities to manage threat of danger and harm to life (Porges, 2009, Dana, 2018). When all three systems are working together in harmony, we experience a greater ease and flexibility in navigating the world and we are able harness our autonomic states in an aligned and time-oriented manner. Psychotherapies that include Polyvagal Theory may focus on growing the capacity to access and use the ventral vagal system and conceptualize cues of safety as ones that can lead to an inner felt sense of safety and support the ability to be within social engagement to counteract the impact of trauma.

According to Porges (2011), after trauma, the socially engaged and connected state of the ventral vagal system may be overridden by a defensive and mistrustful state and a state of immobilization in response to fear, which Dana (2018) states "keeps the autonomic nervous system from finding safety in connection" (p. 32). After chronic, pervasive, and repeated experiences of trauma with close others, the body's reactions and responses to another as threatening and dangerous may shift and become procedurally stuck "on," perceiving most others as triggers to danger or threat to life. This reorients neurophysiology to one of reactive defendedness and guardedness when in proximity to another, with such responses residing in midbrain and limbic system structures that are responsible for emotion and survival, and often outside of conscious awareness and a knowing that it's now safe enough to relate and connect. As Chefetz (2022) opines, within the context of psychotherapy with persons with histories of complex relational trauma and dissociation, "the notion of immobilization and conjuring of both sympathetic activation and parasympathetic deactivation, simultaneously from the tugs and pulls of differently endowed self-states is the stuff out of which confusion in relatedness is present on a physiological level" (p. 68). It's crucial to understand that this automatic defense is one that overrides logic, and the ability to access and be within a ventral vagal state, or social engagement, narrows as a means of ensuring protection and survival.

These neurophysiological foundations are laid early through relationship to early caregivers, who are tasked with creating external safety and providing consistent and predictable care and support to build the scaffolding for the experience of internal safety and affect regulation (Gomez, 2012; Schore 2003a, 2003b; Liotti, 1992). Caregivers are tasked with providing a good enough sense of safety through the consistent and predictable use of emotional availability, attunement, and mirroring responses that are congruent and predictable. When unable to provide this co-regulation, or when done in an unpredictable manner, primary caregivers become the source of distress and danger through incongruency, abuse, and/or neglect. These accumulated experience(s) of such adverse early experiences may coalesce into an internal representation, or Internal Working Models, within the child, compromising the ability to trust that being in relationship to another can be safe. These internal representations and indicators of others as untrusting and dangerous may be further understood as offering a prediction for future relational experience (Brown & Elliott, 2016; Bowlby, 1980a).

As such, Bowlby (1988) offered us a method of understanding the "function and development of human protective behaviour... [that form] inner representational models to explain how prior experience was retained over time and used to guide expectations and future behaviour" (Crittenden & Landini, 2011, p. 30). Through the process of psychotherapy, these inner representational models may be revised and reworked as outdated ways of relating to self, others, and the world. However, this chapter argues that both this process of revision and the experience of a felt sense of safety becomes complicated by the simple notion that accomplishing such reworking is done in relationship to another, as in working with clients who have histories of complex relational trauma, the ventral vagal social engagement system gets turned off or repatterned in response to proximity. As such, complexly traumatized persons may be left with the underlying, automatic defensive strategies in response to therapy to either to fight or flee, to disappear and shut down, or for dissociated identities to come out front as a perceived need for protection from proximity arises. When this occurs, the nervous system is in a state that has incredible advantages in detecting dangerous others and unsafe, threatening conditions, and simultaneously compromised in being connected, specifically to the therapist, to engage in therapeutic work. For survivors of complex trauma and persons living with dissociated identities, "even the proximity to another human being in a small, enclosed space may be activating" (Herman, 2015, p. 58).

Neuroception and Compromised Epistemic Trust

Compromised Epistemic Trust and the process of Neuroception may be considered as additional ways of understanding and recognizing what may be happening in the therapeutic space when danger and threat have been activated by simply being in proximity to the therapist. They also reveal how the possibility of connection and its therapeutic capacity to facilitate change seems to become exiled from the space. Gomez et al. (2016) shared that "regardless of when the trauma occurs, the experience of being rendered powerless by betrayal, within a relationship on which an individual depends, challenges one of the most basic human survival mechanisms—one's orientation toward connection with others" (p. 167-168). As a result of ongoing experiences of relational trauma, wherein betrayal by one's only source of safety occurs, this chapter proposes that the internal working models of others as dangerous and unsafe lend to a *compromised epistemic trust* in the complexly traumatized individual.

Epistemic Trust may be defined as the willingness to take in information and knowledge shared in an interpersonal context and trust that there is personal relevance and generalizable significance to accepting and applying the information (Fonagy & Allison, 2014; Fonagy et al., 2019). This becomes relevant where the therapist is concerned, as the therapist is tasked with providing trauma-specific knowledge through psychoeducation in support of reframing symptoms as manifestations of what has happened to the client, guiding healing as one that is trauma-specific and connects past to present. This is often done within a phased approach to trauma treatment (Courtois & Ford, 2013, 2020; Van der Hart et al., 1989) that uses the therapeutic relationship as both anchor and container, and includes, but is not limited to, the development of emotional, cognitive, and somatic modulation and regulation, working through one's traumatic experiences alongside dissociated identities, and the reworking and revising of internal working models through a new, more secure attachment experience with an emotionally attuned, mentalizing, and available therapist. However, with the notion of relationship to another having become generalized as unsafe and untrusting, the client may be perpetually triggered and experience a compromised ability to receive knowledge and guidance from the helping professional, which may lead clinicians to misunderstand the lack of client openness as resistance to the therapeutic process and healing.

So how does compromised epistemic trust based on outdated internal representations of others as unsafe get activated within the therapy room? Turning back to PVT, the process of Neuroception may offer us a way of understanding what is happening as therapists' endeavor to build the therapeutic relationship through offering connection, attunement, mentalization, and resonance, but encounter perceived barriers in relation to the activation of a client's inner experiences of fear, terror, and shame when in proximity to the therapist. According to Porges (2019), "to effectively switch from defensive to social engagement strategies, the mammalian nervous system needs to perform two important adaptive tasks: (1) assess risk, and (2) if the environment is perceived as safe, inhibit the more primitive limbic structures that control fight, flight, or freeze behaviors" (p. S88). These tasks are accomplished through the process of Neuroception, a term that describes the neural process whereby the brain unconsciously and automatically scans for cues of safety or risk in the environment, a dynamic process that includes external sensory feedback and internal feedback from the viscera, or our 'insides,' and then responds. Furthermore,

> "When the environment is appraised as being safe, the defensive limbic structures are inhibited, enabling social engagement and calm visceral states to emerge. In contrast, some individuals experience a mismatch, and the nervous system appraises the environment as being dangerous even when it is safe. This mismatch results in physiological states that support fight, flight, or freeze behaviors, but not social engagement behaviors" (Porges, 2011, p. S89).

These physiological states are the ones previously described that may show up un the therapy space as paradoxical and perplexing to treating clinicians, whose intentions to 'help' miss the intricately adaptive protective mechanisms that show up and offer us new ways of understanding and engaging. Simply put, when trauma occurs in relationship to others, closeness, and proximity to another becomes *neurocepted* as dangerous and the mind and body responds to manage the threat expeditiously, which includes disengaging from the therapist, the therapeutic process, and the ability to receive knowledge and information shared interpersonally to support healing.

An additional layer of consideration is the inherent imbalance of power in the therapist-client relationship and how this too can trigger client's compromised epistemic trust and ability to engage in therapy. Clients with complex post-traumatic stress and dissociative defenses and adaptations have "...emotional responses to any person in a position of authority have been deformed by the experience of terror" (Herman, 1997, p. 136). As terror, fear, and loss of power and control get activated within the interpersonal interactions of therapy, defensive adaptations, such as avoidance (the urge to flee) or anger (the urge to fight back), may show up to protect and defend against what well intentioned therapists are trying to offer - a good and safe enough therapeutic alliance, knowledge, and strategies to relearn how to live in the present. Courtois & Ford's (2016) assert that "many chronically traumatized clients have learned to "read" and respond to the signals of others- especially perpetrators of abuse and anyone else in a position of power – in an attempt to stay safe and avoid further mistreatment or due to their learned caretaking" (p. 92). Therapists thus find themselves faced with this additional challenge, as their very being serves as a trigger to imbedded experiences of internal working models that stipulate others and relationships are not safe and cannot be trusted as sources of important knowledge. Without this awareness and understanding of therapist as both trigger and solution for the client, there is an additional risk for unnoticed countertransference reactions to occur, which may include but are not limited to, defensiveness and frustration, taking the clients responses personally, hopelessness, and responding in kind. This has the potential to lead to "the worst fears of the person confirmed and reinforced... [with the] possibility of therapeutic change buried and despaired of betrayed defenses are reengaged with a vengeance" (Heckler & Johanson, 2015; Schwartz, 1995).

Transcending Awareness and Operationalizing Safety

This final section of the chapter will focus on the ways in which therapists can use this conceptual frame to harness awareness and understanding within the therapeutic space to create the conditions for healing within relationship to another. Critten & Landini (2011) share that clinician understanding is fundamental, as "when we understand the meanings that distressed people struggle to communicate, a pathway to safety and comfort will be opened" (p. 2). Operationalizing the notion of understanding may include, but is not limited to, expecting to be neurocepted as an unsafe other and a trigger to danger, empathically attuning to client *and* therapist micro expressions and movements that may indicate this process via observable client cues, which offer signals to slow down the pace and shift into a space of 'being with.' This may be further supported through the clinician's multisensory and intentional use of congruent verbal and non-verbal language that convey cues of safety. When proximity brings on a neurocpetion of danger rather than one of safety, cues of safety may be communicated through the eyes, smiles and warm facial expressions, soft prosody, and gestures (Dana, 2018). Through these considerations, clinicians can more mindfully step into the relational field with clients whose relational templates are defined by terror, harm, and abuse. Such mindfulness lends to a greater ability to recognize the relational space as a minefield of triggers to disavowed, disowned, dissociated relational trauma memories and its core organizers of experience, and attune to the need to create early conditions for curious experimentation with social connection and engagement while in proximity to another. In turn, expectations around change becomes paced to the client's level of tolerance in response to the triggered inner experiences and corresponding protective reactions when in proximity to the therapist.

When a therapist is prepared for these relational dynamics, an inner shift may be accessed towards a more humane understanding of the process whereby clients automatically and unconsciously attend to the neuoception of danger, and respond with procedurally learned, automatic defensive adaptations. These defensive adaptations developed out of necessity as a result of early traumatic experiences of both commission and omission within early primary caregiving relationships, as previously discussed, and can be used within therapy to explore the present inner responses and reactions that get activated within the therapeutic relationship. By attending to this, therapists start to build micro-moments of corrective relational experience through a more empathetic, understanding stance that extends inwardly and outwardly. These micro-moments may also be considered as a more implicit method of supporting the client to expand their ventral vagal or social engagement system capacities, which when consistent and predictable across time, build the foundation for the therapeutic relationship to become neurocepted as safer and more trusting. An approach that considers consistency and predictability is crucial, as despite intending to offer clients safety, the process by which they are able to be receive and internalize it is unique to each client and occurs within a more complex process of relearning across time and through repetition. As this more implicit relational work unfolds, therapists both hold the hope for change while also recognizing and authentically accepting that change will not occur quickly.

In addition to holding the understanding and awareness of the therapist as trigger, empathic and mindful attunement can be used to recognize a client's cues of danger and their corresponding defensive adaptations in response to our proximity. According to Shewfelt (2018), attunement is:

> "...the therapist's capacity and sensitivity to notice the subtle cues from the client's tone of voice and prosody, body language, facial cues, and so forth, which convey the moment-to-moment emergence of the client's unconscious experience. It also involves the therapist's capacity to respond with accuracy and sensitivity in a well-timed attuned response, so that the client can feel emotionally accompanied and engaged" (p. 65).

Within the context of such intentional attunement, therapists are offered opportunities to better observe client's unique cues and signs of mobilization and immobilization in response to their presence, as well as the reciprocal cues and responses that follow within them. Observable client cues to mobilization that follow a neuroception of danger may include dilating pupils, a visible and fast carotid pulse, and a quickened breathing, while cues to immobilization may include the pupils constricting, significantly slowed down breathing, collapsed muscle tone and posturing, and a cessation of speaking. In addition to attuning to the client, as mentioned above, therapists are also encouraged to attune to their own autonomic cues and responses as a means of considering the dynamic interplay between the client and clinician's inner and outer experiences. Through this process of reciprocal attunement, therapists exercise their own ventral vagal social engagement system through which a new relational template may be modelled for clients, and with time, consistency, and repetition, the client can begin to join and experiment with matching and adjusting their ventral vagal social engagement system and capacities through a reciprocal process of patterned listening and responding (Dana, 2018), synchronizing into a more engaged and collaborative tempo.

Within this process, however, therapists are encouraged to be mindful of not making assumptions about the client's underlying inner subjective experiences connected to what is being noticed. Instead, therapists are encouraged to ground in the opportunity to simply become curious about what is happening and then adjust as a means of slowing down the process to intentionally build and layer the foundation for healing – the relationship. This is done by engaging in a process of figurative seed sowing around the possibility of a collaborative but titrated process of learning and re-learning ways of co-creating meaning within relationship, as the impact of being in relationship and proximity to another can start to be noticed. Part of this process may include the use of intentional and congruent verbal and non-verbal language that offers new multi-sensory cues of safety in an effort towards building new positive feedback loops within the growing therapeutic relationship.

So why is this important? If therapists are able to create a space that is perceived as safe, or safe enough, there is a greater neurophysiological possibility that distinct regions of the brain can communicate, collaborate, and regulate the social engagement system in order to promote and relearn safety within connection, communication, and engagement (Porges, 2001). To generate an inner felt sense of safety, Porges (2021) further shares three crucial, dependent conditions: the autonomic nervous system not being in a state of defense, an activated social engagement system, and that cues of safety be available through the facial expressions, gestures, and prosody of another. For the purposes of this chapter, the assumption is that proximity to therapist may trigger an automatic state of defendedness, deactivating the social engagement system from the outset. As a result, focus is on a preparatory operationalization of relational safety through the translation of often wordless cues of safety into both verbal and non-verbal language, which includes accompanying tone and prosody, and attends to an importance of offering clients congruent multisensory cues of safety from the outset. Both verbal and non-verbal language in this way is contingent on the other, as relational safety is modelled and offers opportunities for clients to experiment with it and grow the capacity to access and utilize their vagal brake, in turn growing the capacity to inhibit mismatched defensive mechanisms and responses. Considerations are further offered around the use of repetitive and consistent language that conveys choice, predictability, and offers open-ended invitations to engagement, accompanied by a congruent tone as a means of building a neuroception of safety in the therapeutic space. In doing so, therapists endeavor to support clients to re-build compromised epistemic trust within the context of the therapeutic relationship, gently challenging the automatic prediction that all relationships and the information they have to offer are unsafe and untrusting through the provision of new cues of safety. This aligns with Porges (2021), who shares that "by supporting the client's capacity for non-defensive social engagement, a client's reactiveness can be transformed over time [as] in the presence of someone perceived as safe, the client's experience of safety will result in both their defenses being inhibited and in their expressing nonverbal markers of being safe" (p. 179). In practice, this is dynamic and finely tuned to each unique client's presenting cues, symptoms, needs, and history, and will likely be executed in a perfectly imperfect manner.

In turning towards the proposed use of language, it's important to consider that the words we use and how we say and embody those words matter. Language is considered in this chapter as something that transcends words and is also spoken through the body and tone. In alignment with the embodiment of language, Howell (2020) draws on the work of Allan Schore and shares that "affects are conveyed procedurally and implicitly by somatic states, by body rhythms, and by facial expressions in ways that are not accessible to ordinary verbal consciousness" (p. 67). In communicating in an embodied way that strives to achieve congruence between words and body language, sound and prosody are additional considerations for clinicians in conveying congruent cues of safety. Dana (2020) speaks to how "sound is one of the ways the autonomic nervous system experiences the world. When you speak, you are not only creating a story through language, but with prosody (the music of the voice is a felt in rhythm, loudness, and pitch)" (p. 112). In this way, the clinician's use of language is multifaceted and is one that embodies safety through pitch and expression, transcending words, and tasks clinicians with building an awareness of their own cues, affective states, and contingent responses. Without this awareness, there is a greater risk of creating further unnoticed mismatches between words, body language, facial expression, and prosody/tone, thus further triggering a neuroception of danger, rather than safety, in the client. Because neuroception occurs beneath conscious awareness, persons living with complex trauma and dissociated identities are primed to look for cues of danger that exist within the therapist, which may at times allude us in the therapy space. Such cues may include incongruent body language and words, vocal prosody and tone that indicate affective shifts, closed body posturing, quickened breathing, and facial expression that may be experienced as tense rather than soft in its appearance.

With respect to the use of verbal language, consider the use of invitation and predictability as options to engage clients and provide new, curious cues of safety through words. Therapists are encouraged to consider the use of verbal language that focuses on choice, offering options rather than demanding or telling. This may be accompanied by a curious yet soft tone and sense of wonder in its prosody and always offers the right of refusal in therapy, as "...prosody communicates what is beneath the words, the intent of the speaker" (Dana, 2018, p. 146). Verbal language that offers predictability at all steps in the therapeutic relationship may focus on the use of preparatory language cues. This may include providing a step-by-step overview of what to expect or what comes next and allowing clients to decide when any therapeutic exploration or intervention starts and stops. Invitational language is considered as collaborative and inclusive to all dissociated identities and may provide clients with opportunities to exercise agency at a pace that is tolerable and manageable for them. This may include the practice of giving and revoking consent or permission within the therapeutic relationship or sharing when the clinician was misattuned or incorrect in reflection of thoughts or feelings. Invitational language is also open-ended and without expressed expectation, both verbally and non-verbally. The use of such language is dynamic rather than prescriptive in nature, with recognition that any one moment that calls for a certain approach and its accompanying melodic prosody, may not be appropriate in another context or if another dissociated identity emerges that is unable to yet tolerate that same prosody. In this way, therapists are called on to engage in a dynamic interpersonal dance, where they are closely following the client moment-to-moment through attunement, with an awareness and understanding that we are not yet *safe enough* to be followed by the client. This dance, and its ever-shifting choreography, is a gift our clients offer us as a way in to supporting them in their unique journeys to healing (Gomez, 2012). When we are able to see this as a gift, the doors to increased possibilities and routes to healing are illuminated, lending to a softened therapeutic stance and response to the complexities of healing from complex trauma within relationship.

Discussion and Conclusion

The focus of this chapter has been to offer new and seasoned clinicians with a conceptual frame to understand the ways in which the therapeutic relationship can simultaneously function as both a trigger and solution to healing for clients with histories of complex relational trauma and dissociated identities. In this context, *a process of being with* has been highlighted as one that builds the scaffold to support the relationship through which healing unfolds; one where the work unravels to reveal that the possibility of a repatterning of how the past, and its influence on predicting the future, exists within us. Within this process, it has been proposed that an increased awareness and understanding that additional preparatory work may be needed to assist client's with accessing a physiological state that allows for engagement, while working towards the creation of a safe base for healing work to occur. In this way, much therapeutic work is premised as being done in between the lines, both at the outset of therapy and in an ongoing manner; particularly, work that is often wordless and based on a depth of survivor's perception and neuroception that interprets and reinterprets to ensure internal and external safety.

The Polyvagal Theory (Porges, 2003, 2009, 2011, 2017, 2018, 2021) was proposed as the conceptual lens through which we can make meaning of a client's contradictory responses and reactions to proximity to the therapist and the very process of therapy, offering a deeper understanding of the ways in which relational safety exists beyond technique or intervention. The concepts of Neuroception (Porges, 2019) and compromised Epistemic Trust (Fonagy & Allison, 2014) were offered as ways of further understanding the process by which triggering occurs and results in difficulty to take in important information related to healing. The frame offered here offers neurophysiological way of understanding how the internal defense and action systems get activated in the therapy space, orienting the mind and body to respond to the threat of another and the interpersonally shared information that other has to offer. An exploration followed into how adopting such a lens can generate a deeper understanding and sensitivity in approaches to treating complex trauma and dissociation, exploring the use of both non-verbal and verbal language as a means of operationalizing theory into practice and supporting clients in the moment-to-moment process of relational healing in psychotherapy. Attunement and empathic understanding were explored as capacities a therapist may engage in to slow down the therapeutic process to allow for cues of safety to develop when in proximity to the therapist.

This is by no means the only way of understanding and responding to the complex interpersonal dynamics that emerge within therapy. It is with hope, however, that this lens offers new and seasoned therapists with an additional frame for understanding and approaching the complexities of treatment, one that veers away from assumptions of treatment stagnation, client resistance, or a need for a technique or protocol to overcome the complexity of healing within relationship when so much harm was caused within the context of relationship. When we can deeply understand a client's reactions and responses as defensive and protective adaptations, albeit mistimed, rather than as a pushing back against therapy or as indicators that we are not "good enough" therapists, we can truly meet our clients where they are and not where we think they should be.

REFERENCES

Anderson, H. (2016, Spring). Listening, hearing and speaking: Brief thoughts on the relationship to Dialogue. *Psychological Opinions*.

Anderson, Harlene. (2003, August 29). *Listening, hearing and speaking: Thoughts on the relationship to dialogue* [Conference presentation]. Eighth Annual Open Dialogue Conference: What is helpful in Treatment Dialogue, Finland.

Arntz A. (2020). A plea for more attention to mental representations. *Journal of Behavior Therapy and Experimental Psychiatry, 67*, 101510.

APA Presidential Task Force on Evidence-Based Practice. (2006). Evidence-based practice in psychology. *American Psychologist, 61,* 271–285. http://dx.doi.org/10.1037/0003-066X.61.4.271

Badenoch, B. (2017, March). *A symphony of gifts from relational neuroscience: How understanding our brains can support lives of hope and resilience* [Virtual summit presentation]. Neuroscience Training Summit, Sounds True.

Bowlby, J. (1980a). *Attachment and loss, Vol. 3: Loss, sadness, and depression*. NY, NY: Basic Books.

Bowlby, J. (1988*). A secure base: Parent-child attachment and healthy human development*. NY, NY: Basic Books.

Bretherton, I. (1992). The origins of attachment theory: John Bowlby and Mary Ainsworth. *Developmental psychology, 28*(5), 759-775.

Brown, D. P. & Elliott, D. S. (2016). *Attachment disturbances in adults: Treatment for Comprehensive Repair*. NY, NY: W.W. Norton & Company

Chefetz, R. (2022). *Attackments; Subjugation, shame, and the attachment to painful affects and objects* (O. Badouk Epstein, Ed.). NY, NY: Routeledge.

Courtois, CA, and Ford, JD (2013) *Treatment of Complex Trauma: A Sequenced, Relationship-Based Approach*. NY, NY: The Guilford Press.

Courtois, CA, and Ford, JD, eds. (2020). *Treating Complex Traumatic Stress Disorders in Adults, second edition*. NY, NY: The Guilford Press.

Cozolino, L. (2006, 2014). *The neuroscience of human relationships: attachment and the developing social brain*. NY, NY: W.W. Norton & Company.

Cozolino, L. (2010). *The neuroscience of psychotherapy: Healing the social brain (2nd ed.).* W.W. Norton & Company.

Crittenden, P.M. & Landini, A. (2011). *Assessing adult attachment: A dynamic-maturational approach to discourse analysis.* NY, NY: W.W. Norton and Company.

Damasio, A. (2021). *Feeling & knowing: Making minds conscious*. NY, NY: Pantheon Books.

Dana, D. (2018). *The Polyvagal theory in therapy: Engaging the rhythm of regulation (Norton series on interpersonal neurobiology)*. W.W. Norton & Company.

Dana, D. (2019, March/April). The touch taboo: Are we missing a vital source of healing?" *Psychotherapy networker*, Retrieved from: https://www.psychotherapynetworker.org/magazine/article/2345/the-touch-taboo

Dana, D. (2020). *Polyvagal exercises for safety and connection: 50 client centered practices*. NY, NY: W.W. Norton & Company.

Dalenberg, C. J. (2000). *Countertransference and the treatment of trauma*. American Psychological Association.

Dalenberg, C. J. (2004). Maintaining the safe and effective therapeutic relationship in the context of distrust and anger: Countertransference and complex trauma. *Psychotherapy: Theory, Research, Practice, Training, 41* (4), 438-447.

Ellis, A. E., Simiola, V., Brown, L., Courtois, C., & Cook, J. M. (2018). The role of evidence-based therapy relationships on treatment outcome for adults with trauma: A systematic review. *Journal of Trauma and Dissociation, 19,* 185–213. http://dx.doi.org/10.1080/15299732.2017.1329771

Emerson, D., Sharma, R., Chaudry, S., & Turner, J. (2009). Yoga therapy in practice: Trauma-Sensitive Yoga: Principles, Practice, and Research. *International Journal of Yoga* Therapy, 19, 123-128.

Fonagy, P., Luyten, P., Allison, E., & Campbell, C. (2019). Mentalizing, epistemic trust and the phenomenology of psychotherapy. *Psychopathology* 52, 94–103.

Fonagy, P. & Allison, E. (2014). The role of mentalizing and epistemic trust in the therapeutic relationship. *Psychotherapy*, 51(3), 372-380.

Fonagy, P. & Target, M. (1997). Attachment and reflective function: Their role in self-organization. *Development and Psychopathology*, 9, 679-700.

Fosha, D., Siegel, D. J., Solomon, M. F. (2009). *The healing power of emotion: Affective neuroscience, development & clinical practice* (Norton Series on Interpersonal Neurobiology). W.W. Norton.

Fosha, D. (2001). The Dyadic Regulation of Affect. *Journal of Clinical Psychology/In Session*, 57(2), 227-242.

Fosha, D. (2000). *The transforming power of affect: A model for accelerated change*. Basic Books.

Gomez, A. M. (2012). EMDR therapy and adjunct approaches with children: Complex trauma, attachment and dissociation. NY, NY: Springer.

Gomez, J., Lewis, J.K., Noll, L.K., Smidt, A.M., & Birrell, P.J. (2016). Shifting the focus: Non-pathologizing approaches to healing from betrayal trauma through an emphasis on relational care. *Journal of Trauma & Dissociation*, 172(2), 165-185.

Heckler, R.A. & Johanson, G.J. (2015). Enhancing the immediacy and intimacy of the therapeutic relationship through somatic dimension. In Marlock & Weiss (Eds.), Theory and Practice of Body Psychotherapy, 471-479.

Herman, J. L. (2015). *Trauma and Recovery: The aftermath of violence–from domestic abuse to political terror*. NY, NY: Basic Books.

Howell, E. (2011). *Understanding and treating dissociative identity disorder*. NY, NY: Taylor & Francis Group.

Howell, E. (2020). Trauma and dissocation informed psychotherapy: Relational healing and the therapeutic connection. NY, NY: W.W. Norton & Company.

Kinsler, P. J. (2014). Relationships redux: Evidence-based relationships. *Journal of Trauma & Dissociation*, *15* (1), 1-5.

Liotti, G. (1992). Disorganized/disoriented attachment in the etiology of the dissociative disorders. *Dissociation*, *5*(4), 196-204.

Norcross, J. C., & Wampold, B. E. (2019). Relationships and responsiveness in the psychological treatment of trauma: The tragedy of the APA Clinical Practice Guideline. *Psychotherapy, 56* (3), 391–399. https://doi.org/10.1037/pst0000228

Pearlman, L. A., & Courtois, C. A. (2005). Clinical applications of the attachment framework: Relational treatment of complex trauma. *Journal of Traumatic Stress: Official Publication of The International Society for Traumatic Stress Studies, 18* (5), 449-459.

Porges, S. W. (2001). The polyvagal theory: phylogenetic substrates of a social nervous system. *International journal of psychophysiology*, *42*(2), 123-146.

Porges, S. (2003). The polyvagal theory: phylogenetic contributions to social behaviour. *Physiol Behav,* 79, pp. 503–513.

Porges, S. W. (2007). The polyvagal perspective. *Biological psychology*, *74*(2), 116-143.

Porges, S. (2009). The polyvagal theory: New insights into adaptive reactions of the autonomic nervous system. Cleveland Clinic Journal of Medicine, 76(2): S86–S90. doi:10.3949/ccjm.76.s2.17.

Porges, S. (2011). The Polyvagal Theory: Neurophysiological foundations of emotions, attachment, communication, self-regulation. New York, New York: W.W. Norton & Company.

Porges, S. (2017). The pocket guide to the polyvagal theory: The transformative power of feeling safe. New York, New York: W.W. Norton & Company.

Porges, S. W., & Dana, D. (2018). *Clinical applications of the polyvagal theory: The emergence of polyvagal-informed therapies (Norton series on interpersonal neurobiology)*. W.W. Norton & Company.

Porges, S. W. (2021). *Polyvagal Safety: Attachment, communication, and self-regulation*. NY, NY: W.W. Norton & Company.

Schore, A.N. (2003a). *Affect dysregulation and disorders of the self*. New York: W.W. Norton & Company.

Schore, A.N. (2003b). *Affect dysregulation and the repair of the self*. New York: W.W. Norton & Company.

Schwartz, Richard (1995). *Internal Family Systems Theory*. New York: Guilford Press.

Solomon, S.D., & Siegel, D. (2003). *Healing trauma: Attachment, mind, body, and brain*. New York: W.W. Norton & Company.

Van der Hart, O., Brown, P., & Van der Kolk, B. A. (1989). Pierre Janet's treatment of post-traumatic stress. *Journal of traumatic stress*, *2*(4), 379-395.

Non-Suicidal Self-Injury and Suicidality in Dissociative Disorders

by Alexis E. Arbuthnott, Ph.D., R.D. Psych.

Harming the body can become a potent way of coping with psychological pain, though it is also unhealthy and can have significant life-threatening and life-interfering consequences. As people with dissociative disorders (DDs) tend to have an overabundance of psychological pain, alongside underdeveloped skills and resources for coping with internal and external stressors, there is an elevated risk for non-suicidal self-injury (NSSI) and suicidality among this population (Calati, et al., 2017; Tanner et al., 2017; Webermann et al., 2016). It is therefore imperative that clinicians understand the functions of these behaviours and be skilled in responding to their clients in ways that facilitate healthy coping and growth.

This chapter discusses the current research linking NSSI, suicidality and dissociation among people with DDs. Next, the functions of NSSI and theories of suicide are explored within the context of exposure to developmental trauma and managing trauma symptoms. Finally, clinical implications for risk assessment and interventions are outlined.

The term non-suicidal self-injury (NSSI) refers to the "deliberate, self-inflicted damage of body tissue without suicidal intent and for purposes not socially or culturally sanctioned" (International Society for the Study of Self-Injury, 2018), and includes behaviours such as cutting, burning, hitting, and scratching oneself. Suicidality, as discussed in this chapter, encompasses the full continuum of suicidal thoughts and behaviours, including passive thoughts of suicide (e.g., wanting to disappear, not wanting to exist), active thoughts of suicide (e.g., making a suicide plan), suicide preparations (e.g., acquiring the means for suicide, writing suicide notes), suicide attempts, interrupted and aborted suicide attempts, and death by suicide. While NSSI and suicidal behaviour refer to actual behaviour, suicidality itself may or may not include action. A full review of the risk factors and etiology of NSSI and suicidality are beyond the scope of this chapter (see Ford & Gómez, 2015; Nock, 2014).

Both NSSI and suicidal behaviours fall under a larger umbrella of self-harm alongside substance use and other addictions (e.g., gambling, shopping), disordered eating, risky or compulsive sexual behaviours, and other risk-taking behaviours (e.g., speeding without wearing a seatbelt). Whereas other self-harm behaviours may inadvertently cause harm to the body (e.g., accidental overdose alongside substance use, severe malnutrition associated with food restriction), their underlying intent is generally not directly to harm the body. Given the tendency for trauma survivors to substitute alternative symptoms (e.g., behaviours) as a means of managing trauma symptoms, it may be helpful to conceptualized NSSI and suicidal behaviours as sharing functions and treatment considerations with these other forms of self-harm (see Briere, 2019).

A discussion of the definitions of dissociation and etiology of DDs are also beyond the scope of this chapter. However, it is important to note that most DDs (e.g., dissociative identity disorder, other specified dissociative disorder-type 1) are traumagenic in origin, meaning that they develop as a way to cope with chronic adverse events during the developmental period (see Dorahy et al., 2014). Thus, understanding the impact of trauma during the developmental period is important in conceptualizing NSSI and suicidality as symptoms of trauma exposure and disrupted attachment within this population. Survivors of complex trauma have had to deal with a greater cumulative number and severity of adverse life events, experience higher baseline levels of psychological pain, and have experienced disruptions in the normative acquisition of skills for self-soothing, emotion regulation, communication, problem solving, and mentalization (see Herman, 1992; Silberg, 2021). These developmental disruptions have implications for a trauma survivor's reduced access to healthy strategies for coping with stressors, solving problems and connecting with other people.

For people with DDs, some self-states (i.e., alters, parts, aspects, or other ways in which the person may refer to the components of their internal system) may engage in NSSI or suicidality with or without the awareness of other self-states (Brand, 2001). The functions of NSSI and theories of suicide outlined in this chapter apply to both the whole person and to individual self-states. Similarly, interpersonal functions of NSSI and suicidality may apply both to relations with other people as well as to relations between self-states. Understanding the use of NSSI or suicidality as part of these self-states' roles within the larger internal system is essential in helping the client to find healthier ways to cope and in resolving internal conflicts (Brand, 2001; Chefetz, 2017).

Relations Between Dissociation, NSSI, Suicidality

Research consistently demonstrates associations between traumatic experiences and both NSSI and suicidality, with the path between these variables being complex and multifaceted; dissociation appears to be one of several mediators on this path (Ford & Gómez, 2015). Indeed, there is a strong association between dissociation and both NSSI and suicidality (e.g., Calati, et al., 2017; Černis, et al., 2019; Ford and Gómez, 2015). For example, one meta-analysis (Calati, et al., 2017) found that psychiatric patients who reported a history of NSSI or suicide attempts also reported higher levels of dissociation relative to patients without this history. Thus, dissociation may be a transdiagnostic mechanism that increases risk for NSSI and suicidality.

People with DDs may be at a particularly high risk for NSSI and suicidality (Nestor, Brand et al., 2022; Calati, Bensassi, & Courtet, 2017; Tanner et al., 2017; Webermann et al., 2016), with dissociation severity associated with greater NSSI and suicidality (Nestor, Brand, et al., 2022; Webermann et al., 2016). When psychiatric patients with and without DDs were compared in a meta-analysis (Calati et al., 2017), patients with DDs were more likely to report both previous NSSI and suicide attempts. Up to 78% of patients with DDs engage in NSSI, and up to 86% attempt suicide (see Webermann et al., 2016 for a review). Furthermore, 1.8% of the participants in the Patients with Dissociative Disorders (TOP DD) study completed suicide within a 30-month span (Brand et al., 2013). Indeed, DDs may confer a specific and unique risk for NSSI and suicidality beyond that which is conferred by suicide ideation, depression, or PTSD alone (Webermann et al., 2016).

Although people with DDs often initially present for treatment with high levels of NSSI and suicidality, these behaviours tend to decrease as treatment progresses (Brand et al., 2009; 2013). Over a one-year period in the TOP-DD study, 38% of patients in the first stage of treatment attempted suicide, whereas there were no suicide attempts among patients in the last stage of treatment (Brand et al., 2009). Similarly, over a 30-month period NSSI and suicide attempts dropped 5% and 6%, respectively, each month (Brand et al., 2013). Decreases in level of dissociation during treatment is associated with decreases in NSSI and suicide ideation (Lynch et al., 2008). Taken together, these results demonstrate that effective treatment reduces risk of NSSI and suicidality among clients with DDs.

Functions of NSSI

NSSI serves a variety of functions, which can lead to self-harm becoming a primary way of coping with a wide range of internal and external stressors. The reasons for NSSI initiation may differ from the functions that maintain it (e.g., Muehlenkamp et al., 2013; Nock, 2009; Whitlock & Selekman, 2014). While understanding factors surrounding NSSI initiation is important for preventing NSSI in the first place, this chapter focuses primarily on understanding and treating NSSI that is already occurring. Understanding the functions maintaining NSSI is important for two reasons. First, it contextualizes the behaviour as a strategy to meet an unmet need when healthier options are not accessible. This approach reduces shame and self-stigma and increases access to compassionate supports. Second, it assists in identifying and prioritizing interventions that match healthier strategies to NSSI functions. It is unwise to take away a behaviour that was meeting a need without having healthier options to use in its place.

Functions of NSSI generally fall into three broad categories (see Whitlock & Selekman, 2014): psychological (e.g., NSSI as reinforced through intrapersonal or interpersonal consequences) social (e.g., NSSI with an interpersonal goal) and biological (e.g., NSSI as an attempt to restore levels of endogenous opioids to homeostasis). Among trauma survivors, self-harm may have the additional function of reenacting trauma (see Farber, 1997, Yakeley & Burbridge-James, 2018). Functions within each of these categories are discussed in detail below. Of note, however, is the overlap between these models and the tendency for NSSI to serve multiple functions simultaneously (e.g., NSSI with the function of reducing negative affective states through alterations in neurobiology while simultaneously communicating distress) (Whitlock & Selekman, 2014).

PSYCHOLOGICAL FUNCTIONS

The psychological model (Nock, 2009) explains NSSI as being maintained through both intrapersonal and interpersonal functions, which are each composed of both positive (i.e., increasing something that is desired) and negative (i.e., removing something that is aversive or unwanted) reinforcers. Intrapersonal functions include using NSSI to generate sensations or feelings (e.g., anti-dissociation, generating a thrill or rush of energy), as well as the use of NSSI to escape from uncomfortable internal states (e.g., shutting down unwanted emotions, reducing internal tension). With respect to trauma symptoms specifically, NSSI may serve as a distraction from intrusive or disturbing thoughts or rumination, including self-critical, shaming and suicidal thoughts (Ford & Gómez, 2015). People who dissociate sometimes describe the sight of their own blood as grounding, which may have a role in escaping from flashbacks and dissociated states, and the physical pain may reduce depersonalization. Furthermore, NSSI may provide the person with an increased locus of control and a sense of self-efficacy. Interpersonal functions include the use of NSSI to influence others (e.g., to communicate distress in order to elicit care, obtaining resources or rewards) or to avoid punishment or expectations (e.g., preventing others from setting limits or enforcing consequences). Interpersonal functions overlap with the social model of NSSI, and are explored in more depth in that section below.

The most commonly endorsed functions of NSSI are to avoid or distract from psychological pain and to express psychological distress (see Whitlock & Selekman, 2014). In one sample of people with DDs who engaged in NSSI, 62% and 52% of the participants reported engaging in NSSI in response to trauma-related cues and emotion dysregulation, respectively (Nestor, Boi, et al., 2022). Trauma survivors experience high levels of psychological pain resulting from the painful life events that they have endured. Furthermore, trauma during the developmental period disrupts development (see Herman, 1992; Silberg, 2021), which may interfere with the normative acquisition of healthy strategies for self-soothing, emotion regulation, problem solving and communication. Healthy strategies across these domains are initially learned through coregulation and modeling with attuned caregivers, and later through explicit instruction and assistance. When caregivers are absent, abusive or themselves lack healthy strategies across these domains, children do not have the opportunity to learn healthy strategies from their caregivers. Trauma also dysregulates the nervous system, leading to increased emotion sensitivity, reactivity, and a slower return to baseline as a means of maintaining a readiness to respond to potential dangers. Taken together, trauma survivors experiences higher levels of distress associated with a greater number and severity of current and lifetime cumulative stressors, while simultaneously having access to fewer healthy internal and external resources to manage these stressors. Within this developmental context, NSSI can become a one-size fits-all solution for managing psychological pain when healthier strategies were missed during the developmental period.

NSSI is also used to communicate distress both at an internal level (i.e., to themselves) and to other people (Muehlenkamp et al., 2012; Whitlock & Selekman, 2014). The central conflict of dissociation is the need to know and not know at the same time (Howell, 2011). People with DDs are inherently disconnected from aspects of their internal experience, which often includes their own distress. Where people are repeatedly told that painful events did not happen or that they should not feel how they feel, or their pain has been repeatedly invalidated in another way, they may dissociate their pain and internalize this invalidation. NSSI may then be used to make invisible pain visible, or "real." Physical injury may be substituted for emotional injury, or distress related to internal conflicts may be acted out on the body (Brand, 2001; Chefetz, 2017; Farber, 1997). The use of NSSI to express distress to others is discussed within the context of social functions, below.

SOCIAL FUNCTIONS

The social model of NSSI describes NSSI as a tool to meet relational needs (see Whitlock & Selekman, 2014), including obtaining care (via expression of distress), influencing others and social bonding. The use of NSSI for social functions reflects that developmental tasks, such as learning healthy communication and problem solving skills, were either missed or were ineffective in getting needs met during the developmental period. Thus, NSSI reflects the person's creativity in developing strategies to get these needs met as effectively as they are able, with the resources that they have available, within the environment in which they developed. Research is clear that although NSSI may serve social functions, these tend to be secondary to intrapersonal functions such as affect regulation (Muehlenkamp et al., 2013; Whitlock & Selekman, 2014). This highlights the importance of understanding the larger context in which the NSSI occurs, including assessing for the multiple functions of this behaviour.

The use of NSSI to meet social needs can be understood within the context of disrupted attachment. People with secure attachment styles feel connected with others and know how to ask for and receive support from appropriate people and in healthy ways. People with insecure attachment styles have learned that they cannot rely on other people to meet their needs through normative means, and they develop alternate strategies (e.g., excessive independence, clinginess, parentification, dissociation, escalation of maladaptive behaviours) to ensure their needs are met. As a result of relational trauma (e.g., misattunement, abuse, neglect) people with DDs inherently experience attachment styles that are not secure. Indeed, DDs have been linked to a disorganized attachment style in infancy (Liotti, 2006). Furthermore, people with DDs tend to experience high levels of shame (e.g., Dorahy et al., 2013; 2015), may view themselves as a burden to others, and may deny their own needs, all of which make it difficult to directly communicate distress to significant others (e.g., family, friends, support people, clinicians). Rather than using words to express distress and ask for help, NSSI may become a nonverbal means of communicating distress and eliciting needed care. It may be easier to justify asking for help when there is a visible physical need for it, and it may be more difficult for significant others to deny the request for help when there is a visible injury. From this lens, NSSI may serve a care- or connection-seeking function.

Although NSSI can also be used as a means of influencing others beyond merely seeking connection or care (e.g., obtaining resources, preventing the setting of limits and boundaries), this is generally not a primary function of NSSI (Muehlenkamp et al., 2013; Whitlock & Selekman, 2014). Nonetheless, the use of NSSI to influence others again reflects disruptions in attachment and limited access to healthy relational and problem solving skills. This may also reflect difficulties with mentalization (i.e., the ability to understand the mental states of self and others) and empathy, as demonstrated through a limited awareness or understanding of the psychological impact of NSSI behaviours on other people, as well as the objectification of others. Children learn mentalization skills through a caregiver's attunement and early affect mirroring (see Fonagy et al., 2002). Repeated neglect of the child's mental state interferes with the normative developmental of mentalization skills. Furthermore, when a child's body is repeatedly used to meet the needs of others (e.g., via sexualization, as an outlet for adult aggression), the person learns that other people are objects to be used to meet their own needs.

Finally, NSSI may have a social bonding function (e.g., to fit in with others). Social bonding may be more salient in the initiation of NSSI rather than its maintenance (e.g., Muehlenkamp et al., 2013). This highlights the potential social contagion effects associated with NSSI among people who are already at a higher risk (Jarvi et al., 2013), such as those with trauma and dissociation. Thus, when someone is experiencing a high level of psychological pain and they are introduced to NSSI through interactions with their peers or through social media, NSSI may be perceived as a socially acceptable and effective way to manage their pain. Although a secondary gain may include a sense of connection with peers through shared experience, alternate functions (e.g., affect regulation, communication of distress) generally maintain NSSI in those who go on to engage in NSSI repetitively (Muehlenkamp et al., 2013).

BIOLOGICAL FUNCTIONS

Biological models of NSSI highlight the neurobiological alterations that make people more vulnerable for using NSSI to down-regulate high arousal and tension (Groschwitz & Plener, 2012). Neuroimaging and neuroendocrine studies have shown that people who engage in NSSI may have neurobiological alterations affecting multiple biological systems, including those systems related to threat avoidance, learning and motivation, cognition (e.g., memory, perception, attention, language), social processing, as well as arousal and biological regulation (see Schreiner et al., 2015). Many of these neurobiological alterations overlap with those altered through exposure to traumatic stress, particularly changes in the limbic system, hypothalamic-pituitary-adrenal axis, and key monoamine neurotransmitters. These biological changes map onto symptoms of hyperarousal, numbing, dissociation and reexperiencing of trauma (see Weiss, 2007).

On a biological level, NSSI is surprisingly effective in reducing psychological pain, thus its appeal as a means of regulating painful affective states and reducing internal tension. NSSI is often preceded by high emotional arousal and tension, and hyperarousal tends to be reduced following NSSI (Klonsky, 2007). The homeostasis model of NSSI suggests that people who engage in NSSI have lower baseline levels of endogenous opioids (perhaps due to chronic exposure to traumatic environments and adverse experiences), and the release of endogenous opioids via NSSI functions to regulate affect (see Bresin & Gordon, 2013).

REENACTMENT

The role of NSSI as a form of trauma reenactment has received little attention in recent research. Nonetheless, the older psychodynamic frameworks point to the role of NSSI as a means of attempting to differentiate between self and other, define and differentiate body boundaries, and to master severe childhood trauma through psychophysiological reenactments (see Farber, 1997, Yakeley & Burbridge-James, 2018). NSSI may come to be used as a substitute caregiver from which the person seeks soothing and a sense of self. For trauma survivors whose bodies have been violated, the act of NSSI may release not just negative affect and tension, but also symbolically relieve the person from the perceived badness inside themselves (e.g., cleansing or purification, atonement through self-punishment), or discharge rage onto a perpetrator. Through this perspective, the person engaging in NSSI takes on both the roles of the perpetrator and the victim simultaneously and acts out traumatic events and inner conflicts. This model may be particularly helpful in understanding the roles of self-states that claim responsibility for engaging in NSSI.

Theories of Suicide

A large number of theories exists to explain why people intentionally kill themselves (see Gunn & Lester, 2014; Van Orden et al., 2016). Many pathways can lead to suicidality. Thus, rather than a single theory explaining all cases of suicidality, these theories should be considered complementary to each other in understanding suicide. Biological theories of suicide highlight the interaction between physiological vulnerabilities and psychosocial stressors. Cognitive-behavioural theories explain suicide as being driven by maladaptive cognitive styles (e.g., hopelessness, suicidal cognitive mode, state dependent memory, perceptions of entrapment). Developmental and systems theories account for the role of social and family systems as causal factors in suicidality. Escape and interpersonal theories of suicide, which inherently overlap with the aforementioned theories, are discussed in detail below.

ESCAPE THEORIES

Escape theories of suicide (see Gunn & Lester, 2014) underscore the function of suicide as a means to escape from aversive states and situations. From this lens, suicide is viewed as a solution to a problem. Baecher (1975) was one of the first theorists to explain escape-motivated suicides, and posited that suicide may occur when the person has passed the threshold of what they feel they can handle within a given situation (i.e., escape-flight suicide), when they have lost something central to their way of life (i.e., grief-motivated suicide), or when someone is attempting to atone for a real or imagined fault (i.e., punishment-motivated suicide). Baumeister (1990) proposed that suicide is an attempt to escape from aversive self-awareness (e.g., of the self's inadequacy, incompetence, unattractiveness, or guilt) following an inability to meet expectations and where this failure is attributed to negative qualities of the self. The Suicide as Psychache theory of suicide (Shneidman, 1993) explains suicide as a way to stop the unbearable psychological pain caused by deprivation of vital needs. Unfortunately, it is not uncommon for people with DDs to have experienced chronic states of physical and relational deprivation leading to unbearable psychological pain. Furthermore, as discussed earlier, individuals with DDs tend to have an excessive amount of psychological pain, coupled with both a higher level of stressors and fewer internal and external resources to cope with these stressors.

The early escape theories of suicide highlight the role of psychological pain as a precursor for suicidality. However, psychological pain alone is unlikely to be sufficient in generating suicidal behaviour, and a more salient factor may be the ways in which the person appraises their situation. The Cry of Pain model (Williams, 1997) argues that perceptions of entrapment and defeat are key factors leading to suicidality. Research support for this theory has found that perceptions of defeat and entrapment mediate the relation between PTSD symptoms and suicidal behaviours (Panagioti et al., 2013). These results have implications for trauma survivors, as trauma by definition exceeds a person's capacity to cope. The person may have experienced a "freeze" or "submit" survival response during traumatic events whereby they were unable to escape the situation (i.e., entrapment) and they may have lost agency (i.e., defeat) over what happened to their bodies (see Kozlowska et al., 2015). Even when the traumatic event has ended, people may continue to find themselves psychologically and physiologically stuck in a state of inescapable danger. Furthermore, limited knowledge and experience with self-soothing and problem solving skills may contribute to difficulties identifying and accessing alternate "ways out," leading to the perception of suicide as the only possible escape from their pain.

INTERPERSONAL THEORY

Social isolation is one of the most potent predictors of all aspects of suicidality, including suicide ideation, suicide attempts and deaths by suicide (see Van Orden, 2016). The interpersonal (or interpersonal-psychological) theory of suicide (Joiner, 2005; Van Orden et al., 2010) posits that suicidality arises when a person experiences unmanageable feelings of perceived burdensomeness and thwarted belongingness, and the person has the capability for suicide. Both perceived burdensomeness and thwarted belongingness reflect a sense of perceived social disconnection, with thwarted belongingness also including intense loneliness and a perceived lack of reciprocal care.

Trauma impacts relationships. Survivors may have difficulties navigating relational closeness and distance, independence and dependence, and interpersonal boundaries. Some trauma survivors genuinely have few, if any, reciprocal relationships. For others, limited relationship-related object permanence (i.e., the ability to hold another person in mind when they are not physically present) and mentalization (e.g., understanding the mental states of others) may enhance a sense of thwarted belongingness, as it may be difficult for the person to access an accurate mental representation of supportive others when those people are not physically present. Furthermore, many trauma survivors take on a caretaking role (e.g., Liotti, 2017). When a caretaking role is assumed, the person's own needs may be self-perceived as a burden to others. Similarly, some trauma survivors may be overly clingy in relationships and excessively fear rejection and abandonment, which may be self-perceived as being "too much" and may elicit invalidating messages to that effect from others. This perspective aligns with the eusocial theory of suicide which conceptualizes suicide as a perceived self-sacrifice for the good of others (Joiner et al., 2016).

Finally, the third component of the interpersonal theory of suicide is that the person must have the capability for suicide. The capability for the level of self-directed violence necessary for suicide may be acquired through exposure to other forms of violence against the body (e.g., abuse, assaults). Experiencing violence normalizes violence. Capacity for suicide may also be built up through increasingly severe NSSI. Indeed, NSSI is known to be a gateway to suicidal behaviour, and it may confer a unique risk for future suicidal behaviour independent of shared risk factors (Whitlock et al., 2013). The more severe the NSSI, where this NSSI is perceived as effective in meeting the person's needs, the less frightening suicide becomes.

Clinical Implications

The whole person is responsible and accountable for their behaviour regardless of which self-state engages in self-harm or suicidal behaviours. Thus, assessment of suicide risk and interventions targeting self-harm and suicidality need to address the impact of dissociation, increase internal cooperation surrounding safety concerns, and generalize access to healthier strategies across self-states (see Brand, 2001).

RISK ASSESSMENT

Given the high associations between dissociation, NSSI and suicidality, all clients presenting with trauma, dissociation and/or NSSI should be screened for risk of suicide and severe NSSI. Clinicians should be familiar with procedures for thorough suicide risk assessments (e.g., Fowler, 2012). Reassessments as warranted are recommended. The *ideation-to-action* framework (e.g., Klonsky & May, 2014; 2015) explains the shift from suicide ideation to suicide attempt as facilitated by an increase in capacity for suicide, which results from changes in dispositional (e.g., pain sensitivity, blood phobia), acquired (e.g., habituation to experiences associated with pain and injury), and practical (e.g., concrete factors such as knowledge and access to lethal means) factors. As chronic suicide ideation is common among clients with DDs, it is important that clinicians become familiar with their client's baseline presentation and level of suicidality and be vigilant for shifts away from this baseline. In general, three types of risks should be considered when assessing for suicide risk among clients with DDs: (1) risk derived from the person's demographics (e.g., trauma history, sex, gender, age, cultural marginalization, baseline level of dissociation, other diagnoses); (2) risk relative to the person's baseline presentation (e.g., increases in depressive or trauma symptoms, acute increase in NSSI or suicide ideation); and (3) risk associated with current and foreseeable changes in social factors (e.g., changes in employment or financial status, relationships and social supports, medical status), including increases in stressors and decreases in protective factors.

Assessment of suicide risk with clients with DDs should involve language inclusive of multiplicity. Asking the presenting self-state whether they are experiencing any suicide ideation may result in the person denying all suicidality; this may be accurate, as that particular self-state may genuinely not experience suicidality, even in the presence of behaviours with an obvious suicide intent. In contrast, asking whether any part of the person experiences suicide ideation is more likely to elicit information related to suicide risk held by self-states that may not be in direct communication with the clinician, as well as capture suicide ideation that may be more passive or ambivalent in nature. Identifying the self-states associated with suicidality opens opportunities for interventions involving these self-states.

SUPPORT PLAN

A client-centered collaborative approach is essential when developing a plan to support the person's safety. Some people find the term "safety plan" to be condescending and overly simplistic, and clinicians may need to find an alternate description that empowers the client to take an active role in both the creation and implementation of the plan. The client is the expert in what they find both helpful and unhelpful, and clinicians should actively work to promote the client's agency in finding and implementing solutions to assist them in manage internal and external stressors in healthy ways, such that they learn through experience that they are neither trapped nor helpless. Even when a client reports that "nothing helps," the clinician needs to remember that the client has kept themselves alive despite having lived through some exceptionally difficult life events, and thus they must have some level of internal and external resources for having been able to do so.

Support plans should clearly outline the signs and symptoms indicative of an increase in distress that may lead to a crisis (e.g., Stanley & Brown, 2012). Helping the client identify their internal experiences (i.e., emotions, thoughts, sensations, urges) at baseline, when triggered and escalating, and when at crisis may help them to match the appropriate coping strategy to the level of escalation. For example, clients may have more access to strategies for independent self-regulation when triggered and beginning to escalate versus when they are at a crisis level. There may be some merit to the client's report that "nothing helps" when strategies are implemented only at very high levels of distress; at this point the client may be too distressed to access or benefit from healthy coping strategies that may have been accessible and effective at lower levels of distress. Thus, the role of the support plan in preventing crises, as well as in responding to crises, should be emphasized.

In general, the support plan should list the strategies that the client has learned for coping independently, social contacts and social settings that can provide a distraction from suicidal and distressing thoughts, support people who can help resolve the crisis, and mental health professionals (e.g., clinicians) or agencies (e.g., crisis lines, hospital emergency departments) who can provide professional or crisis mental health supports (Stanley & Brown, 2012). Clinicians should also initiate a discussion of how future serious safety crises will be managed by the therapist, such that a predictable plan has been outlined in advance (Brand, 2001). The support plan should be considered a living document, and should be reviewed and revised regularly as the client learns new strategies that are found to be helpful.

Support plans should also include ways of restricting access to lethal means for suicide, to the extent that the client is willing, such as decreasing access to a stockpile of medications, sharps, ropes, firearms, or whatever means for suicide align with the client's specific suicide plan. The intention here is not to get rid of all potentially dangerous objects, as people can get quite creative in finding ways to hurt themselves, but rather to add an extra step between having thoughts of suicide and making a suicide attempt. Increasing the time it takes to obtain the means for suicide may reduce the impact of impulsivity on carrying out a suicide plan, and may provide enough time for the acute stressors to resolve, distress to reduce naturally and support people to respond.

Many clients find it difficult to remember the components of their support plans, or even that they have a support plan, when they are in states of high distress. Thus, having the plan written down and accessible is essential. Clients may find it helpful to keep a copy of their support plan on their cell phones for easy reference (e.g., photo, note, safety planning app). Some clients also benefit from reminders to use their support plans (or even to practice individual strategies within the plan as a means of prevention), such as putting a symbol or sticker on their hand, setting alarms on their phones, or leaving notes for themselves.

Clients may require admission to an acute inpatient mental health unit for a period of stabilization when they are unable to maintain their safety and they are at an imminent risk for suicide or serious self-harm. Ideally the decision to seek a higher level of care will be made collaboratively. However, clinicians may have a legal and ethical responsibility to initiate hospitalization without their client's consent when necessary due to their client's high risk. Potential benefits of hospitalization include the opportunity for diagnostic clarification, more intensive opportunities for building or restoring skills and coping strategies, rapid changes in medications to facilitate symptom reduction, and a reduction in immediate stressors that allow for time and space to focus on mental health concerns. If accessible, clients with DDs may benefit most from care on inpatient units specialized in treating trauma and dissociation. The goal of inpatient care is generally rapid stabilization (Sharfstein, 2009), with the intention of returning the client to care in the community as quickly and as safely as possible.

While inpatient care can be potentially life-saving, it is not without risks. Clinicians should be mindful of the risks of retraumatization (e.g., Cusack et al., 2003), including the potential negative impacts of involuntary hospitalization, perceived coercion, and use of seclusion and restraints (e.g., Akther et al., 2019; Cheize, 2019; Cusack et al., 2003). The current culture of some hospital wards (e.g., frequent staff changes, staff burnout, lack of trauma-informed care) may increase client's distress, and clients with DDs may use dissociation as a means to cope with inherent inconsistencies associated with the system itself (Parry, et al., 2017). Furthermore, the hospital environment may meet needs for the client that are not being met in the community (e.g., safety, care or connection, tangible needs such as access to food, reduced stressors), which may lead to repeated admissions and difficulty generalizing stabilization from hospital to home. Indeed, the transition period immediately following discharge from inpatient care reflects a period of increased risk for suicide (Bojaníc et al.,2020; Forte et al., 2019), and rapid follow-up with a community clinician is strongly recommended (Bojaníc et al.,2020).

STABILIZATION PHASE

Current guidelines (e.g., International Society for the Study of Trauma and Dissociation, 2011) for treating DDs advocate for a three-stage treatment approach. Stage One is a stabilization phase where the goal is to decrease trauma symptoms, increase internal and external safety, and increase healthy coping. Stage Two is the trauma processing phase where the trauma is remembered, worked through, losses are grieved and new meanings are made. Stage Three is about reconnection, both internally (e.g., identity) and externally (e.g., intimacy), and empowerment. These stages are not linear and the therapeutic work weaves back and forth across the stages as warranted. For example, trauma processing is inherently destabilizing, and the therapeutic work may need to periodically return to stabilization as a means of protecting and reestablishing the client's safety and level of functioning.

The presence of serious NSSI and suicidal behaviour necessitates a return to the stabilization phase of treatment. Brand (2001) has outlined five steps to resolve safety concerns among clients with DDs. First, determine the extent to which the person is aware of the NSSI and suicidality. This may require both direct and indirect communication with dissociated self-states. Second, assess the function(s) of the self-destructive urges or behaviours. Third, negotiate a "truce" with the person with respect to NSSI and suicidal behaviours. Fourth, build an alliance with the self-states that threaten NSSI and suicide. Finally, resolve the internal conflict and/or teach healthy alternatives to NSSI and suicide. Note that the pain held by self-states engaging in NSSI and suicidal behaviours may need to be directly addressed and relieved as a prerequisite to reducing dangerous behaviours (see Chefetz, 2017).

Stabilization techniques can be drawn from any therapeutic modality in which the clinician is trained and as clinically indicated by the client's unique presentation, goals and needs. For example, a relational approach grounded in psychodynamic theory may assist both in developing the therapeutic frame from which the client can use the therapist as a secure base, and to facilitate an understanding of the relational factors contributing to NSSI and suicidality. Meanwhile, interventions rooted in neurobiology (e.g., eye-movement desensitization and reprocessing, hypnosis, sensorimotor psychotherapy) may assist the client with containment, establishing a felt-sense of safety, reducing distress and providing alternate options for coping with psychological pain. Given the developmental gaps associated with developmental trauma, dissociative clients may also need to be explicitly taught missing skills (e.g., self-soothing, emotion regulation, communication, problem solving, mentalization) in order to replace NSSI and suicidal behaviours with healthier strategies; to this end, dialectical behaviour therapy-informed interventions may be modified to support clients with DDs (see Foote & van Orden, 2016; Shabb, 2016).

Social support and a sense of connection are potent protective factors against suicide (see Van Orden, 2016) and are core components of healing from trauma (Herman, 1991). Thus, it is imperative that the clients be supported to establish healthy social connections. Social supports may include peers, safe family members, mentors, or healthy online communities. As clients with DDs may have unhealthy relational scripts and limited relational skills, they may also benefit from ongoing support to navigate these relationships.

CLINICIAN SELF-CARE

Patients with DDs may experience multiple crises related to NSSI and suicidality, which may evoke a wide range of reactions (e.g., fear, helplessness, horror, guilt, anger, betrayal) in the clinicians working with these clients (see Brand, 2001). Clinicians need to be mindful of their own countertransference when working with clients who engage in NSSI and suicidal behaviour, and work towards maintaining an empathic but appropriately boundaried stance. Underreacting to suicide risk poses a real threat to the person's life, whereas overreacting may have a negative impact on the client, therapist and therapeutic relationship. Just as connection is essential for protecting clients, therapists should not work in isolation. Having a professional support network ensures that the clinician can consult with colleagues when warranted.

REFERENCES

Akther, S. F., Molyneaux, E., Stuart, R., Johnson, S., Simpson, A., & Oram, S. (2019). Patients' experiences of assessment and detention under mental health legislation: systematic review and qualitative meta-synthesis. *BJPsych open, 5*(3), e37. doi: 10.1192/bjo.2019.19

Baechler, J. (1975). *Suicides*. Basic Books.

Baumeister, R. F. (1990). Suicide as escape from self. *Psychological Review, 97*, 90-113.

Bojanić, L., Hunt, I. M, Baird, A., Kapur, N., Appleby, L., & Turnbull, P. (2020). Early post-discharge suicide in mental health patients: Findings from a national clinical survey. *Frontiers in Psychiatry, 11*, 502 doi: 10.3389/fpsyt.2020.00502

Brand, B. (2001). Establishing safety with patients with dissociative identity disorder. *Journal of Trauma & Dissociation, 2*(4), 133-155. doi: 10.1300/J229v02n04_07

Brand, B. L., Classen, C., Lanins, R., Loewenstein, R., McNary, S., Pain, C., & Putnam, F. W. (2009). A naturalistic study of dissociative identity disorder and dissociative disorder not otherwise specified patients treated by community clinicians. *Psychological Trauma: Theory, Research, Practice, and Policy, 1*(2), 153–171. doi:10.1037/a0016210

Brand, B. L., McNary, S. W., Myrick, A. C., Classen, C. C., Lanius, R., Loewenstein, R. J., & Putnam, F. W. (2013). A longitudinal naturalistic study of patients with DDs treated by community clinicians. *Psychological Trauma: Theory, Research, Practice, and Policy, 5*(4), 301–308. doi:10.1037/a0027654

Briere, J. (2019). *Treating risky and compulsive behavior in trauma survivors.* Guilford.

Calati, R., Bensassi, I., & Courtet, P. (2017). The link between dissociation and both suicide attempts and self-injury: Meta-analyses. *Psychiatry Research, 251*, 103-114. doi: 10.1016/j.psychres.2017.01.035

Černis, E., Chan, C., & Cooper, M. (2019). What is the relationship between dissociation and self-harming behaviour in adolescents? *Clinical Psychology & Psychotherapy, 26*(3), 328-338. doi: 10.1002/cpp.2354

Chefetz, R. A. (2017). Issues in consultation for treatments with distress activated abuser/protector self-states in dissociative identity disorder. *Journal of Trauma & Dissociation, 18*(3). 465-475. doi: 10.1080/15299732.2017.1295428

Chieze, M., Hurts, S., Kaiser, S., & Sentissi, O. (2019). Effects of seclusion and restraint in adult psychiatry: A systematic review. *Frontiers in Psychiatry, 10*, 491. doi: 10.3389/fpsyt.2019.00491

Dorahy, M. J., Brand, B. L., Sar, V., Krüger, C., Stavropoulos, P., Martínez-Taboas, A., Lewis-Fernández, R., & Middleton, W. (2014). Dissociative identity disorder: An empirical overview. *Australian & New Zealand Journal of Psychiatry, 48*(5), 402-417. doi: 10.1177/0004867414527523

Dorahy, M. J., Corry, M., Shannon, M., Webb, K., McDermott, B., Ryan, M., & Dyer, K. F. W. (2013). Complex trauma and intimate relationships: The impact of shame, guilt and dissociation. *Journal of Affective Disorders, 147*(1-3), 72-79. doi: 10.1016/j.jad.2012.10.010

Dorahy, M. J., Middleton, W., Seager, L., McGurrin, P., Williams, M., & Chambers, R. (2015). Dissociation, shame, complex PTSD, child maltreatment and intimate relationship self-concept in dissociative disorder, chronic PTSD and mixed psychiatric groups. *Journal of Affective Disorders, 172*(1), 195-203. doi: 10.1016/j.jad.2014.10.008

Farber, S. K. (1997). Self-medication, traumatic reenactment, and somatic expression in bulimic and self-mutilating behavior. *Clinical Social Work Journal, 25*(1), 87-106.

Fonagy, P., Gergely, G., Jurist, E., & Target, M. (2002). *Affect regulation, mentalization, and the development of the self*. Other Press.

Foote, B., & van Orden, K. (2016). Adapting dialectical behavior therapy for the treatment of dissociative identity disorder. *American Journal of Psychotherapy, 70*(4), 343-364. doi: 10.1176/appi.psychotherapy.2016.70.4.343.

Ford, J. D., & Gómez, J. M. (2015). The relationship of psychological trauma and dissociative and posttraumatic stress disorders to nonsuicidal self-injury and suicidality: A review. *Journal of Trauma & Dissociation, 16,* 232-271. doi: 10.1080/15299732.2015.989563

Forte, A., Buscajoni, A., Fiorillo, A., Pompili, M., & Baldessarini, R. J. (2019). Suicidal Risk Following Hospital Discharge: A Review. *Harvard Review of Psychiatry, 27*(4): 209-216. doi: 10.1097/HRP.0000000000000222

Fowler, J. C. (2012). Suicide risk assessment in clinical practice: Pragmatic guidelines for imperfect assessments. *Psychotherapy, 49*(1), 81-90. doi: 10.1037/a0026148

Groschwitz, R. C., & Plener, P. L. (2012). The neurobiology of non-suicidal self-injury (NSSI): A review. *Suicidology Online, 3*, 24-32.

Gunn, J. F. III, & Lester, D. (2014). *Theories of suicide: Past, present and future*. Charles C Thomas Publisher

Herman, J. L. (1992). *Trauma and recovery: The aftermath of violence - from domestic abuse to political terror*. Basic Books.

Howell, E. F. (2011). *Understanding and treating dissociative identity disorder: A relational approach*. Routledge.

International Society for the Study of Self-injury. (2018, May). What is self-injury? Retrieved from: https://itriples.org/about-self-injury/what-is-self-injury.

International Society for the Study of Trauma and Dissociation [Chu, J. A., Dell, P. F., Van der Hart, O., Cardeña, E., Barach, P. M., Somer, E., Loewenstein, R. J., Brand, B., Golston, J. C., Courtois, C. A., Bowman, E. S., Classen, C., Dorahy, M.,, Sar,V., Gelinas,D.J., Fine,C.G., Paulsen, S., Kluft, R. P., Dalenberg, C. J., Jacobson-Levy, M., Nijenhuis, E. R. S., Boon, S., Chefetz, R.A., Middleton, W., Ross, C. A., Howell, E.,

Goodwin, G., Coons, P. M., Frankel, A. S., Steele, K., Gold, S. N., Gast, U., Young, L. M., & Twombly, J.]. (2011). Guidelines for treating dissociative identity disorder in adults, third revision. *Journal of Trauma & Dissociation, 12*(2): 115–187

Jarvi, S., Jackson, B., Swenson, L., & Crawford, H. (2013). The impact of social contagion on non-suicidal self-injury: A review of the literature. *Archives of Suicide Research, 17*(1), 1-19. doi: 10.1080/13811118.2013.748404

Joiner, T. E. (2005). *Why people die by suicide*. Cambridge, MA: Harvard University Press.

Joiner, T. E., Hom, M. A., Hagan, C. R., Silva, C. (2016). Suicide as a derangement of the self-sacrificial aspect of eusociality. *Psychological Review, 123*(3), 235-254. doi: 10.1037/rev0000020

Klonsky, E. D. (2007). The functions of deliberate self-injury: A review of the evidence. *Clinical Psychology Review, 27*(2), 226–239. doi: 10.1016/j.cpr.2006.08.002.

Klonsky, E. D., & May, A. M. (2014). Differentiating suicide attempters from suicide ideators: A critical frontier for suicidology research. *Suicide and Life-Threatening Behaviors, 44*(1), 1-5. doi: 10.1111/sltb.12068

Klonsky, E. D., & May, A. M. (2015). The Three-Step Theory (3ST): A new theory of suicide rooted in the "Ideation-to-Action" framework. *International Journal of Cognitive Therapy, 8*(2), 114-129. doi: 10.1521/ijct.2015.8.2.114

Kozlowska, K., Walker, P., McLean, L., & Carrive, P. (2015). Fear and the defense cascade: Clinical implications and management. *Harvard Review of Psychiatry, 23*(4), 263–287. doi: 10.1097/HRP.0000000000000065

Liotti, G. (2006) A Model of Dissociation Based on Attachment Theory and Research. *Journal of Trauma & Dissociation, 7*(4), 55-73. doi: 10.1300/J229v07n04_04

Liotti, G. (2017) Conflicts between motivational systems related to attachment trauma: Key to understanding the intra-family relationship between abused children and their abusers, *Journal of Trauma & Dissociation, 18*(3), 304-318. doi: 10.1080/15299732.2017.1295392

Lynch, S. M., Forman, E., Mendelsohn, M., & Herman, J. (2008). Attending to dissociation: Assessing change in dissociation and predicting treatment outcome. *Journal of Trauma & Dissociation, 9*(3), 301-319. doi: 10.1080/15299730802139063

Muehlenkamp, J., Brausch, A., Quigley, K., & Whitlock, J. (2013). Interpersonal features and functions of nonsuicidal self-injury. *Suicide & Life-Threatening Behavior, 43*(1), 67-80. doi: 10.1111/j.1943-278X.2012.00128.x

Nestor, M. S., Boi, C., Brand, B. L., & Schielke, H. J. (2022). The reasons dissociative disorder patients self-injure. European Journal of Psychotraumatology, 13(1), 2026738 doi: 10.1080/20008198.2022.2026738

Nestor, M. S., Brand, B. L., Schielke, H. J., & Kumar, S. (2022). An examination of the relations between emotion dysregulation, dissociation, and self-injury among dissociative disorder patients. European Journal of Psychotraumatology, 13(1), 2031592. doi: 10.1080/20008198.2022.2031592

Nock, M. K. (2009). Why do people hurt themselves?: New insights into the nature and functions of self-injury. *Current Directions in Psychological Science, 18*(2), 78-83. doi: 10.1111/j.1467-8721.2009.01613.x

Nock, M. K. (2014). *The Oxford handbook of suicide and self-injury*. Oxford. doi: 10.1093/oxfordhb/9780195388565.001.0001

Panagioti, M., Gooding, P., Taylor, P. J., & Tarrier, N. (2013). A model of suicidal behavior in posttraumatic stress disorder (PTSD): The mediating role of defeat and entrapment. *Psychiatry Research, 209*(1), 55-59. doi: 10.1016/j.psychres.2013.02.018

Parry, S., Lloyd, M., & Simpson, J. (2017). Experiences of therapeutic relationships on hospital wards, dissociation, and making connections. *Journal of Trauma & Dissociation, 18*(4):544-558. doi: 10.1080/15299732.2016.1241852.

Schreiner, M. W., Klimes-Dougan, B., Begnel, E. D., & Cullen, K. R. Conceptualizing the neurobiology of non-suicidal self-injury from the perspective of the Research Domain Criteria Project. *Neuroscience and Biobehavioral Reviews, 57*, 381-391. doi: 10.1016/j.neubiorev.2015.09.011

Shabb, O. (2016). Considering psychoeducation on structural dissociation for dialectical behavior therapy patients experiencing high-risk dissociative behaviors. *Journal of Trauma and Dissociation, 17*(1), 55-66. doi: 10.1080/15299732.2015.1053657

Sharfstein, S. S. (2009). Goals for inpatient treatment for psychiatric disorders. *Annual Review of Medicine, 60*, 393-403. doi: 10.1146/annurev.med.60.042607.080257

Shneidman, E. S. (1993). Suicide as psychache. *Journal of Nervous and Mental Disease, 181*(3), 145-147.

Silberg, J. L. (2021). *The child survivor: Healing developmental trauma and dissociation* (2nd ed.). Routledge.

Stanley, B., & Brown, G. K. (2012) Safety planning intervention: A brief intervention to mitigate suicide risk. *Cognitive and Behavioral Practice, 19*(2), 256-264. doi: 10.1016/j.cbpra.2011.01.001

Tanner, J., Wyss, D., Perron, M., & Mueller-Pfeiffer, C. 2017. Characteristics of suicide attempts in dissociative identity disorders: A 12-month follow-up study in psychiatric outpatients in Switzerland. *European Journal of Trauma & Dissociation, 1*(4), 235-239. doi: 10.1016/j.ejtd.2017.06.005

Van Orden, K. A., Witte, T. K., Cukrowicz, K. C., Braithwaite, S. R., Selby, E. A., & Joiner, T. E. (2010) The interpersonal theory of suicide. *Psychological Review, 117*(2), 575–600. doi: 10.1037/a0018697

Webermann, A. R., Myrick, A. C., Taylor, C. L., Chasson, G. S., & Brand, B. L. (2016). Dissociative, depressive, and PTSD symptom severity as correlates of nonsuicidal self-injury and suicidality in dissociative disorder patients. *Journal of Trauma & Dissociation, 17*(1), 67-80. doi: 10.1080/15299732.2015.1067941

Williams, J.M.G., 1997. *Cry of Pain*. Harmondsworth Penguin

Whitlock, J., Muehlenkamp, J., Eckenrode, J., Purington, A., Abrams, G B., Barreira, P., & Kress, V. (2013). Nonsuicidal self-injury as a gateway to suicide in young adults. *Journal of Adolescent Health, 52*(4), 486-492. doi: 10.1016/j.jadohealth.2012.09.010

Whitlock, J., & Selekman, M. D. (2014). Nonsuicidal self-injury across the life span. In M. K. Nock (Ed.), *The Oxford handbook of suicide and self-injury* (pp. 133-151). Oxford.

Yakeley, J., & Burbridge-James, W. (2018). Psychodynamic approaches to suicide and self-harm. *BJPsych Advances, 24*, 37-45. doi: 10.1192/bja.2017.6

"The Body is Bad": When Disability and Complex Dissociative Disorders Meet

by Marin Hann, M.A., LPC

"The body is bad." That familiar sentence in my experience with clients in the therapy room is one that has been spoken by clients with various dissociative disorders (DDs). What often follows is an expression of the body being dirty or sexual or a client is dysphoric because the external body does not resemble how they see themselves to be. Yet, once I began working with some clients in the disability community that also have a dissociative disorder, the texture of those words changed.

The first moment those words carried something new underneath I recall feeling the familiar presence of countertransference in the room and I used that as my cue to pay attention to what was happening and to what was about to happen. What I would like to share with the reader is a brief example, which is a composite of exchanges with clients in order to protect client anonymity, that I hope will provide a foundation for the information provided in this chapter. I do not simply want to provide a foundation that can be cognitively understood, but also a foundation that can be felt.

"The body is bad." Those are the firm words that come from a part of my client.

"Can you tell me why you say the body is bad?"

"The body is broken. It does not do what it should do. It tremors and it hurts and it doesn't

do what we tell it to do and so we try to ignore it."

"I see. Do you mean to say that the body is disabled? That you are disabled?" I inquire.

"Yes. I hate it. The body is bad. Disability is bad."

I recognize those words. I have heard them outright but because I have heard them behind other words. "Did someone tell you that disability is bad? How do you know disability is bad?"

They appear to shift their age presentation in front of me from abrupt and emotional to fluid and intellectual in their response, "Well, they don't say it in those actual words. I've had people at school, at the doctor's office, at physical therapy, at church, sometimes even at the grocery store people will tell me things like, 'It's so great to see you out and about' or 'Can I pray for you?' and I know they mean pray for my body to be healed. Sometimes they will use words like disability should be 'overcome' or that I should rise above my physical self. I know there are parts of me that feel that way about the body."

"Do you feel that way?"

"I'm not sure. Sometimes?" They respond with a tone in between a question and a statement.

"I've noticed that it seems that most of the time, although, not all of the time, the language you are using is 'the body' more than you say 'my body' or 'our body.'"

"Hmm. Maybe I'm trying to separate myself from my body. I feel like I've always done that."

"I used to do that all the time. Sometimes I still struggle with that."

Their eyes meet mine, "You do?"

"Sure," I reply, "I didn't do so in the exact same way or use words like 'the body' instead of 'my body,' but I used to be very adamant that I was a person with a disability instead of that I was a disabled person. I didn't like thinking that my disability was part of who I am. Not everyone who uses person-first language is using it to separate themselves from their physical experience, but that's part of why I had used it. It took a long time, but now I am more comfortable with identity-first language and so I say that I am a disabled person because I am proud to be a disabled person. I like that part of me. And without that part of me, then I am not really all of me. So now I have chosen to be proud."

"You're proud of your disability?" a softer voice asks.

"Oh yes!" I confirm. "I didn't used to be. I remember that sometimes I wanted to be, but the way other people talked about disability made me think that it was bad to want to be."

Their exclamation springs into the air, "YES! Yes! Other people think it is a *bad* difference instead of it just being *a* difference. I don't think it's all bad. There are things about it that I don't like, but I don't think that means I don't like all of it or disability as a whole." They pause, "I feel a pull to be separate from my body though and it feels a little bit like I'm coping in the same way that having dissociative identity disorder is a way of coping."

I lean forward, "That is a very profound insight. Inside, you have parts of you that were told certain things about you were bad or you would get punished if you were seen doing them."

"Like reading?" a young voice asks.

"Yes," I agree, "Like reading. A lot of you love to read, but sometimes if you were reading then your parent would hurt you and what they did was wrong. But what happened is that other parts of you made sure that they still loved to read and those parts of you kept the love of reading safe even though other parts were taught by the parent that it was bad."

"But reading isn't bad. Loving words is a huge part of who I am!"

I smile with them, "Yes. It is a huge part of who you are."

"Sooo," they nod, "Maybe that's why it feels the same. We were told in words or in action that disability is bad instead of it being a part of who we are and that is not bad. So that's why we have a part who is in charge of the body and dealing with all the different body things so that everyone else can be separate from that."

"I think that makes sense."

There is a pregnant pause before either of us speak again.

"But there are still parts of me that think those other people are right and that my body is something to be overcome, and sometimes that makes me wonder if I am wrong. That maybe I shouldn't be proud to be disabled." Their voice becomes timid when they continue, "Other parts definitely still think that is very wrong." Their head lowers to look away.

I lean in to ask, "That sounds like it is very painful for both of you. What about it do you think they feel is wrong? Is it your body being different than some other bodies that they feel is wrong or is it something else?"

I wait. I can tell there is a war of thoughts, emotions, and beliefs happening inside. I do not have DID or OSDD myself, but I know that I have had my own war within me. And when they speak again, a different part full of fear wrapped up in anger, I feel the battle begin.

"The body is BAD! It needs help! We should not need help! We can't need help. We were too slow or had too many doctor appointments with doctors who never helped because they never noticed the other problems and the other bad things. Teachers never noticed either. We were good at staying out of the way and not needing anything. But with the body we are a burden. It needs more help than it did. It got worse. We are in the way. We need too much. Needing is bad. We don't need anyone."

It was the first interaction, much like this one, that prompted me to consider disability and dissociation as a relationship that needed dire attention.

Models and Theories of Disability

Just as "Emma Sunshaw" (pseudonym) has so aptly shared the history of dissociative disorders and plurality in those chapters, it is important to highlight the basics of the theories of disability. The medical model of disability entails viewing disability as a problem that exists in a person's body and therefore that means they require treatments to fix the disability or help the person to adapt and function despite it (Goering, 2015; Silvers, 1998). Disability scholar, Lisa Crow, notes how this model holds the belief that "a person's functional limitations (impairments) are the root cause of any disadvantages experienced and these disadvantages can therefore only be rectified by treatment or cure" (Crow, 1996, p. 208). However, this model was created by the non-disabled majority, and so, in response, disability activists and scholars have offered a social model of disability. The social model of disability relies heavily on making a distinction between impairment and disability. Impairment is understood as a state of the body that is non-standard such as lacking a limb, organ, or otherwise typical function or mechanism of the body. Yet, it is crucial to note that such "impairment may or may not be met with a negative evaluation by its possessor" (Goering, 2015). In contrast, disability is the "disadvantage or restriction of activity caused by a contemporary social organization which takes no or little account of people who have physical [or cognitive] impairments and thus excludes them from participation in the mainstream of social activities" (Oliver, 1996, p. 22). The point of this distinction is to emphasize that what is often disabling for someone is how society is structured through things such as social arrangements, institutional norms, architecture, etc (Goering, 2015).

In her book *The Minority Body* (2016), Elizabeth Barnes (an associate professor of philosophy at the University of Virginia who is disabled herself), argues for a view that describes disability as a mere difference, rather than a bad-difference or bad simpliciter—which echoes the points of Anita Silvers (2003) and Sara Goering (2015) that disability can be neutral. Barnes conceptualizes this view while accounting for the missing piece that many critics find in the social model and that is that not every negative experience of disability can be accounted for through a pure social and societal explanation. One way Barnes does this is by acknowledging that many people have "local bad" experiences because of their body difference and yet that does not mean the difference in and of itself is a "global bad". She also accounts for the fact the disability does mean the loss of some intrinsic goods, but provides a striking example of why lacking an intrinsic good does not undermine the mere-difference model:

> "We might, at least insofar as we think abilities like hearing and walking are intrinsic goods, also think the ability to be pregnant and give birth — to grow a new person in your own body! — is an intrinsic good. As abilities go, it is certainly an impressive one. People who are [cisgender] male lack this ability. Nor is there any obvious [cisgender] male-specific ability we can point to that *compensates* [cisgender] men for this lack. [...] And yet we don't tend to think that people who are [cisgender] male are automatically worse off, overall, than people who are [cisgender] female simply because they lack an ability we might count as an intrinsic good. There are plenty of interesting, valuable, enjoyable things about being male — or so I am told, anyway. [These don't 'make up for' the fact that they cannot become pregnant or give birth.] But they make us think that people who are [cisgender] male haven't been given a sorry deal in life." (p. 57-58)

I realize at this point some readers may respond that not all disabilities are congenital. Some disabilities are caused by traumas from medical procedures, natural disasters, and the most personal natured traumas of physical abuse, sexual abuse, and neglect. I agree. And while I cannot begin to adequately summarize the mere-difference view in this chapter better than Barnes could explain it in her own words, I can say that she does address this by introducing the at length discussion with the following quote: "The mere-difference view doesn't deny that many of the things that *cause* disability are bad, even though it denies that disability itself is bad" (p. 68). In the same way, many can agree that trauma that causes multiplicity is bad, but that does not have to mean that the survival skill of dissociating or multiplicity in and of itself must be defined as bad.

Astute readers might be searching for statistics that display the prevalence of trauma among disabled people or a description of the relationship between those with dissociative disorders who also live with disability in another form. Before that is provided, there is a buried history that needs to be unearthed. Too often disabled people have been reduced to statistics and our voices have not been heard. Too often people with a dissociative disorder or who are plural have experienced the same. This chapter is for everyone who is both.

Stories We Are Told

The disability community, which encompasses a rich array of sub-communities within itself, has a unifying motto - "Nothing About Us Without Us" (Charlton, 2011; Pelka, 2012). Those are precious words and a demand that was not easy to come by. A thousand different ways are available to explain how that motto is hard-won in both words and in action. It involves deeply ingrained prejudice, systemic discrimination, long-standing historical oppression, the media that is shaped and run by those in power, etc. (Nielsen, 2013). Though some of this has been and will be mentioned here, this is not the book for that anthropological exploration or sizable account of history nor is it the focus of this chapter. Instead, I would like to explore the experiences of some of my clients, along with so many other people who live as plural, and the motto of the Disability Pride and justice movement through the lens of Miranda Fricker's work *Epistemic Injustice* (2007). Fricker writes of ways that prejudice can cause unique types of harm.

TESTIMONIAL INJUSTICE

One of the primary forms of harm she highlights is testimonial injustice which is when a speaker is not believed or given the credit or reliability due them (where others would be) because they are a member of the group that is being stigmatized. For disability in general, this would be when the majority decides to view the testimony of a disabled person as tainted simply because they are disabled. Many disabled people often find that the non-disabled do not believe us when we say we are proud to be disabled or that we enjoy our lives. Harriet McBryde Johnson (2013), a disability writes activist wrote about this in her *New York Times* essay 'Unspeakable Conversations' and said, "I used to try to explain that in fact I enjoy my life, but it's a great sensual pleasure to zoom by power chair on these delicious muggy streets, that I have no more reason to kill myself than most people. But it gets tedious... [T]hey don't want to know. They think they know everything there is to know, just by looking at me. "

Those who identify as plural or who have been diagnosed with dissociative identity disorder or otherwise specified dissociative disorder (not to mention all other traumagenic disorders on the dissociative spectrum) might experience this more heavily in the professional mental health community. Those who are dissociative often report testimonial injustice when a mental health professional discounts the testimony of their lived experience because the professional inappropriately and unjustly uses their diagnosis as a reason to consider their client an unreliable source for knowledge about their own dissociative experience or they may doubt the possibility that their client's testimony could reliably contribute to our further understanding of dissociative disorders in general. This can be especially true when the competency of the professional is on the line. Kristie Dotson (2011) labels a form of testimonial injustice as 'testimonial smothering' to describe when marginalized groups no longer bother to give testimony because they know the other person will only accept content that supports their competency and perspective (p. 244).

This can be clearly seen in the lasting effects of skeptics of dissociative disorders in the mental health field and beyond. There were three proposed inter-related models that skeptics used in the 1980s to try to discount the existence of dissociative disorders. The iatrogenic model (IM) espouses that dissociation like that of dissociative identity disorder was created by clinicians who believe in repressed memories to the extent that they would use highly hypnotizable or suggestible patients for risky treatments and then implant false memories. The second model, the Sociocognitive Model (SCM), believes that the focus of the media in North American culture on multiple personalities, repressed memories, and childhood sexual abuse is enough to convince suggestible people that they have dissociative conditions when they don't. Finally, the Fantasy Model simply believes that dissociation is a cognitive trait that leads to fantasies/confabulations of experiences of trauma. Despite the fact that numerous studies and decades of research do not support these models (Brand et al., 2016; Dalenberg, 2012; Loewenstein, 2018; Loewenstein, et al., 2017; and Spiegel, et al., 2011) and the fact that the accusation of "False-Memory Syndrome" has never been studied, validated, or operationalized (Loewenstein, 2018; Loewenstein, et al., 2017; Coons, 2010), the testimonies of the skeptics – professional or otherwise – are used to silence those with dissociative disorders which then creates a minefield of barriers for them to be able to seek proper support and community.

The disability population and the population of those with dissociative disorders or who identify as plural have this experience of testimonial injustice in common, as do all marginalized people. However, I fear there is a unique danger when some disabled, dissociative/plural people are confronted with this twice. Often, if one only notices a person's visible disability as Johnson has been witness to, then they are at risk to deem the disability itself as the trauma and are likely to miss the trauma of neglect or abuse, as has occurred with several of my clients and as alluded to in the interaction presented at the start of this chapter. Where does one turn when so much of their experience and existence is labeled as an impossible lie by those in power?

HERMENEUTICAL INJUSTICE

Fricker (2007) also identifies what some may argue to be a more sinister form of epistemic injustice, simply because of its personal, covert, and evasive nature — that is hermeneutical injustice. Hermeneutical injustice is when we harm people by obscuring aspects of their own experience. The schemas and assumptions of the majority make it difficult for members of a marginalized group to even find the language or concepts they need in order to articulate their experiences. Again, the case example at the start of the chapter displays this when the client expresses belief that their disability is not all bad, but then they feel lost and frightened in the message they have received that their body is a burden laden with dangerous needs. Fricker shares: "When you find yourself in a situation in which you seem to be the only one to feel tension between received understanding and your own intimated sense of a given experience, it tends to knock your faith in your own ability to make sense of the world" (p. 163). This type of injustice most often comes from one's limited access to information as well as one's limited access to community, not to mention the fact that our absorption of information takes place in community.

To illustrate how hermeneutical injustice can develop for the dissociative and disabled, one need only glance at the information that is available and most accessible to the masses. The most widespread source of information on dissociative disorders and disability can be found in mainstream media. Unfortunately, this source is also heinously inaccurate. There are several ways this negatively impacts the understanding of disability. As summarized by Hann (2016),

> "In the media, people with disabilities are consistently portrayed as the victim or the villain, someone who must also gain superhuman characteristics from their disability to make it more appealing to an audience, a sentimentalized character overcoming what is displayed as a poor misfortune, a noble or selfless two-dimensional character, an outcast, as a charitable means to an end to help build the integrity and selflessness of an able-bodied character, a tool to inspire others to be grateful or to do better, asexual or struggling with their sexuality, or in recent film as one who sees no value in their life and wishes to die (Dahl, 1993; Wolfensberger, 1998; Young, 2014; Sauder, 2016). Marilyn Dahl (1993) summarizes this media trend well when she says, "Rarely does there appear an average or ordinary person whose disability is incidental." (p. 12)

With such widespread narratives empty of complexity and justice, the community of the disabled are left searching for a true story of their own history, suffering, and hope that the surrounding majority cultures dismiss. This is not even to mention the fact a great disservice of the medical model of disability is to attempt to rob disabled people of a hermeneutic that includes the strength and creativity to overcome adversity—adversity that is not sourced in who we are or how we exist, but in the personal and systemic injustices and trauma inflicted on us by others.

For those with dissociative disorders, the failed representation in the media has been massive – and often reduced to a false depiction of only one dissociative disorder: dissociative identity disorder. To begin with, many depictions in the media do not even name the disorder accurately by calling it "Multiple Personality Disorder," which ceased to be its name in 1994. Still, one of the most dangerous misconceptions is how the horror genre perpetuates the idea that there is such a thing as a "bad alter" or that people with DID are villains and monsters (Reid, 2019). Films such as *Split*, *Glass*, *Fight Club*, and *Identity* serve as examples of such false representation.

Additionally, Hollywood is guilty of depicting the presentation of DID in an obvious and provocative way by pretending that switches between parts/alters are always overt and jarring, usually in order to captivate the attention of an audience. In contrast to this, factor analytic studies with actual real life people have found that this is not the case (Loewenstein, et al., 2017 and Spiegel, et al., 2011). In fact, in his book *Dissociation in Children and Adolescents: A Development Model* (1997), Frank W. Putnam explains that symptoms typically manifest as inner voices or through passive influence that exhibit a state of multiple overlapping states rather than overt switching behavior. Many other researchers find the same to be true in most adult presentations and that elaborate differences in the presentation of parts need not be necessary to the diagnosis (Loewenstein, et al., 2017; Spiegel, et al., 2011; Brand, et al., 2016; and *Everything you need to know about dissociative identity disorder*, 2021).

Yet, here we find the media exploiting the real lives of those with dissociative disorders as some sort of attraction to fascinate the masses. When someone first wonders whether they have dissociative identity disorder or they have been newly diagnosed, this is often the information they have at their fingertips. This is typically in opposition to their own real-life experiences and how they have begun to understand themselves, and this can cause experiences of misattunement, which itself is retraumatizing. If they try to share an experience that is counter to how the majority represents them, they often do not have the language to do so nor the support that they need.

Even though those with dissociative disorders have been working to form communities with one another where they can build a more cohesive structure of their individual and collective testimonies; albeit this also can come with risks such as predators posing as someone with DID on the internet, it is grievous to recognize how mental health practitioners have often influenced why this community has lacked the appropriate access to build culture and peer support until more recently. In their podcast System Speak, a member of Emma Sunshaw's system speaks with another who identifies as a plural system they call a "sisterhood" and they point out the following:

> "We've been isolated from one another and almost actively kept from one another because for the longest time—and still pretty much—professionals have been the gateway to one another [...] We only have these big national conventions once a year or all these other things that are put on by people that aren't multiple. And when we do get together it's like in

> the context of support groups. In other words there's no chance for us to just sit around, hang around each other and be normal without or outside the context of psychiatric treatment" (Sunshaw, 2018).

They go on to explain how they feel that doctors have concerns that if people with dissociative disorders are together they will trigger one another. However, many people who are multiple or plural have been in community together and will attest that this is not the case and that it is not consistent with the fact that dissociative identity disorder and otherwise specified dissociative disorder is built in a way to protect the person from trauma. Dissociative disorders are complex and advanced coping mechanisms and the people who experience the world in this manner may need support, as every human does, but they are a strong, creative, and remarkably resilient community. Regrettably, inexperience and arrogance in the mental health field has robbed many with dissociative disorders of the hermeneutic needed to understand themselves this way just as the larger medical community and medical model of disability has done to the disability community.

If anything is clear and foundational in this chapter, let it be the evil of isolation – especially when done under the guise of professionalism or care-taking, and the power of community. In the profound work *Trauma and Recovery: The Aftermath of Violence—From Domestic Abuse To Political Terror* (2015), Judith Herman does not mince her words and her statements on the importance of community, and the destruction that comes from community being taken away are no different. While she is careful to emphasize that group therapy is done in phases appropriate to the tolerance of the individuals in the group, I believe her words can be accurately applied to the necessity of shared experience.

> "Traumatic events destroy the sustaining bonds between individual and community. Those who have survived learn that their sense of self, of worth, of humanity, depends upon a feeling of connection to others. The solidarity of a group provides the strongest protection against terror and despair, and the strongest antidote to traumatic experience. Trauma isolates; the group re-creates a sense of belonging. Trauma shames and stigmatizes; the group bears witness and affirms. Trauma degrades the victim; the group exalts her. Trauma dehumanizes the victim; the group restores her humanity" (p. 214).

That very quote comes from a chapter on commonality, which is inseparable from testimonial and hermeneutical injustice. I urge us all to embrace the hope of commonality and community, and also to heed this warning: to isolate a group from the healing of their solidarity and the ability to express freely through a sense of belonging is to be no different than the perpetrators who initiated the trauma and abuse in the first place.

With the violence of testimonial and hermeneutical injustice coming from both sides and directed at multiple aspects of their experience, one cannot help but see the complex layers of trauma experienced by a disabled person that also has a dissociative disorder. Adding insult to injury is the truth that this experience of added layers of identity, testimonial, and hermeneutic confusion is more likely in the disability community because of the high prevalence of trauma that disabled people experience.

Disability and the Prevalence of Trauma

The epistemic injustice experienced by minority groups is horrifying when held up next to the fact that disability of many forms is associated with an increased risk of experiencing trauma. This increased risk is often composed of interpersonal trauma which is trauma when an individual(s) personally harm another including, but not limited to, child abuse and/or neglect, assault, and intimate partner violence. In 2012, the Spectrum Institute National Disability and Abuse Project did a national survey on abuse of people with disabilities and published their findings in an article titled *Abuse of People With Disabilities: Victims and Their Families Speak Out.* This was the first ever national survey of this kind and it involved 7289 online responses that were received from all 50 states and the District of Columbia. An overview of some of their crucial findings is as follows:

> "Over 70% of people with disabilities who took the survey reported they had been victims of abuse. More than 63% of parents and immediate family members reported that their loved one with a disability had experienced abuse. Some disability types had a higher incidence of abuse than others. For example, 74.8% of people with mental health conditions reported they had been victims of abuse, while 67.1% of those with a speech disability, 66.5% of those with autism, 62.5% of those with an intellectual or developmental

> disability, and 55.2% of those with a mobility disability reported having experienced such abuse. People with disabilities who were victims reported having experienced various types of abuse. Some 87.2% reported verbal-emotional abuse, 50.6% physical abuse, 41.6% sexual abuse, 37.3% neglect, and 31.5% financial abuse. The rate of sexual abuse varied greatly among victims depending on the type of disabilities they had. Some 47.4% of people with mental health conditions reported they had been victims of sexual abuse, whereas 34.2% of those with intellectual or developmental disabilities, 31.6% of those with a mobility disability, and 24.9% of those with autism reported they had experienced sexual abuse" (Baladerian, et al., 2013, p. 2-3).

The findings reported in this survey are unacceptable and the reality of what they mean is heart wrenching, especially considering the limitation of this survey of the disability community to a single nation, the United States. Further research on the relationship between trauma, dissociation, and disability is sorely needed. There is not yet a current estimate for the prevalence of dissociation within the wider community of various disabilities, but through the mental health field's current understanding of how complex trauma can develop into a dissociative disorder, we can still infer a great deal.

For a number of years various experts in the field of trauma and dissociation wondered if the severity of abuse a child experienced was positively correlated with the likelihood that they would develop DID or OSDD (Steele et al., 2009; Waelde et al., 2009). As shown prior in the statistics of abuse experienced by the disability community, the prevalence of sexual and physical abuse is just under twenty five percent or more – certainly not a number to brush aside. However, other authors and preliminary research has suggested that it may be the chronicity of childhood interpersonal trauma that is more indicative of complex dissociation (Wabnitz et al., 2013; Hagenaars et al., 2011). The same national survey on abuse of people with disabilities done in 2012 and published in 2013 came back with the following results regarding chronicity of abuse:

> "More than 90% of people with disabilities who were victims of abuse said they had experienced such abuse on multiple occasions. Some 57% of these victims said they had been victims of abuse on more than 20 occasions, with 46% saying it had happened too many times for them to even count" (Baladerian, et al., 2013, p. 3).

That is 9 out 10 people reporting that they were abused multiple times and in multiple ways. With such daunting numbers, it is not strenuous to imagine many of these victims having been children suffering with circumstances that required their brain to develop advanced dissociate skills such as trance, amnesia, imaginative absorption, depersonalization, and derealization in order to survive.

This points to a relationship between disability and dissociation that has very little, if anything, to do with internal characteristics and nearly everything to do with the surrounding external environment that so many live with. Yet, I believe there is a reason this connection has gone largely unseen for far too long. The testimonies of the multiple/plural and disability communities being silenced by the majority has been a focal point of what has been presented and that has been intentional. Further results from the survey in the article *Abuse of People With Disabilities: Victims and Their Families Speak Out* reports that over forty percent of victims did not report their abuse and fifty eight percent did not do so because they believed nothing would happen. Some may want to believe this to be a tragic lack of faith in a society and a system that would work to bring justice to these victims. The shameful truth is that in 58.9% of cases when victims with disabilities did report the abuse to authorities, nothing happened. Only 9.8% of the reported cases led to an arrest of the alleged perpetrator. Even when the testimony of the disabled victim was supported by corroborating reports made by non-disabled family members the survey showed that nothing happened as a result of the multiple reports in 42.8% of cases and that the percent of alleged perpetrators who were arrested actually decreased to 7.8% (Baladerian, et al., 2013). One cannot help but wonder the extent to which the oppression of testimonial and hermeneutical injustice is the cause of such a travesty.

Discussion and Conclusion

This chapter has made an effort to show that though there are differences in the painful experiences of those who are multiple or plural and members of the wider disability community, their suffering can often be different hues of a similar color. What has not yet been highlighted is that I believe both communities share a common gift. Humans seem to have this drive to always attempt independence despite the fact that humans are interdependent creatures (Rusbult & Van Lange, 2008; Lamarche, 2021; Diamond, 2007). When those who are multiple or plural find that interdependency is externally dangerous they find interdependency inside the parts of the self and begin to work together as a creative system designed to fill roles for meeting basic internal needs, ensure survival, and enable functional living. Those with DID or OSDD do not have the allowance to avoid creative teamwork and interdependence. Even in moments when parts of the system of the self do isolate, the cascading effect upon the rest of the self can be detrimental and the ability to continue with day to day life unravels quickly. The same can be said for those in the wider disability community and I can speak from personal experience that disability is an excellent teacher and one of its many lessons is the myth of independence that is built from ableism (Chatterjee, 2019). Both communities live in ways that expose the lie of independence. Both communities have a deep well to draw from for interpersonal and intrapersonal knowledge, creativity, the honing of communications skills, and so much more that is rooted in interdependency – their minute by minute life depends on it. The difficulty is that it is in this battle for needs and attachments that their greatest wounds were inflicted.

Under healthy circumstances, true interdependency is real, truthful, beautiful...but when healthy interdependency isn't there, then having needs in a relationship with another human being can feel bad. It can feel awful. It can feel like certain danger and the last desperate breath before our lungs give out. This struggle may lead to a person feeling bad for having needs or for attempting interdependency in the first place. Further, if our body then continues experiencing unmet needs, we might find ourselves saying something like, "The body is bad."

I often offer my clients two related thoughts in hopes of providing them with a new perspective. The first is, "I don't believe feelings lie. I prefer to believe that feelings are often misunderstood." Our emotions are there to give us a very important wordless message and the problem is that we do not always interpret that message accurately. The longer we have to slow down and pay attention to the emotion and share that feeling with others (if we are able and have at least one other person we feel secure with), the more we will be able to grasp the picture being painted. When we first encounter that feeling, that interdependency with someone and having to have a need met by another is dangerous, that emotion is signaling to us that something is new —this is wrong and protection is needed. Now our brain moves away from the more intentional functions of the prefrontal cortex and into the automatic responses of freeze, fight, or flight.

But what if that emotion is not signaling something new anymore? What if a sense of overwhelming dread and fear is signaling the same message of "this isn't safe" every time we are around someone? The emotion is certainly conveying something, and in this context of interpersonal trauma, the message is that interdependency was not safe and relationships were not healthy for far too long. For example, we bleed when we are cut, and it does not matter if what wounded us is gone if the bleeding does not stop. When the bleeding does not stop, we look for external aid to ensure that it does. We do not blame the bleeding because we realize it is telling us that the wound is severe and in earnest need of attention. In this metaphor (I find I utilize metaphor quite generously in the therapy room), bleeding is the feeling or emotion. Emotions are not always trying to express new and immediate danger. Sometimes emotions are signaling that an attachment wound is deep and requires more healing resources than what we have had so far.

The closely related phrase I am known to repeat is something along the lines of, "Emotions are energy. I don't like to say we should control them because it sounds like stuffing them away in a box. Instead, use them! We all use our emotions in healthy, unhealthy, or neutral ways. Use your emotions well." As mentioned before, both communities of people who are multiple/plural and the wider disability community have ample opportunity to understand intrapersonal and interpersonal relationships. When the blinders of independence that humans have are on for the members of these communities, they cannot stay on for long. This is even more true for someone who is dissociative and disabled.

To close, I would like to say this: if the reader of this chapter finds themselves in one or both of these communities, my encouragement is that a secure community for you that emphasizes trust and interdependence does exist. One way to use the energy of your emotion is to find those communities. When you are ready, and you do decide to tell your story to someone, give yourself the grace and the time to discover the best way you know how.

If the reader finds that the descriptions of these communities does not fit their story, my encouragement to you is to focus on the motivation and drive that emotion can provide on listening and making space. This is not your story. This is an invitation to learn and to strive continuously toward being a true ally. Your friend, family member, co-worker, colleague, client, patient, etc. may invite you into something both painful and precious, a piece of a story that they have needed to tell for far too long. I am confident that in their words are truths we all desperately need to hear.

REFERENCES

Baladerian N, Coleman T, Stream J. Abuse of people with disabilities: Victims and their families speak out. 2013. https://www.openminds.com/wp-content/uploads/indres/090113disabilityabusesurvey.pdf. Accessed October 2021.

Barnes, E. 2018. *The minority body a theory of disability*. Oxford University Press.

Brand, B. L., Sar, V., Stavropoulos, P., Krüger, C., Korzekwa, M., Martínez-Taboas, A., & Middleton, W. 2016. Separating fact from fiction: An empirical examination of six myths about dissociative identity disorder. *Harvard Review of Psychiatry, 24*(4), 257-270. doi:10.1097/hrp.0000000000000100

Charlton, J. I. 2011. Nothing about us without us: *Disability oppression and empowerment*. W. Ross MacDonald School Resource Services Library.

Chatterjee, D. 2019, July 4. Independence is an ableist myth: Unlocking the power of community in healing. *The Body Is Not an Apology*. Retrieved October 30, 2021, from https://thebodyisnotanapology.com/magazine/independence-is-an-ableist-myth-unlocking-the-power-of-community-in-healing/.

Coons, P. M. 2010. Try to remember: Psychiatrys clash over meaning, memory, and mind, by P. R. McHugh. *Journal of Trauma & Dissociation, 11*(3), 379-384. doi:10.1080/15299731003783246

Crow, L. 1998. Including all of our lives: Renewing the social model of disability. In J. Morris (Ed.), *Encounters with strangers: Feminism and disability* (pp. 206–226). essay, The Women's Press.

Dahl, M. 1993. The Role of the Media in Promoting Images of Disability- Disability as Metaphor: The Evil Crip. *Canadian Journal of Communication*, 18(1). Retrieved July 2, 2016, from http://cjc-online.ca/index.php/journal/article/viewArticle/718/624

Dalenberg, C. J., Brand, B. L., Gleaves, D. H., Dorahy, M. J., Loewenstein, R. J., Cardeña, E., Frewen, P. A., Carlson, E. B., & Spiegel, D. 2012. Evaluation of the evidence for the trauma and fantasy models of dissociation. *Psychological Bulletin, 138*(3), 550–588. https://doi.org/10.1037/a0027447

Diamond, A. 2007. Interrelated and interdependent. *Developmental Science, 10*(1), 152–158. https://doi.org/10.1111/j.1467-7687.2007.00578.x

Dotson, K. 2011. Tracking epistemic violence, tracking practices of silencing. *Hypatia, 26*(2), 236-257. doi:10.1111/j.1527-2001.2011.01177.x

Goering, S. 2015. Rethinking disability: The Social Model of disability and chronic disease. *Current Reviews in Musculoskeletal Medicine, 8*(2), 134–138. https://doi.org/10.1007/s12178-015-9273-z

Hagenaars, M. A., Fisch, I., & van Minnen, A. 2011. The effect of trauma onset and frequency on PTSD-associated symptoms. *Journal of Affective Disorders, 132*(1-2), 192–199. https://doi.org/10.1016/j.jad.2011.02.017

Hann, M. 2016. *Social trauma theory and the disability minority* [Unpublished manuscript]. Grand Rapids Theological Seminary.

Johnson, H. M. 2013 February 16. Unspeakable conversations. *The New York Times*. Retrieved September 3, 2021, from https://www.nytimes.com/2003/02/16/magazine/unspeakable-conversations.html

Lamarche, V. M. 2021. Interdependent transformations: Integrating insights from relationship science to advance post-traumatic growth and personality change research. *European Journal of Personality*. https://doi.org/10.1177/08902070211022119

Loewenstein, R. J. 2018. Dissociation debates: Everything you know is wrong. *Controversies in Psychiatry Dialogues in Clinical Neuroscience, 20*(3), 229-242. doi:10.31887/dcns.2018.20.3/rloewenstein

Lowenstein, R. J., Frewan, P. A., & Lewis-Fernández, R. 2017. Dissociative disorders. In B. Sadock, V. Sadock, P. Ruiz, & H. I. Kaplan (Eds.), *Kaplan & Sadock's Comprehensive Textbook of Psychiatry* (10th ed., Vol. 1, pp. 1866–1952). essay, Wolters Kluwer.

McLean Hospital. 2021, January 13. *Everything you need to know about dissociative identity disorder*. Everything You Need To Know About Dissociative Identity Disorder | McLean Hospital. Retrieved October 14, 2021, from https://www.mcleanhospital.org/essential/everything-you-need-know-about-dissociative-identity-disorder.

Nielsen, K. E. 2013. *A disability history of the United States*. Beacon Press.

Oliver, M. 1996. *Understanding disability: From theory to practice*. Macmillan.

Pelka, F. 2012. *What we have done: An oral history of the disability rights movement*. University of Massachusetts Press.

Putnam, F. W. 1997. *Dissociation in children and adolescents: A developmental perspective*. Guilford press.

Reid, L. 2019, August 13. Monstrous misrepresentation: Disabilities in the horror genre [web log]. Retrieved September 12, 2021, from https://sites.uab.edu/humanrights/2019/08/13/monstrous-misrepresentation-disabilities-in-the-horror-genre/.

Rusbult, C. E., & Van Lange, P. A. 2008. *Why we need interdependence theory. Social and Personality Psychology Compass, 2*(5), 2049–2070. https://doi.org/10.1111/j.1751-9004.2008.00147.x

Sauder, K. 2016 May 23. 'Why are you complaining? Some people actually feel that way': A critique of 'Me Before You'. *The Huffington Post*. Retrieved July 24, 2016, from https://www.huffpost.com/entry/why-excitement-me-before-you-is-deeply-troubling_b_10108260

Silvers, A. 1998. A fatal attraction to normalizing: Treating disabilities as deviations from "species-typical" functioning. In E. Parens (Ed.), *Enhancing human traits: Ethical and social implications,* 95-123.

Silvers, A. 2003. On the possibility and desirability of constructing a neutral conception of disability. *Theoretical Medicine and Bioethics,* *24*(6), 471–487. https://doi.org/10.1023/b:meta.0000006924.82156.5b

Spiegel, D., Loewenstein, R. J., Lewis-Fernández, R., Sar, V., Simeon, D., Vermetten, E., Cardeña, E., & Dell, P. F. 2011. Dissociative disorders in DSM-5. *Depression and anxiety, 28*(12), E17-E45.

Steele K., Van der Hart O., Nijenhuis E. R. S. 2009. The theory of trauma-related structural dissociation of the personality. In Dell P. F, O'Neil J. A, (Eds.), *Dissociation and the dissociative disorders: DSM-V and beyond*. Routledge: Chapman & Hall, 240–250.

Sunshaw, E., (Producer). 2018, December 11. *Dissociation v. psychosis.* System Speak : A Podcast About Dissociative Identity Disorder [Audio podcast]. https://share.transistor.fm/s/a69842df.

Wabnitz, P., Gast, U., & Catani, C. 2013. Differences in trauma history and psychopathology between PTSD patients with and without co-occurring dissociative disorders. *European journal of psychotraumatology, 4.* https://doi.org/10.3402/ejpt.v4i0.21452

Waelde L. C., Silvern L., Carlson E., Fairbanks J. A., Kletter H. 2009. Dissociation in PTSD. In Dell P. F, O'Neil J. A, (Eds), *Dissociation and the dissociative disorders*. Routledge: Chapman & Hall, 447–457

Wolfensberger, W. 1998. *A brief introduction to Social Role Valorization: A high-order concept for addressing the plight of societally devalued people, and for structuring human services* (3rd ed.). Training Institute for Human Service Planning, Leadership & Change Agentry (Syracuse University).

Young, S. 2014 April. *I'm not your inspiration, thank you very much.* Lecture presented at TEDxSydney, Sydney, AU. Retrieved July 16, 2016, from https://www.ted.com/talks/stella_young_i_m_not_your_inspiration _thank_you_very_much

Dissociation in Autism Spectrum Disorders: An Under-Recognized Symptom

by Katherine E. Reuben, MPH, and Ayden Parish

Autism is a pervasive neurodevelopmental disorder primarily affecting social communication, cognition, and sensory perception. Autistic individuals tend to struggle with nonverbal communication, and many struggle with verbal language as well. Cognitive differences can include highly focused interests and executive dysfunction, and autism often co-occurs with attention deficit hyperactivity disorder (ADHD) or learning disabilities. Recently, attention has begun turning towards the sensory differences reported by autistic individuals, which may include experiencing certain sensations as overwhelming or even painful, having difficulty processing streams of sensory information, and seeking out certain sensations as particularly pleasurable or fascinating. Autism can be diagnosed at any age, and indeed, with the rising awareness of autism over the past decade, many adults are now finding themselves with a new label for their lifelong feelings of alienation and difference. As a difference in neurology, autism cannot be "cured," and many autistic individuals find the idea of curing their neurological differences undesirable and offensive. Nevertheless, autistic traits tend to lead to difficulties and disability in engaging with society.

There are reasons to believe that dissociation is a common experience for individuals with developmental disorders and particularly autism. Several risk factors for dissociation, such as anxiety and trauma, are known to be elevated in autistic populations. Further, dissociative symptoms are reported by many autistic adults in online forums, social media, and blogs. Preliminary research supports that dissociation is a common experience for autistic individuals, especially those that have experienced trauma. This may have important implications for working with the symptoms and coping mechanisms that autistic individuals find relevant to their daily life.

This chapter draws particular attention to the lived experiences of autistic individuals. Often, research on autistic individuals comes from a neurotypical – that is, non-autistic – perspective. Not only are these perspectives less likely to be relevant to the lives of autistic individuals, but they may prove actively stigmatizing by presenting a deficit-focused model of autism. Additionally, autism research and narratives have historically focused primarily on the impacts on and reactions of neurotypical family members. This chapter strives to prioritize the perceptions and needs of autistic individuals in a respectful and collaborative manner. To that end, both authors are themselves autistic, and the chapter highlights the narratives provided by other autistic individuals collected as part of a survey on autism and dissociation.

Risk Factors

ANXIETY

Anxiety is common among autistic individuals, affecting between 11% to 84% (see Steensel et al., 2011). 20% to 57% of autistic youth have been reported to have symptoms of social anxiety specifically (see Wood & Gadow, 2010). The true prevalence is hard to estimate because of a lack of measures validated for this population (Wood & Gadow, 2010) and because some anxiety diagnoses require that an autistic individual have anxiety beyond what might be considered typical for the disorder. General, social, and separation anxiety are to an extent typical features of autism (Steensel et al., 2011).

Anxiety is often associated with dissociation. Depersonalization and derealization are common when individuals with social anxiety disorder are under acute social stress (Schweden et al., 2016) and can be found alongside anxiety in both clinical and non-clinical populations, especially in cases involving panic (Nestler et al., 2015). In fact, anxiety has been theorized to be a key component of depersonalization and derealization (Holmes et al., 2005). Regarding autism specifically, depersonalization and derealization have been found to accompany anxiety in 18% of autistic youth (Storch et al., 2012).

TRAUMA AND POSTTRAUMATIC STRESS

Trauma is known to be a possible cause or risk factor for all possible expressions of dissociation. Severe or chronic trauma, especially child abuse, is recognized as a major or even primary cause of the most severe manifestations of dissociation, such as identity alteration and dissociative amnesia. Dissociation immediately following trauma is common and predicts later symptoms of posttraumatic stress, and many trauma-focused researchers view posttraumatic flashbacks as inherently dissociative (Holmes et al., 2005; Spiegel et al., 2011; Steinberg, 2000; Van der Hart et al., 2006). Likewise, dissociation significantly correlates with posttraumatic stress in autistic adults (Reuben 2022).

Traumatic experiences are unfortunately very common for autistic individuals. Much research has been done on autistic social isolation, lack of caregiver attunement, and peer rejection and harassment. However, autistic adults and especially children are also at an increased risk of neglect, abuse, and assault, including from parents, other family members, disability caregivers, peers, intimate partners, and unknown individuals (Baladerian et al., 2013). This is especially concerning because interpersonal trauma is a better predictor of posttraumatic stress than traumas such as natural disasters or accidents (Breire et al., 2016; Lilly & Valdez, 2016) and is a particularly severe risk factor for dissociation (Holmes et al., 2005; Spiegel et al., 2011; Steinberg, 2000; Van der Hart et al., 2006). This correlation between interpersonal victimization and dissociation has also been found in autistic adults (Reuben et al., 2021).

Disabled individuals in general experience higher rates of interpersonal trauma (Baladerian et al., 2013; Cohen et al., 2006; Hughes et al., 2011; Mitra et al., 2011; Roberts et al., 2015; Smith, 2008). Child maltreatment may be increased because of high levels of parental stress, frustration with the child's disability, or financial strain. Peer rejection and harassment can occur in response to cultural disability stigma. As an adult, the disabled individual may be at higher risk because of their lower socioeconomic status and reduced independence. Predatory individuals may also perceive the disabled individual as more vulnerable and therefore an appealing target (Fisher et al., 2013; Hoover & Kaufman, 2018; McDonnell et al., 2019; Pfeffer, 2016; Roberts et al., 2015; Weiss & Fardella, 2018).

Autistic individuals face additional risks. Due to differences in social communication, autistic individuals often have a difficult time forming close friendships which might otherwise be protective. They may also struggle to recognize when a predator means them harm. Intellectual disability or uneven cognitive profiles, which are common in autism, may worsen difficulties recognizing ill intentions and increase perceived vulnerability. Other emotional or behavioral challenges may also increase the individual's alienation from potential sources of protection, perceived vulnerability, and likelihood of ending up in risky situations. This is true even for individuals who do not meet the full criteria for an autism spectrum disorder (ASD) diagnosis but have autistic traits or other associated risk factors (Chan et al., 2018; Fisher et al., 2013; Haruvi-Lamdan et al., 2020; Hoover et al., 2018; Holtmann et al., 2007; Kerns et al., 2015; McDonnell et al., 2019; Paul et al., 2018; Roberts et al., 2015; Rumball et al., 2020; Schroeder et al., 2014; Weiss & Fardella, 2018).

The types of interpersonal trauma that autistic individuals are vulnerable to are varied. 44%–97.8% of autistic children are bullied; contrary to common perceptions, this victimization may be complex and involve prolonged harassment, property theft or destruction, or group assault. It is also commonly repeated, with almost half of autistic people reporting being bullied 10 or more times (Baladerian et al., 2013; Chan et al., 2018; Griffiths et al., 2019; Hellstrom, 2019; Maïano et al., 2016; Paul et al., 2018; Rose et al., 2015; Schroeder et al., 2014; Weiss & Fardella, 2018). Autistic children are more likely to have reported and substantiated maltreatment (50.4%–80%) compared to neurotypical children, especially autistic children with co-occurring intellectual disability. They have been found to have higher rates of physical abuse (18.5%–57.8%), emotional or verbal abuse (62.2%–79%), and sexual abuse (2.8%–30%) (Baladerian et al., 2013; Chan et al., 2018; Gotby et al., 2018; Griffiths et al., 2019; Hellstrom, 2019; Mandell et al., 2005; McDonnell et al., 2019; Pfeffer, 2016). Conventional crime victimization is also a problem for many autistic children (56.4%–90.9%), as is witnessing violence (30%) (Hellstrom, 2019; Weiss & Fardella, 2018).

Autistic adults also report high rates of sexual violence (24.4%–78%), physical assault (34%–56%), bullying (60%–70%), and emotional abuse from partners (39%) (Brown-Lavoie et al., 2014; Griffiths et al., 2019; Haruvi-Lamdan et al., 2020; Reuben et al., 2021; Weiss & Fardella, 2018). In particular, Brown-Lavoie et al.'s (2014) study of autistic adults found that they were 2 to 3 times more likely to report unwanted sexual contact, sexual coercion, and rape compared to neurotypical adults. Another study by L. Platt et al. (2015) surveyed 350 developmentally disabled adults and found that 63.7% of men and 68.2% of women reported having experienced abuse as an adult. Reuben et al. (2021) also found that autistic women and gender minorities reported especially high rates of sexual victimization.

Because of the high rates of trauma that autistic individuals experience, it should be no surprise that they also describe high rates of posttraumatic stress. Studies have found that 16% to 19% of autistic adults report being diagnosed with posttraumatic stress disorder (PTSD; Griffiths et al., 2019; Reuben et al., 2021), and between 32% and 60% of autistic adults meet criteria for PTSD when screened (Haruvi-Lamdan et al., 2020; Reuben et al., 2021; Rumball et al., 2020). Autistic children have also been found to have more severe posttraumatic stress compared to neurotypical children (Paul et al., 2018; Mehtar & Mukaddes, 2011), although this is not always the case for studies that rely on parent reports (see Brenner et al., 2018).

Even at non-clinical levels, autistic traits predict posttraumatic stress following a trauma (Haruvi-Lamdan et al., 2019, 2020; Roberts et al., 2015). The same social communication differences that make autistic individuals vulnerable to interpersonal trauma can also leave them without support to assist with their healing. Cognitive differences can make the trauma harder to understand, and mental health and emotional regulation difficulties can also exacerbate posttraumatic stress (Chan et al., 2018; Haruvi-Lamdan et al., 2020; Hoover et al., 2018; Holtmann et al., 2007; Kerns et al., 2015; McDonnell et al., 2019; Paul et al., 2018; Roberts et al., 2015; Rumball et al., 2020; Schroeder et al., 2014; Weiss & Fardella, 2018). However, this is an under-recognized connection, and PTSD is not often assessed for in autistic individuals (Kerns et al., 2015; Kildahl et al., 2019).

DISABILITY STIGMA AND SHAME

Trauma is not the only risk factor that can arise from societal responses to autism. While threats to survival and wellbeing are important, there are other more common (and commonly overlooked) experiences that can also heavily shape the autistic individual's view of the world and themself. Disability stigma is one such experience that can be communicated either independently or as part of traumatic experiences (e.g., bullying that is focused on an individual's autism). An important outcome of disability stigma is shame.

Unlike fear, which may result from violence and threats of harm, shame is strongly associated with degradation, boundary violations, and social isolation. Individuals may feel shame not only for what others have done to them but also for who they are. Shame, along with dissociation, is a key symptom of complex PTSD, which results from interpersonal trauma (Dorahy et al., 2013; Herman, 2011; Van der Hart et al., 2006), and both shame and dissociation are predictors of posttraumatic stress severity. Additionally, individuals with clinical levels of dissociation have more trait and state shame (Dorahy et al., 2013).

In addition to reducing the pain and disruption associated with posttraumatic stress itself, dissociation has also been theorized to reduce posttraumatic shame. However, dissociation may additionally co-occur with shame to shift an individual's focus away from traumatic events (e.g., to direct attention and blame internally). This can help to preserve functioning, especially when the trauma is high in betrayal and the relationship with the perpetrator is one that the individual needs to preserve (M. G. Platt et al., 2017). Although not necessarily traumatic, disability stigma may create a similar incentive to focus inward and dissociate, particularly when the shame originates from caregivers.

Overt and Covert Discrimination. A majority of autistic individuals experience bullying during childhood and adulthood. Some of this bullying is likely focused on the traits and behaviors of the autistic individual, while some of it may be motivated by the ASD diagnosis itself. Aubé et al. (2021) found that when shown short videos of autistic children and typically developing children, elementary school children rated the autistic children more negatively and wanted to interact with them less. While this effect decreased in higher grades, the desire to avoid autistic children as measured through an implicit attitudes task did not, which the authors thought might be a particular risk for anti-autistic microaggressions.

In addition to peers, autistic individuals may face discrimination from caregivers, teachers, medical professionals, and even strangers. Griffiths et al. (2019) report on a variety of forms of discrimination experienced by professionally diagnosed autistic individuals, including schools refusing requested accommodations, employers overlooking the individual for employment or promotions despite the individual's qualifications and training, and acquaintances tricking or pressuring the individual into breaking the law or giving someone else money or possessions. While some of these experiences may have happened regardless of the individual's diagnostic status (i.e., may have been motivated by perceived traits of the autistic individual as opposed to knowledge of the individual's ASD diagnosis), others may have been directly motivated by stigma.

Laina Eartharcher, an autistic woman writing under a pseudonym, has used her blog to discuss experiences that she and others have had in which their competence was questioned or others talked down to them only after their autism was disclosed. One of her blog posts also discussed how autism is often described with pathologizing language, such as calling it a "disease" or "devastating," which can lead autistic individuals to perceive that others view them as – or that they *are* – broken or defective. Comments under the post revealed that many autistic adults related to her statements and shared similar experiences (Eartharcher, 2017).

The Double Bind of Diagnosis. There is a surprising lack of literature on the impact of an ASD diagnosis for the affected individual. The few existing studies on this topic highlight immediate reactions of relief, anger, fear, and denial. On one hand, being diagnosed can provide an explanation for one's experiences and therefore reduce confusion and shame. Understanding oneself as autistic provides a path for self-acceptance, whereas a lack of diagnosis leaves room for negative self-assessments such as being "weird," "flawed," "failed," or somehow "wrong." Similarly, a diagnosis may lead to increased support and understanding from family members, teachers, and peers, and having a diagnosis provides the opportunity to access necessary services and accommodations. Late-diagnosed adults in particular, who likely sought out assessment based on their own suspicions, may experience the diagnosis as a relief (Arnold et al., 2020; Humphrey & Lewis, 2008; Jones, 2001; Powell & Acker, 2015; Reed & Osborne, 2012; Smith et al., 2018).

On the other hand, stigma associated with an autism diagnosis can lead to negative feelings about oneself and the world, particularly if it leads to rejection by neurotypical loved ones and professionals (Arnold et al., 2020). How others react to one's autism is important to self-conception and acceptance. One study of 20 autistic youth found that several had negative perceptions of autism prior to their diagnosis, but others developed negative perceptions over time because of bullying, ostracism, or being treated differently by teachers (Humphrey & Lewis, 2008). Concerns of stigma can lead to disidentification with the diagnosis or attempting to hide it from others. Conversely, peer support and acceptance can lead to a positive autistic identity (Humphrey & Lewis, 2008; Smith et al., 2018).

Unfortunately, as commonly highlighted by autistic individuals, messages about autism come from many sources – including professionals, family members, peers, media, and educational resources – and these messages are often very negative (Eartharcher, 2017). Worse, these messages are often aimed at the family of autistic individuals and rarely acknowledge the views or needs of autistic individuals themselves. For example, one woman described a book titled Living with Autism – that was in fact aimed at neurotypical parents – which made autism seem like an "unwanted houseguest." She described how she thought that the book "personified Autism... [the autistic child] has become the 'disorder' and is entirely identified by it" ("Little Sparrow", 2017). An ASD diagnosis may lead to identifying with and being shamed by stigma towards autism, but little is known about how this impacts autistic individuals in the long term.

More research exists on caregiver reactions to the diagnosis and highlights feelings of frustration with the diagnostic process, fears of stigma against themselves and their children, and fears about how autism might impact their family (Smith et al., 2018). Only half of caregivers are satisfied with their child's diagnostic process and the subsequent support and information provided, and the associated caregiving stress can negatively impact the autistic child (Reed & Osborne, 2012). In some cases, caregivers may delay disclosing the ASD diagnosis to their autistic child, which can contribute to denial and further shame surrounding being autistic (Smith et al., 2018; Jones, 2001). A stumbling block for both caregivers and autistic individuals is coming to terms with autism being lifelong (Powell & Acker, 2015; Smith et al., 2018).

Even in the absence of a cure, many autistic people and their caregivers desire treatment for the most difficult or distressing symptoms (Arnold et al., 2020; Humphrey & Lewis, 2008; Jones, 2001; Powell & Acker, 2015; Reed & Osborne, 2012; Smith et al., 2018). A late diagnosis means years or decades without support, and many struggle to get the help that they need even with a diagnosis (Arnold et al., 2020; Powell & Acker, 2015). This, too, may contribute to self-alienation and dissociation. However, an early diagnosis of ASD may lead to the child undergoing applied behavioral analysis (ABA), which many autistic people have reported contributed to their sense of shame, self-alienation, and self-loathing. Although ABA can be combined with other therapies to help autistic individuals cope with stressors without resorting to potentially dangerous behaviors, it is often used to train autistic children to look more "normal" (i.e., neurotypical). This involves using intense behavioral conditioning to discourage unconventional but harmless autistic traits as well as to encourage behaviors that society privileges but which may be experienced as extremely aversive or even painful to the child. Some autism researchers have theorized that ABA might interfere with identity formation because of tension between the conditioning and the individual's natural self. An emphasis on compliance may also leave the autistic child unable to say no and vulnerable to future abuse (Kupferstein, 2018; McGill & Robinson, 2020; Wilkenfeld & McCarthy, 2020).

Masking. Stigma and internalized shame cause many autistic individuals to try to camouflage or "mask" their autistic traits. They may copy neurotypical individuals' speech, dress, body language, and facial expressions as well as try to hide their reactions to overwhelming or aversive sensory stimuli in an attempt to be accepted by others. Masking can contribute to feeling disconnected from or confused about one's true self. It is exhausting and may require engaging in dangerous behaviors (e.g., disordered eating or substance misuse) to maintain. At worst, it may result in suicidality (Bradley et al., 2021; Miller et al., 2021). Masking may be closely related to dissociation for some autistic individuals.

Autistic Burnout. Discrimination and attempts to mask can contribute to "autistic burnout," an experience often described by autistic adults in which an accumulation of life stressors and insufficient support lead to chronic exhaustion, loss of skills, and reduced tolerance to sensory stimuli. A key precursor of autistic burnout seems to include unattainable expectations placed on the autistic individual, such as demands that the autistic individual camouflage or mask their autism, expose themself to aversive sensory stimuli, or engage in unwanted amounts of socialization. All of these may be driven by society's refusal to respect the needs of autistic people and the subsequent internalization of the idea that the autistic person is not allowed to maintain boundaries (Raymaker et al., 2020).

Many autistic people report that a lack of ability to maintain previous levels of functioning induces shame (Raymaker et al., 2020). This may be associated with dissociation, which may in turn worsen burnout by making it difficult for the individual to connect with and respond to their emotional and physiological needs. On the other hand, dissociation may also be a coping mechanism utilized by some autistic individuals to create distance from intense feelings and overstimulation that could otherwise lead to a loss of functioning.

Attachment Disruptions. Autistic traits may be recognized as early as 12–18 months (Szatmari et al., 2016), and severity of autism symptoms predicts lower attachment security, fewer pro-social responses to caregivers, and poorer parent-child interactions. Secure attachment, which 47% of autistic children do achieve, is conversely associated with improved behavior. Both parental sensitivity and insight into their child's needs promote secure attachment. Unfortunately, not only can autism make it more difficult for the child to understand their parent, but the child's atypical communication can make it harder for the parent to understand and respond to their child. Additionally, parents may feel disconnected from their autistic child due to the child's difficulties with eye contact, conversation, and physical contact as well as due to the stress of raising a disabled child (Teague et al., 2017).

Parents of autistic children often face discrimination and exclusion by their communities (Gray, 2020; Kinnear et al., 2016; Liao et al., 2019). Additionally, a lack of sufficient support and resources for coping with their child's symptoms can lead to high levels of stress and depression (Zaidman-Zait et al., 2017). These stressors can increase the perceived difficulty of parenting, reduce parenting quality, increase child behavioral problems, and potentially interfere with the parent-child relationship (Kinnear et al., 2016; Osborne & Reed, 2010; Zaidman-Zait et al., 2017). This is troubling because even subtle emotional unavailability and attachment disruptions as early as infanthood are important predictors of dissociation later in life (Lyons-Ruth et al., 2009).

Unfortunately, the disconnection between parent and child may not remain subtle. When increased parental stress is combined with anti-autistic stigma, this may lead to parental embarrassment, social withdrawal, and associating the child with public shaming, all of which the child might internalize. The child might be further negatively affected if the parent expresses covert resentment or openly blames the child for making their life more difficult. Given the high rates of maltreatment experienced by autistic children, it is likely that for many parents, these stressors lead to a cycle of the parent taking out their frustration on their autistic child, the child's behavioral problems escalating as a result, and the parent responding with more frustration and maltreatment. This cycle might be very hard for the family to break without external help, which is generally not available.

ABSORPTION AND FANTASY PRONENESS

Absorption refers to one's ability to become "absorbed" in fantasy and imagination. While it is unclear to what extent absorption may itself be considered an inherently dissociative experience (see Holmes et al., 2004), studies point towards an association between absorption and other more centrally dissociative factors, such as compartmentalization, as well as with psychopathology more generally (Levin & Spei, 2004; Soffer-Dudek et al., 2015). Fantasy proneness, a related construct, refers to the trait of being drawn to immersive inner fantasy, with highly fantasy prone individuals being inclined towards spending long portions of time engaging in daydreaming or other fantasy-based activities like roleplaying. This, too, shows some correlation with dissociative experiences more generally (Merckelbach et al., 2021).

The stereotypical image of autism is one of a "genius without imagination" (Quirici, 2015). That is, autistic individuals have been typically viewed as having a somehow deficient capacity for imagination and creativity. However, attention to autistic individuals' own narratives uncovers the important role of fantasy and imagination for many. In her study of a summer camp for autistic youth, Fein (2020) argues that these youth identified strongly with fictional characters from literature, video games, and their own creation, to the extent that these fantasies organized how they related socially to one another. These fantasy worlds can further prove deeply personally meaningful for the individual (Visuri, 2018). It may be the case, then, that an interest in fantasy could mediate a relationship between autism and dissociation. Early research also indicates that autistic traits may be specifically associated with pathological absorption in the form of maladaptive daydreaming (West et al., 2020).

Previous Research

Despite these reasons to believe that autistic individuals are at a higher risk of experiencing dissociation, there is minimal existing research on this topic. Three studies have examined dissociation symptoms in autistic youth, and two have surveyed autistic adults. Two of the youth studies found that somatic dissociation is elevated in autistic children (Mahan & Matson, 2011; Sukhodolsky et al., 2008). 18% of autistic youth were also found to experience dissociation as a response to anxiety (Storch et al., 2012).

Zdankiewicz-Ścigała et al. (2021) surveyed 79 autistic adults and 126 neurotypical adults. They found that for both groups, stronger autonomic reactivity predicted higher somatoform dissociation, and alexithymia (specifically difficulties identifying and describing feelings, but not a bias for external focus) mediated this relationship. This relationship was stronger for autistic individuals, who additionally reported higher somatization.

Reuben et al. (2021) surveyed 687 autistic adults and found that 94% had at least one clinically elevated scale on the multiscale dissociation inventory. Emotional disengagement was the most commonly endorsed symptom, affecting 85% of participants. This was followed by depersonalization (72%), emotional constriction (60%), derealization (59%), and memory-related dissociation (53%). Identity disturbances were least common but still endorsed by 26% of participants. Additionally, 32% of participants scored above 35 on the 20-item somatoform dissociation questionnaire.

Dissociation was more severe in autistic adults who had experienced physical assault, sexual assault, or another unwanted or uncomfortable sexual experience, which were endorsed by 72% of the sample. 91% of the autistic adults reported having directly experienced any kind of trauma, for an average of 3.54 unique types of traumas. Additionally, 44% of the adults screened positive for PTSD, including half of those who had experienced assault or sexual victimization. Using the same sample, Reuben (2022) found that autistic adults who met criteria for PTSD had significantly elevated dissociation overall and elevated scores for each unique type of dissociation assessed. These findings support that high rates of trauma exposure and interpersonal victimization increase the risk of dissociation in autistic adults.

Autistic Descriptions of Dissociation

In the survey from Reuben et al. (2021), 351 autistic adults provided further narratives about their experiences of dissociation and/or their understanding of its potential causes or correlates. The participants were given descriptions of different types of dissociation and then specifically asked how they felt that their experiences of dissociation might be influenced by or interact with their autism, other neurodevelopmental disorder symptoms, anxiety, or trauma history. They were also provided the opportunity to share anything else that they wanted known about their dissociative experiences. These responses are still being analyzed and will be presented in more detail in a future study; however, a preliminary analysis is possible and highlights several key areas of interest.

Experiences of Dissociation

Firstly, many individuals described some set of experiences that are very similar to current understandings of dissociation's phenomenology. That is, these autistic adults indeed reported – not only in standardized measures but in prose – the full range of dissociative experiences, from depersonalization and derealization to somatoform dissociation and identity alteration. For example, one individual reports:

> "It just feels like I withdraw from experiencing the outer shell of my body… and retreat into the inside of my body that is unaffected by the outside world. Like a little room behind my eyes, or curling up behind my heart. And I push away too strong sensations or emotions or thoughts. I use my brain to put a wall between myself and the harm. This happens automatically and I really struggle with understanding how I feel." (Cisgender woman, age range 22–25)

Others provided examples of specific, acute dissociative episodes:

> "I just recently, within the month, spoke at a national conference about suicide and I remember the beginning of my speech, my hands looking like they belonged to someone else- and can't remember anything after that, except for pieces here and there of anything the rest of that day, that night and all the next day until evening. I am told my speech was fine, I took a bus tour, had ice cream with people,

> walked back to my hotel in unfamiliar streets, took a taxi to the airport, had a lay-over and made it back to my children safely and that's when I can remember again." (Cisgender woman, older than 51)

That is, dissociative experiences in autistic individuals are not radically different from neurotypical experiences of dissociation. This may have important implications for understanding the etiology and treatment of dissociation for autistic individuals. Nevertheless, responses spoke of a number of particularities to autistic dissociation, namely the effect of autism in trauma and victimization, the influence of conflicting social expectations, coping with sensory and/or emotional overstimulation, and possible overlaps with typical autistic symptoms such as executive dysfunction and face blindness.

Correlates of Dissociation

DISSOCIATION AS A RESPONSE TO TRAUMA

In line with previous research on dissociation, many respondents connected their dissociation to various kinds of trauma.

> "I dissociated near-constantly during a lot of my incredibly traumatic childhood. It's hard for me to even recognize it sometimes because it feels so normal that sometimes I would just completely blank out and not be able to think or remember where I am or what I'm supposed to be doing or how to do basic things. It's like moving through gel, like my

> brain doesn't work right." (Cisgender woman, age range 26-30)

Notably, several provided their understandings of how their autism led to or made them more vulnerable to victimization:

> "I feel that having undiagnosed ASD made me more vulnerable to domestic abuse, which in turn led to dissociative amnesia and identity confusion. Constantly being bamboozled in social situations and trying to adapt myself to fit in has led to identity confusion and alteration. It all ties together - autistic traits lead to me getting into traumatic situations, trying to repress/ change who I am, getting confused... and the situations are more difficult because I'm autistic…" (Cisgender woman, age range 22–25)

Some further described dealing with social isolation, discrimination, and stigma as forms of trauma that led to their dissociative symptoms:

> "Strang[e]ly, the big trauma that I've had doesn't play in as much as the every day little traumas. The isolation of being a [neurodevelopmentally disabled] person. The little times I know I did wrong socially, but didn't have the ability to do right. The times I've messed up at work despite my putting 110% into being correct. Those are the situations that haunt me and make me "flash back" or "go into the bubble."" (Cisgender woman, age range 41–45)

DISSOCIATION AS A RESPONSE TO SOCIAL EXPECTATIONS

Dealing with stigma and discrimination – whether understood as traumatic or not – often leads autistic individuals to put great effort into masking their autistic traits. Further, autistic difficulties in understanding social norms can make interaction with others feel confusing and unpredictable. Responses attributed a range of dissociative symptomatology to these social difficulties. For example, the need to suppress one's natural behaviors and consciously present a "false front" was highlighted as a particularly potent cause of depersonalization and derealization:

> "I feel like I have to 'fake' a lot to appear 'normal', and interacting with humans is a role playing game. This probably contributes to the feeling that none of this is real…" (Gender unknown, age range 31–35)

> "The real person I a[m], was unacceptable and punished in many ways from many sources so I had to learn to put on appropriate personalities, retreat into myself and watch myself "behaving appropriately" as if it was a play that I was putting on... Most of the dissociative symptoms and post-traumatic symptoms I've experienced from childhood stem from my autism being unacceptable, and further traumatic experiences (domestic violence, unwanted sexual behaviour) arose because I had learned to, dissociate from my real feelings and needs and behave how other people found acceptable. Autism, and a lack of knowledge or

> tolerance of it, is central to my experiences with dissociation." (Cisgender woman, age range 31–35)

Others described feelings of identity confusion and even identity alteration due to never being allowed to connect with their "true self" or due to constructing "personalities" to match others' demands:

> "I have spent many decades working hard to mask my odd behavior. This may account for some of the [dissociated] experience[s] I have had and still have--- my simulated / emulated personality impinging on my authentic one." (Cisgender man, age range 51+)

> "I believe my alters experience my autism to different degrees and in different regards. For instance, one alter may be nonverbal and stim by chewing and pulling hair and rocking, while another alter may be very charismatic, abnormally intelligent, and only do small stims (like playing with a spinner ring). Usually, I switch whenever a specific alter seems better-fitted to a task, so one alter might be great for managing emotional distress, while another one is better for socializing with peers, while another one is better for socializing with family." (Trans man, age range 22–25)

Of note, similar experiences with identity confusion and alteration were described by Polly Samuel ("Donna Williams"), a well-known autistic advocate who was diagnosed with dissociative identity disorder related to the traumas she experienced as part of and in response to her autism (Samuel, 2012).

DISSOCIATION AS A RESPONSE TO SENSORY AND EMOTIONAL OVERSTIMULATION

Autism is associated with sensory processing differences such that the world is experienced by many as overwhelmingly bright, loud, or otherwise chaotic. Emotions may also be felt as particularly intense, and many autistic individuals struggle with emotion regulation (Mazefsky et al., 2013). Autistic individuals describe self-stimulatory behaviors, such as rocking and pacing, as ways to control and cope with such overwhelming sensations. Survey responses suggest that dissociation may be another – often maladaptive – coping strategy:

> "Whenever I am in sensory overload it feels like my bodily functions like walking, reacting to people in a crowd, watching out for objects in the way while walking are sep[a]rated from my personality so that I don't have to make conscious decisions about it because my working memory cannot process these AND the sensory overload. I feel dismember[ed] from my body then and can have normal thoughts while my body functions unconsciously… I have a lot of switches in perception of dream-like states, become unaware of my surroundings in dissociative hyperfocus situation, I forget to eat and drink and become overly self-absorbed." (Nonbinary, age range 26–30)

Certain respondents further pointed towards the derealizing effects of having different sensory experiences than those around them – especially when those experiences were then invalidated by others:

> “The world is too much and at the same time distant. I think I dissociate to cope with the "too much" part. Also I've been denied my experiences a lot ("it can't feel that bad") so it feels like I feel things that can't be real since nobody believes them.” (Cisgender man, age range 36–40)

> “I feel like I'm stuck inside a body that doesn't belong to me and I struggle to recognise as mine and I want to learn how to embody it properly, but the fact that people won't explain to me how to use it to communicate… I have no idea what signals this body is sending out to people.” (Nonbinary, age range 31–35)

DISSOCIATION AS OVERLAPPING WITH AUTISTIC TRAITS

While the survey asked participants to reflect on the influence autism had on one’s dissociation, some respondents seemed to struggle with disentangling these two concepts. That is, some described ways in which autistic and dissociative symptoms seemed to overlap and complicate one another. For example, difficulties in shifting focus between activities are understood as a symptom of executive dysfunction, yet one respondent suggested a dissociative tint to their struggles:

> “I never really thought about this until reading the "staring off into space without thinking" item in this questionnaire earlier. At times when I'm preparing to transition to doing some other activity, such as after waking up or when returning to my work from a break, I sometimes do that for

> a minute or two. I never considered that it might have something to do with [Asperger's]." (Gender unknown, age range 22–25)

Another described face blindness (an inability to recognize faces) as interwoven with their experiences of depersonalization:

> "I think my issues with depersonalization are complicated by the face blindness issues I have--I can't recognize my face to start with, and when I'm [dissociating] there's an added layer of su[r]reality layered over it that can make trying to look in the mirror difficult. When looking at other people it's sort of funny--people's face to body p[ro]portions swim in and out and look cartoonish." (Nonbinary, age range 31–35)

Given the lack of research on dissociation in autistic individuals, it is difficult to say how exactly these experiences should be classified. Further research into this topic will no doubt uncover further intersections and elucidate the potential dissociative mechanisms behind these individuals' experiences.

Clinical Implications

Dissociation is common globally, especially among psychiatric patients (Cattell & Cattell, 1974). Specific dissociative disorders can be found in 8.6% to 18.3% of individuals within the general population (Martinez-Taboas et al., 2013). Somatoform dissociation has been found to be especially common (Sar, 2006). However, outside of contexts in which professionals have been specifically trained to recognize and treat dissociation, it is often missed. A lack of awareness about dissociation in the general population, lack of professional education about dissociation, and high rates of comorbidity with other mental health pathology all pose major barriers to the diagnosis and treatment of dissociation (Spiegel et al., 2011; Steinberg, 2000).

Barriers to the recognition of dissociation may be especially likely for autistic individuals. Autism can interfere with one's awareness of and ability to communicate about internal states and can cause a variety of more recognizable symptoms which clinicians may be more inclined to notice and treat. These have been recognized as barriers to diagnosing PTSD (Kerns et al., 2015). Additionally, Baladerian et al. (2013) found that only 55.4% of their autistic sample reported the abuse they experienced, with even lower rates of reporting among survivors of sexual or physical violence. Although research supports that autism increases the risk for interpersonal and complex victimizations – the traumas most closely associated with dissociation – this is under-recognized in practice. Finally, the lack of knowledge of dissociation in autism may itself contribute to dissociation being overlooked in this population, as this potential comorbidity may not even occur to clinicians.

Unfortunately, due to the lack of existing studies on dissociation in autism, it is unknown what the most effective treatments are. At the moment, the most important clinical recommendation is that providers who serve autistic individuals should increase screening for trauma, posttraumatic stress, and dissociation. Additionally, trauma professionals in turn should consider screening more clients for autism. Only once a sufficient number of dissociative autistic individuals have been identified in clinical contexts can treatment best-practices be established. Until then, recognition of the autistic individual's dissociative experiences may in and of itself be helpful through providing space for the individual to be heard and potentially learn other ways to cope with their stressful and traumatic experiences.

REFERENCES

Arnold, S. R. C., Huang, Y., Hwang, Y. I., Richdale, A. L., Trollor, J. N., & Lawson, L. P. (2 "The single most important thing that has happened to me in my Development of the impact of diagnosis scale—preliminary revision. *Autis Adulthood, 2*(1), 34–41.

Aubé, B., Follenfant, A., Goudeau, S., & Derguy, C. (2021). Public stigma of aut spectrum disorder at school: Implicit attitudes matter. *Journal of Autism and Developmental Disorders, 51*, 1584–1597.

Baladerian, N., Coleman, T., & Stream, J. (2013). Abuse of people with disabilities: Victims and their families speak out. *Center for Victim Research Repository*. Retrieved from https://ncvc.dspacedirect.org/handle/20.500.11990/998

Bradley, L., Shaw, R., Baron-Cohen, S., & Cassidy, S. (2021). Autistic adults' experiences of camouflaging and its perceived impact on mental health. *Autism in Adulthood, 3*(4), 320–329.

Brenner, J., Pan, Z., Mazefsky, C., Smith, K., & Gabriels, R. (2018). Behavioral symptoms of reported abuse in children and adolescents with autism spectrum disorder in inpatient settings. *Journal of Autism and Developmental Disorders, 48*, 3727–3735.

Breire, J., Agee, E., & Dietrich, A. (2016). Cumulative trauma and current posttraumatic stress disorder status in general population and inmate samples. *Psychological Trauma, 8*(4), 439–446.

Brown-Lavoie, S. M., Viecili, M. A., & Weiss, J. A. (2014). Sexual knowledge and victimization in adults with autism spectrum disorders. *Journal of Autism and Developmental Disorders, 44*(9), 2185–2196.

Cattell, J. P., & Cattell, J. S. (1974). Depersonalization: Psychological and social perspectives. In S. Arieti (Ed.), *American Handbook of Psychiatry* (2nd ed., pp. 766–799). New York: Basic Books.

Chan, K. L., Lo, C. K. M., & Ip, P. (2018). Associating disabilities, school environments, and child victimization. *Child Abuse & Neglect, 83*, 21–30.

Cohen, M. M., Forte, T., Du Mont, J., Hyman, I., & Romans, S. (2006). Adding insult to injury: Intimate partner violence among women and men reporting activity limitations. *Annals of Epidemiology, 16*(8), 644–651.

Dorahy, M. J., Corry, M., Shannon, M., Webb, K., McDermott, B., Ryan, M., Dyer, K. F. W. (2013). Complex trauma and intimate relationships: The impact of shame, guilt and dissociation. *Journal of Affective Disorder, 147*(1–3), 72–79.

Eartharcher (2017, May 10). Asperger's / autism and microaggression [Blog article]. *the silent wave.* Retrieved from https://thesilentwaveblog.wordpress.com/2017/05/10/aspergers-autism-and-microaggression/

Fein, E. (2020). *Living on the Spectrum: Autism and Youth in Community*. New York, NY: New York University Press.

Fisher, M. H., Moskowitz, A. L., & Hodapp, R. M. (2013). Differences in social vulnerability among individuals with autism spectrum disorder, Williams syndrome, and Down syndrome. *Research in Autism Spectrum Disorders, 7*(8), 931–937.

Gotby, V. O., Lichtenstein, P., Langstrom, N., & Pettersson, E. (2018). Childhood neurodevelopmental disorders and risk of coercive sexual victimization in childhood and adolescence: A population-based prospective twin study. *Journal of Child Psychology and Psychiatry, 59*(9), 957–965.

Gray, D. E. (2002). 'Everybody just freezes. Everybody is just embarrassed': Felt and enacted stigma among parents of children with high functioning autism. *Sociology of Health & Illness, 24*(6), 734–749.

Griffiths, S., Allison, C., Kenny, R., Holt, R., Smith, P., & Baron-Cohen, S. (2019). The vulnerability experiences quotient (VEQ): A study of vulnerability, mental health and life satisfaction in autistic adults. *Autism Research 12*(10), 1516-1528.

Haruvi-Lamdan, N., Horesh, D., Zohar, S., Kraus, M., & Golan, O. (2020). Autism spectrum disorder and post-traumatic stress disorder: An unexplored co-occurrence of conditions. *Autism, 24*(4), 884–898.

Haruvi-Lamdan, N., Lebendiger, S., Golan, O., & Horesh, D. (2019). Are PTSD and autistic traits related? An examination among typically developing Israeli adults. *Comprehensive Psychiatry, 89*, 22–27.

Hellstrom, L. (2019) A systematic review of polyvictimization among children with attention deficit hyperactivity or autism spectrum disorder. *International Journal of Environmental Research and Public Health, 16*(13), 2280.

Herman, J. L. (2011). Posttraumatic stress disorder as a shame disorder. In R. L. Dearing & J. P. Tangney (Eds.), *Shame in the Therapy Hour* (pp. 261–275). American Psychological Association.

Hoover, D. W. & Kaufman, J. (2018). Adverse childhood experiences in children with autism spectrum disorder. *Current Opinion in Psychiatry, 31*(2), 128–132.

Holmes, E. A., Brown, R. J., Manselld, W., Fearone, R. P., Hunterf, E. C. M, Frasquilhoe, F., & Oakley, D. A. (2005). Are there two qualitatively distinct forms of dissociation? A review and some clinical implications. *Clinical Psychology Review, 25*, 1–23.

Holtmann, M., Bolt, S., & Poustka, F. (2007) Autism spectrum disorders: Sex differences in autistic behaviour domains and coexisting psychopathology. *Developmental Medicine & Child Neurology, 49*(5), 361–366.

Hughes, R. B., Lund, E. M., Gabrielli, J., Powers, L. E., & Curry, M. A. (2011). Prevalence of interpersonal violence against community living adults with disabilities: A literature review. *Rehabilitation Psychology, 56*(4), 302–319.

Humphrey, N., & Lewis, S. (2008). Make me normal: The views and experiences of pupils on the autistic spectrum in mainstream secondary schools. Autism, 12(1), 23-46.

Jones, G. (2001). Giving the diagnosis to the young person with Asperger syndrome or high functioning autism: Issues and strategies. Good Autism Practice, 2(2), 65–73.

Kerns, C. M., Newschaffer, C. J., & Berkowitz, S. J. (2015). Traumatic childhood events and autism spectrum disorder. *Journal of Autism and Developmental Disorders, 45*, 3475- 3486.

Kildahl, A. N., Bakken, T. L., Iversen, T. E., & Helverschou, S. B. (2019). Identification of post-traumatic stress disorder in individuals with autism spectrum disorder and intellectual disability: A systematic review. *Journal of Mental Health Research in Intellectual Disabilities, 12*(1–2), 1–25.

Kinnear, S. H., Link, B. G., Ballan, M. S., & Fischbach, R. L. (2016). Understanding the experience of stigma for parents of children with autism spectrum disorder and the role stigma plays in families' lives. *Journal of Autism and Developmental Disorders, 46*, 942–953.

Kupferstein, H. (2018). Evidence of increased PTSD symptoms in autistics exposed to applied behavior analysis. *Advances in Autism, 4*(1), 19–29.

Levin, R. & Spei, E. (2004). Relationship of purported measures of pathological and nonpathological dissociation to self-reported psychological stress and fantasy immersion. *Assessment, 11*(2), 160–168.

Liao, X., Lei, X., & Li, Y. (2019). Stigma among parents of children with autism: A literature review. *Asian Journal of Psychiatry, 45*, 88–94.

Lilly, M. & Valdez, C. (2011). Interpersonal trauma and PTSD: The roles of gender and a lifespan perspective in predicting risk. *Psychological Trauma, 4*(1), 140–144

"Little Sparrow" (2017, May 17). Death of a thousand cuts [Blog article]. *Counting the Ways.* Retrieved from https://countingthewayssite.wordpress.com/2017/05/17/death-of-a-thousand-cuts/

Lyons-Ruth, K., Dutra, L., Schuder, M. R., & Bianchi, I. (2009). From infant attachment disorganization to adult dissociation: Relational adaptations or traumatic experiences? *Psychiatric Clinics of North America, 29*(1), 63–86.

Mahan, S. & Matson, J. L. (2011). Children and adolescents with autism spectrum disorders compared to typically developing controls on the Behavioral Assessment System for Children, Second Edition (BASC-2). *Research in Autism Spectrum Disorders, 5*(1), 119–125.

Maïano, C., Normand, C. L., Salvas, M. C., Moullec, G., & Aimé, A. (2016). Prevalence of school bullying among youth with autism spectrum disorders: A systematic review and meta-analysis. *Autism Research, 9*(6), 601–615.

Mandell, D. S., Walrath, C. M., Manteuffel, B., Sgro, G., & PintoMartin, J. A. (2005). The prevalence and correlates of abuse among children with autism served in comprehensive community based mental health settings. *Child Abuse & Neglect, 29*(12), 1359–1372.

Martinez-Taboas, A., Dorahy, M., Sar, V., Middleton, W., & Krügar, C. (2013). Growing not dwindling: International research on the worldwide phenomena of dissociative disorders [Letter to the editor]. *Journal of Nervous & Mental Disease, 201*(4), 353.

Mazefsky, C. A., Herrington, J., Siegel, M., Scarpa, A., Maddox, B. B., Scahill, L., & White, S. W. (2013). The role of emotion regulation in autism spectrum disorder. *Journal of the American Academy of Child & Adolescent Psychiatry, 52*(7), 679–688.

McDonnell, C. G., Boan, A. D., Bradley, C. C., Seay, K. D., Charles, J. M., & Carpenter, L. A. (2019). Child maltreatment in autism spectrum disorder and intellectual disability: Results from a population-based sample. *Journal of Child Psychology and Psychiatry, 60*(5), 576–584.

McGill, O. & Robinson, A. (2020). "Recalling hidden harms": Autistic experiences of childhood applied behavioural analysis (ABA). *Advances in Autism, 7*(4), 269–282.

Mehtar, M., & Mukaddes, N. (2011). Posttraumatic stress disorder in individuals with diagnosis of autistic spectrum disorders. *Research in Autism Spectrum Disorders, 5*(1), 539–546.

Merckelbach, H., Otgaar, H., & Lynn, S. J. (2021). Empirical research on fantasy proneness and its correlates 2000–2018: A meta-analysis. *Psychology of Consciousness: Theory, Research, and Practice*.

Miller, D., Rees, J., & Pearson, A. (2021). "Masking is life": Experiences of masking in autistic and nonautistic adults. *Autism in Adulthood, 3*(4), 330–338.

Mitra, M., Mouradian, V. E., & Diamond, M. (2011). Sexual violence victimization against men with disabilities. *American Journal of Preventive Medicine, 41*(5), 494–497.

Nestler, S., Jay, E. L., Sierra, M., & David, A. S. (2015). Symptom profiles in depersonalization and anxiety disorders: An analysis of the Beck Anxiety Inventory. *Psychopathology, 48*, 84–90.

Osborne, L. A. & Reed, P. (2010). Stress and self-perceived parenting behaviors of parents of children with autistic spectrum conditions. *Research in Autism Spectrum Disorders, 4*(3), 405–414.

Paul, A., Gallot, C., Lelouche, C., Bouvard, M. P., & Amestoy, A. (2018). Victimisation in a French population of children and youths with autism spectrum disorder: A case control study. *Child and Adolescent Psychiatry and Mental Health, 12*, 48.

Pfeffer, R. D. (2016). Childhood victimization in a national sample of youth with autism spectrum disorders. *Journal of Policy and Practice in Intellectual Disabilities, 13*(4), 311–319.

Platt, L., Powers, L., Leotti, S., Hughes, R. B., Robinson-Whelen, S., Osburn, S., Ashkenazy, E., Beers, L., Lund, E. M., & Nicolaidis, C. (2015). The role of gender in violence experienced by adults with developmental disabilities. *Journal of Interpersonal Violence, 32*(1), 101–129.

Powell, T., & Acker, L. (2016). Adults' experience of an Asperger syndrome diagnosis: Analysis of its emotional meaning and effect on participants' lives. Focus on Autism and Other Developmental Disabilities, 31(1), 72-80.

Platt, M. G., Luoma, J. B., & Freyd, J. J. (2017). Shame and dissociation in survivors of high and low betrayal trauma. *Journal of Aggression, Maltreatment & Trauma, 26*(1), 34–49.

Quirici, M. (2015). Geniuses without imagination: Discourses of autism, ability, and achievement. *Journal of Literary & Cultural Disability Studies, 9*(1), 71–88.

Raymaker, D. M., Teo, A. R., Steckler, N. A., Lentz, B., Scharer, M., Santos, A. D., Kapp, S., K., Hunter, M., Joyce, A., & Nicolaidis, C. (2020). "Having all of your internal resources exhausted beyond measure and being left with no clean-up crew": Defining autistic burnout. *Autism in Adulthood, 2*(2), 132–143.

Reed, P., & Osborne, L. A. Diagnostic practice and its impacts on parental health and child behaviour problems in autism spectrum disorders. Archives of Disease in Childhood, 97, 927-931.

Reuben, K. E. (2022). Posttraumatic stress disorder in autistic adults: Correlates of meeting DSM-5 criteria and predictors of professional diagnosis [Master's thesis, Georgia State University]. ScholarWorks.

Reuben, K. E., Stanzione, C. M., & Singleton, J. L. (2021). Interpersonal trauma and posttraumatic stress in autistic adults. *Autism in Adulthood, 3*(3).

Roberts, A. L., Koenen, K. C., Lyall, K., Robinson, E., & Weisskopf, M. G. (2015). Association of autistic traits in adulthood with childhood abuse, interpersonal victimization, and posttraumatic stress. *Child Abuse & Neglect, 45*, 135–142.

Rose, C. A., Simpson, C. G., & Moss, A. (2015). The bullying dynamic: Prevalence of involvement among a large-scale sample of middle and high school youth with and without disabilities. *Psychology in the Schools, 52*(5), 515–531.

Rumball, F., Happé, F., & Grey, N. (2020). Experience of trauma and PTSD symptoms in autistic adults: Risk of PTSD development following DSM-5 and non-DSM-5 traumatic life events. *Autism Research, 13*(12).

Samuel, P. (2012, June, 6). Dissociative identity disorder, autism, and a conversation [Blog Post]. *Polly's Pages.* Retrieved from https://blog.donnawilliams.net/2012/06/07/dissociative-identity-disorder-autism-and-a-conversation/

Sar, V. (2006). The scope of dissociative disorders: An international perspective. *Psychiatric Clinics of North America, 29*(1), 227–244.

Schroeder, J. H., Cappadocia, M. C., Bebko, J. M., Pepler, D. J., & Weiss, J. A. (2014). Shedding light on a pervasive problem: A review of research on bullying experiences among children with autism spectrum disorders. *Journal of Autism and Developmental Disorders, 44*(7), 1520–1534.

Schweden, T. L. K., Pittig, A., Brauer, D., Klumbies, E., Kirschbaum, C., & Hoyer, J. (2016). Reduction of depersonalization during social stress through cognitive therapy for social anxiety disorder: A randomized controlled trial. *Journal of Anxiety Disorders, 43*, 99–105.

Smith, D .L. (2008). Disability, gender and intimate partner violence: Relationships from the behavioral risk factor surveillance system. *Sexuality and Disability, 26*(1), 15–28.

Smith, I. C., Edelstein, J. A., Cox, B. E., & White, S. W. (2018). Parental disclosure of ASD diagnosis to the child: A systematic review. Evidence-Based Practice in Child and Adolescent Mental Health, 3(2), 98-105.

Soffer-Dudek, N., Lassri, D., Soffer-Dudek, N., & Shahar, G. (2015). Dissociative absorption: An empirically unique, clinically relevant, dissociative factor. *Consciousness and Cognition, 36*, 338–351.

Spiegel, D., Loewenstein, R. J., Lewis-Fernández, R., Sar, V., Simeon, D., Vermetten, E., Cardeña, E., & Dell, P. F. (2011). Dissociative disorders in DSM-5. *Depression & Anxiety, 28*(9), 824-852.

Steensel, F. J. A., Bogels, S. M., & Perrin, S. (2011). Anxiety disorders in children and adolescents with autistic spectrum disorders: A meta-analysis. *Clinical Child and Family Psychology Review, 14,* 302–317.

Steinberg, M. (2000). Advances in the clinical assessment of dissociation: The SCID-D-R. *Bulletin of the Menninger Clinic, 64*(2),146-63

Storch, E. A., Wood, J. J., Ehrenreich-May, J., Jones, A. M., Park, J. M., Lewin, A. B., & Murphy, T. K. (2012) Convergent and discriminant validity and reliability of the pediatric anxiety rating scale in youth with autism spectrum disorders. *Journal of Autism and Developmental Disorders, 42*(11), 2374–2382.

Sukhodolsky, D.G., Scahill, L., Gadow, K.D., Arnold, L. E., Aman, M. G., McDougle, C. J., McCracken, J. T., Tierney, E., White, S. W., Lecavalier, L., & Vitiello, B. (2008) Parent-rated anxiety symptoms in children with pervasive developmental disorders: Frequency and association with core autism symptoms and cognitive functioning. *Journal of Abnormal Child Psychology, 36*(1), 117–128.

Szatmari, P., Chawarska, K., Dawson, G., Georgiades, S., Landa, R., Lord, C., Messinger, D. S., Thurm, A., & Halladay, A. (2016). Prospective longitudinal studies of infant siblings of children with autism: Lessons learned and future directions. *Journal of the American Academy of Child and Adolescent Psychiatry, 55*(3), 179–187.

Teague, S. J., Gray, K. AM., Tonge, B. J., & Newman, L. K. (2017). Attachment in children with autism spectrum disorder: A systematic review. *Research in Autism Spectrum Disorders, 35*, 35–50.

Van der Hart, O., Nijenhuis, E. R. S., & Steele, K. (2006). The haunted self: Structural dissociation and the treatment of chronic traumatization. New York: W.W. Norton.

Visuri, I. (2018). Rethinking autism, theism, and atheism: Bodiless agents and imaginary realities. *Archive for the Psychology of Religion, 40*(1), 1–31.

Weiss, J. A. & Fardella, M. A. (2018). Victimization and perpetration experiences of adults with autism. *Frontiers in Psychiatry, 9*, 203.

West, M. J., Somer, E., & Eigsti, I. (2020, June 3). The association between autism traits and maladaptive daydreaming [Poster presentation]. International Society for Autism Research Virtual Keynote Webinar. Retrieved from https://insar.confex.com/insar/2020/meetingapp.cgi/Paper/34919

Wilkenfeld, D. A. & McCarthy, A. M. (2020). Ethical concerns with applied behavior analysis for autism spectrum “disorder”. *Kennedy Institute of Ethics Journal, 30*(1), 31–69.

Wood, J. J. & Gadow, K. D. (2010) Exploring the nature and function of anxiety in youth with autism spectrum disorders. *Clinical Psychology: Science and Practice, 17*(4), 281–292.

Zaidman-Zait, A., Mirenda, P., Duku, E., Vaillancourt, T., Smith, I. M., Szatmari, P., Bryson, S., Fombonne, E., Volden, J., Waddell, C., Zwaigenbaum, L., Georgiades, S., Bennett, T., Elsabaggh, M., & Thompson, A. (2017). Impact of personal and social resources on parenting stress in mothers of children with autism spectrum disorder. *Autism, 21*(2), 155–166.

Zdankiewicz-Ścigała, E., Ścigała, D., Sikora, J., Kwaterniak, W., Longobardi, C. (2021). Relationship between interoceptive sensibility and somatoform disorders in adults with autism spectrum traits. The mediating role of alexithymia and emotional dysregulation. *PLoS One, 16*(8), e0255460.

Intersectionality of LGBTQ+ and Trauma

by Rose Brown, PhD, and Emily Christensen, PhD

The traumatic experiences of clients who identify as lesbian, gay, bisexual, queer, and questioning (LGBQ+) are situated in pervasive heterosexism and part of overall historical and collective trauma. This chapter reviews terminology and discusses the potential for traumatic response in these clients, especially as a marginalized group – some of whom may also be people of color and/or those from non-affirming religious traditions is exponentially increased. Historical, social, political, and cultural contexts also influence experiences of marginalization. Understanding this, along with a "risk and resilience theory, form a conceptual basis to clarify the reciprocal relationships between LGBQ+ people and their environments. Together, these theories assist in locating optimal intervention points for mental health professionals, ensuring the best possible outcomes for this population" as we advocate for strategies to promote health and mental well-being (Mallinger, 2021).

Terminology

To understand LGBTQ+ issues, one must first understand the terminology utilized in safe and accepting language, as well as increase awareness of what commonly used words actually mean. For example, "sex" has historically been "viewed as fixed, determined by genitalia, and binary (only two options)" (Himes, 2021a). In this sense, people have traditionally been assigned a sex when they are born, either as male or female, and more recently the third biological category generalization of "intersex" – the natural condition of biological or genetic origin when a person is born with both male and female sexual organs or sexual characteristics. This is not uncommon, actually, with about one in every 1,500 births being intersex (Dickens, 2018).

In years past, a physician or parents decided which sex (male or female) an intersex baby should be, and treatment proceeded accordingly from infancy, often including both surgery and socialization to the assigned gender. In many cases, this was traumatic for the intersex person whose internal experience of gender may or may not have matched the assigned gender. Dreger (2012) points out that "one of the first responses to the birth of a child with ambiguous sex by clinicians, and parents, is to "disambiguate" the situation: to assign the newborn's identity as either male or female, surgically modify the child's genitalia to conform believably to that sex identity, and provide other medical treatments (such as hormones) to reinforce the gender decided upon." Dickens writes (2018):

> "The tendency of societies to recognize only male and female genders at birth has resulted in intersex children being subjected to invasive surgery and related, sometimes lifelong, medication to confirm them as male or female. On gaining maturity, some are severely distressed and resentful that early gender assignment was mistaken, particularly

> when excision of testes to enforce femininity or of ovaries to enforce masculinity has denied them procreative capacity. Emerging principles support postponement of such interventions until intersex individuals can make a gender choice for themselves."

Due to these reports of distress, such ethics have been called into question, as well as matters of consent. The depths of this issue is beyond the scope of this chapter, but ought to be sensitively and ethically considered. It is a significant source of trauma for many people born as intersex infants, with many survivors calling it out as genital mutilation. Carpenter (2018) writes:

> "... the World Health Organization (WHO) has reviewed and removed pathologizing classifications and codes associated with sexual and gender minorities from the International Classification of Diseases (ICD). However, classifications associated with intersex variations, congenital variations in sex characteristics or differences of sex development, remain pathologized. The ICD-11 introduces additional and pathologizing normative language to describe these as "disorders of sex development." Current materials in the ICD-11 Foundation also specify, or are associated with, unnecessary medical procedures that fail to meet human rights norms documented by the WHO itself and Treaty Monitoring Bodies. This includes codes that require genitoplasties and gonadectomies associated with gender assignment, where either masculinizing or

> feminizing surgery is specified depending upon technical and heteronormative expectations for surgical outcomes. Such interventions lack evidence. Human rights defenders and institutions regard these interventions as harmful practices and violations of rights to bodily integrity, non-discrimination, equality before the law, privacy, and freedom from torture, ill-treatment, and experimentation. WHO should modify ICD-11 codes by introducing neutral terminology and by ensuring that all relevant codes do not specify practices that violate human rights."

Intersex or not, male or female or not, sex is assigned to most of us at birth. Current, and most helpful, terminology references how a person was "assigned" at birth—leaving space for that individual to define their own gender experience. Thus, when a doctor looks at an infant's genital and assigns that infant the designation of "male," then that infant is "assigned male at birth", "AMAB"; likewise, when the doctor assigns the designation of "female," then that infant is "assigned female at birth", or "AFAB" (Himes, 2021a).

Someone who identifies with a gender that is not congruent with the sex they were assigned at birth may identify as "transgender", or just "trans", with *trans-* meaning "cross or beyond", as in gender that is beyond binary sex assigned to them at birth. That said, "transgender" is a large umbrella term that covers anyone who chooses to use it, including (but not limited to) transsexual persons and non-binary individuals" (Himes, 2021b). As such, trans* refers to any person who is not cisgender (someone whose experience of gender identity and birth sex correspond).[1] It is noted that issues of transition for trans* clients are beyond the scope of this chapter, but the reader would be referred to WPATH (World Professional Association for Transgender Health) Standards of Care.[2]

Clinicians must remember that sex is not the same as "gender", which is "an internal, felt sense of self as either male, female, both, neither, or some other variation" (Himes, 2021a). "Gender identity", then, is whether or not and how one identifies as a particular gender internally, regardless of biological sex (male, female, non-binary, non-conforming, or other identified genders). Thus, one may express their gender identity through "gender expression", such as how masculine or feminine or ambiguous they present themselves to be through chosen name, makeup, hairstyle, clothing choices, behaviors, attitudes, and other means of self-expression (ibid). Pronouns are also an example of this, and "there are profound clinical reasons to ask about, learn to use, and genuinely respect transgender [or any] client's pronouns" (ibid). Further, correct pronouns *always* matter, not just when the client is in session, and that includes in communication "with other professionals, in notes, on insurance paperwork, and in session. Affirmation of an individual's identity and accurate mirroring of their gendered experience is of paramount importance to treatment" (ibid).

---

[1] Using the * is an attempt to be as inclusive as possible. It signifies the "umbrella" part of the term "transgender," meaning that non-binary and other people who might not ever go through physical changes are part of this experience, too.

[2] https://wpath.org/

It also important to remember that gender identity and gender expression are not the same as sexual orientation or attraction. There is same-sex attraction, which is a physical attraction to others of the same sex, just as there is cross-sex attraction for people who identify as straight, or experiencing attraction to the opposite sex or gender. However, culturally it is understood that referring to a person as having "same-sex attraction" pathologizes their experience in a variety of ways. Gay and lesbian people do not experience their physical attractions as something "irregular" or "abnormal". Further, "gay" and "lesbian" are identity expressions, not necessarily sexualized terms. In addition, some people are attracted to more than one sex and/or gender identity, and so may identify as "bisexual" – for which that "more than one" does not have to be the binary genders of male or female. Others may not feel sexually attracted to anyone at all, and they may identify as "asexual" (or "ace"). Others may still be exploring, or "questioning" what they experience and what that means to them. Some may identify as pansexual, which means their sexual or physical attractions are not limited in sexual choice with regard to biological sex, gender, or gender identity. It is important to listen to the client to understand what their identified gender identity or orientation means to them specifically, and how you as clinician can support their identity expression.

Besides sexual attraction, there is also emotional attraction, which may or may not align with their physical attraction experience (Himes, 2021). While some people are emotionally and sexually attracted to men, to women, to non-binary people, or to other genders, other people may be emotionally attracted to one but sexually attracted to the other. Some people may be very specifically attracted to female bodies or male bodies or non-binary expression, but mentally or emotionally be more attracted to the opposite – or even other expressions all together, such as specific body types, attitudes, or emotional expression styles. This can be confusing for a person who is coming to terms with understanding themselves, especially if they are in a non-supportive or traumatizing environment that already is not affirming their experiences or supportive in their "coming out" process that publicly shares their identity expression.

Review of Literature

In a 2018 study, Tyler and Schmitz found that "LGB youth were found to experience more trauma, both in childhood and while homeless in adolescence, than their heterosexual peers. LGB[TQ+] youth were also found to be worse-off in their ability to find shelter than their heterosexual counterparts, and also were significantly more likely to exchange sex for resources, another level of hardship that homeless LGB[TQ+] youth face compared to heterosexual homeless youth." A similar study on adults addressed "hate crime victimization rates as well as associated mental health phenomena among LGBTQ+ individuals" (Cramer, et al., 2018). There is a well-documented correlation between trans* identity and autism (Warrier, et al., 2020; Strang, et al., 2019). Keating and Muller (2019) found that:

> "Compared to participants who did not experience their trauma as related to discrimination, those who did were higher in attachment anxiety, attachment avoidance,

> emotion dysregulation, PTSD, and dissociative symptoms. Biphobia was positively associated with attachment anxiety, emotion dysregulation, PTSD, and dissociative symptoms. Homophobia was positively associated with emotion dysregulation, PTSD, and dissociative symptoms. Transphobia was positively associated with PTSD and dissociative symptoms. Appearance congruence was negatively associated with emotion dysregulation, PTSD, and dissociative symptoms."

Rostosky (et al., 2021) was the first study to explore the LGBTQ+ lived experiences of hypervigilance, and they reported that "participants reported over 30 negative emotions that accompanied hypervigilance (anxiety, fear, and exhaustion were the most common). Negative emotional reactions occurred in public and private settings and with family, coworkers, strangers, and others perceived to be prejudiced. Participants self-monitored and socially withdrew in efforts to protect themselves from stress and risk of harm." Describing this, Cardona, et al. (2021) introduced an emotion-focused conceptualization of minority stress in SGM [sexual and gender minority] people through the lens of traumatic invalidation.

Moleiro, et al. (2021) broaden this by looking at these issues internationally, as well as specifically with migrants, refugees and asylum seekers in contemporary societies. Collins and Levitt (2021) also looked at this in the context of "heterosexism" using a framework of attachment style, defense style, and ego identity. Mallinger (2021) wrote:

> "In addition, heterosexism can be overt or hidden. Covert heterosexism is synonymous with microaggressions. Sue and colleagues [2007] defined microaggressions as casual comments and/or behaviors by people of privilege communicating disparaging messages to marginalized recipients. Microaggressions serve to demean and devalue individuals, whether or not they are intentional. For example, a lesbian adolescent may be told that since she wears make-up, there is no way she can be gay. Consequences of microaggressions for LGBQ individuals include depression, low self-worth, and trauma [Nadal, et al., 2019]. Persistent discrimination at the socio-cultural level directly impacts physical and mental well-being. The perception of oppression, as well as actual experiences of discrimination, are correlated with low self-esteem, depression, and substance abuse among LGBQ youth [Craig and McInroy 2013; Almeida, 2009]."

Further, the topics of sexuality and sexual trauma are often "fraught with silencing and shame. Several of the studies presented in this special issue point to the effects of this silencing. The avoidance, numbing, and dissatisfaction with one's sexuality contribute to a range of negative outcomes including increased risk of suicide" (Smidt and Platt, 2018). Grocott (2021) looks at this institutionally, exploring "perceptions of their college/university's institutional response to reports of sexual violence (e.g., taking a report seriously and taking corrective action), and the perceived impact of reporting sexual violence (e.g., students would support the person making a report)" and reporting that:

> "logistic regression analyses revealed higher rates of sexual victimization among sexual minority students (compared to heterosexual), women (compared to men), and transgender and gender diverse (TGD) students (compared to cisgender). In addition, sexual minority (compared to heterosexual), women (compared to men), and TGD (compared to cisgender) students were more likely to perceive their institution would have a poor response to reports of sexual violence. Women and sexual minority students were also likely to believe that students who report sexual violence would suffer academically."

As for treatment focus, Keskin and Yig (2021) found that "the number of childhood physical and sexual trauma episodes was found to be high in sexual minorities; in particular, the traumatized narratives were found to be associated with an avoidant attachment style ($p > 0.05$)." Himes (2021b) notes that: "there is a marked difference between conceptualizing trauma as an etiology of diverse gender experience (pathologizing explanation), and conceptualizing a type of dissociation as intrinsic to gender dysphoria (non-pathologizing)." Further, those with dissociative responses to these traumas can often benefit from the same relational, psychodynamic, and embodied therapies as other trauma clients. Wilmanns (2021) discussed development of a dance and movement therapy method "designed to contribute to the strengths and limitations dance/movement therapy holds in relation to dissociative symptoms, specifically working within the window of tolerance trauma model and with trans* individuals where the intersection of dissociation can be aligned with gender dysphoria."

Clinical Implications

It is critical to be aware of the level of trauma that people in the LGBTQ+ community have experienced, both historically and individually – especially if they have grown up in unsupportive or even traumatizing environments. Many have experienced some form of shaming, shunning, and other forms of literal or emotional isolation, if not overt harm because of their internal experience of gender identity or external expression of it. As such, "dissociation and fragmentation (in the current cultural context) are often inseparable aspects of [LGBTQ+] experience" (Himes, 2021a). Practitioners play a critical role in advocating for LGBQ rights, "including parity in the areas of health and mental health" (Mallinger, 2021). Professionals can also raise client consciousness, as well as awareness of broader sociopolitical influence. Specifically, clinicians assist clients as they "link their experiences with overt and covert heterosexism" (ibid). For example, mental health workers can "discuss how heterosexism and the resultant stigma and discrimination exacerbate individual stressors" (Russell and Fish, 2016).

To be both more sensitive and more inclusive, Himes (2021a) suggests simple pragmatic changes to clinical paperwork and dialogue. For example, they suggest that if the binary response of male or female is necessary due to insurance requirements, the clinician just clarifies that directly in writing where it asks for the information: "Which sex is listed for you on your insurance? (Unfortunately, we have to submit the sex that matches what is written on your insurance records in order for them to accept our claims. We know that this may not reflect who you are and wish we didn't have to ask)" (ibid). Clinicians can also affirm that a client's chosen name is the appropriate name by inquiring about an individual's legal name. Clinicians could also broaden all of this, allowing clients to express on paperwork their own identities in their own words, by stating something like: "How do you describe your various identities? Feel free to describe in detail or list off a set of terms. (Not nearly exhaustive list of examples: gender queer, POC, poly, trans masculine, immigrant, kinky, female, transwoman, Filipina American, asexual, Jewish)" (ibid).

Further, clinicians can support LGBTQ+ clients providing information and support about "negotiating successful dating relationships and advocating for services promoting physical, sexual, and emotional health,...proactively engage clients in anti-violence outreach, and [address] relationship enhancing skills... [as well as] sex education... and [issues of] intimate partner violence" (Mallinger, 2021; Starks, et al., 2015). Mallinger (2021) also writes that clinicians can:

> "also educate families about the potential deleterious effects of negative reactions [to coming out]. Further, they can provide counseling on integrating political values and religious beliefs which may not be in concert with their child's sexual orientation. Providers must also be sensitive to racial/ethnic and socio-economic variations and their potential impact on parental support.... Practitioners must also understand the impact of historical, political, and

cultural context in the development of stigma and community resilience."

Discussion and Conclusion

Historical, political, and cultural contexts contribute to the risk of adverse outcomes for LGBQ+ clients. Heterosexism intersecting with racism, sexism, and religious bias, negatively impact LGBQ+ people of color, those holding non-Christian beliefs, and/lesbian and bisexual women. Community environment also can create barriers or supports. Developmentally, adolescents are most affected by school experiences, peer and romantic connections, and family relationships. Placement in foster care, homelessness, mental health and substance abuse are among adverse consequences for LGBQ youth and young adults (ibid).

Trauma complicates the already complex experience of LGBTQ+ clients. Additional layers of trauma may add confusion regarding, fear of acceptance of, delay in acceptance of, or difficulty processing diverse gender experience (Himes, 2021b). Gender dysphoria is an aspect of gender diverse experience for some, but not all, transgender people (many gender diverse folks do not experience dysphoria). LGBTQ+ people report extensive discrimination (trauma) from health care providers, which adds to minority stress (more trauma) (Bradford, et al., 2-13; Kanamori and Cornelius-White, 2016; Shipherd, et al., 2010). More specifically, amongst gender dysphoric trans* people, there is a significant prevalence of disorganized attachment (Vitelli and Riccardi, 2010; Lingiardi et al., 2016). Trauma may contribute to pathological types of dissociation in gender dysphoric individuals (Colizzi, et al., 2014; Giovanardi, et al., 2018). Gender dysphoria itself may be viewed as a type of dissociation which is specific to transgender individuals and which is alleviated by GCS [gender confirmation surgery](Colizzi, et al., 2014).

Historically, attempting to find "causation" for diversity in pathological experiences (e.g., childhood trauma) has caused significant harm to marginalized populations" (Himes, 2021b). If gender diversity (including dysphoria) is a natural diversification of human experience, then attempting to explain it through pathological etiology will only continue to replicate the lack of mirroring, rejection, and fear that is clearly linked to minority stress in transgender individuals" (ibid). Mental health professionals' appreciation of the impact of diverse needs and experiences of LGBQ+ clients, combined with use of affirmative practice skills, has the ability to protect [clients] and shift the narrative from risk to resilience" (Mallinger, 2021).

REFERENCES

Almeida, J., Johnson, R.M., Corliss, H.L., Molnar, B. E., &Azreal, D. 2009. Emotional distress among LGBT youth: The influence of perceived discrimination based on sexual orientation. Journal of Youth and Adolescence, 38 (7), 1001-1014.10.1007/s10964-009-9397-9.

Bradford, J., Reisner, S.L., Honnold, J.A., and Xavier, J. 2013. Experiences of Transgender-Related Discrimination and Implications for Health: Results From the Virginia Transgender Health Initiative Study, American Journal of Public Health, 103(10): 1820-1829.

Cardona, N. D., Madigan, R. J., & Sauer-Zavala, S. 2021. How minority stress becomes traumatic invalidation: An emotion-focused conceptualization of minority stress in sexual and gender minority people. Clinical Psychology: Science and Practice.

Carpenter, M. 2018. Intersex variations, human rights, and the International classification of diseases. Health and human rights, 20(2), 205.

Collins, K. M., & Levitt, H. M. 2021. Heterosexism and the self: A systematic review informing LGBQ-affirmative research and psychotherapy. Journal of Gay & Lesbian Social Services, 33(3), 376-405.

Colizzi, M., Costa, R., & Todarello, O. 2014. Transsexual patients' psychiatric comorbidity and positive effect of cross-sex hormonal treatment on mental health: Results from a longitudinal study. Psychoneuroendocrinology, 39, 65–73. doi: 10.1016/j.psyneuen.2013.09.029

Craig, S.L. & McInroy, L.B. 2013. The relationship of cumulative stressors, chronic illness, and abuse to self-reported suicide risk of Black and Hispanic sexual minority youth. Journal of Community Psychology, 41 (7), 783-798. 10.1002/jcop.2157

Cramer, R., Wright, S., Long, M., Kapusta, N., Nobles, M., Gemberling, T., & Wechsler, H. 2018. On hate crime victimization: Rates, types and links with suicide risk among sexual orientation minority special interest group members. Journal of Trauma and Dissociation, 19(4), 476–489.

Dickens, B. M. 2018. Management of intersex newborns: Legal and ethical developments. *International Journal of Gynecology & Obstetrics*, 143(2), 255-259.

Dreger, A. D. 2021. "Ambiguous Sex"—or Ambivalent Medicine?: Ethical Issues in the Treatment of Intersexuality. The Hastings Center Report, vol 28, no 3.

Giovanardi, G., Vitelli, R., Maggiora Vergano, C., Fortunato, A., Chianura, L., Lingiardi, V., & Speranza, A. M. 2018. Attachment patterns and complex trauma in a sample of adults diagnosed with gender dysphoria. Frontiers in psychology, 9, 60.

Grocott, L. R., Leach, N. R., Brick, L. A., Meza-Lopez, R., & Orchowski, L. M. 2021. Institutional response and impact of reporting sexual violence: an examination of sexual and gender minority college students. Journal of interpersonal violence, 08862605211055078.

Himes, H.L. 2021a. Basic Principles & Ethical Guidelines For Trauma Informed Psychotherapy With Transgender Adults. Presentation for 2021 ISSTD Virtual Conference. 10 April 2021.

Himes, H.L. 2021b. Working with Transgender Adults: A Deeper Theoretical Understanding. Presentation for 2021 ISSTD Virtual Conference. 24 October 2021.

Nadal, K.L. 2019. A decade of microaggressions research and LGBTQ communities: An introduction to the special issue. Journal of Homosexuality, 66 (10), 1309-1316.10.1080/00918369.2018.1539582

Kanamori, Y., & Cornelius-White, J. H. D. 2017. Counselors' and counseling students' attitudes toward transgender persons. Journal of LGBT Issues in Counseling, 11(1), 36–51. doi:10.1080/15538605.2017.1273163.

Keating, L., & Muller, R. T. 2020. LGBTQ+ based discrimination is associated with PTSD symptoms, dissociation, emotion dysregulation, and attachment insecurity among LGBTQ+ adults who have experienced Trauma. *Journal of Trauma & Dissociation*, 21(1), 124-141.

Keskin, G., & Yig, G. T. 2021. The Effect of Early Traumatic Experiences on Attachment Styles in Sexual Gender Minority Individuals. Journal of Forensic Nursing, 17(4), 219-228.

Lingiardi, V., Nardelli, N., Ioverno, S., Falanga, S., Di Chiacchio, C., Tanzilli, A., & Baiocco, R. 2016. Homonegativity in Italy: Cultural issues, personality characteristics, and demographic correlates with negative attitudes toward lesbians and gay men. *Sexuality Research and Social Policy*, 13, 95–108. doi:10.1007/s13178-015-0197-6

Mallinger, G. 2021. "Promoting Mental Health among Lesbian, Gay, Bisexual, and Questioning Youth: Implications for Practice." J Ment Health Soc Behav 3.1 2021: 135.

Moleiro, C., Solntseva, S., & Aybar, G. 2021. Culture and Violence Against LGBTQ+ Persons: International Contexts and Issues in Contemporary Societies. In Violence Against LGBTQ+ Persons (pp. 219-230). Springer, Cham.

Rostosky, S. S., Richardson, M. T., McCurry, S. K., & Riggle, E. D. 2021. LGBTQ individuals' lived experiences of hypervigilance. Psychology of Sexual Orientation and Gender Diversity.

Russell, S.T. & Fish, J.N 2016. Mental health in lesbian, gay, bisexual, and transgender youth. Annual Review of Clinical Psychology, 12 (1), 465-487. 10.1146/annurev-clinpsy-021815-093153

Shipherd, J., Maguen, S., Skidmore, W. C. and Abramovitz, S. M. 2010. Potentially traumatic events in a transgender sample: Frequency and associated symptoms

Smidt, A. M., & Platt, M. G. 2018. Sexuality and trauma: Intersections between sexual orientation, sexual functioning, and sexual health and traumatic events. Journal of Trauma & Dissociation, 19(4), 399-402.

Starks, T., Newcomb, M., &Mustanski, B. 2015. A longitudinal study of interpersonal relationships among lesbian, gay, and bisexual adolescents and young adults: Mediational pathways from attachment to romantic relationship quality. Archives of Sexual Behavior, 44(7), 1821–1831. 10.1007/s10508-015-0492-6.

Strang, J. F., Klomp, S. E., Caplan, R., Griffin, A. D., Anthony, L. G., Harris, M. C., ... & van der Miesen, A. I. 2019. Community-based participatory design for research that impacts the lives of transgender and/or gender-diverse autistic and/or neurodiverse people. Clinical practice in pediatric psychology, 7(4), 396.

Sue, D. W., Capodilupo, C. M., Torino, G. C., Bucceri, J. M., Holder, A. B., Nadal, K. L., & Esquilin, M. 2007. Racial microaggressions in everyday life. American Psychologist, 62(4), 271-286. 10.103770003-066X.624.271

Tabashneck, S., & Judge, A. M. 2021. Evaluating LGBT Individuals Who Have Committed Sexual Offenses. Sex Offenders: Identification, Risk Assessment, Treatment, and Legal Issues, 466.

TSER (Trans Student Educational Resources). 2015. The Gender Unicorn. Article online and booklet available for order. https://transstudent.org/gender/. Accessed 8 March 2022.

Tyler, K., & Schmitz, R. 2018. A comparison of risk factors for various forms of trauma in the lives of lesbian, gay, bisexual and heterosexual homeless youth. Journal of Trauma and Dissociation, 19(4), 431–443.

Vitelli, R., & Riccardi, E. 2010. Gender identity disorder and attachment theory: The influence of the patient's internal working models on psychotherapeutic engagement and objective. A study undertaken using the adult attachment interview. International journal of transgenderism, 12(4), 241-253.

Warrier, V., Greenberg, D. M., Weir, E., Buckingham, C., Smith, P., Lai, M. C., ... & Baron-Cohen, S. 2020. Elevated rates of autism, other neurodevelopmental and psychiatric diagnoses, and autistic traits in transgender and gender-diverse individuals. Nature communications, 11(1), 1-12.

Wilmanns, E. 2021. DMT and Dissociation: Opening the Window of Tolerance to Embodiment; Development of a Method.

The Role Misogyny and Patriarchy Play in the Development of Dissociative Disorders, Complex Trauma, and Attachment Injury

by Christine Forner, B.A., B.S.W., M.S.W., R.S.W.

One systemic and intergenerational factor that receives little discussion when we examine the issue of dissociation, complex trauma, and attachment injury is misogyny. "The term "misogyny" is derived from the Ancient Greek word "mīsoguníā" which means hatred towards women. Misogyny has taken shape in multiple forms such as male privilege, patriarchy, gender discrimination, sexual harassment, belittling of women, violence against women, and sexual objectification" (Srivastava, 2017). Conceptually, misogyny is a result of patriarchy, which is "understood in terms of what it does to women" (Manne, 2017, p. 13):

> "I argue that we should think of misogyny as serving to uphold patriarchal order, understood as one strand among various similar systems of domination (including racisms, xenophobia, classism, ageism, ableism, homophobia, transphobia, and so on). Misogyny does this by visiting hostile or adverse social consequences on… girls and women to enforce and police social norms that are gendered either in theory (i.e., content) or in practice (i.e., norm enforcement mechanisms)."

This damage from the patriarchal distain or even full hatred for half of the species, should be, especially in the trauma world, one of our main priorities in prevention and care, but it is not. Rarely are there lengthy discussions on the devastating effect that misogyny has had on the development of our current societies, policies, judicial, economic and medical systems. The impact that billions and billions of our mothers have been raped, enslaved, tortured, held as property, beaten, not given agency over their own bodies, and been through hundreds of attempts at extermination should raise some alarm bells, but it does not (Papa, 2017; Rackin, 2016). The damage that misogyny had and still has on our species is acute and ongoing – and attempts to prevent anything being done about it (Messina, 2019):

> "For centuries, women have weathered storms of underestimation, disrespect, and character assassination, usually at the hands of men. Even after the advent of second-wave feminism, critics have undermined the contributions of women to society and culture. When women suggest an idea, propose change, or develop something that challenges the status quo (especially if the unfamiliar idea shows promise), the men who benefit from existing habits and systems often resist. When women's ideas disappear, violence has been done to their minds and spirits, in psychic blows that cannot heal as the body does…"

The resulting destruction is not just the profound massive amount of harm that has been done and that still occurs, but also the damage caused by the detached attitude that ignores the vital maternal care that a human being needs to be optimal (Bitzer, 2015).

This strange situation of oppression disrupts the attachment and bonding processes through the societal distancing from maternal care (Takševa, 2019). Further, this factors into little research on both victimology and perpetration, outside the anthropological or intersectionality context (Moss, 2003). It is as if there is global general biased blindness to this real, measurable, and tangible agent of profound harm. The fact that misogyny and patriarchy do not often enter consideration in clinical discussions on aetiology, prevention, and healing of traumatic experiences is telling (Messina, 2019).

Misogyny is about 10,000 to 6000 years old (Holland, 2006). It is not a natural state for humans, and to assume so ignores everything we know about the neurobiology of our species (Abi, 2021; Kulish, 2021; Sherlock, 2021). There are several lay theories as to why misogyny and patriarchy exist: that men are stronger, or that it is just part of men's genes, or that men are generally more aggressive. None of these theories are based in scientific accuracy. In actuality, there is a lot of contrary evidence that debunk these myths (Van Valkenburgh, 2021; Harari, 2014; Hoffnung, 2015). The truth is that we do not know exactly when and why misogyny started. There is a general agreement that it did start around the same time as patriarchy, within very similar conditions.

Some posit that misogyny and patriarchy are natural is because it occurs everywhere, and it can be found in almost every single culture around the globe for nearly 10,000 years (Harari, 2014; Holland, 2006).

What is missing from these conversations and general philosophical discussions is the awareness that everything we know comes from deep rooted, unquestioned, generationally, economically and religiously biased concept of what it is to be a human being. The notion of what *it is* to be a human and what *might be possible* are two very different conversations.

When we look through the lens of misogyny and patriarchy, all humans are degraded and downgraded, used as pawns of power rather than living with dignity and purpose through the care of one another. Confronting these ideas, we realize that much of what we think is true, is not. Much of what we know is definitely mis-labelled. The old oppressive arguments about who we think humans are, come from the patriarchy. These arguments about what humans need are entrenched in misogyny. The saddest part of this conundrum is that the solution is quite simple, yet it will never be applied because in a misogynist/patriarchal world, the solution is seen as the enemy or completely disregarded.

How misogyny began, and the subsequent replacement veneration, the patriarchy, should be part of every area that studies human beings. It should be foundational in psychology, medical, psychiatric, social work, marriage and family therapies and any other clinical training program because of the impact that these traumatic reactions have on every single human's mental health, physical health, relational health, climate health, and every other single part of human existence. It is paramount in understanding why human suffering exists in the first place.

It can be stated with a fair amount of certainty that much of what threatens us as a species can be traced back to misogyny (Estok, 2019;

Reardon, 1985; Zeitlin, 1978). There is an excellent argument that psychopathy, in all of its iterations, is created and caused by misogyny and patriarchy. All of the greed that we are supposed to possess as a species, the notion that power is seductive for humans, particularly men, and the detrimental relationship most, if not all, societies have with sexual abuse, in all of its forms can all be linked, directly, to misogyny and patriarchy. Yet, it is never mentioned. There is a gigantic elephant in the room that continues to be willfully ignored on a level that cannot even come close to being described as a cognitive dissonance because it is so much larger than this.

This chapter will be dedicated to describing misogyny and patriarchy from a trauma perspective. Where misogyny and patriarchy likely originated from and what external conditions likely led to the perpetuation and continuation of misogyny and patriarchy. This chapter will also discuss how misogynistic systems are abhorrent to the homo sapien species and how patriarchy became the only substitute in the absence of maternal and paternal care. The main issues raised in this chapter is to highlight the emergent need to address these systems in order to eliminate them. I suggest that misogyny and patriarchy are clearly the root cause of human-to-human harm, which can be traced to a broken maternal and paternal bond. Until we understand the multi-level and insidious damage these beliefs have on all of humanity, likely little will change in the world of complex trauma and dissociation. But, conversely, applying non-misogynistic and non-patriarchal principles to our clinical practices, a world of hope and possibility can come flooding in to heal us all.

Misogyny

There is the often used and too simplistic definition of the word misogyny: the hatred or distain of women. But arguably, misogyny is not that simple, and it is not that cut and dry. How does one attempt to encompass a many millennium long human rights travesty, whose brutality is on such a grand scale, that resulted in all of humanity being unfathomably traumatized? It is difficult for many to see the current realities that are a direct result of misogyny, let alone how to connect the dots from 6000, to 10,000 years of generational neglect and human-to-human harm (Card, 2018; Dillon and Marsoobian, 2018). The problem is so huge, normalized so much, and quite possibly so personally activating that any alternative way of existing was likely lost, even within our collective consciousness and our imaginations, many millennium ago.

When doing a literature review for things like "the origin of misogyny" or "the cause of misogyny", the results are rather dismal. There is no real clear definitive explanation or a definitive start date. Jack Holland (2006) states that "it is hard to be precise about the origins of a prejudice. But if misogyny has a birthdate, it falls sometime in the eight century, B.C." (p. 12). Is this lack of scientific knowledge partly because there is such a deep-seated bias collectively, and generally believing this, is just the way it is? Or is this lack of knowledge based in another bias of the global assumption that believes that this is just an extension of our "uncivilized" past, therefore real scientific rigorous investigation is not really of value? Or is it because there is the assumption that our more primitive nature is rooted in a gendered division of humans, so it is not really worth the investigation?

It is likely that all three issues, plus several more, contribute to the root of why we do not know of the *why*.

There does seem to be a general agreement and default setting that women are weaker and more dependant, while men are generally stronger and are more able to be the provider (Scaptura, 2019). The argument that the biggest separation of men and women is because women are smaller, less assertive, and naturally more dependant due to birthing and rearing children, while men are more violent, sexually driven and greedy are the foundational differences between the sexes. These attributes and arguments all consistently seem to be the reasons that misogyny exists: its just in the genes, and that's the way it is since the beginning of time.

This gargantuan leap, that some members of our species are "weaker and more dependant" as an explanation as to why so many males brutalize and torture their offspring, rape and violate others, steel and hoard resources, frighten and punish large groups of other people, and feel justified in using terror and baffling amounts of cruelty to control whole cultures and societies does not add up. There is still a huge information gap when examining the harmful, neurobiological effects that a misogynistic world has on all humans and their attachment, bonding, and regulation systems. How does the need to be cared for and protected somehow translate to, and in many ways fully sanction, child abuse, rape, murder, torture, profound neglect, and other heinous acts? It simply does not make sense, and there is no evidence to support this theory.

It's a bizarre idea, this notion that brutal violence is justified towards all things categorized as female (and those beings who represent vulnerability because of a need for dependency). This puts those who have violently participated in acts of misogyny in a strange light. In other words, this profoundly species-hating and environmental-sabotaging is rationalized because of perceived weakness and dependency. How can something so mind-boggling severe be explained by something so trivial? This argument is entirely illogical, and few seem to see the absurdity in this colossal myth. Not only does this defy the laws of nature, but this also defies evolution (Abi, 2021; Kulish, 2021; Sherlock, 2021). The reason behind the advent of misogyny does not make any logical sense.

If the reason that everyone is taught to hate women is because of a distain for vulnerability, dependence, and apparent weakness, it implies the passing down of the savage genetic preference: *this person is dependant on me, therefore I must destroy not only their body, but the essence of what make that person a human being*. These acts of forced and coercive control, interpersonal betrayal, child-torture, rape, and murder are so destructive both physically and emotionally that those who participate in these acts and those who suffer these acts often can no longer be a fully functioning human being. These acts most often result in not being able to be a healthy participant in general society (Brookman, 2015; Fox, et al., 2015; Ardino, 2012; Pollack, 2009).

To hate someone or many someone's so much that a compulsion to terrorize, beat and destroy is "unavoidable" because you don't like that they are dependant, vulnerable and weak, and that you just so casually can be violent and aggressive, again just does not add up. In order to hate or be so enraged with someone this much, something else has to be occurring. There has to be something that is much more logical than the flimsy explanation of physical strength or lack thereof, and the responsibility, or lack thereof, of having to care for someone else.

Something cataclysmic had to have occurred a long time ago that resulted in the intergenerational attempted decimation of women and children. Something really bad had to have happened for humanity to turn on itself as it did. Something catastrophic had to have happened for humanity to attack itself from the inside out. Something species-shattering had to have happened because this is exactly what the end result is – we see evidence of the origin in the unfolding.

Sometime about 10,000 to about 8,000 years ago, our species started to turn on itself. A literal war started where an entire species started to do things that went against its own interests and neurobiological underpinnings. All of the unique attributes that make a human a human seemed to have come under attack. This was not because a few men had to take care of their offspring and the person who brought their children into the world. It was not because a few women were not perceived to be as strong as the guy standing next to them. Something dreadful had to have happened that disfigured what we see as male and female. It is a scar that each and every single human on this planet carry, and it is one that bears witness, or that re-enacts, its own origin story through a culture and society that does not value the need of maternal and paternal care.

Patriarchy

The Patriarchy, is too, simply defined as a system of a society in which men hold the power and women are largely excluded from it. Again, too, as with the definition of misogyny, this simpler version does not come close to what the Patriarchy really is and how this system is fueled by fear and profound violence. The truth runs so much deeper.

There are two basic lay theories of why the patriarchy exists: the first being that males are believed to be physically stronger, and therefore they must have a natural inclination to rule; and the second being that when we moved from a hunter-gatherer to an agriculturally based creature, the notion of ownership and the need to protect one's property (along with limited resources) tipped the already precarious power dynamic in men's favour. Basically, men rule because they hit harder simply cannot be the best explanation for thousands and thousands of years of pain, suffering, war, rape, incest, genocide, fascism, colonization, slavery, psychopathy, greed and sanctioned inhumanity.

The theory that men are a violent creature, by nature, and the justification of this violence because of limited resources, is often supported by comparing Homo Sapiens social order, with the social order of Chimpanzees and Bonobos (Hare, 2017; Palagi, et al., 2014; Boesch, 2007). The weak link in this argument, however, is that our neurobiology differs greatly from these two species, that we separated, evolutionarily, some 10 million years ago, makes for a very cherry-picked argument. By extrapolating that humans use violence because Chimpanzees use violence does not pay attention to how Chimpanzees tend to their young. If we are just like Chimpanzees, then why do humans not parent their young like a Chimpanzee? Chimpanzees are not raping, neglecting, beating, starving, and harming their young, en masse, as we humans do. The male chimps are not secretly sexually assaulting their infants and essentially destroying a great deal of the potential that occurs within their species. This failed argument tends to point out that we are just an animal like every other animal without including that we are the only creature who will brutalize and torture its young. These theories that attempt to explain male-dominated violence do not include the fact that humans are doing something that goes against basic fundamental natural laws. These theories that attempt to justify and normalize human-to-human violence ignore that a living thing must put all of its resources into the continuation and perpetuation of the species. In other words, the natural expectation that the creators of life will do everything they can to foster and ensure the continuation of the species, not try to destroy it as patriarchy does.

In what can only be describes as another forced "fitting" of a theory, is the idea that the patriarchy started with the advent of the invention of agriculture. The agricultural theory postulates that the development of male dominance seems to be related to the invention of agriculture which brought out the just below the surface natural need to protect one's new proclaimed lands and resources (Ananthaswamy, & Douglas, 2018). According to this theory, some 10,000 years ago, quite suddenly, when humans proclaimed that this land now has ownership and belongs to someone, men drastically jumped to violence as a way to protect what is "theirs". In turn, they then needed to protect and defend their families and their food from pillaging hoards.

In further exaggeration of both theories, this indicates something genetic that must have already been there because of men's innate need for protection and psychopathic greed. Ultimately, this possessiveness easily led to domestic violence, coercive control, the vilification of women, and the justification of rape. This is a rather large leap in logic! How does the need to have guaranteed resources translate into centuries upon centuries of the most inhumane and cruel acts that one set of humans can do to another set of humans? This is not logical, and is basically saying that all of this cruelty is because men cannot share.

To offer a new proposition of what really happened, we must hold space for recognizing and understanding that most, if not all, the previous theories of why this happened are incorrect. Doing so is difficult, and challenges a status quo that has been in place for a long time. However, it is evident that these theories completely ignore or deny the internal neurobiology of the Homo Sapien. These theories make huge and grossly broad generalizations that are extremely contrary to Homo Sapien biomechanics. These theories also completely ignore and remove the role that dissociation and attachment breaks have on humans.

This cannot be the way we are! Everything inside of us contradicts the idea that randomly, out of the blue, we started to become violent and greedy – especially when there is ample evidence that humans are otherwise (Perkeybile, et al., 2019; Potts, 2003). These theories do not pay attention to the vast amount of anecdotal and scientific evidence of what hurts humans. Simply, if misogyny and patriarchy were "normal" then it would not bother everyone as it does.

So how did misogyny and patriarchy come about if it was not about greed or a "primitive" instinct that was always there? Or only now exaggerated by the newer drive to protect one's land and resources? I will suggest it was a trauma response. If the result is trauma, then why would the instigator not be traumatic? Something had to have happened that was severe, as the response is equally severe.

Vilification of healing and parental care leaving us parentless as a species (the pain of detachment)

Misogyny and patriarchy are so much more than the hatred of women and the natural-assumed higher role of men: *they are the distain and vilification of human care*. It is the dislike and mistrust of kindness, compassion, true empathy, generosity, attunement, connection, dependence and co-regulation. It is very hard to find reference material that supports these foundational, and unique aspect of the human species. A literature review does not reveal an abundance of information that clearly states we are a peaceful creature whose ability to regulate oneself was traumatically ripped away several thousands of years ago and we have been in a massive tailspin ever since.

When one looks for information about humans and human behaviour you will likely come across all sorts of philosophical offerings about personality types and driving forces. Often the driving forces are greed, fighting over resources, and sex. Billions and billions of dollars have been spent on attempting to find these genetic sources of our behaviours and illnesses, without ever seeing that what drives most of our behaviours are symptoms of too much stress, too little soothing, too much pain and too much isolation. Still to this day, even when the information dealing with complex trauma and dissociation is irrefutable (Reinders and Veltman,

2021), you will have a difficult time finding anything that really contradicts what we have deduce about humans for the last 3,000 years or so.

Humans are an allo-parenting species (Emmott, & Page, 2021; Kenkel, Perkeybile, & Carter, 2017). This means that at least four, if not six, adults are required to raise one infant. This also means that, for our species, many others are required to assist the parents in raising our young. This is the opposite of what is found in a patriarchal society. In an allo-parenting society infants are the top priority, as it is with every other single creature that raises its young. Clearly, this is not the case in our current societies as child sexual abuse, neglect, physical abuse, domestic abuse, rape, forced labour, poverty, and racism are extremely normal parts of everyone's life (Ricks, 2018).

In looking at the inner neurobiology of human beings, it is clear from the world of complex trauma and dissociation that we are not violent creatures. We do not tolerate violence well (Freyd, 2003). Humans can adapt to trauma, but they certainly do not do well with the adaptation. It has been well known and verified many thousands of times over, that when anyone at any developmental stage, albeit infant, child, adolescent, adult or elder, is neglected, verbally abused, emotionally abused, spiritually abused, and/or sexually abused, the whole person is affected for a lifetime if not healed (Lamp, 2013; Bonanno, 2011; Delahanty, 2008). It is also very well known and proven quite conclusively that when an infant and child is harmed, or harmed and ignored, or ignored all together, that the brain cannot and likely will not develop completely as it should (Pfluger, 2021; Cassidy and Mohr, 2011). It is also well known that stress, lack of attachment, disorganized attachment, frightening or frightened attachment effect the human being on a profoundly harmful way (Ariav-Paraira, 2021; Dagan, 2021; Venta, and Abate, 2021; Brisch, 2021). It is only a reasonable deduction to surmise that if we are so sensitive to stress, so much so that it interferes with our ability to care and tend to ourselves and our young, a thing that literally threatens the continuation of the species, that human to human harm and human induced traumatic stress is not part of our evolutionary adaptations and defenses.

We are a creature who can do several things that no other creature, that we know of, can do. We can empathize. Empathy is a process where one person can literally experience the inner sensations and feelings of another and realize that these inner feelings and sensations are not ours own but another's (Forner, 2019b). We can attune to and be objective about ourselves and other people. Attunement is very closely linked to fully developed empathy. There are several brain structures that are designed to non-verbally tune into another person for the main reason of knowing, learning, and comprehending how that other person feels (Forner, 2019a). We can communicate our feelings and sensory perceptions with words and written language. We have incredibly sophisticated mechanisms which are designed to be able to communicate to others about feelings, and knowing the feelings of others makes humans feel, act, and function optimally. We can adjust to make our environment suit our needs. We can articulate and remember into the past not just through procedural learning but through autobiographical memory, as well. We can also imagine and think abstractly into the future.

Humans are a being that do not behave like any other creature, even in regard to our social intelligence. We are a creature who feels better when we are seen. How many creatures on this planet, a planet whose biodiversity is build upon predator and prey, feels better when it is intensely looked at, and feels safer when it is empathized with? We are a creature who experiences neurobiological security the more others comprehend us. We are a creature who feels safer being protected and cared for not by just one or two others but many hundreds of others (Emmott, & Page 2021; Kenkel, Perkeybile, & Carter, 2017).

Attachment and the Homo Sapien

For the human being, it is well established that we need people more than we need food (Bowlby, 1977). This is often seen as an odd statement, as many millions can spend days alone but cannot go days without eating. However, that sentiment applies to adults, rather than infants and children. In applying it to infants and the connection to attachment, trauma, and dissociation, the real damage that misogyny creates becomes extremely illuminating. In a recent study by Lasselin (2021), it is shown that inflammation from our central nervous system effects our behaviours. This is not a new discovery in the world of complex trauma and dissociation. There have been studies that show that when humans move into our emergency response systems, like fight, flight, hard freeze, or attachment cry, our central nervous system becomes inflamed (Kendall-Tackett, 2009; Kendall-Tackett, et al., 2003; Kozlowska, Walker, McLean, & Carrive, 2015). Inflammation, as we know, causes pain (Ji, et al., 2016). What seems to not be connected is these two well established facts of the homo sapien. In understanding the correlation between human detachment, relational disconnection, pain, and dissociation a powerful argument for why misogyny has to become our primary focus in the world of trauma, and else where.

When an infant is first born, its only real functioning information systems is the sensorimotor and affective circuitry (Schore, 2019; Zeevi, 2021). The infant is one hundred percent running on instinct. There is zero cognition, zero abstract thinking, zero external awareness or consciousness. An infant just responds to what the central nervous system instructs it to respond to and the central nervous system responds only to need and survival. When that infant first comes into the world it has no control over any of its body or bodily functions. Human infants cannot move on their own for months and even then, it is very uncontrolled gross motor function like waving a hand. It takes nearly a decade for humans to have full control over their fine motor functions. When the human infant first comes into the world all its instinctual underpinnings function as every other living thing on this planet – it tries to survive. For us humans, the first act of survival is to bond!

If you have ever seen an infant placed onto the mother's body directly after birth, you witness the infant's body being directed by millions of years of evolution: it squirms and crawls to the breast. Most assume that the newborn does this to eat. However, if we consider where that infant has just been, inside a space that is full of fluid and likely still attached to the umbilical cord, a biomechanical mechanism that delivers the infants only food source, there is no likelihood that this infant is hungry. Certainly, it will not be hungry enough to instinctually move a body that will not be able to move, fully, on its own for months, in order to find its mother's breast. If it is not driven by eating and nutrition, two extremely powerful needs that will have to be addressed hundreds of thousands of times during that human's life, what would or could be more powerful than food?

Consider that when an infant is first born, it is only capable, instinctually, of this crawl, sucking, breathing, digesting and other biomechanical functions, peeing, and passing waste. Infants cannot pass gas or burp on their own; they cannot regulate temperature; they cannot move on their own; they cannot sleep on their own; and they cannot protect themselves in any way.

At birth, it is not hunger moving that tiny body. It is the need to bond! Attachment theory fully supports this fact (Johnson, 2013; Lamb, 1982). We need to bond with our mothers more than we need to eat, at birth and, in extension, we need to continue this intense, life-saving bond throughout our whole lives. If that bond does not occur, the infant's body can only respond to the emergency that it really is. It is not any different than what it does when it cannot eat. Both events are experienced and felt within the central nervous system as an emergency (Schore, 2019, 2000).

As mentioned above, the central nervous system becomes more and more electrified and inflamed when it is in an emergent state. Neurochemical and neuroelectrical studies of infants and children show that they feel the same as adults do, except these feelings and sensations are happening inside a body that cannot move or cannot move well (Mueller and Tronick, 2019; Schore, 2019; Tronick, 2002). There is also a plethora of research that shows the absolute damage that profound neglect has on infants (Perry, 2008, 2002; Perry and Pollard, 1997). In a patriarchal and misogynistic world, the experience of infants and children are not taken into consideration that much or at all. In a world that is more aligned with our neurobiology, it would be common knowledge that when the bond does not happen instantly, the infant's body automatically notices the absence. It would also be common knowledge that an infant's body goes from discomfort to distress to a state of emergency very quickly.

For us humans, a species that is incredibly weak and vulnerable to the natural world, our one and only defense is other people. We do not have speed, agility, sharp claws, strong and sharp teeth, thick skin, heightened senses, or any other natural innate defense like every other animal that is part of the world of predator and prey. Humans did not escape the reality of the natural world, even if we have adapted our environments, so much so, that many of us never see a real-life predator. But still, because we have a Central Nervous System (CNS), we are part of the world of predator and prey (Barrett and Finlay, 2018). Everything that makes us a species is the same that makes every other species a species. We all have naturally evolved mechanisms that are designed for a species to survive. It is just that humans are the only ones to put all of their defenses into getting along with another person. Empathy is our main defense mechanism! A mechanism designed to comprehend and feel what is occurring inside of our infants. Thus, when an infant feels that they are alone, it very quickly feels the danger of being alone and this danger signal comes straight from the CNS, via the sensorimotor and affective systems (Ogden, et al., 2006; Ogden, 2021).

For infants, as with every other human, when the CNS detects a need, the need is communicated through a sensorimotor reaction via a sensation (ibid). The sensorimotor system is intimately connected to our affective circuitry. Sensation is communicated via affect, or feelings. It is through these feelings that needs are communicated via movement, small sounds, crying, and eventually words, and higher language. It is interesting to note, as referenced above, that sensorimotor and affective circuitry is nearly fully developed at birth, while cognition and imagination will not begin to develop for another 3 or 4 years – and does not reach full maturity until the age of at least 25 or even later (Perrus, Sisk, and Romeo, 2021; Wickrama, et al., 2017; Gogtay, et al., 2004; Lopez, et al., 2008).

When an infant has a need, the only way to detect this need is through the CNS as it becomes inflamed. This inflammation is felt first as discomfort. If this discomfort does not change or is regulated it will soon be felt as pain (Perry, 2008, 2002; Perry and Pollard, 1997; Schore, 2019). This pain is often referred to as shame. Shame is highly dissociative and tied into neglect. (Platt, et al., 2017). Anything that is highly dissociative can only be interpreted as incredibly painful and unbearably frightening. We know this because of all the research that has been done regarding fear and the defense cascade (Kozlowska, Walker, McLean, & Carrive, 2015). If a body that is in major distress – and cannot do anything about this distress in any way – if it is essentially trapped and close to death, and its one and only defense mechanism, other people, are not available, then the only option is to dissociate the pain. For an infant, the only feeling they have is that something is terribly wrong, even with the slightest amount of neglect. Paulsen (2017) in their book *When There Are No Words*, states "the child, who is naturally the centre of his or hers own small universe, interprets the neglect as evidence the child is doing something wrong, "I am bad", "I am unworthy", "I am shameful" (p. 71). For an infant the only feeling they have is that something is terribly wrong, even with the slightest amount of neglect.

Humans are extremely sensitive creatures to maternal stress. Allan Schore (2019) in *The Development of the Unconscious Mind* discusses the vulnerability that male infants have to maternal stress. Male infants are much more dependant on their care givers to regulate their affective and sensorimotor circuitry in early life. Schore postulates that "the stress regulation circuits of the male brain mature more slowly than those of the female in prenatal, perinatal and postnatal critical periods, and that this is reflected in normal gender differences in right brain attachment functions" (ibid, p.89). In other words, we have a great deal of evidence that shows that male infants need their neurobiological affect regulators so much more than female infants. This information shows us that neglect for male infants effect them more than female infants. It has been known for at least a decade that early neglect for male infants is comparable to infant sexual abuse (Teicher & Samson, 2016; Trickett and Putnam, 1998; Trickett and McBride-Chang, 1995).

What do you suppose happens to infants who are forced to disconnect because they just so happen to be born male and are at best highly encouraged, and at worst, violently enforced, not to bond with their mothers? What do you suppose happens to a society where mothers are raped, controlled, forced, impoverished, and killed? Patriarchy generally and globally encourages its male infants and children to be neglected. This pain will need to be coped with and somehow managed. It is well known that the more patriarchal a group, person, organization, system is, the more misogynistic it is (Messina, 2019; Papa, 2017; Rackin, 2016; Holland, 2006). It is also well known that misogyny is the root cause of sexual abuse and torture of our children, as well as domestic abuse (Hill, 2019). That being said, to take this one step further, it is likely that misogyny and patriarchy are the root cause of unfettered capitalism, global climate crisis, war and pillaging, racism, colonialism, sexual objectification, and neglect (Howell and Itkowitz, 2020). These are very bold statements, made with full intention and full purpose. The boldness of this statement resides with the many similarities in the descriptions of masculinity, toxic masculinity, and psychopathy.

Misogyny: the distain of caregiving
Patriarchy: the idolization of psychopathy

When we view misogyny and patriarchy from a lens of attachment and dissociation, then it starts to make sense. How can a creature who is capable of such love, compassion and charity be so capable of horrors, cruelty, and hatred? If one understands that when someone who is harmed so severely and so frequently – and there is no care or care is taken away, shamed away, stolen or when care is not given the authority it needs – then what is left is traumatic dissociation. By understanding what happens to a human when they chronically and continually dissociate, we understand that that person experiences pain that is rather unfathomable and totally intolerable. Dissociation is nature's anesthetic; it is a powerful numbing agent. But it also cuts off or shuts off certain brain structures that are made to help with these painful experiences, such as the vMPFC, default mode network and many other brain structures. When someone moves into the life-saving reaction of dissociation, information from the CNS and body (sensations and affect) is scattered via the thalamus. The insula turns off as well. It is extremely possible to have feelings and sensations that you cannot feel or sense (Lanius, et al, 2018; Lebois, et al, 2021).

When care is provided to someone who is or has dissociated as a way of coping with infant or childhood neglect, the dissociative mechanism is no longer needed. The human body is not designed to dissociate all the time. It wants to be at its original species designated base line: a place of comfort, safety, and security. When kindness, empathy, attunement, generosity, and love are given, all of the dissociative mechanisms stop. When dissociation stops, and the numbing stops, the insula and thalamus start to work properly – which causes all of the previously dissociated pain and suffering to come forward. This causes the person to be flooded with unimaginable, knee-buckling pain. It is actually a pain that we don't really have a name for, but it is real, tangible and often the thing that prevents people from healing. No one has ever died from feeling their feelings, but billions have died in an attempt to not feel this unbearable pain.

Three common ways that humans attempt to stop the pain are abuse of substances to replicate the natural chemicals in the brain; to harm-self in effort to generate the neurobiological reaction of dissociation; or to accomplish the same thing by harming another person. Hurting another, especially a child, is the ultimate form of self-harm. All tied together in a melee of the human experiences of neglect, forced rejection, pain, suffering, underdeveloped or atrophied brain structures, sexual abuse, war, pillaging, distain for all things humane and idolization of all things inhuman is the perfect storm of the ultimate abuse cycle that cannot be seen for what it is.

In a misogynistic world, where harm is invisible or grossly justified, who do you suppose gets blamed for this pain? It is a cycle of violence that will never end. Another side effect of dissociation is that the front brain structures that can help with developing context for the pain, empathy for their suffering, objective distance, maturation of procedurally learned information, affective and bodily regulation of conditioned fear, and many other functions that grow and develop in safe and secure relationships, become underdeveloped or fully atrophied (Forner, 2019a). This is likely the birthplace of psychopathy. The reaction of hurting another, to continually induce a dissociative response so that you do not have to feel the pain of neglect and early attachment rupture, and/or harsh and abusive environments.

Discussion and Conclusion

Misogyny and patriarchy rob us of how to manage ourselves, what is required in leadership, how to trust and be trustworthy, how to regulate ourselves, and eventually, it took away our humanity. As trauma experts, we have to introduce a new broader understanding of the notion of choice. Being abusive goes against everything that makes a human a human. We have to start to educate that early traumas are brutally hard to change and nearly impossible to heal in an environment that assumes that male violence is natural. Misogyny will always create psychopathy.

Patriarchy is a never-ending, self-fuelling engine of misogyny, because it will hurt to apply care when you've been harmed so severely. Care eliminates dissociative barriers. We have to look at psychopathy in a new light and not as a natural default setting. Misogyny, whenever it first happened, was likely some event that made it impossible for people to care for their offspring as they had for hundreds of thousands of years. Patriarchy is a traumatic symptom that has been normalized. In an understandable way, at the same time a feeling of care and healing became vilified.

We now know! We know what abuse, stress and neglect do to infants and children. Misogyny and patriarchy are not that mysterious if you comprehend human attachment, dissociation, and the neurobiological underpinnings of secure attachment. What is needed is to comprehend the absolute power of care, and the urgent need to care for our infants in ways that they are biomechanically and neurobiologically meant to be cared for by the humans around them. We, as clinicians, need to put value, stock, and authority into how powerful it is to be regulated with our clients. We need to be speaking about the utter damage that misogyny has had on us as a species, as it truly is the birthplace of psychopathy and the various other ailments that plague us as a species. We have an opportunity as specialists in these areas. We have an opportunity to help others connect the dots. We have the opportunity to stop the mindless violence and earth-destructing force that comes from a trauma wound that makes us all suffer the unimaginable, yet incredibly common experience, of infant and childhood abuse and neglect.

REFERENCES

Abi Rached, M., Hankir, A., & Zaman, R. 2021. Patriarchal Upbringing in the 21st Century: The Impact Emotional Abuse Related to Parental Styles Has on the Genesis of Gender Inequality and the Development of Unresolved Trauma in Children. Psychiatria Danubina, 33(Suppl 11), 121-132.

Ananthaswamy, A., & Douglas, K. 2018. The Origins of the Patriarchy. New Scientist, 238(3174), 34-35.

Ardino, V. 2012. Offending behaviour: The role of trauma and PTSD. European Journal of Psychotraumatology, 3(1), 18968.

Ariav-Paraira, I., Oppenheim, D., & Sagi-Schwartz, A. 2022. Disrupted affective communication characterizes mothers of infants with disorganized but also ambivalent attachments: An Israeli study. Child Development, 93(1), e59-e70.

Barrett, L. F., & Finlay, B. L. 2018. Concepts, goals and the control of survival-related behaviors. Current opinion in behavioral sciences, 24, 172-179.

Bitzer, J. The pandemic of violence against women – the latest chapter in the history of misogyny. The European Journal of Contraception and Reproductive Health, 20(1): p. 1-3. Published online: 29 Jan 2015 https://doi.org/10.3109/13625187.2015.1005445. Retrieved online 23 February 2022.

Boesch, C. 2007. What makes us human (Homo sapiens)? The challenge of cognitive cross-species comparison. Journal of Comparative Psychology, 121(3), 227.

Bonanno, G. A., & Mancini, A. D. 2011. Toward a lifespan approach to resilience and potential trauma. Resilience and mental health: Challenges across the lifespan, 120-34.

Bowlby, J. 1977. The making and breaking of affectional bonds: I. Aetiology and psychopathology in the light of attachment theory. The British journal of psychiatry, 130(3), 201-210.

Bregman, R. (2020). *Humankind: A hopeful history*. Bloomsbury Publishing.

Brisch, K. H. Attachment and dissociation. In Treating Children with Dissociative Disorders (pp. 7-9). Routledge.

Brookman, F. 2015. The shifting narratives of violent offenders. Narrative criminology: Understanding stories of crime, 207-234.

Card, C. 2018. Challenges of Global and Local Misogyny. Criticism and Compassion: The Ethics and Politics of Claudia Card, John Wiley & Sons.

Cassidy, J., & Mohr, J. J. 2001. Unsolvable fear, trauma, and psychopathology: Theory, research, and clinical considerations related to disorganized attachment across the life span. Clinical psychology: Science and practice, 8(3), 275.

Dagan, O., Schuengel, C., Verhage, M., van IJzendoorn, M. H., Sagi-Schwartz, A., Madigan, S., ... & Cummings, E. M. 2021. Configurations of Mother-Child and Father-Child Attachment as Predictors of Internalizing and Externalizing Symptoms: An Individual Participant Data (IPD) Meta? Analysis.

Delahanty, D. L. 2008. The psychobiology of trauma and resilience across the lifespan. Jason Aronson.

Dillon, R. S. and Marsoobian, A. T. 2018. Criticism and Compassion: The Ethics and Politics of Claudia Card. John Wiley & Sons.

Emmott, E. H., & Page, A. E. (2021). Alloparenting. *Encyclopedia of evolutionary psychological science*, 210-223.

Estok, S. C. 2019. Ecophobia, the agony of water, and misogyny. ISLE: Interdisciplinary Studies in Literature and Environment, 26(2), 473-485.

Forner. C., (2019a) What Mindfulness can learn about Dissociation and what Dissociation can learn from Mindfulness, *Journal of Trauma & Dissociation, 20:1, 1-15*, DOI: 10.1080/15299732.2018.1502568

Forner, C. (2019b). Mindful Attachment: An organic way to work with children who have been through complex trauma and neglect. *Frontiers in the Psychotherapy of Trauma and Dissociation, 3*(1):91–106. DOI:10.1080/15299732.2018.1502568

Fox, B. H., Perez, N., Cass, E., Baglivio, M. T., & Epps, N. 2015. Trauma changes everything: Examining the relationship between adverse childhood experiences and serious, violent and chronic juvenile offenders. Child abuse & neglect, 46, 163-173.

Freyd, J.J. 2003. What is a Betrayal Trauma? What is Betrayal Trauma Theory? Retrieved 23 February 2022 from http://dynamic.uoregon.edu/~jjf/defineBT.html.

Gogtay, N., Giedd, J. N., Lusk, L., Hayashi, K. M., Greenstein, D., Vaituzis, A. C., & Rapoport, J. L., et al. 2004. Dynamic mapping of human cortical development during childhood through early adulthood. Proceedings of the National Academy of Sciences of the United States of America, 101(21), 8174–8179.

Hare, B. 2017. Survival of the friendliest: Homo sapiens evolved via selection for prosociality. Annual review of psychology, 68, 155-186.

Harari, Y.B. 2014. Sapiens: A brief history of humankind. Canada: Penguin Random House

Hill, D. 2019. Marxist education and teacher education against capitalism in neoliberal/neoconservative/
neofascist/times. Cadernos do GPOSSHE On-line, 2(1).

Holland, J. 2006. Misogyny: The world's oldest prejudice. Running Press.

Hoffnung, M. 2015. Theorizing gender differences: Genes or misogyny? [Review of the book Warriors and worriers: The survival of the sexes, by J. F. Benenson]. PsycCRITIQUES, 60(5). https://doi.org/10.1037/a0038458

Howell, E. F. and Itzkowitz, S. 2018. Psychopathy and Human Evil: Brief Descriptions of Articles, Contemporary Psychoanalysis, 54:1, 1-4, DOI:10.1080/00107530.2017.1420349.

Ji, R. R., Chamessian, A., & Zhang, Y. Q. 2016. Pain regulation by non-neuronal cells and inflammation. Science, 354(6312), 572-577.

Johnson, K. 2013. Maternal-Infant Bonding: A Review of Literature. International Journal of Childbirth Education, 28(3).

Kendall-Tackett, K. 2009. Psychological trauma and physical health: A psychoneuroimmunology approach to etiology of negative health effects and possible interventions. Psychological Trauma: Theory, Research, Practice, and Policy, 1(1), 35-48. doi:10.1037/a0015128

Kendall-Tackett, K. A., Marshall, R., & Ness, K. E. 2003. Chronic pain syndromes and violence against women. Women and Therapy, 26, 45–56.

Kenkel, W. M., Perkeybile, M., and Carter, C. S. 2017. The Neurobiological Causes and Effects of Alloparenting. Devepmental Neurobiology, 77(2): 214–232. doi:10.1002/dneu.22465.

Kozlowska, K., Walker, P., McLean, L., & Carrive, P. (2015). Fear and the defense cascade: clinical implications and management. *Harvard review of psychiatry*.

Kulish, N., 2021. The Abject: Clinical Manifestations of Hatred of the Feminine. *Canadian Journal of Psychoanalysis*, 29(1).

Lanius, R.A., Boyd, J.E., McKinnon, M.C., Nicholson, A.A., Frewen, P., Vermetten, E., Spiegel D. (2018). A Review of the Neurobiological Basis of Trauma-Related Dissociation and Its Relation to Cannabinoid- and Opioid-Mediated Stress Response: a Transdiagnostic, Translational Approach. *Current Psychiatry Reports, 20*(12), 118. https://doi.org/10.1007/s11920-018-0983-y

Lamb, M. E. 1982. Early contact and maternal-infant bonding: One decade later. Pediatrics, 0(5), 763-768.

Lamp, K. 2013. Personal and contextual resilience factors and their relations to psychological adjustment outcomes across the lifespan: A meta-analysis.

Lasselin, J. 2021. Back to the future of psychoneuroimmunology: Studying inflammation-induced sickness behavior, Brain, Behavior, & Immunity - Health, Volume 18. https://doi.org/10.1016/j.bbih.2021.100379.

Lebois LAM, Li M, Baker JT, et al (2021): Large-scale functional brain network architecture changes associated with trauma-related dissociation. *Am J Psychiatry*; 178:165–173

Lopez, B., Schwartz, S. J., Prado, G., Campo, A. E., & Pantin, H. 2008. Adolescent neurological development and its implications for adolescent substance use prevention. The Journal of Primary Prevention, 29(1), 5–35.

Manne, K. 2017. Down girl: The logic of misogyny. Oxford University Press.

Messina, K.E. 2019. Misogyny, projective identification, and mentalization: Psychoanalytic, social, and institutional manifestations. Routledge.

Moss, D. (Ed.). 2003. Hating in the first person plural: Psychoanalytic essays on racism, homophobia, misogyny, and terror. Other Press.

Mueller, I., & Tronick, E. 2019. Early life exposure to violence: developmental consequences on brain and behavior. Frontiers in behavioral neuroscience, 13, 156.

Ogden, P. (2021). The different impact of trauma and relational stress on physiology, posture, and movement: Implications for treatment. *European Journal of Trauma & Dissociation*, *5*(4), 100172.

Ogden, P., Minton, K., & Pain, C. 2006. Trauma and the body: A sensorimotor approach to psychotherapy. WW Norton & Company.

Palagi, E., Norscia, I., & Demuru, E. 2014. Yawn contagion in humans and bonobos: emotional affinity matters more than species. PeerJ, 2, e519.

Papa, R. 2017. Finding her in history: Confronting the traditions of misogyny. Springer.

Paulsen, S. (2017). *When there are no words: Repairing early trauma and neglect from the attachment period with EMDR therapy*. Bainbridge Institute for Integrative Psychology.

Perkeybile, A. M., Carter, C. S., Wroblewski, K. L., Puglia, M. H., Kenkel, W. M., Lillard, T. S., ... & Connelly, J. J. 2019. Early nurture epigenetically tunes the oxytocin receptor. Psychoneuroendocrinology, 99, 128-136.

Perrus, K., Sisk, C. L., and Romeo, R., D. 2021. Review: Coming of Age: The Neurobiology and Psychobiology of Puberty and Adolescence. *Journal of Youth Adolescence,* 50, 1738–1740. https://doi.org/10.1007/s10964-021-01439-7.

Perry, B. D. 2008. Child maltreatment: A neurodevelopmental perspective on the role of trauma and neglect in psychpathology.

Perry, B. D. 2002. Childhood experience and the expression of genetic potential: What childhood neglect tells us about nature and nurture. Brain and mind, 3(1), 79-100.

Perry, B. D., & Pollard, R. 1997. Altered brain development following global neglect in early childhood. In Proceedings from the Society for Neuroscience Annual Meeting (New Orleans).

Perrus, K., Sisk, C. L., and Romeo, R., D. 2021. Review: Coming of Age: The Neurobiology and Psychobiology of Puberty and Adolescence. *Journal of Youth Adolescence,* 50, 1738–1740. https://doi.org/10.1007/s10964-021-01439-7.

Pfluger, V., Rohner, S. L., Eising, C. M., Maercker, A., & Thoma, M. V. 2021. Associations Between Complex Trauma Exposure in Childhood/Adolescence and Psychopathology in Older Age: The Role of Stress Coping and Coping Self-Perception. Journal of Child & Adolescent Trauma, 1-13.

Platt, M. G., Luoma, J. B., & Freyd, J. J. 2017. Shame and dissociation in survivors of high and low betrayal trauma. Journal of Aggression, Maltreatment & Trauma, 26(1), 34-49.

Pollack, S. 2009. "You Can't Have it Both Ways": Punishment and Treatment of Imprisoned Women. Journal of Progressive Human Services, 20(2), 112-128.

Potts, R. 2003. Early human predation. In Predator—Prey Interactions in the Fossil Record (pp. 359-376). Springer, Boston, MA.

Rackin, P. 2016. Misogyny is everywhere. A Feminist Companion to Shakespeare, John Wiley & Sons, 2, pp.60-74.

Reardon, B. 1985. Sexism and the war system. New York.

Reinders, A. & Veltman, D. (2021). Dissociative identity disorder: Out of the shadows at last? The British Journal of Psychiatry, 219(2), 413-414.

Ricks, S. A. 2018. Normalized Chaos: Black Feminism, Womanism, and the (Re) definition of Trauma and Healing. Meridians, 16(2), 343-350.

Scaptura, M. N. 2019. Masculinity threat, misogyny, and the celebration of violence in White men (Doctoral dissertation, Virginia Tech).

Schore, A. N. 2019. The Development of the Unconscious Mind (Norton Series on Interpersonal Neurobiology). WW Norton & Company.

Schore, A. N. 2000. Attachment and the regulation of the right brain. Attachment & human development, 2(1), 23-47.

Sherlock, B. 2021. Book review: Trauma in the Creative and Embodied Therapies: When Words Are Not Enough. *Dramatherapy*. 02630672211056103.

Srivastava, K., Chaudhury, S., Bhat, P. S., & Sahu, S. 2017. Misogyny, feminism, and sexual harassment. Industrial psychiatry journal, 26(2), 111–113. https://doi.org/10.4103/ipj.ipj_32_18.

Takševa, T. 2019. One is not born but rather becomes a mother: Claiming the maternal in women and gender studies. *Journal of the Motherhood Initiative for Research and Community Involvement*.

Teicher, M.H. and Samson, J.A. (2016), Annual Research Review: Enduring neurobiological effects of childhood abuse and neglect. J Child Psychol Psychiatr, 57: 241-266. https://doi.org/10.1111/jcpp.12507

Trickett, P. K. and Putnam, F. W. 1998. Developmental consequences of child sexual abuse.

Trickett, P. K. and McBride-Chang, C. 1995. The developmental impact of different forms of child abuse and neglect. Developmental review, 15(3), 311-337.

Tronick, E. Z. 2002. A model of infant mood states and Sandarian affective waves. Psychoanalytic Dialogues, 12(1), 73-99.

Van Valkenburgh, S. P. 2021. Digesting the red pill: Masculinity and neoliberalism in the manosphere. Men and Masculinities, 24(1), 84-103.

Venta, A., & Abate, A. 2021. Insecure Attachment and Related Difficulties. Developmental Psychopathology, 58-86.

Wickrama, K. A. S., O'Neal, C. W., & Holmes, C. 2017. Towards a heuristic research model linking early socioeconomic adversity and youth cumulative disease risk: an integrative review. *Adolescent Research Review,* 2, 161–179. https://doi.org/10.1007/s40894-017-0054-3.

Zeevi, L., Irani, M., Catana, C., Feldman-Barrett, L., & Atzil, S. 2021. Maternal dopamine encodes affective signals of human infants. Social cognitive and affective neuroscience.

Zeitlin, F. I. 1978. The dynamics of misogyny: Myth and mythmaking in the Oresteia. Arethusa, 11(1/2), 149-184.

When it is the Oppressor Dissociating from Harm Caused: Historical Trauma and the Impact of Racism

by Rose Brown, PhD, and Emily Christensen, PhD

"The most common and extreme suffering humankind has ever experienced comes from interpersonal and collective intentional violence" (Blanco, et al., 2016). One kind of collective trauma is historical trauma. Historical trauma is "a social determinant of health emanating from targeted mass group-level harm" (Ortega-Williams, et al., 2021). An obvious and current example of this is during war, such as Russia's invasion of Ukraine, forcing millions of people to flee for their lives. Only a generation ago, we witnessed examples of mass group-level harm in the form of both aggressive oppression (Apartheid) and attempted extinction via genocide (the Holocaust). After 2016, we nearly experienced civil war again – and absolutely did experience a cultural war – in the United States as a result of the administration's aggressive attacks on women, marginalized peoples, people with disabilities, as well as inciting and permitting a culture of violence against non-white-bodied peoples, all of which culminated in the polarizing pandemic response that was ultimately traumatizing for people on both sides of politics. Social psychologist Ignacio Martín-Baró addressed in a preferential way the study of civil war in El Salvador in terms of intergroup hostility and polarization, approaching the aftereffects of war "by means of a theoretical core assumption: that traumatic experience rooted in collective violence (a human-made stressor) should be understood bearing in mind its social roots (pre-traumatic situation), its personal and collective harm (collective injury), and the destruction of the social fabric" (Blanco, et al., 2016).

Historical Trauma has impacted a variety of groups of people. The trauma inflicted on people with disabilities is beyond the scope of this chapter, and elsewhere address both historically (in the chapter on Plurality) and in impact (in the chapter on Disability and Dissociation). In addition, the traumas inflicted due to misogyny, patriarchy, and gender-based violence are covered primarily in the chapter of that topic, as well as a different chapter addressing LGBTQ+ issues specifically. For those reasons, this chapter primarily addresses the trauma of ethnic marginalization. Due to the limitations of this chapter and the personal lived experience of these authors, this chapter focuses on marginalized peoples of the United States, primarily American Indian and Alaska Native (AI/AN) and people of color (Black / African American) with select groups emphasized due to recent research (Filipino Asian Americans as distinct from other Asian Americans). We acknowledge that this is not all-inclusive, and ultimately is similarly applicable to other marginalized peoples in other parts of the world in unique ways.

Impact of Historical Trauma

Beltran, et al. (2018) reported that American Indian and Alaska Native (AI/AN) populations have seen a dramatic increase in cardiovascular disease, despite a history of low rates, and that this has been attributed to how "disruptions to place-based relationships are associated with emotional distress and impact health and mental health outcomes (Ferreira, 2006; Walters, et al., 2011; Whitbeck, et al., 2004), and the impact of historical environmental traumas." Upon study, examples of these specific stressors included "exposure to early life trauma, which is linked to the development of depressive and anxiety disorders, including post-traumatic stress disorder (Libby, et al., 2005); higher risk for racial discrimination (associated with higher diastolic blood pressure and greater risk for hypertension; Thayer, et al., 2017); and disruptions to social and cultural lifeways through forced assimilation and urbanization, which are perceived by AI/ANs to contribute to risk behaviors including interpersonal violence, substance misuse, and poor nutrition (Evans-Campbell, 2008; Walters, et al., 2011a; Walters, et al., 2011b)" (Beltran, 2018). Beltran writes:

> "For many Indigenous peoples, the notion of place is embedded in a profound relationship with ancestral lands and intricate sociocultural and spiritual connections to complex webs of creation. The very definition of health and well-being for Indigenous people is intimately connected with place. Often referred to by Indigenous scholars as "Original Instructions" (Pierotti & Wildcat, 2000), traditional cultural codes of conduct that have shaped tribal health practices are intimately tied to the land, such as hunting and gathering methods, seasonal dietary shifts, land management, and physical engagement with the natural

> world. Moreover, place and land-based practices are "integral to one's sense of being which is also central to both individual and collective spiritual health and wellness," whereas "loss of place (i.e., displacement) is akin to loss of spirit or identity" (Walters, et al., 2011, p. 173). As such, both historical and ongoing disruptions in social, cultural, and physical relationships with place are understood as negatively impacting health and wellness in Indigenous communities and have been cited by scholars as contributing factors to increased stress" (Ferreira, 2006; Walters, et al. 2011; Whitbeck, et al., 2004)

Even the modern relationship with land is complication for indigenous people. Now, because of historical trauma, the land itself has been traumatized. Painful memories of historical trauma reside not only in the minds and epigenetics of the people, but also in the earth beneath their feat. "Related disruptions in family and social cohesion, [are] a noted outcome of historical trauma (Evans-Campbell, 2008). Beltran (2018) shared interviews with elders, in which one "described "political dirtiness" and "getting attacked by your own family members" as a painful part of being on tribal land." In the same breath, she also described reservation land as "the place where those same family members come together to pray and celebrate" (ibid). She said:

> "You know what? It's both good and bad for me. It's like one of the worst places for me, and it's one of the best. It's one of the worst, because it has historical trauma here. And it has the boarding school. It has like death on the roads. It

> has dead relatives. It just has the hard aspects. Political dirtiness. The trying to fight for tribal rights, but the struggle… And it also has the ceremony when tables come together and people celebrate. It also has that aspect, that we know we're family. We know we're connected, and we love each other. We come together when we need to. But it's also very devastating when you're going through a hard time like say, your job, because these are your family and, you know, get attacked by your own family members. It's harder."

Contemporary Western ideology and lifestyles are oriented to time, progress, and products while those of Indigenous peoples are oriented to relational qualities of place (Walters, et al., 2011; Pierotti and Wildcat, 2000). Thus, we see both historical and ongoing trauma from the displacement and forced migration of indigenous peoples. Their dissociation in response to these traumas is not only internal, but also a dis-association from their literal grounding skills through both identity and practice, culturally and spiritually.

Native communities had industries such as mining, irrigation, agriculture, and even transportation; however, in contrast to many contemporary industries, they used the land so that it could regenerate (Cajete, 2000). The tribe involved Beltran's 2008 study, for example, previously had successful sustainable fishing and timber industries that worked in accordance to the seasons and ensured ongoing abundance (Krohn & Segrest, 2009; Thrush, 2000). One of the elders he interviewed explained changes to the land as a result of colonization and subsequent industry:

> "Well, you know we conceded all this land to the United States government, and they raped our resources. Like this used to be a great, great timber industry and fishing industry, and they destroyed it all. You look at the mountains, you won't see no more trees. You look in the water, you don't see no more salmon" (2008).

Modern development and the resulting disconnection from traditional healthy behavioral practices changed the way people obtain and prepare food and thus, how they relate to it, as shared by another elder, "It's just different now from when I was growing up. It really is. It used to be part of us and we used to hunt, fish. They'd kettle mussels and sit there [by] the fireplace and now it's all different" (ibid). Tribal members also discussed with Beltran the impacts of colonization on food preparation and physical health (ibid):

> "People around here... everything's fried if you go in their [homes]. [Before] my cousins, they were growing their food, they were canning all these fruits. You don't see that anymore. They go to [the grocery store] and buy the junk food. What do you call that? Top Ramen? They don't have time. And it's so busy here. I've never had that stuff...the ingredients... all salt..... I just learned [from] my grandfather [who] hunted. He had fruit trees. We grew our own chickens and my mother made bread. We used to pick the berries... And I don't see 'em doing that anymore. Now it's through [the grocery store]. We used to eat everything off the land, eat the berries, the cherries. I don't think we had

> microwaves. We had the old wood stoves, we cooked out of it, [we'd] make bread in the oven and it'd come out perfect. I think it's all the fast food they're eating."

These experiences associated with Western land development and imposition of Western diet and eating behaviors anchor tribal narratives in a space of loss and diminishing opportunities for healthy development and healthy elder years.

Besides these examples, racial discrimination "not only contributes to increased blood pressure, but is also linked to a constellation of additional risk factors across racial minority groups, including increased cortisol levels" (stress hormones; Beltran, 2018; Berger & Sarnyai, 2015; Thayer & Kuzawa, 2015), higher allostatic load (Brody, et al., 2014), and lower heart rate variability (Wagner, et al., 2015). "AI/ANs experience a substantially greater burden of PTSD and related symptoms than U.S. Whites" with "combat experience and interpersonal violence were consistently cited as leading causes of PTSD and related symptoms. PTSD was associated with bodily pain, lung disorders, general health problems, substance abuse, and pathological gambling. In general, inciting events, risk factors, and co-morbidities appear similar to those in the general U.S. population" (Bassett, et al., 2014). Webb reports (2022):

> "Two studies[3] have suggested that altered resting-state connectivity of nodes in the salience network (SN), such as the amygdala, insula, and connected sensory-processing regions (eg, thalamus, visual cortex), are associated with

[3] See Clark, et al., 2018 and Han, et al., 2021

racial discrimination. Han and colleagues found differential insula connectivity in older Black adults reporting greater racial discrimination (2021). In the context of the SN, the insula is involved in perceptions of self-awareness as well as determining the valence of external stimuli, particularly stimuli tied to social situations.[4] Altered functional connectivity between the insula and regions implicated in vigilance (e.g., intracalcarine cortex, supplementary motor area) was associated with a greater number of experiences of racial discrimination, whereas reduced connectivity between the insula and dorsolateral prefrontal cortex was associated with fewer discriminatory experiences. These vigilance regions have been implicated in other social constructs frequently associated with the experiences of racial discrimination, including behavioral response-selection to emotional stimuli and mistrust. In a racially, ethnically, and sexually diverse sample of adults (10% White, 72% Black, 23% Hispanic, 32% gay or bisexual), greater social discrimination was associated with greater spontaneous resting-state connectivity between the amygdala, another key node of the SN, and various other regions, including the insula. Interestingly, Clark and colleagues found the most robust association with social discrimination was greater connectivity between the amygdala and thalamus."

[4] See Han, et al., 2021; Masten, 2011; and Singer, 2009

Further, research has shown that even when controlling for income and reported PTSD symptoms generally, there is "greater connectivity between the amygdala and thalamus was associated with greater exposure to discrimination (t(97) = 6.05; false discovery rate (FDR)–corrected P = .03). Similarly, racial discrimination was associated with greater connectivity between the insula and precuneus (t(97) = 4.32; FDR-corrected P = .02)" (Webb, et al., 2022). The implications of this explain not only the extent of damage caused by historical trauma neurobiologically, but also the pervasive impact externally in community.

Impact of Racism

In looking at the impact of racism, we can examine the excluded of the excluded: when one group is lumped in with a greater group as part of racism. These issues of marginalization and dis-association from community cause additional trauma, as well. For example, research on Asian Americans "tends to focus explicitly on East Asian Americans, namely, Chinese and Japanese Americans" (Agbayani-Siewert, 2004; David and Okazaki, 2006; Nadal, 2004, 2011, in Nadal, et al., 2012). This can lead to "generalizing these two groups' experiences to apply to all Asian American ethnic groups" (Nadal, et al., 2012). In addition, this also results in issues of other non–East Asian American groups (e.g.,Filipinos, Vietnamese, Asian-Indians, and others) remaining unknown, "resulting in the lack of culturally competent services for these subgroups... Moreover, these other ethnic groups may feel marginalized in the Asian American community, leading to tensions and conflict within the panethnic group" (Nadal, et al., 2012; Espiritu,1992; Nadal,2011).

Complicating things further, "when counselors assume that Asian Americans are all the same, they fail to recognize the unique experiences that may occur because of ethnicity, phenotype, and religion, as well as other variables such as social class, gender, sexual orientation, and immigration status" (Nadal, et al., 2012). This develops into a myth that all Asian-Americans fit into the constraints of stereotypes: that all of them are highly (and easily) educated, that they are all good citizens, and that they can all achieve the American Dream (Nadal, et al., 2012). By default, this then "Others" a variety of marginalized groups, as if they must be opposing due to categorization of other false myths: that people with disabilities cannot be educated easily, that people of color are not good citizens, or that Latinx cannot become productive members of society. These racist ideas are examples of microaggressions.

The term "microaggression" was originally coined in the 1970's (Pierce, 1978). The term was re-introduced in 2007, and defined then as "brief and common place, daily verbal, behavioral, or environmental indignities, whether intentional or unintentional, that communicate hostile, derogatory, or negative racial slights and insults toward people of color" (Sue, et al., 2009, p.271). A "theoretical taxonomy of the types of microaggressions was also introduced, with categories including assumption of criminality (i.e.,experiences in which people of color are assumed to be dangerous or deviant), second-class citizen (i.e.,experiences in which people of color receive substandard service compared with their White American counterparts), and alien in one's own land (i.e.,experiences in which people of color are assumed to be foreign born and or "not American enough")" (Nadal, et al., 2012). In considering Filipino Asian-Americans, Nadal (et al., 2012) identified several themes of lived experience due to racial microaggresion: use of racist language, assumption of stereotypes, exclusion from the greater Asian-American community, assumption of universal experience, and mistaken identity. Additional traumatic themes included being "alien" in one's own land, being viewed by both self and others as second-class citizens, the invalidation of interethnic differences, the sexualization of women, the de-masculinization of men, pathologizing cultural values and traditions, and the too-often assumption of criminality or deviance (Nadal, et al., 2012; Rivera, et al., 2010; Sue, et al., 2009).

These examples are only some examples of the greater trauma of more covert racism. That said, racism is common experience that involves many realms (Bonilla-Silva, 2014; Carter, et al., 2013; DeLilly, 2012; Nadal, 2011; Nadal, et al. 2014; Nadal, et al., 2011; Shams, 2015). There has never been a time in history where racial discrimination has been more critical (Tynes, et al., 2012). Racism is destructive and traumatizing, and "can destroy self-confidence and identity, lead to internalization of discriminatory messages, prevent achievement of potential, and affect mental health due to the barriers in accessing and receiving mental health care" (Hemmings and Evans, 2017; see also Anderson, 2013; Evans, et al., 2015; Williams, et al., 2012; Williams and Williams-Morris, 2000). Researchers reported that "the effects of racially motivated verbal and physical attacks on racial minorities have remained underdeveloped in research, reflecting the fact that this element of social disadvantage has not been adequately explored" (Hemmings and Evans, 2017; see also Brondolo et al., 2009; Brown, 2008; Carter and Forsyth, 2009; Carter, et al., 2013; Fernando, 2012; Garcia and Sharif, 2015; Thompson and Carter, 2013; Tynes et al., 2012).

Issues in Recovery

As described in other chapters of this work, relational trauma is the worst, with the greatest impact neurobiologically. If healing comes through connection, including experiences of attunement and tending to relationships, then healing historical trauma is only going to come through offering dignity, compassion, and respect for these communities – and most importantly, connection to those community experiences, practice, and culture. However, while connection to community is critical for those who have experienced trauma, "yet many interventions do not build on or in some cases disrupt positive connections to community" (Schultz, et al, 2016a). This is absolutely a gap in most services provided by most white-bodied clinicians, leading to increased misattunement even in attempts to help, and adding to the retraumatization of people who have already endured historical trauma. Community-informed efforts toward healing and re-associating people to their cultural context have "the potential to be more effective and sustainable in reducing the impact of trauma on families and societies" (Schultz, et al, 2016a). Understanding this is a vital part of trauma recovery, especially for "racial and ethnic groups [who are] experiencing ongoing systemic" trauma (Ortega-Williams, et al., 2021).

Thus, connecting through community offers a framework for most all survivors that enables post-traumatic growth to focus on "positive shifts in individuals coping with trauma" (Ortega-Williams, et al., 2021). A powerful example of this is the self-study in which tribal members re-walked the Trail of Tears to consider its effect on contemporary tribal health (Schultz, et al., 2016b). Qualitative data from tribal members suggest that "engagement with place and experiential learning, particularly the physical and emotional challenge of the Trail, facilitated changes in health beliefs, attitudes, and behaviors" (ibid). In this way, tribal narratives literally suggest a path "to reconciling disrupted relationships to place by illuminating opportunities for adapting and re-integrating place-based traditional cultural practices to contemporary contexts" (Beltran, 2018).

Another powerful example of individuals healing and preventing further trauma by returning to community was the organization of Black Lives Matter. This was in direct response to the traumatic impact of living "in a world where Black lives are systematically and intentionally targeted for demise" (2019). This movement is "an affirmation of Black folks' humanity, our contributions to this society, and our resilience in the face of deadly oppression" (ibid). The Black Lives Matter web page on *Herstory* reads (ibid):

> "Black liberation movements in this country have created room, space, and leadership mostly for Black heterosexual, cisgender men — leaving women, queer and transgender people, and others either out of the movement or in the background to move the work forward with little or no recognition. As a network, we have always recognized the

> need to center the leadership of women and queer and trans people. To maximize our movement muscle, and to be intentional about not replicating harmful practices that excluded so many in past movements for liberation, we made a commitment to placing those at the margins closer to the center."

Benard (2004) described resilience as a developmental capacity to adapt and survive through harsh surrounding circumstances by resisting threats to homeostasis. "Clients of color demonstrate resilience when they resist potentially oppressive threats" (Danzer, 2012). "Positive identification with one's blackness is vital to AAs' development because their black selves are constantly attacked by the pervasive influence of white racism, which sends subde, yet powerfully negative messages about blackness in the mainstream media and everyday social interactions" (Danzer, 2012).

Historical and collective trauma, then, can be defined using Blanco's 2016 model of "an expanded 4-dimension theoretical argument on psychosocial trauma: (a) pre-trauma conditions based on social distress, (b) shared network of fear leading to breakdown of core social assumptions, (c) the outgroup as a target of negative emotions, and (d) destruction of family ties and community networks." This broader and multi-layered perspective can be used alongside assessment tools. The African American Historical Trauma questionnaire was checked for internal consistency and factorial validity, and found to have 30 items with Cronbach's $\alpha = .91$. Correlations between factors ranged from .32 to .52, which provides "a step toward an empirical understanding of African

American historical trauma" (Williams-Washington and Mills, 2018). These issues highlight the disparity between health care needs and the actual provision of appropriate and helpful services. Studies have looked at counselor competency using the Race-Based Trauma Survey for Counselors, and found that "although most participants reported working with clients who had symptoms associated with race-based trauma, many had not received training in identifying and treating race-based trauma among individuals of color" (Hemmings and Evans, 2018).

In attempting to intervene in trauma, "psychology must overcome the mutually constitutive interaction between the (dis)order of a given macro or microsocial context, and the mental health of the persons living in it" (Blanco, 2016). Further, mechanisms through which community connectedness operates in such contemporary contexts "include accountability, community norming, and belonging and identity" (Schultz, et al, 2016a). "By revitalizing traditional cultural practices related to place, tribal members are identifying cultural health behaviors with great potential for improving... health" (Beltran, 2018).

In the same way, "Afro-centric values include interdependence with nature and other living things, a deep sense of spirituality, emotional expression, direct communication, and expressing one's true emotional self through dance, music, and other creative arts" (Danzer, 2012; see also Parham et al., 1999; Robinson, 1995; Lum, 2003). The theory of resilience has been tested and validated. Markstrom, Sabino, Turner, and Berman (1997) found a correlation between the presence of resilience and ego strength, which Markstrom and Kalminar (2001) equate -with positive ethnic identity for people of color. "The relationship between resilience and positive ethnic identity may suggest that a resilience-oriented therapeutic approach may help people of color develop more positive ethnic identities" (Danzo, 2012). This perspective is doubly important because it provides white-bodied therapists with a less presumptuous way to work with people of color through an Afro-centric lens (Parham et al., 1999).

That being said, clinicians must be cautious in making assumptions about support networks. For example, going to the bar can be "community" and give elders a new "circle" from which to lament and teach and connect with tribal members, but also behaviorally leads to increase of addiction and diabetes-related health risks (Beltran, 2018). We see this happen virtually with the online community and dissociation: when the survivor community is only gathering on social media groups out of hunger for community, the focus too often quickly deteriorates into trauma-dumping, trauma-bonding, and trauma-bickering, retraumatizing all who are involved (Christensen, 2021). What makes a unique and healthy community for any group is the emphasis on dignity, boundaries, vulnerability, and responsiveness to focus on healing. Healing needs a culture of attunement and compassion for it to be supportive and helpful, and the safety is prerequisite. Jones, et al. (2022) emphasizes:

> "Religion is a cultural factor impacting disclosure of abuse. African Americans traditionally rely on religion for meaning and support in facing trauma, and religious institutions are credited for providing effective coping spaces (Bryant-Davis et al., 2015). However, these institutions can also conceal Black pain and sexual trauma and function as a cultural

barrier to reporting sex crimes. Additional religion-related barriers include the power of religion/religious leaders; use of religion to justify abuse; belief that religious leaders will not act in the best interest of participants; fear of harm from abuser, particularly when the perpetrator is a religious leader; and fear of backlash from the religious community following disclosure (Perry-Burney et al., 2014). Patriarchal ideology has significant implications in the suppression or censure of sexual violence because patriarchy is embedded in religious texts that sanction social patterns and subjugate women (Ruether, 1982). Patriarchy is a sociopolitical structure that justifies and promotes male domination of women's bodies. Patriarchy silences women, including those who have survived sexual traumas. Silencing sexual trauma also fuels victim-blaming ideology including myths about harassment and violence that favor the perpetrator and foster poor coping among survivors. Black female trauma survivors, in particular, are routinely shamed and disempowered from sharing their trauma narratives.

Clinical Implications and Discussion

Ethically, counselors must comply with the Multicultural Counseling Competencies of the American Counseling Association (see Arredondo, et al.,1996; Sue, et al., 1992), by which they demonstrate knowledge, awareness, and skills when working with different racial and ethnic populations. When applying an ethical framework to these population, foundational principles still apply: doing no harm; promoting welfare; self-determination and autonomy; fidelity, faithfulness, and keeping promises; justice, equality, and fairness; and veracity and truthfulness (American Counseling Association, 2014). Doing no harm is non-maleficence, while avoiding the doing of harm by promoting welfare is beneficence. Autonomy references the client's right to choose their own course of action, which could be referenced developmentally as self-determination. Fidelity has to do with honoring commitments made to clients, which includes adhering to the other foundational principles as described above. Justice means providing equal treatment to all people, which includes the work of acknowledging our own bias and privilege in both the therapeutic relationship and the therapeutic process. Veracity refers to being truthful and acknowledging errors rather than deceiving or participating in the microaggressions of oppression, the misattunement of dismissing lived experience from the patient's perspective, or failing to grasp the impact of the patient's cultural perspectives and meaning. These values are common to all the helping professions (Corey, Corey, and Callahan, 2010).

Clinicians must become knowledgeable about "recognizing the influences of colonialism, family values, and experiences of microaggressions on identity development and mental health. Counselors must be aware of their own attitudes, biases, and assumptions" (Nadal, et al., 2012). Several studies have found that victims of microaggressions may feel immediate distress, while experiencing potential long-term mental health problems (Sue, et al., 2008, 2009). Thus, when clients discuss micro-aggressions, it is crucial for counselors to ensure that these clients verbalize their reactions thoroughly, instead of repressing or internalizing potentially damaging emotions (Nadal, et al., 2012). This applies to research, as well, not just the clinical setting: biases often influence the types of questions asked and how the data were interpreted – or exclude entire populations all together (ibid), and yet applying treatment to all. Researchers have used the term "race-based trauma to describe the emotional, psychological, and physical reactions to personal experiences with harassment and discrimination that cause pain" (Hemmings and Evans, 2018; see also Carter, 2007; Evans, et al., 2015). To provide effective treatment, counselors must be educated and trained to acknowledge race-based trauma (Bryant-Davis & Ocampo, 2006; Carter, 2007; Carter & Sant-Barket, 2014; Sue & Sue, 2003). Clinicians must utilize an "intersectional framework acknowledges that single-issue oppression does not exist; racism and other '-isms' symbiotically produce injustices" (Jones, et al., 2022; see also Collins, 2000).

The actual trauma healing and recovery process occurs in stages that parallel Maslow's hierarchy of needs (Herman, 1996). "First, the trauma survivor needs to escape physical danger and seek an environment that is safe and stable. Once physical safety has been re-established, the survivors' emotional needs can be met more effectively. The trauma survivors' highest priority emotional need is to rebuild a core of trust and safety that was shattered by the trauma. Trust and safety can be re-built through the reassurance, patience, support, and nurture of caring others, including the survivor's therapist" (Danzer, 2012). Finally, over time and through relational connection, emotional safety is re-established and "gradually allows the survivors' mind and body to re-route energy to deprived systems, facilitating trauma survivor's physiological recovery (ibid; see also Lieberman & Van Horn, 2008). However, for those who have endured the collective trauma of racism or other historical traumas, it may be difficult to establish safety when the trauma is ongoing and/or repetitive. Racism (and ableism) is (are) traumatic for marginalized peoples, and it impacts them "in ways that parallel how women and children are affected by chronic physical abuse" (Danzer, 2012).

REFERENCES

Agbayani-Siewert, P. 2004. Assumptions of Asian American similarity: The case of Filipino and Chinese American students. Social Work, 49,39–51.

American Counseling Association. 2014. ACA Code of Ethics. Alexandria, VA.

American Psychological Association. 2017. Ethical principles of psychologists and code of conduct.

Anderson, K. F. 2013. Diagnosing discrimination: Stress from perceived racism and the mental and physical health effects. Sociological Inquiry, 83, 55–81.

Bassett, D., Buchwald, D. & Manson, S. Posttraumatic stress disorder and symptoms among American Indians and Alaska Natives: a review of the literature. Soc Psychiatry Psychiatr Epidemiol 49, 417–433 2014. https://doi.org/10.1007/s00127-013-0759-y

Beltran, R., Schultz, K., Fernandez, A. R., Walters, K. L., Duran, B., & Evans-Campbell, T. 2018. From ambivalence to revitalization: Negotiating cardiovascular health behaviors related to environmental and historical trauma in a Northwest American Indian community. American Indian and Alaska Native Mental Health Research, 25(2), 103-128.

Benard. 2004. Resiliency: What have we learned San Francisco, CA WestEd.

Berger, M., and Sarnyai, Z. 2015. "More than skin deep": Stress neurobiology and mental health consequences of racial discrimination. Stress, 18(1), 1-10. https://doi.org/10.3109/10253890.2014.989204.

Black Lives Matter. 2019. Herstory. http://blacklivesmatter.com/herstory/. Accessed online 5 March 2022.

Blanco, A., Blanco, R., and Díaz, D. 2016. Social (dis)order and psychosocial trauma: Look earlier, look outside, and look beyond the persons. American Psychologist, 71(3), 187–198. https://doi.org/10.1037/a0040100

Bonilla-Silva, E. 2014. Racism without racists: Color-blind racism and the persistence of racial inequality in the United States (4th ed.). Lanham, MD: Rowan & Littlefield.

Brody, G. H., Lei, M.-K., Chae, D. H., Yu, T., Kogan, S. M., & Beach, S. R. H. (2014). Perceived discrimination among African American adolescents and allostatic load: A longitudinal analysis with buffering effects. Child Development, 85(3), 989–1002. https://doi.org/10.1111/cdev.12213

Brondolo, E., Gallo, L. C., & Myers, H. F. 2009. Race, racism and health: Disparities, mechanisms, and interventions. Journal of Behavioral Medicine, 32, 1–8.

Brown, T. N. 2008. Race, racism, and mental health: Elaboration of critical race theory's contribution to the sociology of mental health. Contemporary Justice Review, 11, 53–62.

Bryant-Davis, T., Ullman, S., Tsong, Y., Anderson, G., Counts, P., Tillman, S., ... Gray, A. 2015. Healing pathways: Longitudinal effects of religious coping and social support on PTSD symptoms in African American sexual assault survivors. Journal of Trauma & Dissociation, 16(1), 114–128. doi:10.1080/15299732.2014.969468 PMID:25387044

Bryant-Davis T., & Ocampo, C. 2006. A therapeutic approach to the treatment of racist-incident-based trauma. Journal of Emotional Abuse, 6, 1–22.

Carter, R. T., Mazzula, S., Victoria, R., Vazquez, R., Hall, S., Smith, S., . . . Williams, B. 2013. Initial development of the Race-Based Traumatic Stress Symptom Scale: Assessing the emotional impact of racism. Psychological Trauma: Theory, Research, Practice, and Policy, 5, 1–9.

Carter, R. T., & Forsyth, J. 2010. Reactions to racial discrimination: Emotional stress and help-seeking behaviors. Psychological Trauma Theory, Research, Practice and Policy, 2, 183–191.

Carter, R. T., & Sant-Barket, S. 2014. Assessment of the impact of racial discrimination and racism: How to use the Race-Based Traumatic Stress Symptom Scale in practice. Traumatology, 21, 32–39.

Clark US, Miller ER, Hegde RR. 2018. Experiences of discrimination are associated with greater resting amygdala activity and functional connectivity. Biol Psychiatry Cogn Neurosci Neuroimaging, 3(4):367-378. doi:10.1016/j.bpsc.2017.11.011

Corey, G., Corey, M.S., Callahan, P. 2010. Issues and Ethics in The Helping Professions. New York: Brooks-Cole.

Danzer, G. 2012. African-Americans' historical trauma: Manifestations in and outside of therapy. Journal of Theory Construction & Testing, 16(1), 16.

David, E. J. R., and Okazaki, S. 2006. Colonial mentality: Are view and recommendation for Filipino American psychology. Cultural Diversity and Ethnic Minority Psychology, 12,1–16.doi:10.1037/1099-9809.12.1.1

DeLilly, C. R. 2012. Discrimination and health outcomes. Issues in Mental Health Nursing, 33, 801–804.

Espiritu, Y.L. 1992. Asian American panethnicity: Bridging institutions and identities. Philadelphia, PA: Temple University Press.

Evans, A. M., Hemmings, C., Burkhalter, C., and Lacy, V. 2015. Responding to race related trauma: Counseling and research recommendations to promote post-traumatic growth when counseling African American males. Journal of Counselor Preparation and Supervision, 8(1). doi:10.7729/81.1085

Evans-Campbell, T., and Walters, K. 2006. Catching our breath: A decolonizing framework for healing Indigenous peoples. In: R. Fong, R. McRoy, C. O. Hendricks (Eds.), Intersecting

child welfare, substance abuse, and family violence: Culturally competent approaches (pp. 91-110). Alexandria, VA: Council on Social Work Education Press.

Fernando, S. 2012. Race and culture issues in mental health and some thoughts on ethnic identity. Counseling Psychology Quarterly, 25, 113–123.

Ferreira, M. L. 2006. Love in colonial light: History of Yurok emotions in Northern California. In Ferreira, M. L., and Lang, G.C. (Eds.), Indigenous peoples and diabetes: Community empowerment and wellness (pp. 357-386). Durham, NC: Carolina Academic Press.

Garcia, J. J., & Sharif, M. Z. 2015. Black lives matter: A commentary on racism and public health. American Journal of Public Health, 105, 27–30.

Han SD, Lamar M, Fleischman D, et al. 2021. Self-reported experiences of discrimination in older Black adults are associated with insula functional connectivity. Brain Imaging Behav., 15(4):1718-1727. doi:10.1007/s11682-020-00365-9

Hemmings, C., and Evans, A. M. 2018. Identifying and treating race-based trauma in counseling. Journal of Multicultural Counseling and Development, 46(1), 20-39.

Jones, V. N., Dopwell, D. M., & Curry, L. C. 2022. Silenced, Shamed, and Scatted: Black Feminist Perspective on Sexual Trauma and Treatment With African American Female Survivors. In Research Anthology on Racial Equity, Identity, and Privilege (pp. 601-622). IGI Global.

Libby, A. M., Orton, H. D., Novins, D. K., Beals, J., & Manson, S. M. 2005. Childhood physical and sexual abuse and subsequent depressive and anxiety disorders for two American Indian tribes. Psychological Medicine, 35(3), 329-340. http://dx.doi.org/10.1017/S0033291704003599.

Lieberman, A, Be Van Horn, P. 2008. Psychotherapy with infants and young children-.Repairing the effects of stress and trauma on early attachment. New York, NY: The Guilford Press.

Lum, D. 2003. Social work practice and people of color (5th ed.). Florence, KY: Wadsworth Publishing.

Markstrom, C, & Kalmanir, H. 2001. Linkages between the psychosocial stages of identify and intimacy and the ego strengths of fidelity and love. Journal of Theory and Research, 1(2), 179-196.

Markstrom, C, Sabino, V., Turner, B., & Berman, R. 1997. The psychosocial inventory of ego strengths: Development and validation of a new Eriksonian measure. Journal of Youth ana Adolescence, 26(6), 705-733.

Masten CL, Telzer EH, Eisenberger NI. 2011. An FMRI investigation of attributing negative social treatment to racial discrimination. J Cogn Neurosci, 23(5):1042-1051. doi:10.1162/jocn.2010.21520

Nadal, K. L. 2004. Filipino American identity development model. Journal of Multicultural Counseling and Development, 32,45–62.doi:10.1002/j.2161-1912.2004.tb00360.x

Nadal, K. L. 2011. Filipino American psychology: A handbook of theory, research, and clinical practice. New York, NY: Wiley.

Nadal, K. L., Issa, M. A., Leon, J., Meterko, V., Wideman, M., and Wong, Y. 2011. Sexual orientation microaggressions: "Death by a thousand cuts" for lesbian, gay, and bisexual youth. Journal of LGBT Youth, 8,16. doi:10.1080/19361653.2011.584204

Nadal, K.L.,&Sue, D.W. 2009.AsianAmericanyouth.InC.S.Clauss-Ehlers(Ed.),Encyclopedia of

cross-cultural school psychology(pp.116–122).NewYork,NY: Springer

Nadal, K. L., Vigilia Escobar, K. M., Prado, G. T., David, E. J. R., & Haynes, K. 2012. Racial

microaggressions and the Filipino American experience: Recommendations for counseling and development. Journal of Multicultural counseling and development, 40(3), 156-173.

Ortega-Williams, A., Beltrán, R., Schultz, K., Ru-Glo Henderson, Z., Colón, L., and Teyra, C. 2021. An integrated historical trauma and posttraumatic growth framework: A cross-cultural exploration. *Journal of Trauma & Dissociation*, *22*(2), 220-240.

Parham, T., White, J., & Ajamu, A. 1999. The psychology of bkeks: An African centered perspective (3rd ed.). Upper Saddle River, NJ: Prentice Hall.

Perry-Burney, G., Thomas, N. D., & McDonald, T. L. 2014. Rural child sexual abuse in the African American church community: A forbidden topic. Journal of Human Behavior in the Social Environment, 24(8), 986–995. doi:10.1080/10911359.2014.953413

Pierce, C., Carew, J., Pierce-Gonzalez, D. and Willis, D. 1978. An experiment in racism: TV commercials. In C. Pierce (Ed.), Television and education (pp.62–88). BeverlyHills, CA: Sage.

Pierotti, R., and Wildcat, D. 2000. Traditional Ecological Knowledge: The third alternative. Ecological Applications, 10(5), 1333-1340. Retrieved from http://www.jstor.org/stable/2641289?origin=JSTOR-pdf

Rivera, D. P., Forquer, E. E., and Rangel, R. 2010. Microaggressions and the life experience of Latina/o Americans. In D. W. Sue (Ed.), Microaggressions and marginality: Manifestation, dynamics, and impact (pp.59–83). NewYork, NY: Wiley.

Robinson, L. 1995. Psychology for social workers: Black perspectives. New York, NY: Roudedge.

Ruether, R. R. 1982. Feminism and patriarchal religion: Principles of ideological critiques of the Bible. Journal for the Study of the Old Testament, 22(22), 54–66. doi:10.1177/030908928200702207

Schultz, K., Cattaneo, L. B., Sabina, C., Brunner, L., Jackson, S., and Serrata, J. V. 2016a. Key roles of community connectedness in healing from trauma. Psychology of Violence, (6)1, 42-48. http://dx.doi.org/10.1037/vio0000025

Schultz, K., Walters, K. L., Beltrán, R., Stroud, S., & Johnson-Jennings, M. 2016b. "I'm stronger than I thought": Native women reconnecting to body, health, and place. Health & Place, 40, 21-28. http://dx.doi.org/10.1016/j.healthplace.2016.05.001

Shams, T. 2015. The declining significance of race or the persistent racialization of Blacks? A conceptual, empirical, and methodological review of today's race debate in America. Journal of Black Studies, 46, 282–296.

Singer, T, Critchley, HD, Preuschoff, K. 2009. A common role of insula in feelings, empathy and uncertainty. Trends Cogn Sci, 13(8):334-340. doi:10.1016/j.tics.2009.05.001

Sue, D. W., Bucceri, J. M., Lin, A. I., Nadal, K. L., and Torino, G. C. 2009. Racial microaggressions and the Asian American experience. Asian American Journal of Psychology, S,88–101.doi:10.1037/1948-1985.S.1.88

Sue, D. W., Nadal, K. L., Capodilupo, C. M., L in, A. I., Torino, G. C., and Rivera, D. P. 2008. Racial microaggressions against Black Americans: Implications for counseling. Journal of Counseling & Development, 86,330–338.doi:10.1002/j.1556-6678.2008.tb00517.x

Sue, D. W., & Sue, D. 2003. Counseling the culturally diverse (4th ed.). New York, NY: Wiley.

Thayer, Z. M., Blair, I. V., Buchwald, D. S., and Manson, S. M. 2017. Racial discrimination associated with higher diastolic blood pressure in a sample of American Indian adults. American Journal of Physical Anthropology, 163(1), 122-128. https://doi.org/10.1002ajpa.23190.

Thompson, C. E. and Carter, R. T. 2013. Race, socialization, and contemporary racism manifestations: Racial identity theory. Mahwah, NJ: Erlbaum.

Tynes, B. M., Umana-Taylor, A. J., Rose, C. A., Lin, J., & Anderson, C. J. 2012. Online racial discrimination and the protective function of ethnic identity and self-esteem for African American adolescents. Developmental Psychology, 482, 343–355

Wagner, J., Lampert, R., Tennen, H., and Feinn, R. 2015. Exposure to discrimination and heart rate variability reactivity to acute stress among women with diabetes: Racial discrimination and heart rate variability. Stress and Health, 31(3), 255-262. https://doi.org/10.1002/smi.2542

Walters, K., Beltrán, R., Huh, D., & Evans-Campbell, T. 2011a. Dis-Placement and Dis-Ease: Land, place, and health in American Indians and Alaska Natives. In: Takeuchi, D. (Ed.), Expanding the boundaries of place. New York: Springer.

Walters, K. L., Mohammed, S. A., Evans-Campbell, T., Beltrán, R. E., Chae, D. H., & Duran, B. 2011b. Bodies 'on't just tell stories, they tell histories: Embodiment of historical trauma among American Indians and Alaska Natives. Du Bois Review: Social Science Research on Race, 8(01), 179-189. http://dx.doi.org/10.1017/S1742058X1100018

Weaver, H. N. (1999). Indigenous People and the Social Work Profession: Defining Culturally Competent Services. Social Work, 44(3). 217-225. Retrieved from https://www.ncbi.nlm.nih.gov/pubmed/10321132

Webb, E. K., Bird, C. M., deRoon-Cassini, T. A., Weis, C. N., Huggins, A. A., Fitzgerald, J. M., ... & Larson, C. L. 2022. Racial Discrimination and Resting-State Functional

Connectivity of Salience Network Nodes in Trauma-Exposed Black Adults in the United States. JAMA network open, 5(1), e2144759-e2144759.

Whitbeck, L. B., Adams, G. W., Hoyt, D. R., and Chen, X. (2004). Conceptualizing and measuring historical trauma among American Indian people. American Journal of Community Psychology, 33(3/4), 119-130. http://dx.doi.org/10.1023/B:AJCP.0000027000.77357.31

Williams, D. R., Haile, R., Mohammed, S. A., Herman, A., Sonnega, J., Jackson, J. S., & Stein, D. J. 2012. Perceived discrimination and psychological well-being in the USA and South Africa. Ethnicity and Health, 17, 111–133.

Williams, D. R., & Mohammed, S. A. 2009. Discrimination and racial disparities in health: Evidence and needed research. Journal of Behavioral Medicine, 32, 20–47. doi:10.1007/s10865-008–9185-0

Williams, D. R., Neighbors, H. W., & Jackson, J. S. 2008. Racial/ethnic discrimination and health: Findings from community studies. American Journal of Public Health, 9, 29–37.

Williams, D. R., & Williams-Morris, R. 2000. Racism and mental health: The African American experience. Ethnicity & Health,5, 243–268.

Williams, J., & Keating, F. 2005. Social inequalities and mental health: An integrative approach. In A. Bell & P. Lindley (Eds.), Beyond the water towers: The unfinished revolution in mental health services 1985–2005. London, England: Sainsbury Center for Mental Health.

Williams, M. T. 2013, May 20. Can racism cause post-traumatic stress disorder? Implications for DSM-V. Retrieved from https://www.psychologytoday.com/blog/culturallyspeaking/201305/can-racism-cause-ptsd-implications-dsm-5

Williams, M. T., Malcoun, E., Sawyer, B. A., Davis, D. M., Nouri, L. B., Bruce, S. L. 2014. Cultural adaptations of prolonged exposure therapy for treatment and prevention of posttraumatic stress disorder in African Americans. Behavioral Science, 4, 102–124

Williams-Washington, K. N., & Mills, C. P. 2018. African American historical trauma: Creating an inclusive measure. Journal of Multicultural Counseling and Development, 46(4), 246–263. https://doi.org/10.1002/jmcd.12113

"Dr Who, a Tardis, and a relocation": Women with Dissociative Identity Disorder reflect on barriers to identifying and disclosing their trauma

by Mary-Anne Kate, PhD, Graham Jamieson, PhD, and Warwick Middleton, MD

When the grim histories of people with Dissociative Identity Disorder (DID) come to light, many people wonder how these abuses can have gone on for so many years undetected. Surely if it was that bad, the child would tell someone, and that person would tell the authorities, and the perpetrators would be jailed? For some onlookers, the lack of effective intervention seems to confirm a disconcertingly widespread belief that the abuse simply didn't happen – the person with DID is unstable and detached from reality or is making it up for attention, money, or some other secondary gain. As Judith Herman (1992) warns, "It is very tempting to take the side of the perpetrator. All the perpetrator asks is that the bystander do nothing. He appeals to the universal desire to see, hear and speak no evil. The victim, on the contrary, asks the bystander to share the burden of pain." In this chapter, the reader is asked to share the burden of pain with twelve women with DID struggling with the aftermath of severe childhood abuse as we try to understand the complex and multifaceted reasons why they were not able to disclose their abuse or seek safety during childhood.

Disclosures of a dozen women with DID

I recount the words of the brave women who spoke to me about their own experiences as part of my doctoral research[5]. The co-authors of this chapter, my PhD supervisors Graham Jamieson and Warwick Middleton, each attended three of the interviews. The women were inpatients attending a trauma and dissociation program at a private psychiatric hospital in Australia. The women ranged in age from their mid-thirties to mid-sixties with most being women being in their forties and fifties. Eleven of the women were biological females, and one was a transwoman. A couple of the women had grown up in poverty, a couple were from working-class backgrounds, and at least half were from middle-class backgrounds. All but one of the women disclosed experiencing sexual abuse. For the majority, one or more of the perpetrators was a family member. Most recounted physical abuse and emotional neglect. The abuse and family dysfunction persisted throughout their childhoods. Their histories of abuse were consistent with the literature on DID (Kate, et al., 2021; Middleton and Butler, 1998). Only one of the women found a safe haven during her childhood – and that was not until the year she turned 18.

The impact of the abuse on the lives of these women is pervasive. Nearly all women described being in and out and out of hospitals for

---

[5] This project, *Understanding the factors that assist or hinder the identification and treatment of childhood trauma and dissociation, and experiences of justice in a sample of people with a Dissociative Disorder,* was approved by the Australian Human Research Ethics Committee (HE14-208) and the research committee of Belmont Private Hospital, Brisbane.

decades, and most had numerous suicide attempts that would land them in the intensive care unit. For example, Simone tells me:

> "I am aiming for this to be the first Christmas and New Year's in 8 years that I'll have been out of hospital."

The women struggled with depression, PTSD, anxiety, self-harm, and some with borderline symptoms, anorexia and other disordered eating. Nearly all had chronic health conditions that appeared somatic or epigenetic such as migraines, irritable bowel syndrome, chronic pain, autoimmune disease, and gynaecological problems. The women's presentation was consistent with other research on DID (Brand, et al., 2013).

Most of the women had been in relationships, and the majority had children of their own. Three of the women felt the safest option was to avoid intimate relationships. Many of the women had experienced relationships where there was (often extreme) intimate partner violence, and some disclosed sexual assaults and violence during their adult life. This is consistent with research that finds histories of child abuse and dissociation increases the risk of revictimization across the lifespan (Zamir, et al., 2018).

Many women spent years, often decades, in the mental health system before their dissociation was detected, which is also consistent with other research (Spiegel, 2011). Most recounted ineffective mental health treatment, including a lack of, or ineffective, psychotherapy, and being overly medicated. Many of the psychiatrists did not consider DID as a possibility, often because they did not "believe in DID". Some of the women were diagnosed incorrectly with schizophrenia. For others, the focus of treatment was on comorbid conditions like depression, anxiety, borderline, or PTSD. Some women had health issues related to their treatment. For example, Carol developed diabetes following the rapid weight gain resulting from commencing the medication Olanzapine to reduce the voices of her alters; and Kylie revealed:

> "I've had about 60 rounds of ECT [electroconvulsive therapy], three or four psychoses, and I really wanted to study science and maths, and my memory is just shot. I used to know the periodic table by heart, balancing chemical equations…"

Kylie, like many of the women, was incredibly bright, insightful, and articulate. Many of the women reported being straight-A students at school. Rosemary was an exception as she has a mild intellectual disability which may have arisen from a head injury given the intense physical violence she experienced from a young age. For most women, their lives began to unravel in their late teens and early twenties when they were first living away from their abusive families. Still, many attempted or completed university. Undergraduate studies included psychology, nursing, law, music, child welfare, and education. The majority of women sought careers in health and social care, such as nursing and physiotherapy. Around half had worked in roles aimed at nurturing and protecting children, including as a child protection officer, play therapist, domestic violence officer, behavioural therapist, and youth worker. One woman worked as a nurse and a domestic violence officer while also studying psychology. These women were powerfully motivated to save children from abuse and neglect. Earlier research at the trauma and dissociation unit had also found the women gravitated towards careers in health care (Middleton & Butler, 1998). One woman was a successful lawyer, another a talented musician, another had been in the military, and a couple had done various low skilled jobs even though they were clearly bright.

Tragically, despite their intelligence, skills and knowledge, at the time of the interview, most had not worked for many years due to their mental health struggles and physical health issues and were living on a government disability pension. Many did not foresee returning to the world of work, and this was crushing for them. Many were articulate and engaged throughout the interview, which seemed a stark contrast to their low level of functioning, chronic suicidality, and lengthy inpatient stays. For example, Jacqueline explains:

> "My life seems to have been a series of being knocked down, getting back up and getting knocked down, and that just seems to be the process through my whole life… at the moment, I'm pretty neurologically stuffed up, so even if I wanted to work, I couldn't. I shouldn't have worded it that way [as] I would love to go out tomorrow and start a job."

Gillian, who was ambitious with her music and studies, told me:

> "When I got really sick and started facing everything, I just couldn't work. I was just switching and dissociating all the time, in and out of hospital like a yo-yo and eventually, they put me on a disability support pension, and that was about the only time I had a moment realizing that all this was real.

> I kept waiting for one day when someone would come and say 'it's over now'."

Cynthia put it starkly:

> "At the moment, our job is to survive to see our kids grow up."

Even finding the will to survive was exceptionally difficult for many. As Alison shares:

> "I just wanted to die. Like I've always had this, just let me die. I just want to die. And I still just lie there and go this world has been so cruel. God, this world has been so cruel."

It is devastating to see the potential of these women lay dormant – for themselves, their families, and society. What can be done to prevent this from happening? I asked them if they could imagine any circumstances during their childhood in which they would have felt it was safe to disclose their abuse or escape from it.

Women with DID have been forbidden, punished, ridiculed, and shamed for speaking their truth. In this chapter, a dozen brave women tell their own stories in their own words. I have changed all identifying details, including names, to preserve their confidentiality. I acknowledge how difficult, painful, and triggering it was for these women to tell me their stories. Yet, all the women were highly motivated to speak with me in the hope that I could help to shine a light on the experience of people with DID to save others from their fate.

As you will read, the barriers to disclosure and seeking safety can seem insurmountable. It is not as simple as the fear of not being believed or the consequences of speaking out, although these are both valid reasons. The picture is complicated by the women's dissociation and doubting their reality, their loyalty to family, the invisibility of their abuse, the complicity of perpetrators and others, the inclination to turn a blind eye, gaslighting, their abuse seeming unbelievable, and a myriad of other reasons. Crystal's answer encapsulates how just formidable the barriers are. She tells me that, for her to speak out, it would have taken something out of this world, like "Dr Who, a Tardis, and a relocation."

The abuse was normalized

For some of the women, the abuse was so pervasive that it seemed normal. Many of the women had multiple perpetrators, including family members. Some experienced organized abuse that included seemingly upstanding community members. Even if the child sensed the abuse was wrong, they may still perceive it to be normal. The child may not consider adults to be trustworthy, which is understandable given the number of adults the child knew who were abusing them, colluding with the abusers, or on friendly or congenial terms with the abusers. Naomi explains that abuse was simply a feature of her childhood:

> "Just not realising that what they were doing is like called abuse."

Alison is a survivor of extreme familial and organized abuse through a fraternal organization. She explains:

> "It was ritualistic and happened all the time. It wasn't a one-off scary thing. It is a thing that happens in my family.
>
> "My father was involved, so it was my grandfather, then my father and my cousin… multiple men doing multiple things to you at the multiple same time ... a neighbour got me, a builder got me, someone else got me."

Belinda's abuse was so pervasive that she was surprised when she went to school to discover all males weren't sexually abusive:

> "Because I was being abused every day, I just thought it was a normal thing… I didn't understand why nothing was going on at school, like with the boys. I think my 'normal' from as long as I can remember. Um, whether it was boys or men. Basically, pretty much sexual stuff every day. Basically yeah. Pretty much. Um, so yeah it was so… it sort of took me out of that normal situation – what I thought was a normal situation…. And I sort of thought it was normal having all these voices in my head…. Because that's just normal."

This warped view was echoed by family members. Belinda reveals what happened when she disclosed to her aunt as an adult:

> "My aunt told me off for telling… she just said that she was abused when she was younger, and it didn't have an impact on her life, and I had no right to say anything. Mum sided

> with her. She walked off. Yeah, she disowned me, again [laughs dryly]. I've been disowned a few times by my mother over the years."

Loyalty

Many of the women were surprisingly loyal to their parents, despite coming to terms with the abuses their parents had perpetrated or enabled. The loyalty was apparent in childhood too. The fear of breaking up the family was reason enough not to speak out, as Alison recounts:

> "I didn't want to break up my family and siblings. My dad went to jail for what he did and I'm still struggling to… I'm dancing around the subject as I don't want to get in trouble even now… it is hard because he is still alive and part of my life, and I find it really hard to say much about him because I still have that fear that I don't want him to go to jail. I just can't do it."

I asked Alison if it would help or make any difference if he ever apologised for abusing her. She answered:

> "No, I would rather he just think I don't remember."

It was more important for Alison to salvage the relationship with her parents. As she explains:

> "I have to – for my mum. She relies on him. She had an abusive past herself and she relies on him. Like, I don't think she'd survive without him, her second husband, and she put

> all her hopes into him. And she actually picked a similar husband as to what she did the first time. For my mum's sanity, I can't bring myself to kind of describe exactly what he did, and that's so hard because then I have to go and see him. You know, I don't hug him or anything, but I have to help him down the stairs and drive him places and be the good daughter facade. That's what I do. I put on my lovely little fake hat and face and do what any daughter needs to do."

Despite their abusive behaviour, Kylie told me that during her childhood:

> "I was protective of my parents. I'd even stick up for them."

Naomi felt it was important to be loyal. She recalls:

> "Believing that it's wrong to speak badly of your parents."

Belinda felt similarly:

> "I don't think I would have talked. Because I felt like it was dishonoring them and even more so once we got into church with mum."

Keeping the family unit together is still an important consideration for Simone:

> "I'm not quite sure what direction I am going to take when I start to deal with that with younger trauma with my family. I've seen people who have cut ties with their family, which I know is how it will have to be with me as I know my family

> unit will stay as a unit. That's very important to them, which means if I started talking about it, I'd basically have to accept that they would no longer be in my life. I don't know if that's worth it."

Not speaking out because of loyalty is a significant barrier highlighted by Alison and Simone, who still feel this way, despite being independent adults who are aware of their trauma history and its impact.

I was the one that was bad, not them

To seek help, you must believe you are worthy of saving. Yet some of the women expressed sentiments that they didn't deserve to be saved, were "less than", subhuman, of no value, fundamentally flawed, deserving of bad treatment, and even evil. Naomi most clearly expressed this perspective. She spoke in a little girl's voice that was so quiet it was almost a whisper. Naomi was apologetic throughout the interview feeling her valuable contribution was not worthwhile. She recounts:

> "I always believed it is all my fault. That it wasn't them and was always me, and it was always my fault why these things happened. Everything was my fault. So, yeah. I was the one that was bad and not them."

Naomi's describes her feelings the first time she ever met with a therapist when she was a university student:

> "I walked in and said, 'There is something very wrong with me, I need your help to fix myself. I keep ruining my family.

> I'm really bad, and I'm really evil, I am really wicked. I wrecked my family, and I need you to help me to fix myself.' That is what I said to her… I felt like I was being evil… how dare I make somebody think those of things of my family or my parents?"

I asked Naomi if therapy helped her get a more realistic perspective. She responded:

> "I still believe it is all my fault. I still believe I am really bad and yucky and evil."

I then asked Naomi if she now understood it was not her fault. She reveals that she found the idea that the abuse was her fault less frightening than the truth of her situation:

> "I find that really hard. I find that really scary. Because on one level, somewhere in me, I do know that. But on another level, I find it incredibly hard to accept because it is terrifying… to think that you have no control and no power, and that is really, really scary…. I think I hide myself from that sometimes from… like I think if I hold onto the fact that if I was different it could all be different, and I still do believe that. But I think that maybe sometimes holding on to that is… I see that as less painful than the truth if that makes sense… there's no hope… and I can't deal with all that emotion…
>
> "I still want to hold out hope that I'm evil and it is all my fault and something is wrong with me and I can fix it and I

> can go home, and they will be loving and supportive and accepting and things can be… I still want to believe it is all my fault that if I could just be different that they would be different towards me. I thought there was something wrong with me… Yeah, if I could be different somehow then they were going to accept me and not hurt me that it would be the family you would always hope to have sort of thing… But I didn't know about me what it was that I needed to change, but I just knew… I just had this idea that if I could just be different everything would be alright."

Alison also felt that she was bad and that if the secret of the abuse got out, she would be the one going to jail, not the perpetrators:

> "I felt like the world had just given up on me…. I had sinned early on, and this was God's punishment to me…. I was evil, and I committed these sinful acts and was going to hell and I didn't want anyone to know that.

> "That would be scary talking to the police when you were little…. I didn't want to go to jail. I was doing these things, and I didn't want to go to jail. It wasn't the other way around."

Kylie was treated by her parents as a second-class citizen and a nuisance. This resulted in her feeling the abusive treatment was her fault:

> "I didn't know how to tell my friends, 'I am a really bad person. This is why my parents have to do this with me.' That was the thought process."

Kylie recounted examples of the type of parental behaviours that made her believe she was not worthy of care and protection.

> "They used to lock me in a rumpus room for no reason, because [my mother] didn't like me at all. She'd just get sick of me, and they'd play happy families upstairs and bring my meal down to me.
>
> "There was a period of time between 12 and 14 when every school holidays, I was banned from the house. My dad worked in the city… he would leave at seven in the morning on the dot. Because I was a nuisance to my mum, he would drop me off in the city and pick me up at 6 pm. And I would walk around the city and sleep in the botanical gardens. And I remember him yelling and berating me for all the things I'm doing to my mum and all the trouble I create and bring on my family on the drive, and I couldn't get away from him. He'd let me out and I'd be absolutely sobbing and hysterical."

During these long days in the city, Kylie was given no money and recalls walking in circles, crying. She couldn't bear it. She explained:

> "I would beg my mum, 'If I take a packed lunch? I won't go near you. I won't go near you! Can I please just stay in the forest all day and I'll take some books? Please, please, I'll stay there as long as you want, please don't make me go to the city!' The city was daunting to me… I wish I knew what I did wrong."

It is only with hindsight that Kylie now realizes that she did nothing wrong and was like “a scared little mouse”.

Belinda’s mother also treated her like an outcast:

> “I was actually more made to stay away from the house... after my youngest brother was born. So, there’s nine and a half years between me and the youngest in the family... just roaming around the streets. I’ve been doing that before then... actually, probably as long back as I can remember... I was more the invisible child.”

The lack of maternal care and compassion was evident following the first suicide attempt of three women. When Gillian attempted suicide at thirteen, her mum came to the hospital and yelled at her. Kylie had a similar experience when she revealed to her mum at age 19 that she was suicidal:

> “Well, I rang up my mum... and I said “mum, mum, I’m suicidal,” and she slammed the phone down. They couldn’t break me because I dissociated... I was put on suicide watch.”

Belinda became homeless after her first suicide attempt:

> “I tried to commit suicide just before I was 17, and I got put into a psych hospital, and I got into major trouble from mum for it, and then I got kicked out of home.... I was living on the streets.”

Her mother's reaction was not surprising as Belinda was accustomed to her mother's lack of care when she was hurt or unwell:

> "I wasn't taken to the doctor for injuries, so it didn't really matter. So, if I had a sprain…, if I was covered in bruises or whatever, it wasn't noticed. If I caused the bruises myself or somebody else caused them it was neither here nor there."

Carol's mother was dismissive of her first hospitalisation.

> "When I was 20, I went into hospital. She wouldn't see me at all and said I was looking for attention."

The lack of maternal care and compassion was a theme that was woven tightly though all of the women's stories. Their mothers were non-protective and often colluded in, or perpetrated, the abuse. Their mothers were cold, unemotional, and unavailable. Their mothers' reactions to their first suicide attempt are characteristic of this and would appear to reinforce the belief that their lives did not matter and that they were not worthy of saving.

A lack of faith in authority figures

Despite the severity of the abuse, some women did not trust authority figures to assist or protect them. For some this was based on their own negative experiences, including authority figures being involved in the abuse itself. Alison had no faith in the police or the justice system to help her. As she explains:

> "And at that time when [my suicide attempt at 17] happened, I'd actually just gone through another assault from being on a date… I did have to get a hospital because he'd actually used a knife… they said about taking it to police to be charged but I didn't because I thought people would find out about what happened about my cousin and it'd be my fault… I think because like in the legal system basically they always like turn things around to make the victim whatever. They can, yeah, sort of put the blame back there."

During the entire interview, Tracey's head was turned away from me, her eyes were rolled upwards with her irises barely visible. Tracey shared with me that her general practitioner (GP) failed to notice and report her abuse despite the frequency and severity of her injuries. She suspects this may have been because her doctor was also involved:

> "We hold our GP accountable given the fact he was our family doctor for all those times, and he hadn't noticed anything. Or if he did. I don't know if he is one of our perpetrators actually, so. We get the flashbacks from him. So, we are still questioning how trustworthy he was."

Tracy also recalls a strange childhood incident that should have raised red flags with the police. As she explains:

> "We got pushed through a window, but in our memory, we were just playing on a road. Don't know why we were playing on a road but playing on a road playing chasey, but [in reality] we had been knocked through the window. I had

> my sisters there, and one of them pulled us out of the window, and we walked to the library and we were bleeding down the arm and everything, and I had just not acknowledged anything. The only awareness we had was when she said, 'Where is all the blood coming from?'
>
> "I said, 'I don't know.' Then we blanked out a bit.
>
> "Then we had to go on to the local police station and burst into tears to them, going. 'Oh my God, we've broken one of your windows – one of your shop windows.'
>
> "They were like, 'Are you going to go home?'
>
> "We were like, 'We don't ever want to go home.' But they didn't pick up any radar on that either. That is another time that external bodies may have [asked], 'Why doesn't a child that age want to go home?' Especially when you've got major injuries."

For Gillian, her abuse went unnoticed even when the police became involved with her family due to the domestic violence. She explains that the police did:

> "Zip. Nada. Nothing [despite] rifles in the house, evidence – a couple of times my mother was bleeding. She had this cut on her lip. I just remember yeah, usually at night-time and the police would come to the house, but nothing ever changed. Nothing was ever done."

Rosemary's teachers noticed she had bruises and welts when she eventually took off her jacket in the summer heat. The school contacted child welfare. She explains that contacting the authorities didn't improve things:

> "I was told not to take my jacket off so people couldn't see… [child welfare got involved] but that didn't help that much, it just seemed to make things worse… yeah, in big trouble. It didn't really help calling the police, family services. I used to tell them, 'next time you've got a bright idea – don't,' or tell the teacher that, as it made it worse at home."

Cynthia had a controlling mother who sexually exploited her throughout her childhood for considerable financial gain. This extended to permitting men, for an additional fee, to inflict physical injuries during the sexual abuse. She reveals:

> "Some of the guys our mum sent us off with weren't all that gentle, so we'd come back a bit beat up or a bit hurt. We were generally kept home until they fixed, so. And she had a doctor friend who used to sort of patch us up and stitch us up if that was needed so it was never sort of taken to an outside… the doctor was well-known. My dad's police friend was quite well known where we grew up. [Even now, we] can't trust the police, well we don't. A lot of our younger parts don't. Even those of us that think there are probably good ones out there."

These women grew up in an environment that made it exceptionally difficult to trust adults, particularly authority figures, who may have been able to assist them.

Flying under the radar at school

Nearly all of the women described flying under the radar at school. Many of the women were A-grade students, although a couple struggled academically or socially. On the whole, the women described themselves as being good students who were generally not disruptive in class. Some described daydreaming during class. A couple had dissociative episodes. Some presented with physical injuries or fairly obvious tell-tale signs of abuse such as sexualised behaviours that were not age appropriate. Yet, the abuse was not detected, and where there were suspicions, these were not addressed effectively.

> "I think that when I was at school, at least our school, it seems that all that mattered to the teachers was that you keep to the rules, so like, behave in class, and if you got grades like your writing and maths right, then that is all they are worried about. They didn't really worry about the social or emotional kinds of things like they do now in schools." – Naomi

> "I was the perfect prefect and then derailed, so to speak. But I knew how I felt, and I knew how I felt walking home and walking to school, and I had the masks on and nobody knew… I think some of my perfect report cards started

saying "marks good, but she's looking out the window a lot" or stuff like that." – Gillian

"[In relation to her eating disorder going unnoticed] People don't care as long as you're doing good grades. You slipped through the system. If you're a good kid who always does the right thing and does all your work perfectly then they don't notice."
– Cynthia

"I got in trouble for drawing a picture when I was in fourth class. It was apparently a bit too explicit.... I got into trouble. Umm, why did I get into trouble?" – Belinda

"The teachers didn't notice anything. Even a child crying saying, 'Don't send me home, don't send me home!' It should have rung alarm bells." – Tracey

"A year eight teacher came close near me and lifted his hand for some reason, and I ducked, and he said, 'You know I'll never ever hit you,'... and I had wondered in hindsight why he didn't ask me a bit more about why I ducked or did a response like that." – Carol

"The society and culture was set up in such a way that everything that happened to us was acceptable. Spare the rod, spoil the child... If I went to school [in the present day] and they saw the welts my father had left on me? Of course, it would be different." – Crystal

Alison's sexualized acting out was noticed. However, she did not feel safe enough to disclose her abuse. As she explains:

> "One teacher noticed my behaviour. I always had a boyfriend, and I always wanted to kiss them. My behaviour was quite sexual compared to other people that age I'm guessing. She and another teacher sat me down and asked if someone was hurting me. That's the only person who ever noticed."

I asked Alison, "How did it feel to be asked? And when you were in your school persona were you aware of the abuse?" She recounts:

> "I was petrified, and I said, 'No, no.' [she replied], 'Are you sure? You won't get into trouble.'"

I then asked Alison, "What would have happened if someone had really pursued that, would you have been able to go along with it?" She explained:

> "I think if I knew what the outcome would be. At that stage, I thought I was in trouble, so as a child, I was like, 'No. No. No one is hurting me.' I wish I had said yes. I wish I had the trust where I could say, 'Yeah, you're right.'… It would be nice if someone could sit down with me one-on-one in the class as two teachers coming to me in the classroom asking if someone was hurting me… it wasn't the right setting to say, 'We've noticed some things and we are really worried about you, can you tell me about what is going on at home?' That would have been much better than me thinking I was in

> trouble for kissing a boy. It is really lovely that she did pick it up, but I just wish she had done more to make it stop back in grade four rather than it going on for another three or four years, and it got more violent each time. It would be nice if there was more education about what happens in that situation, who to talk to, that you won't get into trouble. There was no school counsellor.

Gillian did not feel able to open up to her teacher about her abuse, despite her genuine concern and direct questions. She explains:

> "When I was thirteen, I first attempted suicide, and when I was in the hospital one of the teachers came up to see me… she asked me behind the curtains when no one was around. At the time, I didn't understand why. But now I do. She must have been sus[picous]. She said, 'Why does a thirteen-year-old try to kill herself?' Because I did it at school in the toilets before school started. And she kept asking me was there any reason, and I kept saying, 'no', as I was too terrified to tell why."

Two of the women reported that school itself was not a safe place as they were sexually abused by teachers. In addition to Simone, who was ritualistically abused by her teacher, Cynthia reveals:

> "We were an A student. We had to be… [My mother] got quite upset that I got a B instead of my usual A plus. So, she went up and saw the teacher, and the teacher basically said that I hadn't quite applied myself as well as I could, but if mum wanted to, the teacher was willing to give us some

> tutoring after school, so yeah. The teacher that [sexually abused me] that my mother saw was a female, and that was in younger high school. The second teacher [that abused me] was male and we were a lot older."

Nearly all of the women felt the teachers would have noticed the signs of abuse if they were more attuned and attentive and had approached them in a trauma-informed way. Most were hopeful that societal shifts meant that it was currently more likely that abuses like theirs would be picked up in the school setting.

The ostrich family and turning a blind eye

Gillian's whole family turned a blind eye. She ponders:

> "I think I have a whole family of dissociators as they would have grown up with domestic violence, obviously, and learned to be .. what do you call it? Head in the sand, ostriches. The ostrich family."

Some of the women described their mother turning a blind eye. Simone explains:

> "In an ideal world, my mum would have done something about it… she had a fair idea that something very wrong was going on under our roof."

Cynthia describes her grandma turning a blind eye:

> "My grandma had some idea that something was going on. But in our family, you don't talk about that stuff."

Alison's parents turned a blind eye to the terrifying abuse inflicted on her by her cousin. She explains:

> "I tried to tell my parents that I hated living there, but I was told not to be a trouble-maker and to be appreciative that you have somewhere to live."

I asked her if she explained exactly what was happening. She said:

> "No, just that he was horrible to me. They didn't want to know that he was hurting me. Like just, 'Go tell his mum.' They just didn't want to know… they never listened. They were always drunk. There would be no way. It was clear that… I was petrified of him… I know my mum knew because my aunt would find [describes compelling evidence] but they were totally oblivious. They didn't want to know."

Kylie explains her sisters turned a blind eye to her father's abusive treatment of her:

> "My sisters were bystanders. They copped a tiny bit. Nothing like me. And there's even been conversations they've sort of said, 'The stuff did happen, and child protective services should have been called.' Because some of the things he did were just so weird. The punishments and the rules were so weird."

Kylie's abusive parents also turned a blind eye to her abuse by her uncle. Kylie tried to tell her parents about it when she was 15. Although she could not reveal all the details, saying only that he watched her get undressed. Her parents initially intervened but then let her uncle have full access to her on family holidays again. Belinda's mother literally turned a blind eye to her abuse:

> "Mum walked in one time when something was happening and just closed the door and never said nothing. And she read my diary once. When I was in like my first year in high school… I had a diary, and I knew she'd read it because it was left open. And she wouldn't look at me, and I just thought it would be a good opportunity to talk to her, and she's just like, 'I don't have time. Don't have time to talk to you.' Umm, and yeah, she wouldn't even look at me.
>
> "I was getting abused basically every day…. by my uncle and my older cousin and his friends and stuff."

Belinda told me both of her parents knew of the abuse from her uncle and cousins, so I asked her what they did with this knowledge. She replied:

> "Nothing. I know when dad was dying, he did tell me that, 'when you got abused, [your mother] didn't want to lose her sister over it.'"

Jacqueline's parents turned a blind eye to the abuse she experienced from her grandfather:

> "Yeah. I'd say, 'I don't want to go.' I'd be in tears. But nope, I'd still be sent there. You're talking about I'd be sent back to my parents with stitches on my private parts… it happened when I was really young. I went back to the house, and my parents saw it and said there was nothing. This sentence fits my father perfectly: "I don't want to know." See, my parents are experts at… they live on the theory that if you ignore something long enough, it will go away. And it's not an issue until you actually acknowledge it, and that was in everything, not just abuse."

The family members failed to protect their children from the abuse they knew about or suspected. This is likely to be a key reason the abuse continued throughout these women's childhoods.

Knowing that abuse is a secret not to be shared

Direct threats were not always necessary to ensure secrecy. Some of the women instinctively knew not to tell. As Cynthia explains:

> "It's just you don't tell. Like, I mean if you're told, 'You don't tell.' If you've got people in your family who know but they're not telling. Then it wouldn't have occurred to us that it was okay to tell because everyone we knew that knew about it wasn't helping us. So, why would you? It's not normal. You know if people who do know aren't going to save you… I honestly don't think there would have been any situation where we would have told… if everyone else in the

> family that does know doesn't do anything then, why? How do you even think it could be different? How do you know it's not normal?.... We knew we weren't like other kids. We knew there was something wrong about us. But we just didn't know what. And if you're not allowed to socialize too much, then you don't know what other kids' houses are like."

Naomi understood from an early age that she must remain silent about her homelife:

> "When I was in kindy, I already knew that I was bad and unlovable and that I was not allowed to talk to adults or share my feelings on the outside and not just talk about home and all those things."

Jacqueline explains that there were no circumstances that would have led her to disclose her abuse:

> "I wouldn't have done it. There is nothing that I can think of that would prompt me to talk about that stuff."

It was clear to these women from a young age that telling the secret wasn't an option. Even if people who potentially can help notice and ask the right questions in a trauma-informed way, these women may still have been unable to have disclose their abuse during childhood.

Fear

The more severe abuse the women experienced, the greater the risk in disclosure and the greater the need for protection. For many women, the perpetrator seemed all-powerful. Often the perpetrator's actions demonstrated how dangerous they were and the risk to personal safety if the abuse was disclosed.

For Gillian, it was simply too dangerous for her or family members to disclose her father's abuse:

> "I didn't even get to think that as everyone's lives were at risk. So, you didn't mention it. It wasn't even EVER a consideration to tell anyone because they would be killed. And there was enough evidence of things being killed and stuff happening to mum that did happen. That was enough to go, 'Oh yeah, he will follow through with his threats.'
>
> "When I was four, he said he was going to kill my eldest sister, and he had rifles and knives. Sneaky things too – not obvious bashing so people would know she was a beaten wife. He did sick and twisted things.
>
> "Umm, she told me that when they went on a holiday to Italy – I stayed with my sister, I must have been 12 or 13 – they were on this lookout cliff thing, and he went to push her off the cliff. But it was like push-pull, push-pull. Um, what's that called? I don't know what you call it? Terrorising? Yeah, terrorising. Getting a kick out of scaring her. Obviously, he didn't go through with it.

> "Often we were piled in the car and driven to the police, and no one ever did anything. And then once the three older kids left and I was on my own, mum and I would get into her car and go to her one niece's place and hide out for a while ... He had stuck a dead sparrow with a match through its head under her pillow with a note saying: 'You're next.'
>
> "And umm, she finally thought, she was already sleeping in another room, 'Stuff this. I'm going.' And obviously things got worse when she got home from work, but I was never told. Yeah, and he hunted us down and found us where we were hiding, and he had a gun."

When I asked Alison if her cousin threaten her about disclosure, she revealed a similar story to Gillian:

> "He made it clear that he would kill me. He had a gun. He would use it in the most horrific ways. Then he would shoot at me, and held me over a cliff. I had every reason to believe he would [kill me]. He killed cats in front of me."

Carol's father also threatened her with a gun. She explains:

> "Dad was either shooting at us, or pointing the gun, or cleaning it, or ranting and raving cos he was drunk. He sneered a lot at us and… he'd say he would 'shoot us all.' And he did shoot at us. So, we had to run and hide in the grass. And that was another fear because there were brown snakes [a deadly species]."

Belinda needed assurances that she would never be returned to her family. She explains:

> "I was terrified of my family. They would have to totally guarantee me that I'd never see my family again. As soon as I was behind closed doors and away from other people, I would just get into so much trouble. And it would be physical, emotional and mental, and withdrawal of things. The only way would be for child protective services to take me away.
>
> "This is my mum's exact voice: 'Don't you dare talk about us to anyone else... So you talk about us to anyone else? Don't you dare!'... If stuff was going on, she would pull me into a room by my hair and aggressively whisper threats to me.
>
> "Yeah, I remember going to school. My mum would get into these rages and grab your face and pull it so hard your lips would start bleeding, and I had to make up stories about how that happened."

Naomi learned that it was not safe to discuss her father's abuse with her mother, as when she tried:

> "She'd tell my father what I'd said, and of course, he would come and hurt me for telling and stuff that I had said. Whatever, yeah. And now I see that as a betrayal as she knew. She knew he'd come and hurt me if she said stuff like that to him. So, I kind of think. How could... how could...

> how could your mum do that to you, knowing what her husband was about to do to her child?"

Naomi stopped disclosing the abuse.

> "When I was eight, the things that my dad did were so extreme that I learned to shut my mouth forever and not to speak again. I can't think of anything that would have given me my voice when I was so terrified of knowing the consequences of speaking.
>
> "I had never presented anywhere for help. I never knew it was okay to ask for help. And I thought it was very wrong to ask for help, actually. And very wrong to talk about anything. And indeed, in the past [laughs nervously], I believed that my life would be in danger if I talked about anything."

In some cases, the perpetrator threatened to hurt others if the child did not comply. Alison was fiercely protective of her younger brother. As she explains:

> "When someone has gun, and threatening to kill my little brother, threatening to do things to my little brother, 'Don't do that, do it to me instead.'"

Cynthia too, protected her brother from physical abuse:

> "I love my brother dearly. We spent most of our childhood protecting him because he was always used as a threat that they'd beat him if I didn't behave."

Gillian was protective of her whole extended family. As she explains:

> "So, I protected all my brothers and sisters, my mother, my nephews and nieces... sometimes I wish I had the concentration and the motion to write that exactly the kind of things that happened and for how long and why I never spoke of the threats to save not only your lives but your kids' lives."

It was apparent that some perpetrators were capable of serious bodily harm, and even murder. Understandably, these women were petrified at the prospect of disclosing.

Finding a safe place

For many women, the only reasonable prospect of the abuse stopping was leaving their family permanently and not being found. It is unsurprising some thought of running away. Kylie would have liked to, and she said:

> "I always dreamt of running away, but I was too scared."

Rosemary unsuccessfully tried to put her plans of escape into action:

> "I used to try to escape to my cousin's place all the time... they lived on a farm. You didn't get... inappropriate cuddles at the farm. I always remember having lots of clothes packed away, or hidden, or putting heaps of clothes on."

Rosemary's plans did not go unnoticed by her cousins who observed, "You've got heaps of clothes," but they advised her, "You can't stay here."

Belinda did run away frequently, but she had nowhere safe to go:

> "I was running away from the time I started high school… Sometimes, I didn't come back… I'd sleep on the streets."

The women's recollections suggest that they needed a place that they felt was safe and where they would be cared for. For example, Carol explained that providing safe, comfortable housing and food, in particular, may have motivated her to tell:

> "Food. That sounds strange, but we didn't have a lot of food so we might have got one meal at night sometimes there was fruit there. So, I was very hungry a lot at the time. And even living in a house like, oh the caravan was so small that you really had to roll on the spot."

For Alison, even the prospect of being sent to a children's home was daunting. She explains:

> "I knew I wasn't safe. I knew I wouldn't be believed. I didn't know what would happen to me – we had seen a children's home where people had their kids taken off them – I'd seen that, and in the end, it is better what you know than what you don't know."

The only person who found a safe place during childhood was Cynthia. It was not through her actions, only her receptiveness to a generous and bold offer. The young woman who assisted Cynthia to leave her parents provided material and emotional support. There was no involvement from the authorities, and Cynthia never had to disclose her abuse. As she explains:

> "I was involved with a youth group at that point, and one of the youth group leaders seem to realize something was not right. And then one day, we were playing volleyball and my sleeves fell back and she saw our cuts and that. Yeah, and um, yeah, says she basically said, 'did we want to live with her?'
>
> "And we went, 'Yep.' But there's no way my parents would allow it. So, she basically went and told my parents she was taking us. Yeah, so we went and moved in with her sort of towards the end of that would have been the year we were 18, the year after high school."

This highlights the importance of the child knowing that there is a safe place to go where they will be cared for, and that protection is not conditional on disclosing the abuse.

The unbelievable truth

Even in a post #Me Too movement world, relatively straightforward stories of abuse are still often met with disbelief. Yet, the women's abusive experiences were frequently bizarre and extreme – the truth was often unbelievable. Crystal explains:

> "I know I was labelled as a liar. I know I was labelled as wicked… perhaps it was because I talked about things that other people couldn't accept as being reality. So, therefore, I must be lying. It is like my family treat me now…. my own children – children that I have carried and birthed – I am a liar. You know, if they can do that now with all the knowledge and understanding they have, why wouldn't people back then do the same thing?"

Simone recounts being ritualistically abused by a teacher at her school during year eight when she was twelve. She describes her experience as unbelievable.

> "He was certainly very bright. He threw pretty much every form of programming at me that he could, including hypnosis. He had the ritual thing happening. He had the cultish elements like, 'I have a direct line to God.' Umm, he used religious dogma. He used indoctrination techniques. He used punishment and reward techniques. He threw in… he had a sadistic bent very much so. When I write it out in dot points – which one of my parts tends to do that for me - I can sort of hand it over to people in a really detached way and look at my struggle to… it is kind of like watching a 60 Minutes episode where it is so far removed from reality that you just can't actually imagine it. You know, yeah. In terms of people believing it. No, No."

When the teacher began to develop a close relationship with Simone, another girl who he abused tried to warn her about the teacher. Simone feels it is unlikely that she or any other survivors would come forward as they would not be believed either:

> "The trauma-bonding issues are just phenomenal. It is one thing to sit in the room and allow people to call him my abuser, and it is entirely different thing to even consider taking that to the police. If someone else came forward, I would probably come forward in support of them. But I really can't see that happening. I really can't. I think they wouldn't have been believed. I think they would have been shut down and not believed... He was just that well-liked and that respected."

On a more optimistic note, some women felt confident that the response to disclosures would be more supportive these days. For example, Jacqueline expressed:

> "Back then it was the eighties. What would people in the public think if they heard that? They would assume I was a tattle-tale, a storyteller, you know. Like these days, people would be straight on it and reporting it, but back then the whole... it was a lot easier to blame the child than it was to address those issues."

The apparently normal family

Many of the women independently described how the family presented themselves as upstanding members of the community to the outside world despite the marked family dysfunction behind closed doors.

> "We were a white-collar family and everything was behind closed doors… At parent-teacher meetings, my parents would be the smiling, perfect parents." – Kylie

> "It's all about what the public think. It doesn't matter what happens inside those walls, but as soon as the public can see you… cos to my parents that's what mattered is what others thought of us… Not so much perfect, but normal. Whatever a person deems to be normal." - Jacqueline

> "My father was the patriarch. The head of the house. A good and wonderful person and could do no wrong in the eyes of others. – Crystal

> "Definitely, there was one face for… when you were out in public. It's all show – one face to the world and completely different behind closed doors… my dad would go around saying how perfect he is. He believes he is the perfect person, the perfect parent, the perfect everything. They believe… they would never admit to anything not having been right." – Naomi

> "My parents were pillars of the community." – Cynthia

This facade persisted into the women's adult lives. For example, Carol explains:

> "Mum thinks I've come in here for depression, and she says, 'Well why are you depressed?'
>
> I said, 'Well, we had a bit of a dysfunctional family when we were younger.'
>
> She said, 'No, we didn't. We were normal.'

The women all doubted their childhood memories of abuse. It seems plausible that the stark difference between their parents' public persona and their abusive behaviours behind closed doors made it much more difficult to reconcile the reality of their situation. This, in turn, is likely to have reinforced their dissociative structures.

Gaslighting: jet fuel for dissociation

Gaslighting is a form of emotional abuse where the perpetrator makes the victim question their sanity, perception of reality, and memories. The result is that the victim becomes confused, anxious, and unable to trust themselves. Gaslighting appears to be an active ingredient in dissociation as it is specifically designed to deny the objective lived experience while creating the perpetrator's desired narrative and reinforcing their position of power. Naomi's experience with her mother is consistent with gaslighting. She recounts:

> "I doubt myself so much because my mother always said to me, 'It's not real. It didn't happen. Something is wrong with you.' She always said that to me when things happened. So, I learned to really doubt my own experience.

> "I think we… one of the siblings I think…and we all were saying we remember this, and we all had exactly the same details… we were all fitting with what we were remembering, and my mother said to us… 'We all had a vivid imagination.' And that was all of us together… saying the same thing…. Other times she would say, 'You are crazy,' and that kind of thing. 'It's not real. It didn't happen. Something is wrong with you.'… And then I go back to, 'I must be making it up.' Yeah, because it's too hard to comprehend. It's nothing that makes any sense.

Kylie's mother would also reframe her experience in a way that seemed to go beyond straightforward denial. In relation to her uncle's sexual abuse, her mother would say, "He didn't do that. It's all in your head. It's all in your head. You're making it up. How dare you make that up?" Kylie's family physician picked up something wasn't right with her and gave her a questionnaire that confirmed Kylie's clinical depression. Kylie said, "Oh, okay, but I've felt this way forever." She spoke with her mother about this and the fact she'd always felt this way. This is her mother's reaction:

> "My mother said, 'How dare you! You had a really, really, happy childhood, how dare you go to a GP and tell stories'…

> and then the next day she rang me and said I didn't have it. I didn't join the dots about my family, [my doctor] did.
>
> "I also understand that one of the criteria with DID is that you hide it so well. You learn to hide it as your family teaches you to hide it."

Rosemary's parents would call her crazy and threaten to put her in a notorious mental institution:

> "They were always going to threaten to put me [there]. 'You know what the issue is – you're crazy, you need to go there.'"

Rosemary's parents had some awareness that the neighbour she stayed with before school was sexually abusing her. Rosemary also, "acknowledged a little bit", to the neighbour's wife, who would sometimes say, "Don't go into his room, then." Rosemary explains:

> "I did tell my mum… sometimes she would say, 'Don't go next door.'

Rosemary did follow her mother's advice and no longer went next door. However, this changed when Rosemary's mother needed the neighbours to provide childcare for Rosemary again. Her mother would ask, "Why don't you want to go over there?", or say, "You're making up stories," as if her mother either didn't know or remember about the abuse about which Rosemary had already told her.

Gillian explains how her father rescripted the story of her suicide attempt at age 13 as soon as he arrived at the hospital. She believed he knew his version of the story was "delusional". Gillian explains:

> "Dad was there and was already saying they drugged her at school, wrong crowd, get her out of the school, stuff like that… That's just what everyone was told. And then I got taken out of school."

The impact of gaslighting seems pervasive, leading to chronic self-doubt about the abuse. For example, it seems that the narrative expressed by Crystal's parents has become firmly embedded in her own:

> "There are times that I still can't come to terms with I am a survivor. I am just a liar that gives outrageous stories and to behave in ways that otherwise wouldn't be acceptable or reasonable."

The best-kept secret: a secret from themselves

Ironically, the belief that recovered memories of abuse are false, and people with DID are delusional, or deliberately lying for attention or other gains, appears most prevalent amongst those with DID. People with DID find it extremely difficult to trust their memories, even those that are objectively verified. This makes sense when we consider that the very impetus of the fragmentation of the personality is to hide the horrific, unknowable, and inescapable truth from the self. The scepticism about DID is encapsulated well in this quote from Tracey, who had studied psychology:

> "I mean I wasn't a believer in DID either, so. That's what we were taught at university – DID doesn't even exist – it's a load of garbage."

Many women struggled with their DID diagnosis, and what accepting it entailed. Crystal was also wary of false memories. She explained:

> "[My therapist] talked about things that happened in my childhood that I don't trust at all. I am terrified of. For lots of reasons. One of them is that my whole family deny my father has ever, or could ever, have done anything inappropriate to anyone. Another is because False Memory Syndrome was becoming a big thing. So, I wondered if he'd implanted suggestions that I ran with because it created a pleasant space between us as therapist or client. I don't know. One is that I don't remember what I said to him. I don't know what it is. I wish I could get hold of his notes, I wish I could find out.
>
> "There are whole chunks of my life and whole chunks of my memory and thought that are dominated by Bartholomew – I refer to this being that lives inside of me called Bartholomew – who is like an image of my father who won't allow me to remember lots of things."

Later in the interview, Crystal switched to a non-verbal personality that lives in the mirror and wrote, backwards in mirror image, an account of an abusive episode. After the interview, Crystal retracted the written statement. She apologised for wasting our time and described herself as "a drama queen, self-seeking, narcissistic bitch," advising us that her non-verbal personality was "a pathological liar and nothing she says is true." Despite the years of therapy, there were strong divisions between the parts that accepted the abuse was real and those that did not.

Kylie describes being in denial, despite her memories:

> "There is a lot in my childhood… and the things that I do remember seem so surreal like they happened to someone else, so I don't want them to be me and don't accept DID, and then I go round in circles.
>
> "I'm still in denial about [DID]. I spoke with the nurse manager yesterday, and she said that I am still in denial with what I went through."

Gillian discusses how difficult it was for her to accept the abuse and the dissociation:

> "[My therapist] eventually warmed to the idea of what dissociation was at this end of the scale. Because it took him a while to get me to accept the abuse full stop. And then it was accepting the dissociation. And then it was accepting the parts. And I just kept saying "No, no, no! Bull****, bull****! I don't have that!"
>
> "One day we taped it on a similar thing to that [points to my audio recorder] on a mini-cassette and taped a couple of

> sessions. And umm, yeah. I listened to them back and was like 'aaggghhh'. But it took a fair few years, probably eight... and I went, 'Oh my God, this is me or me's' [me plural]. And no wonder – this is why! Then you'd be really upset as that meant everything that happened was true. Because there was still a part that was saying 'Nothing happened.'"

Tracey, who was taught DID was "garbage" at university, understandably found it difficult to accept the information her therapist was advising she had relayed to him during previous sessions:

> "He started telling us things that I can gather now, now that I can reflect on it, telling us that the father had done things to us and the mother had done things to us. And we told him he was a big, fat liar, and we didn't want to see him ever again. But we didn't know we had parts. So, and they didn't tell us anything about that, so we didn't trust him anymore telling us these stories... I would struggle as I couldn't remember saying it. So, it was like are you telling me lies? Why are you lying to me? Why would I make up those things about people and say nasty things about people? I wouldn't do that."

Naomi describes her struggle accepting that the abuse occurred:

> "I don't want to believe those things happened. I don't want to accept those things happened. I don't want it to be real, but then why the hell would you make it up? Like you wouldn't do this to yourself. What else explains what is

> going on? I don't know. but… but [sighs] when I have alters who really strongly know what happened and know that what happened was wrong, there is a lot of conflict in there about that sort of stuff."

Cynthia explains how confronting it was to be presented with medical information that was consistent with her abuse and how she'd prefer to be wrong:

> "We had a colonoscopy which came back normal except that we've got a lot of scarring inside from damage they think probably growing up… it was terrifying because it meant that maybe I wasn't making it all up. Because there was always this hope that maybe your head is just really screwed."

These women's accounts show how difficult it is to accept that any abuse occurred despite years of therapy discussing their traumatic histories. Furthermore, some women remained resistant to the idea they had been abused by family members and others, even when there was compelling evidence to indicate the abuse had occurred. Their reluctance to accept their abuse is a stark contrast to the accusatory view that robust, false memories of sexual abuse can occur if the therapist merely raises the possibility with the client that they were abused as a child. Further, scientific studies have debunked this false memory claim repeatedly (Kate, et al., 2020; Crook, 2019; Dalenburg, et al., 2012).

Conclusion

The accounts of these women suggest that it is not only extremely difficult but potentially dangerous for children living in situations where there is severe and chronic abuse to disclose this or seek safety. After listening to their stories, it is understandable that none of these women were able to escape from their abusive lives. To do so, they had to realise the abuse was wrong and adults in authority are trustworthy, which is incredibly difficult to do when those supposed to love and protect them are actively hurting them or allowing this to occur. The women had to believe they were worthy of saving, the abuse was not their fault, or they were not somehow complicit. They needed to cast aside their innate loyalty to their parents. Even if these conditions existed, they would have needed trusted adults to notice and effectively intervene, including providing protection and a safe place to live. Yet, this rarely happened. For all but one of the women, their abuse went undetected or unaddressed despite the red flags. Most feared their abuse was literally unbelievable, so there was no point in trying to disclose it. Indeed, these women had a lifelong struggle believing it themselves due to the extreme and often bizarre nature of the abuse and their dissociative structures to hide these unknowable secrets from themselves.

The women's difficulty in believing and accepting their abusive histories appears to be compounded by two factors. Firstly, gaslighting. Parents invalidated their child's reality and told them they were crazy, and it didn't happen. Secondly, all of the women reported that their parents presented as normal to the outside world, even as upstanding members of the community. Yet, behind closed doors, their parents were abusive and dysfunctional. This juxtaposition would make it difficult for the women, and potentially others, to accept the reality of their abuse.

It is difficult to imagine a set of circumstances that would have enabled these women to disclose their abuse during childhood. However, there was a somewhat hopeful sentiment expressed by many of the women who believed that, with greater societal awareness of childhood abuse and mental health issues, children being abused today were more likely to be believed and supported. Being unable to disclose their abuse was, in itself, another aspect of the trauma they endured.

These women's stories highlight the importance of accepting that incest, organized abuse, and sadistic abuse do occur, and that children experiencing this maltreatment will have multiple barriers preventing them disclosing their abuse. Family members, teachers, those in health and social welfare, the police, community members, and society more generally, can all play a role. People should be aware of, and attuned to, the red flags that are indicative of abuse. When these are noticed, steps should be taken to make the child feel safe, help them understand it is not their fault and they are not in trouble, and that they will be believed and protected. Child protection and legal systems must be trauma-informed, including having a robust understanding of what childhood dissociation looks like and the multiple barriers to disclosing abuse.

These women bravely shared their stories in the hope that at least one child could be saved from a fate such as theirs. My wish is that their stories are heard by many and change minds, policies, and practices. The rich insights they have given us about the formidable barriers to disclosing abuse and finding protection provide us with valuable knowledge that can inform strategies that assist children living in abusive situations navigate their way to a safer future.

REFERENCES

Brand, B. L., McNary, S. W., Myrick, A. C., Classen, C. C., Lanius, R., Loewenstein, R. J.,

Pain, C., & Putnam, F. W. 2013. A longitudinal naturalistic study of patients with dissociative disorders treated by community clinicians. Psychological Trauma: Theory, Research, Practice, and Policy, 5(4), 301-308. https://doi.org/10.1037/a0027654 0.

Crook, L. S., & McEwen, L. E. 2019. Deconstructing the lost in the mall study. Journal of Child Custody, 16(1), 7-19. https://doi.org/10.1080/15379418.2019.1601603.

Dalenberg, C. J., Brand, B. L., Gleaves, D. H., Dorahy, M. J., Loewenstein, R. J., Cardeña, E., Frewen, P. A., Carlson, E. B., & Spiegel, D. 2012. Evaluation of the evidence for the trauma and fantasy models of dissociation. Psychological bulletin, 138(3), 550-588.

Herman, J. L. 1992. Trauma and Recovery: the aftermath of violence - from domestic abuse to political terror. Basic Books.

Kate, M.-A., Jamieson, G., & Middleton, W. 2021. Childhood Sexual, Emotional, and Physical Abuse as Predictors of Dissociation in Adulthood. Journal of Child Sexual Abuse, 1-24.

Kate, M.-A., Hopwood, T., & Jamieson, G. 2020. The prevalence of Dissociative Disorders and dissociative experiences in college populations: a meta-analysis of 98 studies. Journal of Trauma & Dissociation, 21(1), 16-61. https://doi.org/10.1080/15299732.2019.1647915

Middleton, W. & Butler, J. 1998. Dissociative identity disorder: an Australian series. The Australian and New Zealand Journal of Psychiatry, 32(6), 794-804.

Spiegel, D., Loewenstein, R. J., Lewis-Fernández, R., Sar, V., Simeon, D., Vermetten, E., Cardeña's, E., & Dell, P. F. 2011. Dissociative disorders in DSM-5. Depression and Anxiety, 28(12), 1119. https://doi.org/10.1002/da.20920

Zamir, O., Szepsenwol, O., Englund, M. M., & Simpson, J. A. 2018. The role of dissociation in revictimization across the lifespan: A 32-year prospective study. Child Abuse & Neglect, 79, 144-153. https://doi.org/10.1016/j.chiabu.2018.02.001

Diet Culture and the Double Bind

by Annie Goldsmith, R.D.,
including a clinical interview with Cassie[6]

The double-bind is an oft-cited factor in the formation of complex trauma. Put simply, a double bind is a situation in which a person is stuck between two choices, both of which result in negative consequences (Erickson and Rossi, 2011; Watzlawick, 1963). It is a "no win" situation. In the context of complex trauma the options the person has are often both perceived to be life threatening (Sar and Ozturk, 2008). This situation might present as a child who is experiencing abuse from their primary caregiver; the double bind for the child is that the very person they depend on for meeting basic survival needs is also terrifying and a source of pain (Herman, 1992). Judith Herman refers to this double bind as a form of betrayal trauma: "The child faces a formidable developmental task: to find a way to form primary attachments to caretakers who are either dangerous or negligent. She must find a way to develop a sense of basic trust and safety with caretakers who are untrustworthy or unsafe" (Herman, 1992). It is under these conditions that dissociation may become a primary survival strategy. Laurie Kahn (2006) writes: "dissociation allows the traumatized individual to continue functioning in these double bind relationships without having to notice the inherent contradictions."

[6] Cassie provided consent to include her interview in this chapter. She herself requested her name be used as a co-author to this chapter. She also reviewed the final draft of this chapter for lived experience sensitivity.

In this chapter, a case will be made for how diet culture puts people (especially people who live in larger bodies) into a double bind. We also propose that this, in turn, leads to the formation of complex trauma. We posit that a weight-inclusive, social-justice-informed approach to medical and mental health care is imperative to support whole-person healing.

Diet Culture, Fatphobia and Weight Stigma: A Brief Overview

What exactly is Diet Culture? While there is no one official definition, I will cite the description put forth by Ragen Chastain, a well known advocate in the anti-diet space. She lists the following as characteristics that define Diet Culture (Chastain, 2022):

- Diet Culture conflates size and health, pathologizing some body sizes (namely larger ones);
- Diet Culture encourages following external rules about what, when, and how much to eat;
- Diet Culture suggests that people are more or less good/moral/worthy based on body size;
- Diet Culture creates thin privilege, which makes thinness a gatekeeper for jobs, benefits, comfort, and accommodation;
- Diet Culture suggests movement as a punishment for, or prevention of, being fat, rather than for fun or personal goals; and
- Diet Culture views fat people as less valuable and more risk-able.

In sum, Diet Culture pathologizes fatness and creates consequences for those who do not meet society's standards of thinness (Laraia, 2021). Further, thinness does not represent health long-term, nor does a high body mass index predict mortality in the elderly (Grabowski and Ellis,

2001). Additionally, Diet Culture's negative impact intensifies for those who hold additional intersecting marginalized identities, such as BIPOC, LGBTQ+, disabled and/or neurodiversity – this will be further addressed and explored later in this chapter.

Critics of this conception of Diet Culture argue that pathologizing fatness has nothing to do with assigning value or morality to body size, and everything to do with health. They name the well-documented association between higher body weight and disease incidence (Lassale, et al., 2018) as evidence that increased fatness causes illness. Following that premise, body size itself is a disease that must be "cured."

The idea that fatness is an independent causal risk factor for disease is so ingrained into the cultural zeitgeist that the premise is rarely questioned. The history of how we got here as a society is not well publicized, but important to know if one is to take a critical view of these issues. And we *should* take a critical view, because these beliefs are the foundation upon which modern medical care rests.

While it is outside the scope of this chapter to take a deep dive into this history, the works of Christy Harrison (2019), Dr. Sabrina Strings (2019) and Lucy Aphramor and Dr. Lindo Bacon (2014) are excellent resources for further reading. They reference the Body Mass Index (BMI), an equation with which modern western medicine currently evaluates whether someone is medically at risk due to their weight. A brief overview reveals that the BMI was invented by Adolph Quetelet, a Belgian astronomer and statistician in the 19th century. He intended for the value to assess averages on a population level, and never intended for the value to be applied to individuals (Nuttall, 2015).

In the 1970's, a researcher named Ancel Keys revived Quetelet's index and called it the Body Mass Index, or BMI (ibid). His position was that the BMI was not a perfect tool, but that it more closely predicted a person's body fat percent than the other available assessment tools at doctor visits. Keys was somewhat of a celebrity scientist in his day, and it was not long before BMI became well known and regarded as a proxy for fatness – and by extension, health.

Absent from the BMI's rise to fame is a shred of peer-reviewed evidence that it can be reliably used as a diagnostic predictor at the individual level. On the contrary, research indicates that anywhere from 30-50% of higher weight people are considered what is called "metabolically healthy obese" (in other words, fat and healthy), while around 25% of smaller-bodied people are considered "metabolically unhealthy normal weight" (Mathew 2016). These are large swaths of the population whose health status is miscategorized if BMI is the primary diagnostic tool upon which we are relying.

If the BMI is such a poor predictor of health for individuals, and has never been verified in the scientific literature as a valid diagnostic tool, why have we adopted it so completely into our standard medical practice? Again, that history is long and complicated. It is suggested that the roots of anti-fatness lie not in medical truth, but rather racism, classism, capitalism, and misogyny (Harrison, 2019; Strings, 2019; and Bacon & Aphramor, 2014). Anti-fatness was woven into the fabric of western culture long before the medical community got on board. But the sanctioning of anti-fat sentiment by the medical community certainly took things to a whole new level. By the time obesity was officially classified as a disease by the American Medical Association (AMA) in 2013, very few people thought to question the decision. Yet interestingly, in declaring obesity a disease, the AMA was going against the 2012 recommendation of the Council on Science and Public Health - the very committee it had assigned to investigate the issue. The Council concluded in its report that not enough evidence exists to accurately define obesity (as BMI is a poor diagnostic tool) or categorize it as a disease. Ultimately, they recommended against adopting the resolution (AMA Report of the Council on Science and Public Health, 2012).

While society at large tends to erroneously conflate population level trends with applicability to the individual, it is worth addressing that yes, on a population level higher weight is associated with poorer health (Lassale 2018). It is easy to fall into the trap of assuming causality from association, especially when the data supports a belief one already holds. This is known as confirmation bias – the tendency to interpret new evidence as confirmation of one's existing beliefs or theories. The scientific method attempts to ward off the pitfalls of confirmation bias by reminding us that "correlation does not equal causation" – or that just because two things tend to happen together does not mean that one necessarily *causes* the other. While this distinction may seem like semantics, it has huge implications for patient care, because the cause of illness is what we target for treatment. If we assume body size is the cause of illness, reduction of body size in form of dieting or surgery becomes the recommended treatment. As we will explore further, this has massive, often devastating implications for larger-bodied people.

If we hypothesize that higher weight does not *cause* poor health, why might we see this association? While some potential confounding variables are sometimes factored into statistical analyses in studies on weight and health (education, smoking, diet, physical activity), it is worth noting that multiple significant and likely contributors to this disparity are virtually always left out. The one that will be focused on for the remainder of this chapter is a person's experience of weight bias and stigma on an institutional, interpersonal, and/or intrapersonal level (Tovar 2017; Bacon & Aphramor, 2011). There is a growing understanding and body of research that tells us that people who live in larger bodies are routinely subjected to weight-based discrimination, bias, and stigma across cultural and interpersonal venues. This discrimination has a measurable impact on physical health through multiple paths.

One well-documented way in which weight stigma impacts health outcomes is related to the literal health care services higher weight patients receive (Lee & Pause, 2016; Bacon & Aphramor, 2011; and Puhl, 2010).[7] Many medical providers hold fatphobic attitudes and both explicit

---

[7] It is important to note that Puhl's full body of work, while making an explicit case for reducing societal weight stigma, also contains implicit fatphobia. Puhl is Deputy Director at UConn's Rudd Center for Food Policy and Obesity, an organization that posits, and is aligned with other organizations that posit, that "obesity" is a disease. These organizations advocate for kinder treatment of fat people, while also supporting and promoting weight loss interventions. Absent from Puhl's work is any commentary on how the conception of "obesity" itself is flawed and stigmatizing. Ragen Chastain commented on Puhl's work: "her point of view comes from a eugenics position - which is to say that she claims that she doesn't want to stigmatize fat people, but still supports the idea that we should be eradicated/prevented."

and implicit weight bias, which directly impacts patient care. Research shows that clinicians spend less time with fat patients, perform fewer preventative and diagnostic tests, and report being frustrated by their patients when they fail to lose weight, despite the fact there is no evidence that long term significant weight loss is possible for the majority of the population (Lee & Pause, 2016). It is no surprise to learn that research also shows that higher-weight patients routinely engage in health care avoidance; they are acutely aware of the of the discrimination they will likely encounter which deters them from bothering to seek care, and/or they cannot bear the shame of yet one more lecture from a doctor about the failure that is their body (ibid). Because of this, higher weight patients often don't present for medical care with symptoms until they are in later stages of disease progression and more likely to have a poor outcome. Or, when they do present with symptoms they are "diagnosed as fat" and diagnostic testing is denied, while the symptoms are blamed on the patient's size and therefore the patient themselves.

Another way that weight stigma impacts health is related to the stress that holding a marginalized identity and facing discrimination has on the body. While it is important to name that the histories regarding anti-blackness and anti-fatness are distinct[8], it is worth considering that holding these marginalized identities may have commonalities when it comes to health. Public health research paints a compelling picture about the links between experiencing race-based oppression and disease risk. These elevated risks hold when BMI is controlled for in studies. Puhl (2010) writes

---

[8] Sabrina Strings (2019) makes a compelling case that anti-fatness is rooted in racist origins.

that "these findings have led researchers to conclude that racism may act as a psychosocial stressor that elevates cardiovascular responses and in turn impairs health" (p. 1023). Further research provides a framework for understanding the physiological mechanisms that may be responsible for race-based health disparities, namely chronic stress that forces the body into a perpetual sympathetic response of the autonomic nervous system (Mays, et al., 2007). The impact of this stress is referred to in the literature as *allostatic load*, which is defined as the adverse adaptation of multiple physiological systems in response to chronic stressors (Vadiveloo & Mattei, 2017). There is evidence to suggest that this same dysregulatory process may be occurring in people who have perceived experiences of weight-based discrimination and internalized weight bias. Vadiveloo and Mattei (2017) found that the 10-year risk of high allostatic load was *doubled* in those who had experienced perceived weight discrimination.

The situation becomes even more dire for those who experience the cumulative impact of oppression based on multiple aspects of their identity. This is a concept known as *intersectionality*, a term coined by Columbia Law School professor Kimberlé Crenshaw. Crenshaw was the first to write about how those who hold multiple marginalized identities – for example female AND black – experience unique and particularly insidious forms of discrimination and erasure compared with those who hold only one marginalized identity (Crenshaw 1989). When it comes to issues of weight, folks who are fat *and* black, and/or trans, and/or disabled will encounter greater discrimination than fat, white, cis, able-bodied folks due to their additional lack of privileges in areas additional to body size. From this we can extrapolate that they are also at greater risk for health disparities (Gomez, 2019). Black and Hispanic people tend to have higher BMIs then their white counterparts, in part because BMI standards are based on a sample of adults living in Britain in the 1980's – hardly representative of black and Hispanic genetic heritage (CDC, 2022; Harrison, 2019; Strings, 2019; and Bacon & Aphramor, 2014). Yet, in a cruel irony, they are likely to have *body size* be identified as the cause of their health problems, which is a strikingly dystopian form of gaslighting by the western medical system.

Taking all of this into account, one may start to speculate on how much fatness itself is responsible for poor health outcomes in higher-weight people, versus the impacts of stigma and discrimination. For those interested in further reading, the works of Peter Muennig (2008) provide additional evidence and arguments in support of this perspective.

The Double Binds

In the next section of this chapter, I will build the case that diet culture creates a no-win situation in which a person may be caught between two survival threats: lack of biological safety though malnourishment, and lack of relational and physical safety through social and/or institutional rejection.

Weight loss as a threat to survival

We must first unpack why intentional weight loss attempts are perceived, if not always cognitively, then somatically, as a threat to survival. This requires further challenging of culturally accepted norms around how we understand the concepts of optimal nutrition and weight and the premises they are built upon historically. Recall the shaky foundation upon which BMI was established as standard medical practice? There is more to that history and how the BMI cutoffs were established.

In current practice, the BMI categories are as follows: <18.5 kg/m^2 = underweight; 19-25 kg/m^2 = normal weight; 25-30 kg/m^2 = overweight; >30-35 kg/m^2 = obese. Nuttall (2015) outlines how the BMI categories were initially established by the World Health Organization (WHO) in 1995 based on research conducted by Rosenbaum, et al. on the adult population in Great Britain in 1980 – hardly a representative sample of human diversity. Their survey looked at population distribution of height and weight and did not link BMI to health measures in any way. Nuttall (2015) goes on to note that this BMI distribution has not even been replicated in other studies! In fact, at the time the US had different, higher BMI cutoffs for overweight based on National Health and Nutrition Examination Survey (NHANES) data that defined overweight as >85th percentile for BMI based on population data – still not linked to health outcomes. Yet, in 1998 the National Institute of Health (NIH) made the decision to shift to the lower cutoffs, ostensibly to "bring [the US] into line with the...WHO guidelines" (Nuttall, 2015). The more sordid part of the story is that many of the people involved in this policy change had financial ties to the weight loss and diet industries and stood to make a hefty profit from the millions of Americans who became "medically overweight" overnight (Harrison 2019).

This history is important to understand because it highlights how BMI cutoffs are based on flimsy, un-replicated, and unsupported research. They are, for all intents and purposes, largely arbitrary. To the more cynical among us, these cutoffs may seem to be set intentionally low to create a market for the weight loss industry and justification for insurance companies to cover all manner of weight loss surgeries and drugs. Additionally and paradoxically, by making "obesity" a medical diagnosis, insurance companies could also then consider it a pre-existing condition on the basis of which they could deny coverage. Fat activist Ragen Chastain speaks to this experience: "for over a decade I was unable to secure health insurance as a self-employed person because insurers were allowed to consider my existence a pre-existing condition that rendered me ineligible for coverage and affordable care" (2022).

Weight is a largely heritable trait, and the best research we have to date estimates that weight is about 65% determined by genetics (Speakman, 2011). Set point theory posits that each individual human body has a weight and body fat percent range that it is biologically pre-disposed (ibid). Size diversity, just like diversity among virtually all other human physical characteristics, is a normal and expected part of human diversity. Upon consideration, the idea that body size would be the *one* physical characteristic for which all humans should exist in a narrow range defies our understanding of the natural world.

Conventional wisdom tells us weight loss is straightforward: a simple calculation of energy in versus energy out, and theoretically easy to achieve. Yet, when we look at the actual data on studies of weight loss interventions, we see a very consistent pattern that Dietitian and researcher Fiona Willer has dubbed "the Nike swoop of weight regain" (Nordmo, et al., 2019; Bacon and Aphramor, 2011; Stunkard and McLaren-

Hume, 1959). Regardless of the type of diet, study participants on average lose 5-15% of their body weight at the 6-month mark, and then slowly re-gain it over the next 2-5 years (Nordmo et al 2019). No well-designed study to date has demonstrated any weight loss interventions that result in significant weight loss that is maintained 5 years post-intervention.

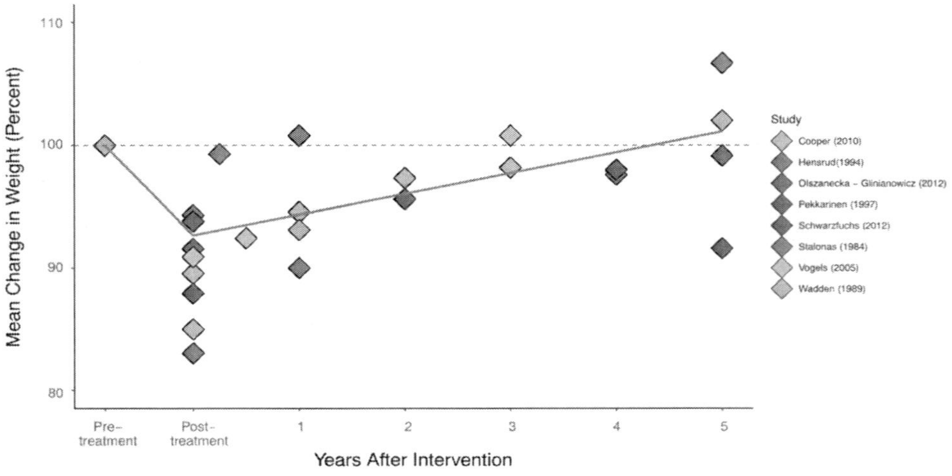

The "Nike Swoop" of Weight Regain
(Nordmo, 2019)

Furthermore, research also suggests that one third to two thirds of dieters will regain more weight than they lost and end up at a higher weight than they started (Mann et al 2007). Dieting may in fact be exacerbating fatness, the very thing it endeavors to eradicate. Advocate Ragen Chastain is a "fat activist" in the movement proudly reclaiming *fat* as part of the vital knowledge of one's own body and lived experience (Matacin and Simone, 2019; Sima, 2016; Cooper, 2013). She states: "while there is nothing wrong with being fat or getting fatter, there is something wrong with an intervention that has the opposite of the intended effect the majority of the time and is prescribed to up to 70% of the population. When we talk about an obesity epidemic, what we may actually have is a dieting epidemic" (Chastain, 2022).

Some dieters are aware of the abysmal "success" rates of their endeavors but hope they will be in the lucky 2-5% who seem to be able to lose weight and keep it off. Others don't know that weight regain is a scientifically predicted outcome; they simply believe they are failures. However, all dieters must attempt to take in less energy than they expend – which will be less and less over time as the body fights to resist catabolizing itself (Keys, 1944). One of the ways the human body has learned to adapt to the threat posed by starvation is by slowing metabolic rate in response to an ongoing caloric deficit. Ancel Keys' seminal Minnesota Starvation experiment, in which participants were put on "semistarvation" diets of approximately 1600 kilocalories/day, revealed that resting energy expenditure decreased by about 40%/day under these starvation conditions (Manfred, et al., 2015). When we look at doubly labeled water studies, which can objectively measure the resting energy expenditure of a person in a day, we find that cis men on average need around 3500 kcal/day, while cis women need around 2600 kcal/day to maintain energy balance and meet basic physiological needs (Boushey, et al., 2017). Yet, turn to the nearest women's magazine, fad diet, or medically supervised diet, and you will find that caloric intake recommendations range anywhere from 500-1500 kcal/day to induce weight loss. No wonder rates of "successful" weight loss are so low.

This is not a failure of the dieter; *it is a triumph of the body*. It is survival. After all, how can the body know that less food is being consumed intentionally, versus reflecting food scarcity in the environment? Modern day humans are the descendants of ancestors who survived millennia of cycles of famine and food scarcity. If our bodies had not learned how to adapt and build resiliency to survive the threat of famine, we likely would not have survived as a species.

Can we classify dieting as trauma? Trauma involves engagement of the fight/flight/freeze response of the autonomic nervous system (Porges, 2017). This system is engaged when a person detects a threat to physical safety (ibid). The neuroscientist Dr. Stephen Porges has coined the term *neuroception* to describe the process by which neural circuits distinguish whether situations or people are safe, dangerous, or life-threatening (2017). Even if a person is consciously choosing to restrict their food intake, the nervous system is likely detecting threat at a subconscious level and responding accordingly. The Keys starvation experiment provides good support for the notion that a significant energy deficit induces psychological changes consistent with trauma. Findings showed that the starved participants, who in part were chosen for the study because they were in very good mental health, developed what the researchers called "semi-starvation neurosis" in the context of caloric restriction (Glucksman and Hirsch, 1968; Schiele and Brožek, 1948). This neurosis was characterized by hypochondriasis, depression, and hysteria as measured by the Minnesota Multiphasic Personality Inventory (MMPI) (Laessle, 1988). Two of the participants failed to complete the study and were hospitalized because of "severe decompensation and 'pre-psychotic' symptoms" (Eckert, 2018). Fascinatingly, in the re-feeding phase of the study, the men's improvement in depression scores (measured using the

MMPI) correlated with the increase in number of calories they received (ibid).

Dietitians in the eating disorder field are heartbreakingly familiar with the risks that malnutrition poses to the safety of the human body. According to the National Eating Disorder Association, Anorexia Nervosa has a higher mortality rate than any other mental illness (when including addiction as mental illness, it is second after opiate overdose). Many of us have worked with patients whose nutrition status has necessitated medically supervised inpatient re-feeding to avoid complications such as electrolyte abnormalities, hypoglycemia, and cardiac arrest. Sadly, many of us see clients die from their illness. To be clear, these medical complications occur in people of *all* body sizes, from very thin to super fat. No matter the body size, starvation is a threat to survival. While dieting *may* occur on a less extreme scale than a diagnosed eating disorder, it nonetheless involves subjecting the body to a chronic starvation state which is perceived by the body as life-threatening.

Staying fat as a threat to survival

Given the realities of dieting and weight loss, it stands to reason that when confronted with this data higher-weight folks might easily let go of the futile pursuit of weight loss and focus instead on life-enhancing self-care behaviors that include nourishing the body well. However, I have observed in my clinical experience as a weight-inclusive dietitian that this is not necessarily the case. Even when clients fully cognitively grasp the science and social context of dieting and diet culture, fear around accepting their larger body often provides a significant barrier to normative eating. Given our cultural climate, that fear is valid, justified, and rooted in a trauma response.

We live in a fatphobic society. Much evidence for that has been laid out in the earlier sections of this chapter (though if you need academic evidence to know that we live in a society that discriminates based on weight, you are not paying attention). There are many, many ways that people living in fat bodies experience discrimination – some are institutional, some are cultural, some are blatant and some microaggressions. For larger-bodied people, this discrimination often begins in childhood and is reinforced within the family system, medical system, and society at large. Courtois and Ford (2013) write: "Complex traumatic stressors involve relational/familial and interpersonal forms of traumatization and exposure that are often chronic and include threats to the integrity of the self, to personal development, and to the ability to relate to others in healthy ways…. Additionally, complex trauma may be based on and associated with the victim's very identity, including such immutable characteristics as a race, ethnicity, skin color, gender, genetic and medical conditions and physical limitations" (p.10). I would argue body size be added to this list.

Aubrey Gordon (2020) goes into great detail about the ways fat people experience the trauma of fatphobia in her book "What We Don't Talk About When We Talk About Fat". She describes how on airplanes fat people are bullied, ridiculed, and even kicked off flights because of their size. Most brick-and-mortar stores don't carry plus size clothes (sizes 16-28) and almost none carry extended sizes (30 plus); many fat people can only find clothes that fit online, and usually for a much higher price tag than their straight-sized counterparts (ibid). An estimated 70% of women in the US are a size 14 or larger, but plus size options account for only 20% of the marketplace (Ashley, 2020). Almost never do we see a person of size as the lead romantic interest in movies or TV shows. Many built spaces are not made to accommodate larger bodies: theater seats, restaurant booths, and academic lecture hall seating.

All of this sends a message to fat people: *Your bodies do not belong here, and your comfort does not matter.* Gordon (who lives in a fat body) writes in her book that:

> "There is a minefield of abuse reserved for the very fat. I have come to view the world through the prism of that abuse, negotiating my days around reducing it. *Who will shout at me? Which doctors will refuse to see me? Which dates will mock my body? Which strangers will photograph me, make a meme of my skin?* I avoid eye contact with strangers, knowing that our locking eyes are too often misconstrued as an invitation to shout or detail their judgements of my body. I deploy a charm offensive, calming agitated aggressors before they have a chance to unleash their fury. I have learned how to keep abusers at bay alone, knowing that no one else will intervene to support or defend me. I have developed this sad and necessary skill set because, in my soft and certain marrow, I know that the abuse faced by fat people is not understood to warrant a reckoning."

Many fat people engage in dieting or performative wellness behaviors: only ordering salads in social settings, or signing up for boot camp exercise programs, or always turning down dessert in public. These behaviors may continue even when people are aware that their efforts are very unlikely to result in sustained weight loss. We might understand this behavior as a form of *fawning*, a trauma response coined by therapist Pete Walker, characterized by trying to please or appease the person who is the source of the threat, because they are also responsible for taking care of you. If a fat person performs the behavior of dieting and concedes the defectiveness of their body, then they can appease their doctor/spouse/coworkers/family members in attempt to avoid further abuse and rejection and maintain attachment in the relationship(s). But just as in all abusive situations, attempts by the victim to protect themselves by placating the abuser do not work – the abuse happens anyway (Herman, 1992).

And fawning in the form of dieting comes at a life-threatening cost – starvation.

It is my deep hope that the arguments put forth in this chapter will be enough to convey how deeply traumatizing diet culture and weight stigma are to people who are victim to it. Following that, it becomes clear that a weight-inclusive, non-diet approach to treatment for people in ALL bodies is critical to support healing and the *only* ethical treatment framework when it comes to issues of body size.

We as clinicians are critical players in supporting clients' access to healing. If we collude with diet culture, we gatekeep healing and perpetuate harm and abuse. If we offer a framework of weight inclusivity, social justice, and body liberation, we can do much to support our clients in accessing these elements (Matacin and Simone, 2019). In the next section of this chapter, we provide an interview with a client with lived experience in a larger body, and the impact that weight inclusive treatment has had on their recovery journey.

Healing Diet Culture Trauma through Self-Acceptance and Self Love: Cassie's Story[9]

A: Hi, Cassie! How does it feel to have the opportunity to talk about your story and share it with others who can learn from your experience?

C: I am so excited to be able to share my story in the hopes that people may relate to it and realize they can seek support, that they're not alone, and most importantly, I hope they can realize that they are not the problem.

A: I am so grateful for your willingness to share. Let's start at the beginning: tell me what your relationship with food and body was like growing up in your family?

---

[9] Annie Goldsmith as "A" is interviewing, and Cassie as "C" is responding as a person with lived experience.

C: I have an older sister who is a little less than 2 years older than me, and we were completely different in every way. Growing up I was always bigger than her, and it was pretty obvious to see that we were treated differently, too – by our parents, by friends, by a lot of people. In middle school, I started to notice how differently we were treated when it came to food. At home we would have snack boxes with our names on them. My box would have nuts and 100 calorie packs while my sister's had leftover Halloween candy and "fun" snacks. I started to notice that my relationship with food was also different. Whenever I was alone, I found myself going into the pantry and fridge to try and find something that would satisfy me, because meal after meal I was never satisfied. Sometimes a piece of cheese would be enough, or a handful of chocolate chips, but sometimes it would be all of that in one sitting plus ten other things. [I remember] going to a friend's house and getting to have mac and cheese for dinner, which is something that never happened in our family. We pretty much had chicken and veggies every night – the things that society deems "healthy".

(C): It was hard because I observed my parents struggle with their bodies and food, always making comments about how they needed to lose weight or telling themselves *I can't have this* or *I can't have that*, and then telling the same things to me.

I remember a turning point being Thanksgiving of 2012. I woke up late and was making breakfast around 11:30 (we usually eat our holiday meal around 4:00). My Dad came in and asked what I was doing. When

I told him I was making breakfast, he asked me why. He said, "We are going to eat in five hours."

I said, "Okay, but I'm hungry now." I remember being confused about why he would say that.

I made a peanut butter and banana sandwich, and I remember there being comments from both my parents about how much peanut butter I was using and about my eating in general. I remember just breaking down and starting to cry.

My Dad got angry and stormed outside. I didn't understand why he was so mad about a damn sandwich on Thanksgiving! There were so many things that I just didn't understand at that time.

He called me outside 20 minutes later. He told me his own story about eating, and about his relationship with food growing up. He told me that seeing me get bigger and bigger broke his heart every day.

After this conversation, I felt like I had disappointed him and my entire family. I remember thinking that I had to fix myself – only then would my parents be happy, and only then would I be happy.

Then and there, [my Dad and I] agreed to start Weight Watchers together. I had just turned 13, and I was so young that I had to get a doctor's note approving the diet.

This doctor was also a big part of my relationship with my body. I remember she would disapprovingly show me graphs of my weight going up. I remember being so confused, like, *I'm growing! Isn't that what I'm supposed to do?* But she would compare my chart to my sister's and tell me how mine was a straight line up while hers was more gradual. So, I started Weight Watchers. At 13 years old, I was being told what to eat, how to eat, how much to weigh. Being told in 8th grade that you need to lose forty pounds to be considered "normal" definitely fucks with you.

A: Do you remember what it was like to start dieting?

C: At first, I was so excited. I was like, *Finally I'll be a smaller size! Boys will like me! I'll be able to share clothes with my friends!* I remember going around and writing the number of Weight Watchers points with a sharpie on all the food boxes in the house. I remember I lost ten pounds the first week and everyone told me I was so amazing and strong. I did Weight Watchers with my dad for two years. I got to my goal weight, but not because I was following the diet. I had just started dating my first "boyfriend" and I was so nervous about it all the time. When I would sit with him at lunch, I didn't eat. I would text him and talk to him all the time, which distracted me from eating. Everyone was praising me for doing such a great job, but they didn't know I was just starving myself.

I remember coming home the day I got to my goal weight and my sister was sitting with her friends eating pizza. I went to grab a slice and my mom said, "Cassie, you just got to your goal weight. What's going to be better, the taste of the pizza or how great you will feel being in a bikini this summer?"

There were so many mixed emotions there. I was happy because I was finally getting approval from my mom and I needed that validation. I felt like she was finally proud of me. But I also remember just going, *Damn, is this how it's going to be for the rest of my life?* and feeling so stuck.

[That's when] my eating disorder started to get really bad. I was restricting so much that I started to binge whenever I had the chance – to the point that I felt sick. [I was] eating double meals because I had to hide the fact that I had eaten already. It didn't feel physically good, but emotionally, it felt great, like this high and this thrill from eating foods that satisfied me [but without] people not knowing about it. My parents would say [that] I was obviously because my weight was going up. I would suppress my memory of the food that I was binging on to the point that I would convince myself that I wasn't binging and I was eating "on program". It was scary.

A: You would block out knowing about your own eating?

C: Yeah. I would suppress it so much that I genuinely would forget I binged on a box of chocolate the night before. My parents noticed my weight starting to increase and told me that if I wanted to stay on Weight Watchers, I needed to start paying for it myself. My Dad wasn't doing it anymore, which made it easy to lie about following the diet. I lied to everyone, even myself. But at the time it felt like the only thing I could do to survive.

A: What do you think would have happened if you hadn't been performing this dieting behavior for people?

C: I was too scared to think what would happen. I remember going to the dermatologist around that time for bad eczema and they told me to go on the keto diet and my eczema would be healed. This was around the time I was diagnosed with polycystic ovarian syndrome (PCOS), too, and the diet was also prescribed to those with PCOS. I was told that PCOS was my fault due to my weight. I was told that if I didn't get my weight under control and with the PCOS diagnosis, I would never be able to have children. I was 15 years old at the time. It was traumatizing.

I just kept thinking that I was such a failure because of everything that was happening to me as I gained weight. That same year, I also broke my knee playing football on the beach. I twisted my body to catch the ball but didn't turn my leg. The doctors told me the severity of my injury was because of my weight. It messes you up so much to hear that everything is related to your weight. You can't escape your weight, ever. Someone is always bringing it up.

I did keto with my parents, and both of them lost a significant amount of weight. I stayed the same weight. I was still binging. Once again, I felt like such a failure – it was working for everyone else, so why wasn't it working for me? Why couldn't I just harness up enough willpower to not binge? Why couldn't I just stick to the damn diet?

I was suppressing what was going on behind the scenes. I was blacking out during binges. I wasn't even aware of my own eating. I was completely out of tune with my body.

I went to college and my weight kept going up, despite the fact that I was active doing swimming and theater and not binging as much. My parents told me that if I wasn't going to commit to a diet, I needed to find something else to try to address my weight. My mom did some research and found a nutritionist in Charlotte and set up an appointment. I was nervous as I'd never been to a nutritionist or dietitian before.

I went with my mom and dad, and that was the first time I met you. Anytime I had gone to medical appointments with my parents in the past, my game plan had always been *Shut your mouth. Let them talk.* They always had so much to say about me. It hurt to hear the things they thought about me, but it was easier to shut up and listen than to share my thoughts. When you started to talk about "Health at Every Size" (HAES) and not focusing on weight loss, I remember thinking *What the hell is this woman talking about? What the fuck is this?? She is insane!!* It was inconceivable to me that a health professional was saying I didn't have to diet or try to lose weight anymore.

Before I go on, I want to say that I know my parents did everything they did because they thought it was the best thing for me. Their actions contributed to my trauma and my eating disorder, but I also know it's not their fault. I don't resent them. They love me so much, and at the end of the day, all they want is for me to be the happiest and healthiest version of myself.

A: What's coming up for me is that they are also a product of our culture and have their own body and diet culture trauma, and this is really a form of intergenerational trauma.

C: Yes, absolutely. Diet culture is everywhere and most people partake in it some way or another.

A: Let's go back to that first meeting we had. I was introducing you to some ideas that were really new to you! What was that experience like?

C: When we first met and you were telling [me and my parents] about HAES and not focusing on weight loss as a part of treatment, I was so confused! After the meeting, I told my parents that I didn't think I was ready for what you were talking about. I liked what you were saying about focusing on healing my relationship with food, but I wanted to lose a bunch of weight first. This is before I knew that you can't separate those things out. I remember my parents just breathed a sigh of relief and said, "Thank God, because we feel the same way."

I went back to college and found another dietitian who basically told me I was too far gone in my eating disorder for her to help me. It was enough of a shock for me to decide that I needed to commit to another diet – this time paleo. I told myself I was going to lose a hundred pounds, then reach back out to you because I really did want to have a different relationship with food.

I went on the paleo diet, and I was the most unhappy version of myself I have ever been. I lost thirty pounds in a couple months, but I was never so depressed in my entire life. I hated school. I hated being far from home. I hated everything about it.

A: How much do you think your dieting and how you felt about your body impacted that experience?

C: So much! My best friend at that college was so beautiful, and when I was with her I felt like the fat best friend, the designated ugly fat friend of the group. It was so clear to me how I was treated as a plus size human in this world as opposed to how I saw her treated by others.

Like I said earlier, I was so depressed, and one day it hit me that I needed to do what was best for me if I was going to survive – because every day was a struggle to survive. I wanted to be happy more than I wanted anything. I decided to transfer to college in Charlotte, fifteen minutes from my parents. I was determined to focus on my own healing.

That's when I made an appointment with you. I figured I had nothing to lose. I knew what I was doing wasn't working for my mental or physical health. I moved and I got a dog, who couldn't care less how much I weigh. I started seeing you, and then [my HAES therapist] a month later. My life has completely changed since then!

A: Tell me about the process of unlearning and untangling your relationship with diet culture and the ways it has impacted you.

C: At first, I thought, *I still don't know if I believe this*. But I was at such a vulnerable place in my life that I told myself that it didn't matter if I believed it. What I was currently doing was so detrimental to my mental health that I needed to try something radically different.

A: You really hit diet "rock bottom".

C: Yeah, and it was terrifying! As cheesy as it sounds, when you hit rock bottom there's only way to go, so I had to go in with an open mind to try and unlearn all this diet crap. What else was I supposed to do?

At first, there were things you would say that I would be like, *How did I not realize that? How did I not realize that restricting was the reason I was binging? How did I not see it? It's so clear!*

I remember one day craving grapes. I realized I couldn't recall the last time my body had craved a fruit. I was learning to listen to it! When I was giving myself everything I wanted and needed, my body had the answers! It was trying to tell me this whole damn time! I just needed to listen! When I was restricting, my body was trying to tell me something by binging. I just wasn't understanding what it was saying.

A: I'm curious, how has your experience with your parents evolved throughout your recovery and self-acceptance journey?

C: I think that's the hardest part of it all for me, because all I've ever wanted is to have a good relationship with my parents. I'm finally at a point in my life where we are in a good place. That being said, body and food are still sensitive topics. We can talk about it, but both my parents and myself have to walk on eggshells with each other about it at times. They accept that this is my journey, but they don't think it could ever be the journey for them.

A: So there is some cognitive dissonance there.

C: Yeah. But I will say, my parents genuinely want to be there to support me. Whenever I bring something up related to this journey they go and research it, not to prove me wrong, but to try and really understand. They have taken workshops about the non-diet approach to try and understand how to best support me. That's all I can ask for, really.

A: What I am hearing is that they have really embraced and accepted the choices you have made for yourself about how to eat and how to relate to your body. That they are finding more acceptance maybe not of themselves, but of you. Do you feel accepted by them, just as you are?

C: I feel accepted, I do. And I feel loved. But I know it's still hard for them to see me in a plus sized body. Mostly because both of them have lived in plus sized bodies and know [what it's like] to be oppressed, and that there are obstacles in life that make it harder. When I went to Yankee stadium with my dad, I know it was hard for him to see me uncomfortable in the seats that were too small. Even if he could understand it was the seats that were the problem, not me or my body, it still sucks to see your daughter hurting. I think they just want me to be in a smaller body for life to be easier. The way my parents would love me in a smaller body or a larger body would never change. But for so long I thought it would.

A: That brings me to my next question. What has changed for you in your life? How is life different for you now that you have internalized a Health at Every Size framework?

C: Everything. It has changed everything, from my friendships to my sense of self-worth. It has helped me re-find my love for fashion and writing. It's helped me find a passion for cooking. It has given me this power. I can now go to gatherings with friends and actually enjoy the company and presence of people. I can go to a family event and do the same.

Not loving yourself and your body stands in the way of literally everything. You can't enjoy life without accepting your body. And it's ok to not love it every day, because we aren't perfect, no one is. But the work that I've done to get where I am? I'm happy pretty damn often.

A: What piece of advice would you share with clinicians working with patients in larger bodies? What would you want them to know?

C: Please, please, please educate yourself, so you don't create a barrier with your clients. One bad experience with a provider perpetuates this disconnect from all providers. No matter a person's body size, we all need to be cared for to ensure that we are healthy and happy. There are going to be a lot of unhealthy and sad people out there if this distrust continues. If as a provider you are tempted to suggest weight loss as a solution, think about if a person in a smaller body was presenting with the same symptoms, and what you would suggest to them. Apply that logic across the board.

A: That is absolutely brilliant, Cassie! Thank you so much for your willingness to share your story.

REFERENCES

American Medical Association. 2012. Report of the Council on Science and Public Health. Retrieved 14 February 2022 https://www.ama-assn.org/sites/ama-assn.org/files/corp/media-browser/public/about-ama/councils/Council%20Reports/council-on-science-public-health/a13csaph3.pdf

Ashley, B. 2020. What happened to plus size? Vogue Business. Retrieved online at https://www.voguebusiness.com/ fashion/what-happened-to-plus-size on 14 February, 2022.

Bacon, L., Aphramor, L. Weight Science: Evaluating the Evidence for a Paradigm Shift. *Nutr J* 10, 9 (2011).

Bacon, Lindo and Aphramor, Lucy (2014). Body Respect: What Conventional Health Books Get Wrong, Leave Out, and Just Plain Fail to Understand about Weight

Boushey, C. J., Spoden, M., Delp, E. J., Zhu, F., Bosch, M., Ahmad, Z., Shvetsov, Y. B., DeLany, J. P., & Kerr, D. A. (2017). Reported Energy Intake Accuracy Compared to Doubly Labeled Water and Usability of the Mobile Food Record among Community Dwelling Adults. *Nutrients*, *9*(3), 312.

Centers for Disease Control (CDC). 2022. https://www.cdc.gov/obesity/data/adult.html. Retrieved 14 February, 2022.

Chastain, Regen. 2022. Recognizing and resisting diet culture. National Eating Disorders Association Blog. Retrieved 14 February 2022. https://www.nationaleatingdisorders.org/blog/recognizing-and-resisting-diet-culture.

Cooper, C. (2013) 'A Quick and Dirty Intro to Fat Activism', [online], was available: http://forbookssake.net/2013/07/03/a-quick-and-dirty-intro-to-fat-activism/ retrieved online 14 February 2022.

Crenshaw, Kimberle "Demarginalizing the Intersection of Race and Sex: A Black Feminist Critique of Antidiscrimination Doctrine, Feminist Theory and Antiracist Politics," University of Chicago Legal Forum: Vol. 1989: Iss. 1, Article 8.

Courtois, C.A. and Ford, J.D. 2013. *Treatment of Complex Trauma: A Sequenced, Relationship-Based Approach*. New York, New York: The Guilford Press.

Erickson, M. H. and Rossi, E. L. 2011. Varieties of Double Bind. *American Journal of Clinical Hypnosis*, Volume 17(1975)(Issue 3), Pages 143-157. Published online: 20 Sep 2011. https://doi.org/10.1080/ 00029157.1975.10403733.

Glucksman, M.L. and Hirsch, J., 1968. The response of obese patients to weight reduction: a clinical evaluation of behavior. Psychosomatic Medicine, 30(1), pp.1-11.

Gomez, J.M. 2019. What's the harm? Internalized prejudice and cultural betrayal trauma in ethnic minorities. American Journal of Orthopsychiatry, 89(2), 237-247.

Grabowski, D. C. and Ellis, J. E. 2001. High Body Mass Index Does Not Predict Mortality in Older People: Analysis of the Longitudinal Study of Aging. Journal of the American Geriatrics Society, Volume 49(7):968-979. https://doi.org/10.1046/j.1532-5415.2001.49189.

Harrison, Christy (2019). Anti-Diet: Reclaim Your Time, Money, Well-Being, and Happiness Through Intuitive Eating.

Herman, J. L. 1992. Trauma and recovery, New York: Basic Books.

Kahn, L. 2006. "The Understanding and Treatment of Betrayal Trauma as a Traumatic Experience of Love." Journal of Trauma Practice, Vol.5(3) © 2006 by The Haworth Press, Inc.

Laraia, B. A., Leung, C. W., Tomivama, J., Ritchie, L. D., Crawford, P. B., and Epel, E. S.. 2021. Drive for thinness in adolescents predicts greater adult BMI in the Growth and Health Study cohort over 20 years. *Obesity: A Research Journal*, Volume 29, Issue 12, Pages 2126-2133. https://doi.org/10.1002/oby.23285

Laessle, R.G., Schweiger, U. and Pirke, K.M., 1988. Depression as a correlate of starvation in patients with eating disorders. *Biological Psychiatry*, 23(7), pp.719-725.

Lee, J. A., & Pausé, C. J. (2016). Stigma in Practice: Barriers to Health for Fat Women. *Frontiers in psychology*, *7*, 2063.

Matacin, M.L. and Simone, M., 2019. Advocating for fat activism in a therapeutic context. Women & therapy, 42 (1-2), pp.200-215.

Mays, V. M., Cochran, S. D., & Barnes, N. W. (2007). Race, race-based discrimination, and health outcomes among African Americans. *Annual review of psychology*, *58*, 201–225.

Muennig P. (2008). The body politic: the relationship between stigma and obesity-associated disease. *BMC public health*, *8*, 128.

Muennig, P., Jia, H., Lee, R., & Lubetkin, E. (2008). I think therefore I am: perceived ideal weight as a determinant of health. *American journal of public health*, *98*(3), 501–506.

Müller, M. J., Enderle, J., Pourhassan, M., Braun, W., Eggeling, B., Lagerpusch, M., Glüer, C. C., Kehayias, J. J., Kiosz, D., & Bosy-Westphal, A. (2015). Metabolic adaptation to caloric restriction and subsequent refeeding: the Minnesota Starvation Experiment revisited. *The American journal of clinical nutrition*, *102*(4), 807–819.

Nuttall F. Q. (2015). Body Mass Index: Obesity, BMI, and Health: A Critical Review. *Nutrition today*, *50*(3), 117–128.

Porges, S. W. (2017). *The pocket guide to the polyvagal theory: The transformative power of feeling safe.* W W Norton & Co.

Sar, V. and Ozturk, E. 2008. What Is Trauma and Dissociation? *Journal of Trauma Practice*, Volume 4 (2006), Issue 1-2, Pages 7-20. Published online: 15 Oct 2008.

Schiele, B.C. and Brožek, J., 1948. " Experimental neurosis" resulting from semistarvation in man. *Psychosomatic medicine*.

Simic, Z., 2016. Fat as a feminist issue: A history. In Fat sex: New directions in theory and activism (pp. 31-52). Routledge.

Speakman, John et al. Set points, settling points and some alternative models: theoretical options to understand how genes and environments combine to regulate body adiposity. *Dis Model Mech* (2011) 4 (6): 733–745.

Strings, Sabrina (2019). Fearing the black body: the racial origins of fatphobia. New York: New York University Press.

Stunkard, A., McLaren-Hume, M. (1959). The Results of Treatment for Obesity: A Review of the Literature and Report of a Series. AMA Arch Intern Med., 103(1):79–85. doi:10.1001/archinte.1959.00270010085011

Tovar, Virgie (2017). Take the Cake: 3 levels of fatphobia. https://ravishly.com/3-levels-of-fatphobia. Retrieved 14 February 2022.

Watzlawick, P. 1963. A review of the double bind theory. *Family Process*, 2(1), 132–153. https://doi.org/10.1111/j.1545-5300.1963.00132.

Weiderpass, E., Wennberg, P., van der A, D. L., Arriola, L., Benetou, V., Boeing, H., Bonnet, F., Colorado-Yohar, S. M., Engström, G., Eriksen, A. K., Ferrari, P., Butterworth, A. S. (2018). Separate and combined associations of obesity and metabolic health with coronary heart disease: a pan-European case-cohort analysis. *European heart journal*, *39*(5), 397–406.

Parenting with Dissociation

by Alexis E. Arbuthnott, Ph.D., R.D. Psych.

People are not born knowing how to parent effectively. Parenting blueprints are developed in part through the process of being cared for by significant attachment figures in childhood and adolescence (Nurmi, 2004; Simpson & Rholes, 2019; and Van Rosmalen, et al., 2016). When children are securely attached to their caregivers and receive healthy parenting throughout their development, they are more likely to develop parenting blueprints that allow them to respond to their own children in ways that promote their child's secure attachment and healthy development (Hornor, 2019; Snyder, et al., 2012). Unfortunately, survivors of complex trauma may have missed out on experiencing consistently healthy caregiving. For these parents, parenting blueprints may include models of ineffective parenting practices, or key parenting skills may be missing (Curran, 2019; Luke, et al., 2004). Furthermore, ongoing trauma symptoms may interfere with a parent's ability to self-regulate and use effective parenting strategies. Unresolved trauma may resurface as learned unhealthy parenting strategies, intolerance of their child's behaviours, and difficulties with self-regulation within the context of parenting stressors (George, 1996). These parenting behaviours may, in turn, have an effect on the developing child (see Lang & Gartstein, 2018; Siegel & Hartzell, 2014). Indeed, parents who have experienced severe childhood abuse self-report lower parenting self-efficacy and less satisfaction as parents, relative to parents without this history of abuse (Baiverlin & Blavier, 2020).

Some of these parents may benefit from additional supports to promote their growth, effectiveness and satisfaction as parents.

The impact of unresolved trauma on parenting ability and capacity is on a continuum (see Wamser-Nanney & Sager, 2021). Although dissociation does not necessarily impact a parent's ability or capacity to parent, it has the potential to make parenting more difficult. Many parents who dissociate are phenomenal parents who may occasionally find certain aspects of parenting to be challenging. Other parents may find that they are generally able to provide good care for their children, but that they have varying levels of difficulties across multiple domains of parenting. There are also parents who are themselves so traumatized that they are consistently unable to meet the needs of their children, or who may harm their children. It is important to note that the parenting ability and capacity of parents who have not experienced complex trauma or dissociation also fall along this same continuum; thus, parenting challenges are not unique to this particular population.

It is essential to recognize that while parents have a central role in shaping a child's development, additional factors outside of the parent's control also influence the child's outcomes. For example, key people in the child's life beyond parents (e.g., coaches, teachers, mentors, extended family, older siblings) may play a role in shaping the child's understanding of, and future interactions with, themselves and the world around them. Peers may similarly take a central importance and influence during the adolescent years as youth explore their identity and begin to separate from their parents. Unexpected difficult or tragic events (e.g., deaths, accidents, illnesses, other traumatic events) during the developmental period may create stressors for both the child and their parent, and impact the child's development. Finally, the child's genes and biological factors may influence the child's temperament and nervous system, which may then influence how the child interacts with the world and predisposes the child to certain positive or negative outcomes. The child's outcomes are ultimately influenced by a host of biological and environmental factors, of which parenting may be one component.

This chapter outlines key considerations for clinical work with parents who dissociate with the intention of supporting healthy parenting and child development. Normative parenting tasks leading to healthy child development are described first, followed by a discussion of the role of parents as a secure base for healthy child attachment. This chapter then reviews the research on the relations between a parent's history of trauma and dissociation, parenting, and child wellbeing. Finally, this chapter closes with a discussion of clinical implications for supporting parents who experience dissociation.

Parenting Tasks

A full review of child development is beyond the scope of this chapter. Rather, an emphasis is placed here on the overarching framework for how parenting supports healthy child development. Normative child development may be disrupted when a parent's unresolved trauma history interferes with their ability to complete these parenting tasks effectively (Chambers, 2017).

Newborn infants are completely dependent on their caregivers for survival. At birth, caregivers are responsible for meeting all of the infant's needs, as the infant is not yet capable of meeting their needs themselves. These needs include the infant's basic physical needs (e.g., food, shelter, safety from physical harm to their bodies), as well as their emotional (e.g., soothing) and relational (e.g., connection) needs. A caregiver's attunement to the infant ensures that the right needs are met at the right time (Ainsworth et al., 1974). Parenting tasks at the infant stage involve regulating the infant's nervous system through coregulation, and helping the infant organize and integrate their experience using both language (i.e., nonverbal communication, providing a narrative) and actions (e.g., meeting the infant's tangible needs) that reflect the infant's experiences back to the infant. A fundamental task during infancy is the provision of a secure base from which the infant learns that their needs can and will be met.

As infants grow into children and then adolescents, caregivers continue to play a key role in ensuring that these basic needs are met. Caregivers also become responsible for helping children learn limits and boundaries, they model healthy self-regulation and communication, and they support the young person's individuation and developing identity. Over the course of the child's development, the responsibility for meeting the young person's intrapersonal and interpersonal needs is gradually transferred from the caregiver to the young person such that the young person develops into a fully functional adult with a full repertoire of healthy strategies for caring for themselves, navigating relationships, and ensuring their own ongoing survival and the survival of their potential offspring.

There are no perfect parents. Striving for perfection may set parents up for experiencing shame and guilt when they are not able to attain this goal. Rather, the goal becomes for parents to meet the child's needs *enough* of the time that the child learns they can depend on the parent. More specifically, infants demonstrate statistical learning (see Lany & Saffran, 2013), which means that parents needs to demonstrate appropriate parenting behaviours consistently *enough* that the infant is able to identify an underlying pattern in their relationship with their parent (Woodhouse et al., 2020).

As with all relationships, ruptures within the parent-child relationship are inevitable. When parents successfully resolve these ruptures, even some of the time, children benefit. For example, research has found that when a parent is able to hold their crying infant until soothed even 50% of the time, the child later displayed increased attachment security (Woodhouse et al., 2020). In this study, the parent's behaviour at the end of the crying spell was more important in predicting healthy development than the parent's behaviour at the onset of the infant's crying, thus demonstrating that the repair may be far more important than the rupture in developing an expectation of future parent behaviour. Repairs are also associated with greater child self-control (Kemp et al., 2016; Scholtes, Lyon, & Skowron, 2020) and may be a part of the parent-child coregulation process that helps children develop self-regulation (Kemp et al., 2016). Finally, the process of parent-initiated repair following a rupture is associated with a reduced risk of child maltreatment (Scholtes, Lyon, & Skowron, 2020; Skowron, Kozlowski, & Pincus, 2010).

Parents as a Secure Base

Attachment theory (Main and Solomon, 1990; Ainsworth and Bell, 1970; Bowlby, 1969) posits that children are born with an innate attachment system designed to keep dependent children close to their parent, and thus safe and cared for, in times of stress or danger. A reciprocal caregiving system may drive a parent to behave in ways that promote this proximity and the provision of comfort when the parent perceives their child to be stressed by an internal (e.g., hunger, fatigue) or external (e.g., dangerous animal, menacing stranger) situation (Chambers, 2017). Although the caregiving system begins to mature in late adolescence, it develops most during the transition to parenthood (i.e., pregnancy, birth, post-partum period) (Simpson and Rholes, 2019). Both biological changes (e.g., hormonal changes such as increases in oxytocin, structural changes in the brain) and prior attachment experiences may promote maturation of this system (Lenzi, et al., 2015). Together, the child's attachment system and the parent's caregiving system interact to create the environment for attachment security, which works to ensure the child's survival (Bowlby, 1969).

The core of attachment security is the child's ability to use the parent as a *secure base* (Bowlby, 1969; 1988). A secure base provides a foundation for the child to alternately explore their surroundings and then return to the parent when distressed such that their parent acts as a safe haven. The ability of the caregiver to meet the needs of the child on both sides of the attachment-exploration continuum is associated with the development of the child's secure attachment with the parent (see Woodhouse, et al.,

2020). Experience has taught these children that they can expect that their parents will be responsive to their needs.

A child's experience of security within the parent-child relationship has been linked to the parent's ability to coregulate the child (Ainsworth, et al. 1978; Lyons-Ruth & Spielman, 2004). Coregulation of the child's emotional and physiological needs is essential because the child's exploration becomes impossible when the child is too distressed or dysregulated to safety explore (Woodhouse, et al., 2020). In order to coregulate the child, the parent needs to be able recognize the child's cues and then respond to them appropriately (Ainsworth, 1978; Woodhouse, et al., 2020). Thus, parental reflective-self functioning (Fonagy, et al., 1991), or the parent's ability to understand the child's underlying mental states and intentions, is an essential part of parenting effectively.

The majority of the research looking at parenting behaviours that support a secure attachment has focused on parental sensitivity (Ainsworth, et al., 1974). Parental sensitivity requires that a parent be aware of their infant's signals, accurately interpret these signals, and then provide an appropriate and prompt response to them. An emphasis is placed on moment-by-moment attunement of the parent towards the child in order to ensure that the parent responds to the child's needs appropriately. Parental sensitivity has been found to impact infant attachment; however, this effect may be modest (de Wolff & van Ijzendoorn, 1997), which suggest that parental sensitivity does not tell the whole story about how infants become securely attached to their parents. Furthermore, the concept of parental sensitivity does not necessarily generalize across cultures and socioeconomic statuses where a moment-by-moment parent-to-child attunement and prompt responses may not be culturally relevant.

More recent research has begun to focus on parenting behaviours that support the parent's *secure base provision*, or their ability to meet the needs of their child on both sides of the attachment-exploration continuum even in the presence of high levels of insensitive parenting behaviours that may occur along the way (Cassidy et al., 2005; Woodhouse, et al., 2020). Although secure base provision and parental sensitivity both require that parents attune to their child's needs and respond to these needs appropriately, secure base provision allows for a broader conceptualization of effective parenting that may transcend cultural and economic differences. Rather than requiring parents to attune to all of their infant's signals at all times, secure base provisions require parents to attune to *key* infant signals, such as signals indicating the need for attachment or bids for social connection.

Similarly, rather than requiring a moment-by-moment match between the child's needs and the parent's responses, there is greater specificity about parenting behaviours that directly meet the infant's attachment and exploration needs. Parenting behaviours that directly meet the infant's attachment needs include responding when the infant is crying but not necessarily when the infant is fussing, and avoiding frightening behaviours in response to infant distress. Parent behaviours directly meeting the infant's exploration needs include allowing the child to remain in a calm state, not deactivating exploration through intrusive parent behaviours, as well as anticipating and preventing child stress and dysregulation. Of note is that promptness in parent responses is not necessarily required within the construct of secure base provision, but rather the emphasis is on the resolution of the child's distress and the ratio of appropriate parental responses.

Parenting Styles

Parenting styles are used to classify a parent's typical parenting behaviours across the attachment-exploration continuum. The most widely known method of organizing parenting behaviours classifies parenting into four distinct styles—authoritative, authoritarian, permissive, and uninvolved—across the dimensions of parent responsiveness and parent demandingness (Baumrind, 1967; Maccoby & Martin, 1983). Parental responsiveness is also known as parental warmth and refers to the extent to which a parent expresses affection towards, and accepts affection from, their child. Parental demandingness can be conceptualized as parental control and refers to the extent to which parents actively promote respect for rules and social conventions. Authoritative parenting involves high parental warmth and high parental control. Authoritarian parenting involves low parental warmth and high parental control. Permissive parenting involves high parental warmth and low parental control. Uninvolved parenting involves both low parental warmth and low parental control.

A more recent conceptualization of these parenting styles within the child psychotherapy field uses animal metaphors to encourage parents to aspire to a more balanced approach to parenting. Originally developed as part of the New Maudsley Approach for treating eating disorders in youth

(Treasure & Smith, 2007), and later adopted into Emotion Focused Family Therapy (see Lafrance, et al., 2019), many parents find these animal metaphors to provide a more relatable model of parenting styles. This model classifies parenting across the two dimensions of emotional expression and caregiving style, with three animal metaphor options within each dimension. The ideal level of parent emotional expression is captured through the Saint Bernard, which symbolizes warmth and calmness, as opposed to a jellyfish (where too much expressed emotion such as displays of anxiety and anger may overwhelm the child) or an ostrich (where parents may avoid their child's emotional needs). The ideal caregiving style is captured through the dolphin, which symbolizes the provision of just enough direction through gentle guidance, as opposed to the rhinoceros (where parents may exert too much control, direction, or coercion), or the kangaroo (where parents may provide too much smothering and prevent a child's exploration).

Parenting behaviours that most effectively promote a secure base align best with the authoritative parenting style, and thus also with the Saint Bernard and dolphin caregiving styles (see Jones & Cassidy, 2014; Larzelere, et al, 2013). Here, the parent recognizes their child's signals, understands their child's needs, and responds to these needs appropriately. Thus, both the child's exploration and attachments needs are met within the context of a structured and supportive environment. Securely attached children learn healthy self-regulation through coregulation by their caregivers, and they learn healthy relationship skills through their caregivers' modeling and explicit teaching.

Insecure Attachment

Less effective or inconsistent parenting styles may inhibit the child's use of the parent as a secure base. A child's attachment to a caregiver develops in response to specific experiences with their caregiver (Bowlby, 1969). When a parent is consistently not able to interact with their child in ways that lead to the child's experience of security within the parent-child relationship, the child may develop an insecure attachment to the parent. When the parent is consistently preoccupied with their own needs, does not recognize their infant's signals, is not able to interpret these signals, and/or does not respond appropriately to meet their infant's needs, infants may develop one of three insecure attachment styles with their parent: avoidant, anxious-ambivalent, or disorganized (Ainsworth, et al., 1979; Main & Hesse, 1990). Infants with an avoidant attachment do not seek support or comfort from their parents, may avoid or ignore their parents, and may prefer to attempt to meet their needs on their own. Infants with an anxious-ambivalent attachment with their parent seek support from their parent through frequent proximity-seeking or clinging behaviours while simultaneous displaying behaviours rejecting the caregiver (e.g., pushing away or hitting the parent).

Infants may also develop a disorganized attachment with their parent when the parent behaves in ways that are frightening to the child, including when parents themselves are frightened, dissociated, sexualizing the child, or engaging in other frightening or atypical behaviours (Lyons-Ruth et al, 1997; Main & Hesse, 1990). The secure base is intended to ensure the child has a safe haven in times of distress (Bowlby, 1969).

However, when the parent is frightening or frightened, it creates a paradox whereby the child is afraid of the very parent from whom they need to seek comfort (Main & Hesse, 1990). Indeed, frightening caregiving behaviour is linked to disorganized attachment in infants (Madigan et al., 2006). Infants with disorganized attachment do not know what to do to get their needs met, and they display inconsistent and contradictory responses including freezing and self-soothing behaviours (e.g., rocking, pacing, head banging). Of note is that disorganized attachment itself is linked to the use of dissociation in children as a means of coping with a frightening environment (Liotti, 2006).

Attachment styles are formed in infancy (Ainsworth, 1974; 1978; Bowlby, 1969). However, as children mature they become increasingly able to grasp their parent's motivations and plans, and they become more capable of altering their behaviour to illicit desired behaviour from their parent (Ainsworth, 1989). Thus, as children age, the parent-child relationship becomes more about the parent-child interactional dance than about parenting behaviours alone. As children learn to predict their parent's responses, including developing an awareness about which of their signals, or cues, will or will not be attended to, children increasingly behave in ways that are most likely to ensure their needs are met. Children may cue parents to meet their genuine needs, or they may miscue parents (e.g., failing to cue an actual need, or cueing parents to meet a need that parents may deem more acceptable than the child's actual need) when they do not anticipate that parents will appropriately meet their needs (see Powell, et al., 2012). For example, children with avoidant attachments may no longue cue their needs to their parent, whereas children with anxious-ambivalent attachments may need to signal more extreme attachment needs via more extreme behaviours before the parent responds.

Interestingly, the majority of children who initially display a disorganized attachment style in infancy demonstrate a shift from behaviours associated with this attachment style into more organized behaviour typically consisting of either punitive-dominant (e.g., competitive or aggressive) or care-giving behaviours towards the attachment figure (see Liotti, 2006, 2017). These child behaviours reflect the activation of the child's other motivational systems (e.g., social ranking and caregiving systems) and the deactivation of their attachment system within the parent-child relationship. Both types of child behaviours invert the parent-child relationship and serve as a defensive process to maintain organization within the family relationships. However, controlling-punitive and caregiving strategies, respectively, are associated with a child's increased risk for developing externalizing and internalizing disorders (Moss, et al., 2006).

Parenting with Dissociation

The foundation of secure base provision is the parent's ability to recognize and respond to their child's signals at both ends of the attachment-exploration continuum, and to avoid behaviours that frighten their child. This inherently requires parents to have some level of awareness about their child's needs, as well as sufficient self-regulation to respond to their child's needs with enough consistency that their child experiences a healthy parenting pattern. The conundrum for parents who dissociate is that dissociation is a form of dysregulation that interferes with present-moment awareness. Thus, when a parent is in a state that is not fully aware of the present-moment, the parent may not be able to attune to the child sufficiently to parent effectively. As the parent's state of dissociation fluctuates, so too does their present-moment awareness and ability to self-regulate, and thus their parenting ability may similarly fluctuate. The term "state" is used here to describe both a dissociative state (e.g., a transient state in which the parent is not fully aware of the present-moment) as well as a personality state (e.g., alters, parts of self, aspects), as these have similar effects on children, albeit to different degrees (Lin, 2021).

Parents who frequently switch between states may be experienced by the child as inconsistent, confusing, or frightening (Lyons-Ruth et al, 1997; Peterson & Boat, 1997). Children may observe parents in an unresponsive trance, or they may observe changes in voice tone, facial expression, or behaviour that does not fit the situation (Blizard, 2006). Early literature about children of parents who dissociate in the presence of their children reported that these children may display either "forced shifting" (i.e., the child transfers from one state to another) or parentification to accommodate for their parent's switch from a caregiving state to an alternate state (Peterson & Boat, 1997). Forced shifting reflects the child's perception of an appropriate response to the parent within the situational cues, such as shifting into a parental role in response to the parent's switch into childlike or frightened state. When the child becomes responsible for the wellbeing of the parent, this forced shifting becomes parentification.

Children with a parent who visibly dissociates may worry both about the safety of their parent, as well as their role in caring for their parent.

Although a parent's level of dissociation has not been associated with inconsistent parenting styles (Chu & DePrince, 2006), it has been associated with inconsistent parenting behaviours (e.g., Chu & DePrince, 2006; Collin-Vézina, et al., 2005; Mann & Sanders, 1994). Parents with high levels of dissociation may provide more permissive parenting (Mann & Sanders, 1994), including difficulties applying discipline (e.g., Chu & DePrince, 2006; Collin-Vézina, et al., 2005; Mann & Sanders, 1994), less monitoring and supervision of their child (Collin-Vézina, et al., 2005), and more corporal punishment (Collin-Vézina, et al., 2005). With respect to meeting the child's emotional needs, higher levels of dissociation are associated with lower levels of parental warmth on factors such as acceptance of their child and child-centered parenting (Mann & Sander, 1994), as well as lower levels of positive reinforcement (Collin-Vézina, et al., 2005). Furthermore, mothers with higher levels of dissociation self-report higher levels of parenting stress (Williams, et al., 2021).

Multigeneration Dissociation and Child Maltreatment

Although parent dissociation has been linked to their child's use of dissociation (e.g., Lewis et al., 2020), this relation may be better accounted for through the parent's overall profile of trauma symptoms (Chu & DePrince, 2006) and emotion dysregulation (Lewis et al., 2020). For example, one study looking at mother's dissociation, mother's inconsistent use of parenting styles, child's betrayal trauma history, and mother's betrayal trauma history found that only the parent and the child's betrayal trauma histories were uniquely associated with the child's dissociation (Chu & DePrince, 2006). Indeed, a model of multigenerational dissociation highlights the role of re-enactment of abuse, followed by denial that this trauma occurred, as being the driving force behind intergenerational transmission of dissociation (McCollum, 2015). Thus, the re-enactment of betrayal trauma may better account for the transmission of dissociation from parent to child than the parent's own dissociation.

Research examining the intergenerational transmission of abuse among parents who are perpetrators has found that dissociation may mediate the link between parent trauma history and subsequent child maltreatment (Egeland & Susman-Stillman, 1996). For examples, mothers who were abused as children and who abuse their own children report higher levels of dissociation than mothers who broke the intergenerational cycle of abuse (Egeland & Susman-Stillman, 1996). Furthermore, the manner in which these groups of mothers recalled their care as children differed, with currently abusing mother recalling their care as children in a fragmented and disconnected fashion, whereas those who broke the cycle of abuse displayed more integration of their experiences into a coherent view of self. Finally, mothers who displayed higher emotional reactivity and more self-attacking introjects were at a higher risk for abusing their children (Skowron, Kozlowski, & Pincus, 2010).

Beyond Dissociation

Models explaining the intergenerational transmission of trauma strongly highlight that parenting behaviours associated with unresolved trauma symptoms—beyond mere dissociation—predict adverse child outcome (see Lang & Gartstein, 2018). Furthermore, although parent dissociation has been correlated with specific parenting behaviours, it has not been found to predict a poor parent-child relationship when other parent and child variables are controlled (Collin-Vézina, et al., 2005). Studies that examine only the relation between dissociation and parenting variables do not adequately capture parenting strengths and challenges among parents who experience dissociation. Indeed, many research studies do not measure the parent's overall trauma symptoms, nor do they account for current trauma symptoms beyond dissociation, when assessing for the impact of dissociation on parenting. For example, one study (Williams, et al., 2021) assessing observations of mothers' parenting behaviours found that a higher level of dissociation was associated with lower maternal sensitivity and a higher level of maternal intrusiveness; however, when the mother's trauma history was assessed alongside dissociation, dissociation was no longer found to have a unique impact on parenting behaviours. These results suggest that the parent's unresolved trauma history—of which dissociation may be one symptom among many—may be more salient in impacting parenting behaviours than dissociation itself.

Similarly, although dissociation is one form of emotion dysregulation, most studies do not assess either a broader conceptualization, or alternate forms, of emotion dysregulation alongside dissociation. However, other forms of emotion dysregulation are prevalent among trauma survivors (see Dvir, et al., 2015). Research on the impact of posttraumatic stress symptoms and parenting has found links between trauma-related emotion dysregulation and parenting beyond dissociation (e.g., Gurtovenka & Katz, 2020; Kumar, et al., 2020). For example, trauma-related alterations in arousal and reactivity are related to more negative parenting beliefs about both the child and the parent, including more negative parenting perceptions and unrealistic beliefs regarding children's development (Wamser-Nanney & Sager, 2021).

The parenting relationship may itself trigger the parent's trauma symptoms in a variety of ways (e.g., see Blizzard, 2006; Schechter et al., 2008). First, children may behave in ways that are reminiscent of the parent's trauma history. For example, a child's behavioural display of frustration, rage, terror, or despair may remind parents of their perpetrator's dysregulated behaviours. Alternately, a child's insecure attachment behaviours may be reminiscent of the parent's own disorganized behavioural responses as a child who was subjected to interpersonal violence. In these cases, the parent's priority may shift from caring for the distressed child to the need for self-preservation. This temporary loss of present-moment awareness may interfere with recognizing the child's needs and coregulating the child, and the parent may behave in ways that are frightening to the child when survival defenses (i.e., fight, flight, freeze, submit) are activated. Other ways in which the parenting relationship may trigger parent trauma symptoms include aspects of the child's development that align with the parent's trauma history, such as when the child's age or developmental stage aligns with that at which the parent experienced their own trauma. Finally, even a parent's own appropriate parenting may trigger grief as parents come to terms with their own childhoods and both the positive and negative aspects of how they themselves were parented.

Clinical Implications for Supporting Healthy Parenting

Most clinicians providing individual therapy with parents who dissociate are trained as adult clinicians, and these therapists may not feel comfortable assessing the needs of the dissociative parent's children or in providing parenting interventions. However, assessing the needs of the family—and the children specifically—and intervening accordingly may improve parent and family functioning, increase parenting ability and capacity, and halt any potential intergenerational transmission of trauma and dissociation. Conversely, clinicians working primarily with children may become aware of a parent's dissociation through working with the child, and these clinicians should be prepared to understand and support these parents in their parenting. In this case, a referral for the parent to work with an individual therapist should be considered to help the parent address other challenges that they may be experiencing in relation to their dissociation or other mental health symptoms. Several key steps are recommended for supporting dissociative parents, and addressing the needs of their children, as outlined below (see also Peterson & Boat, 1997, for recommendations from the early literature).

Clinical Implications for Supporting Parents Who Dissociate

The therapeutic relationship sets the stage for the therapist to model a secure base provision that the parent can then incorporate into their own caregiving blueprints. Here the therapist acts as both a secure base and a safe haven, which the parent then has the opportunity to internalize and replicate. The therapist models healthy caregiving, including both attending to the parent's emotional needs and setting limits, and helps the parent to learn missing skills that may increase both parenting competence and confidence, and that may lead to improve parent and family functioning.

The provision of psychoeducation about attachment, child development, and the impact of both trauma symptoms and dissociation in making parenting more challenging may help to reduce parent shame and guilt regarding any self-perceived deficits in their parenting. Parents may also benefit from psychoeducation about the role of parents in providing a secure base for their child, and the goal of recognizing and meeting their child's key attachment and exploration needs enough of the time that children perceive a pattern of healthy caregiving. In cases where parent and children have reversed roles, such as in the case of parentification of children, parents may benefit from psychoeducation about ensuring that adults are caring for adults (i.e., either the parent is caring for themselves, or another adult is caring for the parent) and ensuring that children are not responsible for caring for adults.

Using a phase-oriented approach, parents should be supported in providing appropriate caregiving for their children within the first (i.e., safety and stabilization) phase of trauma treatment. The same interventions used to assist parents to achieve stabilization in other areas of their lives may be helpful for achieving stabilization within the parenting domain. Specific skills for increasing emotion regulation (e.g., skills for orienting, grounding, tolerating distress, and modulating emotions) may decrease parental reactivity and increase parenting consistency. Similarly, negative cognitions related to self and others, and specifically those related to parenting and child development, may need to be explicitly addressed. Finally, given the role of secrecy and denial in the intergenerational transmission of trauma, parents may benefit from education and skills for improved family communication—particularly in relation to discussing sensitive topics. Trauma processing, when the parent is ready for this, may also assist with integrating the parent's trauma history into their sense of self and reducing the extent to which the parenting relationship may trigger unresolved trauma.

Having an external support system in place ensures that both the parent and the child have people that they can rely on within different settings (e.g., home, school, community). This is not a recommendation unique to working with dissociative parents, but rather reflects the recognition that raising a child is hard work and takes a community. Parents should be encouraged to identify support people both for themselves, who may be able to assist with parenting during times of high stress, and for their child. Having identified support people ensures that the child has appropriate avenues of accessing support when their parent's resources available for parenting tasks may be more limited, such as during periods of increased stress or temporary destabilization.

During the course of therapy, the parent may need to make decisions around setting boundaries or cutting off contact with their own family members who may have harmed them (Paterson & Boat, 1997). However, sometimes these extended family members have become important support people to the child. If the parent chooses to reduce contact between the extended family member and the child, it is essential that parents be supported in explaining this change to the child and that the child be supported through the loss of this relationship.

Some parents may also become aware of a negative impact of their parenting on their children through the process of psychotherapy, and this new awareness may trigger considerable shame and guilt. Helping parents to understand the impact of their own trauma history on their parenting, and providing parents with tangible ways to change their parenting behaviours, may be helpful in reducing guilt. These parents will also need support to process their grief related to what both the parent and the child may have missed out on. It may be an option to support parents through an attempt at a repair with their child. Parents are irreplaceable to their children, even when they are not currently parenting in ways that support healthy child development. When parents are able to recognize and take ownership of ruptures, and are wanting and able to making changes, their children may benefit.

Clinical Implications for Supporting Children of Parents Who Dissociate

Therapists working with a parent who dissociates should directly ask about the child's wellbeing and general level of functioning. Information can be obtained directly from the parent, through observations during family sessions, or, if appropriate, from third parties (e.g., schools, the child's counsellors) with the parent's consent. If there are concerns about the child's mental health or level of functioning, the therapist should consider making a referral for the child to a child therapist knowledgeable about dissociation who can further assess and provide appropriate interventions for the child. In such cases, it is likely prudent to coordinate the family's care—including parenting interventions—with the child's therapist. Children should be provided with age-appropriate information about trauma and dissociation that helps them to make sense of their observations of, and interactions with, their parent.

The relation between parent and child functioning is bidirectional; not only does the parent's mental health affect the child, but the child's mental health and wellbeing also affects the parent's mental health and wellbeing. When children are themselves having mental health or behavioural difficulties, more intensive parenting supports may be warranted. Parenting interventions that use a trauma-informed approach may be particularly beneficial to parents when their own children are displaying challenging behaviours or mental health concerns, including: the Circle of Security Intervention (see Powell, et al., 2014); Attachment, Self-Regulation, and Competence Model (see Blaustein & Kinniburgh, 2010); and Emotion Focused Family Therapy (see Lafrance et al., 2019). Each of these interventions coach parents in secure base provision by teaching skills for addressing the child's needs at both ends of the attachment-exploration continuum. Specific skills that parents may find helpful include: setting limits, collaborating with their child, identifying and validating their child's emotions, taking their child's perspective, communicating effectively, helping their child learn to self-regulate, realigning appropriate parent and child roles, supporting the child's increasing independence, and fostering the child's developing sense of competence and identity. Parents may also benefit from learning skills specific to maintaining their self-regulation when faced with stressful parenting situations.

The responsibility of a therapist to protect children outweighs a parent's right to privacy and confidentiality. In the spirit of protecting children, and as mandated by law, the therapist who suspects that their client or another adult in the child's life (e.g., family members who may have perpetrated against the parent) is harming or neglecting the child needs to report this to the appropriate child protection authorities. Note, however, that mandated reporting of suspected child protection concerns coupled with misconceptions that people with dissociative disorder are dangerous as portrayed in popular media, may make parents who dissociate hesitant to disclose parenting challenges. Thus, it is essential that therapist create a space in which parenting challenges are normalized through psychoeducation about why parenting challenges are so prevalent among this population. An emphasis should be placed on collaboratively addressing these challenges so as to increase the parent's sense of competence and confidence in their parenting, while simultaneously improving family functioning.

Conclusion

Parenting is hard work. This work is made exponentially more challenging when parents do not have models for healthy parenting, and they experience trauma symptoms that may interfere with using effective parenting strategies. Nonetheless, parents have a key role in guiding their child's development. Not all parents who dissociate have difficulties with parenting, but some do. When parents who dissociate find that their symptoms interfere with their parenting, they may benefit from interventions targeting this area of their functioning. Improved parenting may have a positive impact on the parent, child, and family system.

REFERENCES

Ainsworth, M. and Bell, S. 1970. Attachment, exploration, and separation: Illustrated by the behavior of one-year-olds in a strange situation. *Child Development*. 1970; 41: 49-67.

Ainsworth, M. S., Bell, S. M., & Stayton, D. F. 1974. Infant–mother attachment and social development: Socialization as a product of reciprocal responsiveness to signals. In M. M. Richards (Ed.), *The integration of a child into a social world,* pp. 99–135. Cambridge University Press.

Ainsworth, M., Blehar, M., Waters, E., & Wall, S. 1978. *Patterns of Attachment: A Psychological Study of the Strange Situation.* Erlbaum.

Ainsworth, M. S. 1989. Attachments beyond infancy. American Psychologist, 44(4), 709-716. doi: 10.1037/0003-066X.44.4.709

Baumrind, D. 1967. Child care practices anteceding three patterns of preschool behavior. *Genetic Psychology Monographs, 75*, 43-88.

Blaustein, M. & Kinniburgh, K. 2010. *Treating traumatic stress in children and adolescents: How to foster resilience through attachment, self-regulation, and competency.* Guilford Press.

Blizard, R. A. 2006. Prevention of intergenerational transmission of child abuse: A national priority, *Journal of Trauma & Dissociation, 7*(3), 1-6. doi: 10.1300/J229v07n03_01

Bowlby, J. 1969. *Attachment. Attachment and Loss,* Vol. I. Basic Books.

Bowlby, J. 1988. *A Secure Base: Clinical Applications of Attachment Theory.* Psychology Press.

Cassidy, J., Woodhouse, S. S., Cooper, G., Hoffman, K., Powell, B., & Rodenberg, M. 2005. Examination of the precursors of infant attachment security: Implications for early intervention and intervention research. In L. J. Berlin, Y. Ziv, L. Amaya-Jackson, & M. T. Greenberg (Eds.), *Enhancing early attachments: Theory, research, intervention, and policy*, pp. 34–60. Guilford Press.

Chambers, J. 2017. The neurobiology of attachment: From infancy to clinical outcomes. *Psychodynamic Psychiatry*, 45: 542-563.

Chu, A., & DePrince, A. P. 2006. Development of dissociation: Examining the relationship between parenting, maternal trauma and child dissociation. *Journal of Trauma & Dissociation, 7*(4), 75-89. doi: 10.1300/J229v07n04_05

Collin-Vézina, D., Cyr, M., Pauzé, R., & McDuff, P. 2005. The role of depression and dissociation in the link between childhood sexual abuse and later parental practices. *Journal of Trauma & Dissociation, 6*(1), 71-97. doi: 10.1300/J229v06n01_05

Curran, T., Meter, D., Janovec, A., Brown, E., & Caban, S. 2019. Maternal adult attachment styles and mother–child transmissions of social skills and self-esteem, *Journal of Family Studies*, 1-15. 10.1080/13229400.2019.1637365

De Wolff, M., & van IJzendoorn, M. H. 1997. Sensitivity and attachment: A meta-analysis on parental antecedents of infant attachment. Child Development, 68, 571-591. doi: 10.2307/1132107

Dvir, Y., Ford, J. D., Hill, M., & Frazier, J. A. 2014. Childhood maltreatment, emotional dysregulation, and psychiatric comorbidities. *Harvard review of psychiatry, 22*(3), 149–161. doi: 10.1097/HRP.0000000000000014

Egeland, B., Susman-Stillman, A. 1996. Dissociation as a mediator of child abuse across generations. *Child Abuse & Neglect, 20*(11), 1123-32. doi: 10.1016/0145-2134(96)00102-0

Fonagy, P., Steele, M., Steele, H., Moran, G. S., & Higgitt, A. C. 1991a. The capacity for understanding mental states: the reflective self in parent and child and its significance for security of attachment. *Infant Mental Health Journal,12,* 201–218. doi: 10.1002/1097-0355(199123)12:3<201::AIDIMHJ2280120307>3.0.CO;2-7

George, C. 1996. A representational perspective of child abuse and prevention: Internal working models of attachment and caregiving, *Child Abuse & Neglect*, Volume 20, Issue 5, Pages 411-424. https://doi.org/10.1016/0145-2134(96)00016-6.

Gurtovenko, K., Katz, L. F. 2020. Post-traumatic stress, mother's emotion regulation, and parenting in survivors of intimate partner violence. *Journal of Interpersonal Violence, 35*(3-4), 876-898. doi: 10.1177/0886260517690874.

Hornor, G. 2019. Attachment Disorders. *Journal of Pediatric Health Care*, Volume 33(5):612-622.

Jones, J. D., & Cassidy, J. 2014. Parental attachment style: Examination of links with parent secure base provision and adolescent secure base use. *Attachment & Human Development, 16*(5), 437-461. doi: 10.1080/14616734.2014.921718

Kemp, C. J., Lunkenheimer, E., Albrecht, E. C., & Chen, D. 2016. Can we fix this? Parent-child repair processes and preschoolers' skills. *Family Relations, 65*(4), 576-590. doi: 10.1111/fare.12213

Kumar, S. A., Franz, M. R., Brock, R. L., & DiLillo, D. 2020. Posttraumatic stress and parenting behaviors: The mediating role of emotion regulation. *Journal of Family Violence, 35*, 417–426. doi: 10.1007/s10896-019-00124-5

Lafrance, A., Henderson, K. A., & Mayman, S. 2019. *Emotion-focused family therapy: A transdiagnostic model for caregiver-focused interventions.* American Psychological Association.

Lang, A. J., & Gartstein, M. A. 2018. Intergenerational transmission of traumatization: Theoretical framework and implications for prevention. *Journal of Trauma & Dissociation, 19*(2), 162-175. doi: 10.1080/15299732.2017.1329773

Lany, J., & Saffran, J. R. 2013. Statistical learning mechanisms in infancy. In J. Rubenstein & P. Rakic (Eds.), *Comprehensive developmental neuroscience: Vol. 3. Neural circuit development and function in the brain* (pp. 231– 248). Elsevier. doi: 10.1016/B978-0-12-397267-5.00034-0

Lenzi, D., Trentini, C., Tambelli, R., & Pantano, P. 2015. Neural basis of attachment-caregiving systems interaction: insights from neuroimaging studies. *Frontiers in Psychology, 6*, Article 1241. doi: 10.3389/fpsyg.2015.01241

Larzelere, R. E., Morris, A. S., & Harrist, A. W. (Eds.). 2013. *Authoritative parenting: Synthesizing nurturance and discipline for optimal child development.* American Psychological Association.

Lewis, J., Binion, G., Rogers, M., & Zalewski, M. 2020. The associations of maternal emotion dysregulation and early child dissociative behaviors. *Journal of Trauma & Dissociation, 21*(2), 203-216, doi: 10.1080/15299732.2019.1678211

Lin, C. 2021. Parental attachment and dispositional gratitude: The mediating role of adaptive narcissism, *Current Psychology*, 10.1007/s12144-021-01465-5.

Liotti, G. 2006. A model of dissociation based on attachment: Theory and research. *Journal of Trauma & Dissociation, 7*(4), 55-73, doi: 10.1300/J229v07n04_04

Liotti, G. 2017. Conflicts between motivational systems related to attachment trauma: Key to understanding the intra-family relationship between abused children and their abusers. *Journal of Trauma & Dissociation, 18*(3), 304-318, doi: 10.1080/15299732.2017.1295392.

Luke, M.A., Maio, G. R., and Carnelley, K. B. 2004. Attachment models of the self and others: Relations with self-esteem, humanity-esteem, and parental treatment. *Personal Relationships*, 11(3):281-303.

Lyons-Ruth, K., Easterbrooks, M. A., & Cibelli, C. D. 1997. Infant attachment strategies, infant mental lag, and maternal depressive symptoms: Predictors of internalizing and externalizing problems at age 7. *Developmental Psychology, 33*(4), 681–692. doi: 10.1037/0012-1649.33.4.681

Lyons-Ruth, K., & Spielman, E. 2004. Disorganized infant attachment strategies and helpless-fearful profiles of parenting: integrating attachment research with clinical intervention. *Infant Mental. Health Journal. 25,* 318–335. doi:10.1002/imhj.20008

Maccoby, E., & Martin, J. 1983. Socialization in the context of the family: Parent-child interaction. *Handbook of Child Psychology Vol. 4. Socialization, Personality, and Social Development, 4*, 1-101.

Madigan, S., Bakermans-Kranenburg, M. J., Van Ijzendoorn, M. H., Moran, G., Pederson, D. R., & Benoit, D. 2006. Unresolved states of mind, anomalous parental behavior, and disorganized attachment: A review and meta-analysis of a transmission gap. Attachment & Human Development, 8, 89–111. doi: 10.1080/14616730600774458

Main, M., & Solomon, J. 1990. Procedures for identifying infants as disorganized/disoriented during the Ainsworth Strange Situation. In M. T. Greenberg, D. Cicchett, & E. Cummings (Eds.), *Attachment in the preschool years: Theory, research, and intervention* (pp. 121–160). University of Chicago Press.

Mann, B. J., & Sanders, S. 1994. Child dissociation and the family context. *Journal of Abnormal Child Psychology, 22*(3), 373-388.

McCollum, S. E. 2015. Multigenerational dissociation: A framework for building narrative. *Journal of Trauma & Dissociation, 16*(5), 563-576. doi: 10.1080/15299732.2015.1030717

Moss, E., Smolla, N., Cyr, C., Dubois-Comtois, K., Mazzarello, T., & Berthiaume, C. 2006. Attachment and behavior problems in middle childhood as reported by adult and child informants. *Development and Psychopathology, 18,* 425–444. doi: 10.1017/S0954579406060238

Nurmi, J.-E. 2004. Socialization and self-development: Channeling, selection, adjustment, and reflection. In R. M. Lerner & L. Steinberg (Eds.), *Handbook of adolescent psychology* (pp. 85–124). John Wiley & Sons Inc.

Peterson, G., & Boat, B. W. 1997. Concerns and issues in treating children of parents diagnosed with dissociative identity disorder. *Journal of Child Sexual Abuse, 6*(3), 1-14.

Powell, B., Cooper, G., Hoffman, K., & Marvin, B. 2014. *The Circle of Security Intervention: Enhancing attachment in early parent-child relationships.* Guilford.

Schechter, D. S., Coates, S. W., Kaminer, T., Coots, T., Zeanah, C. H., Davies, M., Schonfeld, I. S., Marshall, R. D., Liebowitz, M. R., Trabka, K. A., McCaw, J. E., Myers, M. M. 2008. Distorted maternal mental representations and atypical behavior in a clinical sample of violence-exposed mothers and their toddlers. *Journal of Trauma & Dissociation, 9*(2), 123-147. doi: 10.1080/15299730802045666

Scholtes, C., Lyons, E., & Skowron, E. 2021. Dyadic synchrony and repair processes are related to preschool children's risk exposure and self-control. Development and Psychopathology, 33(3), 1072-1084. doi:10.1017/S0954579420000358

Siegel, D. J., & Hartzell, M. 2014. *Parenting from the inside out: How a deeper self-understanding can help you raise children who thrive*. TarcherPerigee.

Simpson, J.A. & Rholes, W. S. 2019. Adult attachment orientations and well-being during the transition to parenthood, *Current Opinion in Psychology*, Volume 25, Pages 47-52.

Skowron, E. A., Kozlowski, J. M., & Pincus, A. L. 2010. Differentiation, self–other representations, and rupture–repair processes: Predicting child maltreatment risk. *Journal of Counseling Psychology, 57*(3), 304–316. doi: 10.1037/a0020030

Snyder, R., Shapiro, S., & Treleaven, D. 2012. Attachment theory and mindfulness. *Journal of Child & Family Studies*, 21:709-717.

Treasure, J., & Smith, G. 2007. *Skills-based learning for caring for a love one with an eating disorder: The New Maudsley Method.* Routledge.

Van Rosmalen, L., van der Horst, F., & van der Veer, R. 2016. From secure dependency to attachment: Mary Ainsworth's integration of Blatz's security theory into Bowlby's attachment theory. *History of Psychology*, 19: 22-39.

Wamser-Nanney, R., & Sager, J. C. 2021. Posttraumatic stress symptoms and beliefs regarding parenting and children's development among trauma-exposed parents. *Journal of Trauma & Dissociation, 22*(1), 89-106. doi: 10.1080/15299732.2020.1787295

Williams, K., Moehler, E., Kaess, M., Resch, F., & Fuchs, A. 2021. Dissociation links maternal history Of childhood abuse to impaired parenting, *Journal of Trauma & Dissociation.* doi: 10.1080/15299732.2021.1934938

Woodhouse, S. S., Scott, J. R., Hepworth, A. D., & Cassidy, J. 2020. Secure base provision: A new approach to examining links between maternal caregiving and infant attachment. *Child Development, 91*(1), e249-e265. doi: 10.1111/cdev.13224

Securefulness: A Care-Centered Approach to Therapy

Lisa Danylchuk, M.Ed., LMFT, E-RYT, IAYT
and Christine Forner, B.A., B.S.W., M.S.W., R.S.W.

In this chapter, we will introduce *securefulness* as a new concept and a source of healing that highlights overlapping principles of mindfulness and secure attachment. We will recognize mindfulness concepts that have been practiced for centuries and pair them with attachment theory, along with current knowledge derived from neurobiological studies. We hope to clarify how both therapist and client can consciously use these principles to foster a deep and dignified experience of therapeutic healing.

As mindfulness practices have become woven into mental health care, providers have developed increasing awareness of the benefits of trauma and attachment-informed approaches. While we continue to think of trauma, attachment, and mindfulness as separate, there are striking commonalities that are important to name in a cohesive and comprehensive manner. With this recognition, securefulness was born.

Securefulness is a combination of the theory and research surrounding secure attachment and the theory, research, and best practices of trauma-informed mindfulness. Securefulness is a new concept which recognizes the connections between the biopsychosocial process of attachment and the neurological, psychological, and social impacts of mindfulness practices. In recognizing these commonalities, we connect the brain structures that drive human beings to connect with the benefits many report as a result of mindfulness, and suggest how clinicians can harness this theoretical model within the therapeutic relationship.

In learning to harness the power of co-regulation, empathy, attunement, therapist internal regulation, therapist internal awareness, and presence without judgment, the secure, mindful therapist can tap into and assist even the most harmed human in self-regulating and seeking post-traumatic growth. These foundational principles of securefulness address essential needs of human beings, and from here we can identify a new model of human connection, and a foundation for profound healing.

Safe Relationships and Human Safety

When we are young the world is small, and we seek to explore its edges. We crawl away from our caregiver to reach a new distance, and we look back to see if they are still there to support us. When we look back to find a smile, we can choose to return, or to continue crawling away, exploring the edges of our newfound world. If we look back, and the caregiver is gone, our safety net disappears along with them. Who will help if they are not there? How will our basic needs be met without them? If we look back and they are angry or dysregulated, our exploration becomes wrong in our young minds, and our world stays small.

As developing infants and children, our life depends on others who care for us, ensure our basic needs are met, and prevent us from doing things like crawling into a road, or other places that we wouldn't know are dangerous without prior experience. The simple presence of a caring adult helps us to feel safe to explore ourselves and the world. Our physical lives depend on this relationship, and our sense of the world depends on their ability to attune, soothe, and redirect us.

As we grow, safety in relationships becomes less about physical dependence and more about acceptance of identity. Can we be ourselves in this space, with this person present? Will we be threatened, harmed, or encouraged if we share our truest and deepest selves? We begin to explore these edges in childhood and continue throughout adolescence. When we can express a true aspect of ourselves – a thought, a feeling, a quirky sense of humor – and it is met with appreciation or reciprocity, we are able to settle more deeply into our own skin. When we are met with judgment, harshness, or criticism, we learn to hide, often behind a cloak of shame, and protect these tender parts of ourselves.

Mindfulness practices encourage us to notice, without judgment, what arises in our minds and hearts as we sit, walk, or engage in a particular practice. Mindfulness teaches us to be kind to ourselves, to identify our physical needs for safety, but also to identify mental fluctuations as they become apparent, meeting them with compassion and presence. How is this different from parenting, or re-parenting ourselves? In these mindfulness practices, we are simply providing a safe container for ourselves to be, for our minds to filter through experiences and information, and for feelings to digest without naming them bad or wrong. Mindfulness teaches us to experience safety within ourselves – the safety that we needed all along to grow. If we did not receive this security and support from our primary caregivers, this practice provides the essential relational nutrients we need to feel loved and supported. Through mindful practices, we learn to give these nutrients to ourselves. Of course, it's much easier to learn these skills when we have someone who can model them within a relationship.

The Mindful Aspect of Securefulness

Traditional mindfulness is often described as "a deep state of relaxation in which one is engaged in an active mental state requiring great attention" (Lazar et al., 2000). It is often seen as a family of self-regulation practices that involve training, attention, and awareness (Forner, 2009, 2019). A classic definition of mindfulness is that it involves the practice and development of awareness in combination with the skill of being in a present-moment experience with a compassionate, non-judgmental stance (Kabat-Zinn, 1990). Mindfulness meditation, when used as an agent of change, has three main components to the psychological process "(1) awareness, (2) of present experience, (3) with acceptance" (Germer, 2006, p. 13). But this process often only refers to the client as the one learning how to manage the skill of mindfulness. In practicing securefulness with survivors of complex trauma and dissociation, the person who is being instructed to be in a mindful state is the therapist or clinician.

This is what delineates a mindful state from a secureful state. A secureful state occurs when you are using mindful qualities that originate from brain structures that are mainly found in the front parts of the human brain (the ventral medial prefrontal cortex, or vmPFC) which are extremely relational in nature. These structures seem to be "built" to assist one person in helping another regulate their central nervous systems (Forner,

2017; Forner, 2019). To gain a fuller comprehension of the state of therapeutic securefulness, it is essential to comprehend what is occurring when someone is utilizing mindfulness in conjunction with human bonding. For humans, this state of safe relational empathic connection starts with mindfulness.

The image of someone sitting, with legs crossed and eyes shut, focusing on their breath, noticing the ebbs and flows of thoughts then returning to the breath as the way to sustain a state of mindfulness is likely the most common notion of mindfulness meditation. Focusing on the breath, or doing a body scan and then returning to the stabilizing focus-point of the breath, is one of the most popular forms of meditation. Securefulness goes beyond this simple mental focus to involve somatic and relational awareness.

The foundational principle of securefulness, in a therapeutic setting, is the essential combination of the secure human attachment dynamic that occurs when at least one person in the dyad is in a state of mindfulness attention to the present moment, with acceptance. In this state of mindfulness, we are in a deep state of attunement with self and other. This is not traditionally what one assumes when hearing the word mindfulness, and yet the process of therapeutic attunement precisely matches the three-part definition of mindfulness outlined above – awareness of the present moment experience with acceptance. In securefulness, the process is simply occurring in a dyad.

Since there are a variety of mindfulness practices, it is important to differentiate body-based mindfulness from thought-based mindfulness practices. Sensorimotor Psychotherapy defines a body-based practice as:

> "…orienting and attending to the ebb and flow of the present internal experiences. Awareness and attention are directed towards the building blocks of present experiences: thoughts, feelings, sensory perceptions, inner body sensations, muscular changes, and movement impulses as they occur in the here and now." (Ogden, Minton, and Pain, 2006, p. 193)

This definition defines the embodied mindfulness practices that lend themselves to securefulness. As we move beyond a pure focus on thinking and become more aware of sensations, affect and intuition, rapport and embodied therapeutic connection can occur. This approach assists both the clients and the therapist to become aware of how the the central nervous system is functioning, how it may be operating in response to historical trauma, and what it needs to feel safer in the here and now.

A state of securefulness postulates that the state of mindfulness, different from ordinary consciousness, is the foundation of what is required for meaningful change (Cahn & Polich, 2013; Goleman & Davidson, 2018; Shapiro, 1980; Siegel, 2017). This "different state" is an embodied state where the mind is not just focused on thoughts, but on sensations, affective information, and intuition of both the client and oneself as the therapist. In this process, the same brain structures that are responsible for mindful states are engaged during interactions with the client. Mindfulness is one of the few therapeutic interventions that not only change the function of the brain but also the structures of the brain (Hölzel, Carmody, et al., 2011; Forner, 2019; Kang et al.,2013; Lazar et al., 2000, 2005; Luders et al., 2009). There are very few interventions that alter the structure of the brain. This speaks to the power of mindfulness for both the clinician and client.

Mindfulness is much more than a tool to enhance one's mental clarity. Mindfulness utilizes key brain structures and large networks that are designed to promote self-awareness and emotional regulation (Doll, Holzel, Boucard, Wohlschlager, & Sorg, 2015; Farb, Segal, & Anderson, 2012; Young et al., 2018). Other prominent structures that are activated during mindful states and within those who engage in a regular mindful practice include the medial and ventral prefrontal cortex (vmPFC), the posterior parietal cortex in the default mode network, and the amygdala and insula in the salience network (Farb et al., 2012; Forner, 2019; Holzel et al., 2007; Hölzel, Carmody, et al., 2011; Hölzel, Lazar, et al., 2011; Kang et al., 2013; Lazar et al., 2000, 2005; Luders, Toga, Lepore, & Gaser, 2009; Siegel,2007, 2010). When we look at what these brain structures do in relation to how we think, function, and relate to one another, we can see how much they have to offer therapists, clients, and the process of therapy itself.

When the Therapist is Mindful, Securefulness Can Occur

To foster secure attachment, a parent needs to be in a mindful, attuned state, and many adults benefit from fostering this mindful, attuned state for themselves. We believe that mindfulness and human attachment systems are not only coincidentally related, but that they engage the same systems and thus are more similar than different. The same brain structures that are robust and active within individuals who routinely meditate are the same brain structures that are robust and active within individuals who are securely attached (Siegal, 2007). As a result of both, we can connect via empathy, attunement, interoception, and intuition (Forner, 2019a). These innate human skills seem to be a vital and necessary way for us to regulate our bodies and our emotions. These skills, when applied within a therapeutic setting serving very traumatized people, can impact the relational journey in profound ways. If the therapist maintains a secureful state, the person who is close to them will begin to feel the shared regulation, also. This is what our central nervous systems, along with the ventral medial prefrontal cortex, the insula, the default mode network and the salience network are designed to do.

Research on mindfulness indicates that humans who participate in daily mindful states become more present, more accepting, and less negatively judgmental of their client's experiences (Brenner & Homonoff, 2004; Germer, et al., 2005; Forner, 2009). Brenner and Homonoff (2004) reported that when a therapist frequently meditates, they tend to be more focused on the client during the time in the therapeutic process, rather than on other personal issues or their own concerns (Epstein, 2006;

Forner, 2009). Those practitioners who practice mindfulness learn that "it's how you relate that makes a difference" (Epstein, 2006). In neurological terms, the ventral medial prefrontal cortex (vmPFC) and the default mode network help us interpret and put meaning to our inner sensations and feelings during this process of focusing on the client and relating to their journey. This is a process of knowing, feeling, and in many ways sensing other people's internal experiences.

There are nine basic brain functions that are dominant in those who meditate, and in those who are securely attached (Badenoch, 2008; Marks-Tarlow, 2012; Panksepp, 1998, 2002; Perry & Szalavitz, 2010; Porges, 1998, 2003, 2011; Schore, 1994, 2003a, 2003b, 2019; Siegel, 1999, 2007, 2010; 2012, 2017). These nine brain functions are remarkable, especially when you comprehend that they seem to be designed for the sole purpose of understanding, regulating, co-regulating, and gaining deep compassion via empathy and attunement to our fellow humans, (especially our very young humans). The nine functions are as follows: (1) Body regulation, (2) Attuned communication, (3) Emotional balancing, (4) Response flexibility, (5) Empathy, (6) Insight, (7) Conditioned fear modulation, (8) Intuition, and (9) Morality (Badenoch, 2008; Forner, 2019a; Marks-Tarlow, 2012; Panksepp, 1998, 2002; Perry & Szalavitz, 2010; Porges, 1998, 2003, 2011; Schore, 1994, 2003a, 2003b; Siegel, 1999, 2007, 2010; 2012; Siegel & Bryson, 2007; pp. 42–44; 2011).

These nine brain functions are the key to understanding the connection between mindfulness and secure attachment that create a secureful state. Notably, these nine brain functions and the structure that create them cannot grow well, or at all, when we are alone and/or when we are frightened or unsafe. Even more important is the understanding that these structures become overdeveloped, underdeveloped, or fully atrophied when a human being goes into a state of active or inactive defense (Lebois, et al., 2021; Lanius, 2015; Lanius, Lanius, Fisher, & Ogden, 2006; Lanius, et al., 2018). It is also vital to understand that these structures function very well when we are safe and they do not function well or at all when we are scared, experiencing threat and when we are in real or perceived danger. In other words, a safe environment and safe and secure relationships are key to developing the state of securefulness.

The Relational Brain and Securefulness

In gaining a comprehensive foundational understanding of the theory and clinical use of securefulness, a description of what our brains are capable of is useful. Humans have several information processing systems, and these systems are utilized in ways of managing the environment and ourselves. These are not official structures, but the following analogies are a good way of understanding what different mode networks do when humans are in different situations or modes of operation.

It is beneficial to understand securefulness by viewing humans in survival modes, thinking modes, and relating modes. Different structures and networks manage these various ways humans manage themselves. For example, when in survival mode, we tend to not be in relational mode, even though we can use some of the relational networks. This reflects in Polyvagal Theory, which notes the activation of the dorsal vagal complex (DVC) in survival mode, and the presence of ventral vagal complex (VVC) function when someone is engaged in relational connection (Porges, 1998, 2003, 2011). We can apply this state difference to survival mode and thinking mode. There are times when in survival mode we can still think, but that thinking mode can be enormously affected by a person being in survival mode. It is also fair to say that the more, or greater severity, of someone's survival or the more the person is in danger the less they can think. What is very interesting is that when someone is fully in relational mode, we will not be in survival mode, at all, and our thinking becomes quite different. Relational modes are heavily influenced by safety and security and herein lies the power of securefulness.

In neuroimaging studies, it has been found repeatedly that various brain regions, and thus functions, are strongly affected by how safe and secure we feel and, conversely, how frightened or enraged we feel (Lebois, et al., 2021; Lanius, 2015; Lanius, Lanius, Fisher, & Ogden, 2006; Lanius, et al., 2018). These studies show that when a human is in an emergency response, a cascade of defense mechanisms ensues, such as hard freeze, flight, fight, panic, tonic immobility, shame, fawning, and/or complete submission. Various brain structures turn on, others turn off, and in cases of inactive defense, information get cut off by the insula (Lebois, et al., 2021; Lanius, 2015; Lanius, Lanius, Fisher, & Ogden, 2006; Lanius, et al., 2018). Some brain structures become hypo-aroused, others will become hyper-aroused depending on the type of threat or danger, the age of the person being threatened or placed in danger, and the resources around the person who is being threatened, or is in danger. It is important to know that all information about ourselves and our lives comes from the central nervous system. When someone is in an inactive defense that person's bodily information (sensation and affect) can get cut off from other parts of the brain. When someone's body goes into an active defense, certain brain structures and modes get shut off as a way to survive a life-threatening event (Kozlowska, Walker, McLean, & Carrive, 2015; Lanius, et al., 2014).

This is a very important aspect of understanding and utilizing securefulness. When a person is in an active defense, where moving away from danger, or towards safety, or a hard freeze where being still and invisible is deemed the best action or fight, where self-preservation occurs from using all your body to fight the predator, the front brain structures and mode networks go offline. This does not mean that they cannot speak or think, it means that higher brain functions such as organization, focus, intentionally, and other brain functions do not work well, or at all.

When someone goes into an inactive defense such as tonic immobility, or a passive frozen, or shame, or fawning, or complete submission the person can still think, but the feelings and or sensations can either be missing or become hyper, where thoughts race. It is important to know that when a human being goes into survival mode their relating brain goes offline or has information cut off. It is also important to know that all information that is coming from the body and environment is, as a hard-wired process, intended to be managed by the relating brain. Because for us, the physically defenseless creature that we are, relating is how we protect ourselves. Relating is how we obtain and achieve homeostasis. Regulation for us, all comes from relating to other people and to ourselves. This is our version of thick skin, sharp teeth, or strength and speed. So when even the most severely traumatized person seeks help, because securefulness is such a natural part of keeping each other safe, the client's neurobiology will be impacted by being with another who is truly safe, non-judgmental, aware, present, and regulated.

The relating brain, which is the slowest growing, last to develop, and is incredibly sensitive to survival stress, or stress of any kind, is dependent on another person. We are no different than the domesticated cow, horses, goats, cats, dogs, and all the other animals who we have bred to be unwild - who, many, are now fully dependent on humans for their survival. But instead of breeding domesticity into a species, we evolved to be domesticated. It is in our everything, and this is a very important part of organically understanding the power that our mindful attunement and connection to one another, or securefulness, has in assisting others in healing.

Regulation of Fear in the Body

The relating brain is very powerful when it is fully developed (Farb et al., 2012; Holzel et al., 2007; Hölzel, Carmody, et al., 2011; Hölzel, Lazar, et al., 2011; Kang et al., 2013; Lazar et al., 2000, 2005; Luders, Toga, Lepore, & Gaser, 2009; Siegel, 2007, 2010). These relational structures are hard-wired into the human being and, when safe and secure, they become the "strongest". Meaning they are intended to regulate our instinctual fear responses and reactions. Inside of us are formidable structures that are designed to calm, soothe, settle, manage, and move through the fear we experience as infants, children, and in near-death/dying experiences. These structures are intended to alter or stop the bullet train of the sympathetic nervous system reactions of the active defense system, and the breaks of the inactive system of dissociation. These brain structures can take us out of our survival brain so that we can separate the wild environment we evolved in, into the tame environment we need to be in to bond and attach to our infants and other humans, as protection from predation and a key component to our survival. It is a powerful tool for our infants and young, whose vulnerability is extreme. The relating brain, technically, can settle down every fear that our central nervous system experiences.

We know this from studying those who have dedicated their life to learning to meditate. These individuals have a remarkable ability to stay calm; this is an essential skill when raising our young. Human infants have no window of tolerance, they have no ability to calm themselves down, and they have no ability to comprehend what is happening. They do however have the ability to feel what we feel as adults, both physically and emotionally. As stated before, fear is very contagious for humans. It is very important to be able to keep calm, settle and not get frightened when our young go into more fear-based reactions.

This is also an incredibly strong ingredient to working with very traumatized people. Staying regulated and knowing how to stay regulated by using securefulness can assist others who are not able to do so on their own. Many survivors are keenly hyper-focused on other people's fear, as other people's fear usually ended with a mass amount of suffering or neglect, or both. Our fear, or our clients' affect, or of their stories, or our own fear in our lack of abilities can trigger a client into a response of further dissociation or intense fawning. Extremely traumatized clients need our regulation and calm, so that they can learn from it, have a shared experience with it or borrow from us, as an example, of how to move through very terrifying feelings. Therapist-induced regulation is a powerful tool.

Regulation of Emotion and Response Flexibility

The relational brain is capable of both regulating and tolerating affective information. Affective information is data that is supplied by sensorimotor material that is found within the body via the central nervous system and the facia. At birth, we are born with both our sensorimotor and affective circuitries nearly fully developed, meaning that what we feel, both sensations and feelings, as adults is the same as when we are infants (Ogden, 2021; Teicher, & Samson, 2016; Tronic 2011; Schore, 2019). It is because the sensorimotor information system is based on our most basic, and vital needs, like bonding and attachment, food, hydration, temperature, rest, sleep, and activities. The exception between infancy and adulthood is that we are completely incapable of meeting these needs, or even knowing what these needs are as infants and children. When a need occurs in the body of an infant or a child the only way that child has to communicate its needs is automatic movement and automatic affective information, like crying, cooing and other rudimentary sounds (Lanius, et al., 2014; Montgomery, 2013; Ogden, et al., 2006; 2015; Panksepp, 1998, 2002; Perry & Szalavitz, 2010; Porges, 1998; Schore, 1994, 2003a, 2003b).

Being able to regulate one's own affect or emotion can be quite difficult. Affective information can be astoundingly strong. Emotional information can be as potent or more potent than physical pain. The feelings that infants feel are no different than the feelings that adults feel. Being able to manage one's own feelings, to be able to settle them, or let them do what needs to be done, when near death, takes a very strong vmPFC. Being able to stay mindful and not flip into survival is a tricky thing when recalling past frightening experiences and memories. Affect and sensorimotor information feels the same as it did when the original incident occurred, primarily because the body and survival brain structures are not able to cognitively tell time. Yet, in order to move past a frightening event, there needs to be some type of higher processing. For us humans, we feel safer when we know what happened, as much as we need to sequence or discharge the neurochemicals and neuroelectrical charges of a traumatic/frightening event. Fear, abandonment, rejection, isolation, vulnerability, terror and rage are all feelings humans have. The relating brain is capable of being one step removed, but still present, aware, attuned to and empathic of another's and one's own affective information. This makes sense as affective regulation is vital in being able to go from an infant/child who has no affective control or regulation abilities, to an adult who is wise and capable of managing others and one's own affect.

Response flexibility is the ability to be one step removed from one's affective and sensorimotor information as well as being able to take a mental pause. This is the equivalent of your mind saying, "Hey wait! Is this happening now, or is this a memory?" This is very important to be able to assess and discern if the thing that the affect and sensory information is communicating, via sensation and feelings, is a memory, or a response that needs to be regulated and processed. What is meant by processes is the movement of sense perceptions and affective information being moved from the experiential parts of our memory/self (body) to the context and meaning making parts of our self (mind and relating). It is the process of being able to be one step removed from those experiences/feelings/sensations so that we do not get "lost" or stuck in a past experience or a fearful experience.

When a therapist is in their relating brain that holds and maintains regulation of one's sense perceptions and affect, it is much easier to be curious and one step removed from the affect of another person. This brain ability is lacking in survivors of complex trauma and dissociation. This could be why flashbacks are so profoundly challenging. The affect, experience and sense perception of the incidents are naturally needing to be processed, but they cannot fully get processed because there is no mental pause that says, "This is old stuff. This feeling is a memory and cannot really hurt me anymore."

Procedural Learning and Conditioned Fear Response

A conditioned fear response is a response that has become procedurally learned from the past that has not been regulated or processed. There are a lot of terrifying things that happen to children when they are little. Being small and stuck inside your body, with no way to regulate out of it, is scary unto itself. The relating brain is great at updating these "files" of fear.

The connections between body, mind and brain are complex. If you have ever been on a trampoline, and then move back to the ground, there is always a sensation that feels quite strange. What this sensation is, is a lag between what is happening in our conscious awareness and what the central nervous system (CNS) is experiencing. Our CNS is a predictive organ (Barrett, 2017). It predicts the future event/s based on what is happening or what happened before. If the CNS predicts a bouncy floor, until it experiences something different, it will continue to predict the bouncy floor. So when we get off, even though we can see, and know, that we are no longer on the trampoline that has a bouncy floor, our bodies, until they experience the solid ground, will predict the bouncy floor. It isn't until there is another and different experience that the CNS can and will predict the solid ground. This lag happens all the time. The mind and body, without the relational brain, especially if the person has experienced a lot of fear, overwhelm, and lack of care, are quite separate. This notion that our thinking brain can change these deep, instinctual body responses to lived experiences is rather, well, unscientific.

The secureful therapist is a lot more in tune with what is happening in their bodies because they have worked hard in communicating and managing their own procedurally learned and conditioned fear responses and have learned how to regulate their own internal experiences. This leads to things being much clearer on the notion of transference and countertransference. The counter-transference part is reduced, and it becomes easier to differentiate the therapist's internal projections from what is happening for the client, over time.

Attuned Communication and Empathy

Attuned communication is this amazing thing in which those who are securely attached, those who meditate, those who are well regulated, and those who are secureful are skilled. Things like our mirror neurons and other brain structures can literally hone in on another's central nervous system and bodies to gather information and attune to the information that is being experienced and communicated by the other. This is a wonderous mechanism that is part of a human being. It is very important when our young spend the first three years of their lives sensing and feeling without a lot of cognitive or zero mindful skills. Attunement is like an invisible radar that tunes into another person's inner experiences. It is part of how we understand and comprehend one another. A therapist that is skilled in securefulness is able to more clearly feel what their clients are feeling and be able to be one-step removed from these inner experiences and then be able to regulate themselves. We can, as a species, feel what others are feeling. This is good news, as clients commonly express a need to feel understood despite having been lived through uniquely harsh experiences.

As simple as securefulness may sound, it is not common and not easy to achieve or sustain in a world that is full of traumatized human beings, stressful events, realities of being part of a capitalistic world, as well as many other factors that are part of misogyny and patriarchy. Dissociation, or disconnection to self and others, is one of the ways we have survived 10,000 years of chronic, continual, and pervasive traumatic, abusive, waring, impoverished situations. Dissociation of one's feelings and sensations, because of a lack of skilled regulators (parents) is extremely common. For those who have experienced infancies and childhoods that are full of torturous experiences or profound neglect, dissociation is the only way to survive. Learning to attune to humans who have been through the most horrible forms of human torture, child abuse, and neglect is not an easy thing to do.

Practicing securefulness can really help. Being able to regulate one's feelings and sense perception, even the most terrifying and brutal, is extremely beneficial. It can also assist the person who is terrified, who comes to your office for help, to be with someone who is fully accepting of others' experiences, because it can be regulated. Please note, regulated is different than tolerated. One is more of a full embodied experience and the other is a state of mind that runs the risk of being disconnected. The body can still react to the other person's internal experience and have a tolerant mind. The skill of mindfulness, applied to another person can be very effective because this transfer of information can go both ways. It is a way of helping without using words.

Most people think that empathy is the ability to conceptualize what another person is feeling. In actuality, empathy is so much more than this. It is the ability to feel another person's feelings. It is the other half of attunement. When we are with our young, their inner world is quite frightening, as the literal vulnerability that they feel is rather large. But all that these tiny humans have to communicate their inner world is a handful of cries, coos, and – if in real danger – an attachment cry. A parent is supposed to be able to sense into and feel their infants and small children's bodies and then decipher what is going on in there. It is literally the ability to feel, as close to exactly as possible, what another person is feeling. This is an amazing mechanism that can make us feel connected and felt.

This skill is powerful with traumatized clients. So many traumatized humans have so much difficulty putting the right words to describe how they are feeling. The reasons for this are many, such as infant or childhood neglect, gaslighting, or the lack of anyone putting words, meaning and context to their inner feelings and sensations. It is extremely common for a perpetrating parent and/or the parent who aligns with the perpetrating parent to say things like, "This is love; this doesn't hurt; you're just fine; that didn't hurt; or I'll give you something to cry about." This can lead a survivor to not have the correct words to describe their inner experiences. This can feel very frightening as it can also be quite confusing. It is also important to understand that all these parents are missing empathy themselves. Their offspring end up with internal experiences that are confusing, dissociated, nameless, without internal context or meaning, and eventually bring those feelings to therapy. It can be healing to finally have that empathy and compassion provided – for the feelings, the people, and the whole of the harmful experiences.

Without securefulness, the therapist and the client can easily become triggered, overwhelmed, and lost in these feelings that are seeking an empathic, attuned, regulated connection. With a therapist being secureful, the therapist can have one "foot" in the land of trauma and another "foot" in the land of safety, security and grounded regulation. This type of secureful empathy can be like a life-raft and compass in a huge storm.

Intuition, Instinct and Morality

The ability to go into one's body, to sense and feel around, is a valuable skill in learning to comprehend what it is that one is feeling and sensing. It is important in putting context and meaning to what is happening. Insight is the capacity to have inner awareness, introspection, and inner-sensing – not only have perception but *neuroception*. Neuroception is the brain's ability to have automatic detection of environmental information, even prior to conscious awareness (Porges, 2003, 2011).

The secureful brain also has the ability to be mindfully connected with another, while feeling a grounded sense of internal safety. Being able to go inside of oneself and distinguish and differentiate between the wild instinctual reaction that comes from the CNS and the intuitive information that comes from the ether, is an amazing skill. Our instinctual bodies do what needs to be done to survive predation. Our intuitive, relating being is part of something so much larger.

It is well known that even decades after a mother has given birth, the infant's stem cells are still found in her (Bianchi, Zickwolf, Weil, et al, 1996; Chan, Gurnot, Montine, et al, 2012). It is postulated that the reason for this is so that whatever is happening inside the child is felt inside the mother as well. But how are we supposed to know the difference between what our infants and children are feeling and our feelings and sensations? This ability is found inside the relating brain, reached through the state of securefulness.

If you put together all of those capacities of the relating brain that we previously described, you end up with a human being who is able to regulate their bodies, regulate their fear, manage, regulate and communicate emotional or affective information. You then have a human being who is also able to take this sensory information and translate it into sophisticated context and meaning. One who tends to look at this information from a nonjudgmental kind of place, from a place of curiosity, to be able to look at another human being, and feel that other human being's feelings, and then make sense of it. Securefulness describes the deepest form of human connection, and it is a powerful ally when working with traumatized human beings.

Conclusion

Recall the image of an infant at the opening of this chapter, scooting along on the floor to explore the edges of their world. It is the moment they turn around to reconnect that determines their next move. We cannot force them out the door to learn the front yard alone, yet in time, they will venture to this point. Similarly, when working with clients in private practice, we can provide a safe anchor for the client to look to and determine – how far is it safe-enough to go today? At what point might I feel overwhelmed by fear, and at what point do I feel exhilarated in my exploration?

As mental health clinicians, we can learn from our clients cues when they have stepped beyond a threshold of familiarity or safety, and we can provide a safe space for them to return to as “home base”. If we meet them with a strict agenda for their personal exploration, we usurp the feelings of empowerment that come with discovering oneself. If we disregard their process of exploration, or fail to provide an anchoring presence, they will likely not feel safe enough to explore. When we can attune to and help identify their feelings and needs moment to moment, we help them learn to make decisions about when to step forward, and when to step back. By honoring where they are and communicating safety through as many means as we possibly can – the environment, our language, our own self-regulation and approach, we allow them to go beyond places that feel safe to explore the unknown, feel into curiosity, and even engage in play.

This anchored caring presence, then, allows our clients to feel into previously uncharted territory, and attune to parts of self that may have felt distant, or even exiled from their awareness. When we, as providers, are in a state of caring for others, we engage what Polyvagal Theory describes as the Ventral Vagal Complex (VVC), or the myelinated vagal pathway. From this socially engaged place, our bodies are more oriented to connection, and less oriented to fear. When we are in a state of care, our biology is impacted, which impacts communication (verbal and nonverbal) and sends cues of safety to our clients. By grounding ourselves in care, we protect ourselves from diving into the throws of trauma, and we orient our clients to healing pathways in the brain and body. Our self-regulation allows us to become a metaphorical light house that the client can see amidst any emotional storm.

Fear is a contagious emotion. Infants, toddlers, small children, and traumatized people, who live in a near-constant or constant state of terror, can spread this fear to other people, parents and therapists are no exception. Because our central nervous systems speak to one another all the time, even if we are not aware of this form of communication. It is a good reminder that for the relating brain to fully develop these fears need to be regulated. As a therapist, being regulated yourself, and staying in a neutral state, is far more effective than any language you may or may not use.

Securefulness is compassion, non-judgement, and connection. Some might call this love, a word that we rarely use in clinical settings for fear of misunderstandings between platonic and romantic manifestations. Perhaps we can, at least, re-centralize the concept of caring for one another (Danylchuk, 2022) which despite being more difficult to study, has such clear implications for relational healing. With a foundation of care layered with a practice of securefulness, we can address the harm done by disconnection, neglect, and relational harm. Through a practice of mindful attunement to self and other, and through the practice of securefulness, we can foster healing together.

REFERENCES

Badenoch, B. (2008). Being a brain-wise therapist: A practical guide to interpersonal neurobiology. New York, NY: W.W. Norton & Company.

Barrett, L. F. (2017). How emotions are made: The secret life of the brain. Houghton Mifflin Harcourt

Bianchi, D. W., Zickwolf, G. K., Weil, G. J., Sylvester, S., & DeMaria, M. A. (1996). Male fetal progenitor cells persist in maternal blood for as long as 27 years postpartum. Proceedings of the National Academy of Sciences, 93(2), 705-708.

Brenner, M. & Homonoff, E. (2004). Zen and clinical social work: A spiritual approach to practice. Families in Society: The Journal of Contemporary Social Services, 85(2), 261-269.

Cahn, B. R., & Polich, J. (2013). Meditation states and traits: EEG, ERP and neuroimaging studies. Psychology of Consciousness: Theory, Research, and Practice, 1(S), 48–96

Chan, W. F., Gurnot, C., Montine, T. J., Sonnen, J. A., Guthrie, K. A., & Nelson, J. L. (2012). Male microchimerism in the human female brain. PLoS One, 7(9), e45592.

Danylchuk, Lisa (2022). The Centrality of Care, Journal of Trauma & Dissociation, 23:1, 1-7, DOI: 10.1080/15299732.2022.2028465

Doll, A., Holzel, B. K., Boucard, C. C., Wohlschlager, A. M., & Sorg, C. (2015). Mindfulness is associated with intrinsic functional connectivity between default mode and salience networks. Frontiers in Human Neuroscience, 9, 461. doi:10.3389/fnhum.2015.00461

Emmott, E. H., & Page, A. E. (2021). Alloparenting. Encyclopedia of evolutionary psychological science, 210-223.

Epstein, M. (2006). Thoughts without a thinker: Lessons for psychotherapy from meditation. In C. Germer, J. Plat & R. Siege (Eds.), Meditation in psychotherapy (pp. 9-10). Boston, Harvard Medical School, Department of Psychiatry Cambridge Health Alliance.

Farb, N. A. S., Segal, Z. A., & Anderson, A. K., (2012). Attentional modulation of primary interoceptive and exteroceptive cortices. Cerebral Cortex Advance Access, 23(1), 114–126.

Forner. C., (2019) What Mindfulness can learn about Dissociation and what Dissociation can learn from Mindfulness, Journal of Trauma & Dissociation, 20:1, 1-15, DOI: 10.1080/15299732.2018.1502568

Forner, C. (2017). Dissociation, Mindfulness and Creative Meditations: Trauma-informed practices to facilitate growth: New York, NY: Routledge.

Forner, C., (2009). Psychotherapeutic creative, concentration and contemplation meditation: Examining a treatment option for clients who have dissociative identity disorder (Unpublished Master's Thesis for the Faculty of Social Work). University of Calgary, Calgary, Alberta, Canada.

Germer, C. (2006). Why meditate? Which method? In Germer, C., Plat, J. & Siege, R. (Eds.), Meditation in psychotherapy (pp. 14-30). Boston, MA: Harvard Medical School, Department of Psychiatry Cambridge Health Alliance.

Goleman, D. & Davidson, R., (2018). Altered Traits: Science reveals how meditation changes your mind, brain and body. New York: Avery

Holland, J. (2006). A brief history of misogyny: The world's oldest prejudice. Hachette UK.

Holzel, B., Lazar, S., Gard, T., Schuman-Oliver, Z., Vago, D., & Ott, U. (2011). How does mindfulness meditation work? Proposing mechanisms of action from a conceptual and neural perspective. Perspectives on Psychological Science, 6(6), 537–559. doi:10.1177/1745691611419671

Holzel, B., Ott, U., Hempel, H., Hackl, A., Wolf, K., Stark, R., & Vaitl, D. (2007). Differential engagement of anterior cingulate and adjacent medial frontal cortex in adept meditators and non-meditators. Neuroscience Letters, 421, 16–21. doi: 10.1016/j.neulet.2007.04.074

Holzel, B. K., Carmody, J., Vangel, M., Yerramsetti, S. M., Gard, T., & Lazar, S. W. (2011). Mindfulness practice leads to increases in regional brain grey matter density. Psychiatry Research Neuroimaging, 191(1), 36–43. doi: 10.1016/j.pscychresns.2010.08.006

Kabat-Zinn, J. (1990). Full catastrophe living: Using the wisdom of your body and mind to face stress, pain and illness. New York: Dell Publishing.

Kang, D. H., Jo, H. J., Kim, S. H., Jung, Y. H., Choi, C. H., Lee., U. S., ... Kwon, J. S. (2013). The effect of meditation on brain structure: Cortical thickness mapping and diffusion tensor imaging. SCAN, 8, 27–33.

Kenkel, W. M., Perkeybile, A. M., & Carter, C. S. (2017). The neurobiological causes and effects of alloparenting. Developmental neurobiology, 77(2), 214-232.

Kozlowska, K., Walker, P., McLean, L., & Carrive, P. (2015). Fear and the defense cascade: clinical implications and management. Harvard review of psychiatry.

Lanius, R., Lanius, U., Fisher, J., & Ogden, P. (2006). Psychological trauma and the brain: Toward a neurological treatment model. In P. Ogden, K. Minton, & C. Pain (Eds.), Trauma and the body: A sensorimotor approach to psychotherapy (pp. 139–161). New York, NY: W.W. Norton & Company.

Lanius, R. A., Wolf, E. J., Miller, M. W., Frewen, P. A., Vermetten, E., Brand, B., & Spiegel, D. (2014). The dissociative subtype of PTSD. Handbook of PTSD: Science and practice, 234-250.

Lanius RA: Trauma-related dissociation and altered states of consciousness: a call for clinical, treatment, and neuroscience research. Eur J Psychotraumatol 2015; 6:27905

Lanius, R.A., Boyd, J.E., McKinnon, M.C., Nicholson, A.A., Frewen, P., Vermetten, E., Spiegel D. (2018). A Review of the Neurobiological Basis of Trauma-Related Dissociation and Its Relation to Cannabinoid- and Opioid-Mediated Stress

Response: a Transdiagnostic, Translational Approach. Current Psychiatry Reports, 20(12), 118. https://doi.org/10.1007/s11920-018-0983-Z

Lazar, S., Bush, G., Gollub, R., Fricchione, G., Gurucharan, K., & Benson, H. (2000). Functional brain mapping of the relaxation response and meditation. NeuroReport, 11(7), 1581–1585. doi:10.1097/00001756-200005150-00042

Lazar, S., Kerr, C., Wasserman, R., Gray, J., Greve, D., Treadway, M., & Fischl, B. (2005). Meditation experience is associated with increased cortical thickness. NeuroReport, 16(17), 1893–1897. doi: 10.1097/01.wnr.0000186598.66243.19

Lebois LAM, Li M, Baker JT, et al (2021): Large-scale functional brain network architecture changes associated with trauma-related dissociation. Am J Psychiatry; 178:165–173

Luders, E., Toga, A. W., Lepore, N., & Gaser, C. (2009). The underlying anatomical correlates of long-term meditation: Larger hippocampal and frontal volumes of grey matter. Journal of Neuroimaging, 45(3), 672–678. doi: 10.1016/j.neuroimage.2008.12.061

Marks-Tarlow, T. (2012). Clinical intuition in psychotherapy: The neurobiology of embodied response. New York: W.W. Norton & Company

Mech, L. David. 1999. Alpha status, dominance, and division of labor in wolf packs. Canadian Journal of Zoology 77:1196-1203. Northern Prairie Publication 1078. Northern Prairie Wildlife Research Center, Jamestown, ND. See at < http://www.npwrc.usgs.gov/resource/2000/alstat/alstat.htm >. May 16, 2000. Northern Prairie Wildlife Research Center, 8711 37th Street SE, Jamestown, ND 58401-7317
http://www.mnforsustain.org/wolf_mech_dominance_alpha_status.htm

Miller, L. F. (2015). Fine-tuning the ontology of patriarchy: A new approach to explaining and responding to a persisting social injustice. Philosophy & Social Criticism, 41(9), 885-906.

Montgomery, A. (2013). Neurobiology essentials for clinicians: What every therapist needs to know. New York: W.W. Norton & Company.

Ogden, P. (2021). The different impact of trauma and relational stress on physiology, posture, and movement: Implications for treatment. European Journal of Trauma & Dissociation, 5(4), 100172.

Ogden, P., Minton, K., & Pain, C. (2006). Trauma and the body: A sensorimotor approach to psychotherapy. New York: W.W. Norton & Company

Panksepp, J. (1998). Affective neuroscience: The foundations of human and animal emotions. New York: Oxford University Press.

Panksepp, J. (2002). At the interface of the affective, behavioural and cognitive neuroscience: Decoding the emotional feelings of the brain. Journal of Brain and Cognition, 52(1), 4–14. doi:10.1016/S0278-2626(03)00003-4

Perry, B. D., & Szalavitz, M. (2010). Born for love: Why empathy is essential and endangered. New York: HarperCollins Publishers.

Porges, S. W. (1998). Love: An emergent property of the mammalian autonomic nervous system. Journal of Psychoneuroendocrinology, 23(8), 837–861. doi:10.1016/S0306-4530(98) 00057-2

Porges, S. W. (2003). The polyvagal theory: Phylogenetic contributions to social behaviour. Journal of Physiology & Behaviour, 79, 503–513. doi:10.1016/S0031-9384(03)00156-2

Porges, S. W. (2011). The polyvagal theory: Neurophysiological foundations of emotions, attachment, communication and self-regulation. New York: W.W. Norton & Company.

Püschel, H. P., Bertrand, O. C., O'reilly, J. E., Bobe, R., & Püschel, T. A. (2021). Divergence-time estimates for hominins provide insight into encephalization and body mass trends in human evolution. Nature Ecology & Evolution, 5(6), 808-819.

Schore, A. (1994). Affect regulation and the origin of the self. Mahwah, NJ: Lawrence Erlbaum Associates, Inc. Publishers.

Schore, A. (2003a). Affect regulation and the repair of the self. New York: W.W. Norton & Company.

Schore, A. (2003b). Affect dysregulation and the disorders of the self. New York: W.W. Norton & Company.

Schore, A., (2019). The development of the unconscious mind. New York: W.W. Norton & Company

Shapiro, D.H. (Ed.). (1980). Meditation: Self-regulation strategy and altered state of consciousness (1st ed.). Routledge. https://doi.org/10.4324/9780203785881

Siegel, D. (1999). The developing mind: How relationships and the brain interact to shape who we are. New York: Guilford Press.

Siegel, D. (2007). The mindful brain: Reflections and attunement in the cultivation of wellbeing. New York: W.W. Norton & Company.

Siegel, D. (2010). Mindsight: The new science of personal transformation. New York: Bantam Books.

Seigel, D. (2012). The developing Mind: How relationships and the brain develop who we are (2nd ed.) New York, NY: The Guildford Press.

Siegel, D., (2017). Mind: A journey to the heart of being human. New York: W.W. Norton & Company

Siegel, D., & Bryson, T. P. (2011). The whole-brained child: 12 revolutionary strategies to nurture your child's developing mind. New York, NY: Delacorte Press.

Skoglund, P., & Mathieson, I. (2018). Ancient genomics of modern humans: the first decade. Annual review of genomics and human genetics, 19, 381-404.

Spikins, P., French, J. C., John-Wood, S., & Dytham, C. (2021). Theoretical and methodological approaches to ecological changes, social behaviour and human intergroup tolerance 300,000 to 30,000 BP. Journal of archaeological method and theory, 28(1), 53-75.

Skoglund, P., Thompson, J. C., Prendergast, M. E., Mittnik, A., Sirak, K., Hajdinjak, M., ... & Reich, D. (2017). Reconstructing prehistoric African population structure. Cell, 171(1), 59-71.

Teicher, M.H. and Samson, J.A. (2016), Annual Research Review: Enduring neurobiological effects of childhood abuse and neglect. J Child Psychol Psychiatr, 57: 241-266. https://doi.org/10.1111/jcpp.12507

Tronick, E., & Beeghly, M. (2011). Infants' meaning-making and the development of mental health problems. American Psychologist, 66(22), 107–119. doi:10.1037/a0021631

Young, K. S., Van Der Velden, A. M., Craske, M. G., Pallesen, K. J., Fjorback, L., Roepstorff, A., & Parsons, C. E. (2018). The impact of mindfulness-based interventions on brain activity: A systematic review of functional magnetic resonance imaging studies. Neuroscience and Biobehavioral Reviews, 84, 424–433. doi: 10.1016/j.neubiorev.2017.08.003

History of Plurality and the Online Community

Emily Christensen, PhD, LCPC, S

Plurality is a conceptual experience developed into a collective culture, with roots in the shared experiences of ancient indigenous practices, some philosophical and religious practices, and the clinical context of trauma-based disorders. Plurality is an umbrella term that anyone with any kind of experience of multiplicity can self-identify with, but it can also have specific political and cultural connotations. It may include, but is not limited to, a clinical context from a psychological perspective, and is often based in a broader anthropological understanding.

Historical Context of Plurality

There are several aspects of the clinical experience that have historically contributed to the development of Plurality as a culture. Traditionally, the clinical perspective has focused on *dyadic trauma*, meaning trauma caused by one against another such as in cases of child abuse inflicted by a caregiver. Often, this trauma is *intergenerational*, meaning this dyadic trauma happens in patterns over generations, such as in cases of victims of child abuse growing up and choosing partners who then continue the abuse cycle by hurting them or their children (or an original abuser harming the grandchildren). To simplify, dyadic trauma is about what happened in the past, while intergenerational trauma is about what is happening again.

In addition to this, there is *historical trauma*, which is about what is still happening to us because of what has already happened to us. Examples of this include the changing shape of slavery over decades, forced migration, colonization, internment camps, genocides, misogyny, immigrant labor, boarding schools for indigenous children, the destruction of cultural practices, or the loss of native languages. Historical traumas are shared by communities, carried across generations, and inflicted on specific groups of people (based on race, creed, ethnicity, gender, identity, or disability). The effects linger on descendants and result in cumulative trauma such as higher rates of physical and mental illnesses, substance abuse, and erosion of families. Historical traumas threaten the vibrancy of entire cultures.

Thus, within historical trauma, there is also *collective trauma* — what happened to us together. These traumas are more specific to time and shared experience as part of the overall history shared by a group. For example, black history shares an immense amount of historical trauma, but one of the specific collective traumas would be the 1921 Tulsa Race Massacre in Oklahoma. Another example would be the historical traumas of colonization, genocide, forced migration, and boarding school experiences of indigenous cultures; within this overall history is the collective trauma of the Trail of Tears specifically. Intersectionality shows up in collective trauma as well, especially with disability and LGBTQ+ groups.

One of these disability groups would be the Blind, who despite obvious personhood had fight to be included as citizens as recently as the Civil Rights movement in America. In 1968, the Braille Monitor declared, "Those of us who are blind are — need we say it once again — citizens as well. We wish to be treated as other citizens are treated, for all ordinary and general purposes." Most recently, with the world moving online, the Blind community often struggles with access simply through lack of awareness of their seeing peers, as screen readers only have access to what is described. Images and graphics on social media, websites, and in professional presentations cannot be "read" if not described explicitly or in image descriptions.

Likewise, the Deaf community has demanded that since people with disabilities are also citizens, they ought to have the same rights as other citizens. When the International Congress on the Education of the Deaf convened in Paris in 1878, no Deaf people were allowed to attend or testify. The Congress ruled against using sign language in Deaf Schools, a policy that was not revoked unto 2010. Today, the Deaf community still has to fight for interpreters during live news such as inclement weather, natural disasters, or pandemic coverage. The captioning of online material was made law in 2016, and still does not happen consistently. Despite these and other collective traumas, the Deaf community were leaders in the Civil Rights movement, as well as the first group to declare their own culture via research-based evidence of their own language and social norms.

Like the Blind and Deaf and other disability groups, the Mobility group also endured collective trauma. Mobility groups struggled to bring awareness that as citizens with rights, they needed access to the world around them. Even today, "accessible restrooms" means one thing to able-bodied businesses and another thing to someone who needs room for assistive devices, wheelchairs, or adult-size changing tables. Like other disability groups, they were often assumed to be intellectually impaired or developmentally delayed in some way, which led to being institutionalized. That in itself has its own collective traumas, from being shackled to beds because of understaffing to being targeted for experiments and euthanasia – some of which was, perhaps, at its worst during the Holocaust.

Neurodiversity groups built on what these other groups had challenged and defined for themselves. They declared that if they were also citizens with rights and access, then they get to decide for themselves what access looks like. They united together against support organizations that did not represent them accurately or ethically. They challenged language, initially changing to first-person language as a matter of dignity, declaring it more respectful to say "Person with Autism" instead of "Autistic Person". Following this, they shifted back, reclaiming "Autistic" as part of Pride so that "They are / I am autistic" became the expression most culturally appropriate. In these ways, a group of people previously stigmatized for a "lack of social skills" actually managed to develop its own culture and support network in powerful and effective ways – something that is following in other communities, like with disordered eating.

LGBTQ+ groups have also been targeted both historically. Their civil rights are precious at best, and dangerous at worst, due to the polarization of acceptance and rejection in so many areas of their lives: religiously, politically, and publicly. Collectively, an entire generation endured (and grieved) the HIV/AIDS crisis of the 1980's. They also too often endure shared experiences of betrayal trauma and/or isolation from family and loved ones. They experience subtle but wearying microaggression, and they are at risk for experiencing aggression and victimization. Further, the impact of politics does not guarantee their safety, as laws change and are challenge everything from where they can live to who they can marry. This results in a tug of war feeling that leads to instability, as they feel "now it's safe…" then "it's not safe anymore…" to "when will it stay safe?" which gives them a collective trauma of safety and stability being for some, sometimes, but not for everyone all the time.

Other collective traumas unite people as a group through the trauma itself, such as with natural disasters like fires, earthquakes, hurricanes, or tornadoes. The coronavirus pandemic was an example of this globally, though experiences during the pandemic may have been very unique. Some endured long quarantines, while others didn't seem bothered by it at all. This incongruence between the two became divisive in some areas, like America, where people politicized the experience in attempt to gain advantage over others during the crisis. This seems to have added to the level and acuity of experienced trauma on both sides, not because of severity of the pandemic, but because of the misattunement between people taking sides against each other causing deep relational ruptures that many struggled to repair. In contrast, there were lower rates of mental health stressors reported in places where communities viewed keeping each other safe as an act of charity or ethical responsibility – not because the people were "good" to each other, but because of the attunement between them and the congruence of that agreement for safety.

Clinical Context for Plurality

Applying these types of traumas to the treatment setting reveals some interesting shared experiences for patients struggling with dissociation. Those with childhood trauma already come to treatment with dyadic trauma, and many are further traumatized during the process of trying to find a therapist who can actually help. Reinders (2020) reported that in the average time from seeking treatment to receiving a correct diagnosis of Dissociative Identity Disorder (DID), the average person receives four incorrect diagnoses, spends seven to twelve years in mental health services, experiences years of inefficient pharmacological treatment, and endures several experiences of hospital admission. This speaks to the additional layer of intergenerational trauma experiences in the treatment setting, through difficulties due to diagnostic manual changes; managed care limitations; inappropriate or inadequate treatment models being passed down to new clinicians; and the decrease in quality education that too often skips psychodynamic training in favor of quick fix tools, fad modalities, and tricks of the trade that do not adequately address relational trauma.

Patients with dissociation have endured historical trauma in the clinical setting already, even if they are not aware of this. As Reinders mentioned, these patients often already have a history of misdiagnosis. This not only adds fresh trauma, but also can complicate or exacerbate symptoms. "Patients... are often dismissed, or misdiagnosed with relapse, or diagnosed with a new medical condition" (National Institute for Health and Care Excellence, 2020).

Many also have a history of traumatic therapeutic experiences by clinicians. There is also the layer of exploitation in case studies, traditional demonstrations, and modern presentation, all in the name of research and treatment development, but leaving patients feeling exposed by default, vulnerable at best, and violated at worst. There may be other un-intended consequences, as well.

Even in the classic painting of Charcot at the Salpêtriére, the painting on the background wall demonstrates the "swoon" that Blanche Wittman appears to be experiencing. Does the painting influence Wittman's swooning behavior? Or does it reflect the common experience observed by Charcot at the Salpêtriére? Or is it both, art reflecting science as it always has, but also some comfort of resonance for Wittman? Regardless, it is not a surprise, then, that many patients now expose themselves in similar ways on social media or YouTube, either out of trauma re-enactment, in defense of themselves, or in effort to reclaim their own story in their own words.

Further, while consent is "informed", patients do not necessarily have a voice in choosing treatment, and even that informed consent may be severely limited – patients may know about specific techniques or modalities, but not understand the critical nature of the psychodynamic process, for example. Thus, they may search for or end up with a therapist under "EMDR" or "trauma-informed", but not realize that a therapist with such tools may not actually know how to navigate relationships – which is where their trauma is going to show up, both in life and in treatment. Further, if a therapist is unaware of these issues themselves, they do not have access to the information with which to "inform" the patient as part of consent.

Therapy trauma can occur during treatment when a clinician is unaware of ruptures due to lack of psychodynamic training or not tending to relationship or transferences issues. Misattunements can also cause therapy trauma, such as a patient feeling dismissed when a therapist overrides a patient's preferences during treatment. This would include treatment planning and treatment goals, such as pushing for integration as an active goal rather than a natural process. As such, "the therapist must avoid assuming that he or she knows the correct answer in advance. The therapist's role is not to lead the client to a particular conclusion, but to walk the client step-by step through the process" (Gold, 2009).

There is also a history of oppression in the treatment setting itself that ought to be acknowledged, with the power dynamic a default in treatment if not explicitly addressed as done by more experienced clinicians. This imbalance shows up in other areas as well, including racial disparities in research – with "most research on traumagenic dissociation done on upper middle class white women plucked from private pay offices and corporate run hospitals of privilege" (Itterman, 2021). Lack of institutional courage and transparency adds to the power imbalance as well, creating collective wounds between clinicians and patients, as well as a level of betrayal trauma when not repaired. In advocating for the dignity of patients as people, Salter and Hall (2021) stated that "shame is the emotional correlate of attachment failure, child abuse and neglect; however, it is also a socially located and politically structured experience that is exacerbated by public policy, professional practice, and government-decision making."

This is the background of how Plurality developed as a culture and a movement. It takes Sassoon's 1917 *A Soldier's Declaration* and applies to the lived experience in the treatment setting (Fussell, 1983):

> "I am a [plural], convinced that I am acting on behalf of [plurals]. I have seen and endured the sufferings of the troops, and I can no longer be a party to prolong these sufferings... These [plurals] refused to be forgotten. Moreover, they refused to be stigmatized. They insisted on the rightness, the dignity of their distress."

Plurality is meant to re-establish the power of lived experience, the independence of survivors, and the community of shared experience. Historical trauma consists of three factors: the widespread nature, traumatic events resulting in a collective suffering, and the malicious intent of those inflicting the trauma (O'Neill, Fraser, Kitchenham, and McDonald, 2018). In this context, plurality address clinical microaggressions that impact treatment: ableism blocking clinicians' self-awareness of that malicious intent, the lack of cultural humility in uncovering it, and the impact on patients as additional trauma. It is a call to action in response to implicit bias in treatment, or the idea that "associations outside our conscious awareness lead to a negative evaluation of a person based on the irrelevant characteristics such as race or gender [or diagnosis]" (FitzGerald & Hurst, 2017).

In a recent interview, Kluft (2021) pointed out that, in the past, the therapy office was the only outlet and safe space to explore trauma and dissociation and the healing process. This made therapy itself a single-point focused experience, with natural pacing between sessions. Now, however, therapy is only part of a diffused-focus experience because the survivor also has access to more published works; more online resources; virtual support via tele-meeting platforms; social media groups; and peer-advocacy gatherings; blogs, podcasts, and YouTube; both professional and lived experience conferences; and organizations of resources by survivors themselves, such as Blue Knot Foundation, Beauty After Bruises, An Infinite Mind, or The Plural Association. There is a general "meaning-making process" that happens when social groups interact with each other – and emotion, specifically – which creates "new and binding understandings of social responsibility" (Alexander, et. al., 2004). This opens opportunity for patients to advocate for and participate in their own healing at a whole new level. "Playing an active role in their own recovery can be especially important for individuals with complex trauma histories, because their symptoms can reduce individual autonomy and self-direction... Clients recognize that they have the opportunity to become active agents for change in their own behalf" (Jackson, Nissenson, and Cloitre in Courtois and Ford, 2009).

There are, naturally lessons to be learned in the process. Safety is always an issue, especially with those who have already experienced trauma. It takes practice to learn safety in relationships, and that applies to online relationships – even in peer groups or support groups specific to dissociation. Psychoeducation regarding online safety is absolutely beneficial, while forbidding or preventing access may not be. It is an important developmental task for any person to learn what is useful and what is not, what is helpful and what is not, and what is beneficial and what is not. "Without this experiential foundation, the person is likely to experience instability in [not knowing] about personal preferences and values, depending instead on changes in the immediate environment and body states" (Follette, Iverson, and Ford, 2009). In the context of an experienced and educated traumatologist, and with the safety of adequate attention paid to the psychodynamic processes, such psychoeducational support adds both internal and external resources, which increases safety for the patient, resulting in improved functioning and exponential healing of traumagenic dissociation.

History of Plurality

"The systematic study of psychological trauma therefore depends on the support of a political movement... powerful enough to legitimate an alliance between investigators and patients and to counteract the ordinary social processes of silencing and denial" (Herman, 2015). The politics of Plurality developed through intersectionality with disability and LGBTQ+ groups, as well as advocacy for safer and more effective treatment. The Blind declared "we are citizens", and the Deaf declared "we have rights", and the mobility group declared "we want access", and the neurodiversity group demanded they get to decide what access looks like. The LGBTQ+ groups petitioned for keeping their rights and access, so hard-won.

From this, the Plural community cried, *Nihil de nobis, sine nobis!* – or, "Nothing for us, without us!" *Nihil de nobis, sine nobis* is a Latin slogan used to communicate the idea that no policy should be decided by any representative without the full and direct participation of members of the group(s) affected by that policy. This involves national, ethnic, disability-based, mental health, and other marginalized groups. It originated in Central European political traditions in 1505, and has since become a motto representing democratic norms and transfer of power to the people. It was used by an East European activist at an international disability rights conferences in the 1960's, and then used again in early 1970's by disability advocates Michael Masutha and William Rowland in South Africa. It was adopted in English in the 1980's by James Charlton for disability activism in America, and then taken up specifically by the GLBT community during the HIV/AIDS crisis. Charlton then published a book about its meaning and use in disability advocacy in 1998, as did David Werner. The Plural Community taking up this motto was a statement that no longer would it be acceptable to define dissociation without the lived experience component, create treatment guidelines without lived experience input, and research dissociation without diverse participants and fair compensation. The adoption of this motto was "Plurality" as radical acceptance, the "behavioral activation [as] primary mechanisms for changing trauma-related patterns..." (Follette, Iverson, and Ford, in Courtois and Ford, 2009, p, 267). It empowered Plurals to advocate for themselves, while also committing them to their own treatment in safely at a level of engagement never before seen in the history of treatment. "Acceptance involves taking things as they are and not becoming so wrapped up in trying to fix problems (or people) that obvious solutions are overlooked" (Ibid, p. 271). This new kind of dignified acceptance was a form of Pride, without the avoidance of multiplicity itself, cracking through barriers of denial and opening new opportunities for vulnerability in supportive environments of peer support during the decades of waiting for, seeking out, and finding the correct treatment and diagnosis. "To accept is not to be passively resigned or hopeless, but to be actively involved in understanding things as they are, rather than as one wishes or demands they should be" (Ibid, p. 272).

Plurality is more of a cultural designation than a clinical one, and more anthropological than psychological. It is an overall umbrella term for all those experiencing multiplicity, regardless of being from or caused by trauma, culture, religious experience, or philosophical understanding. It was originally intended to be inclusive: many people years or longer for an appropriate clinician so they can receive an accurate diagnosis; many people are aware of their experience of multiplicity, but do not have access to treatment; many people do not have privilege enough to pay for treatment; most people dissociate, even if not all people have DID; and other cultures and faith traditions include dissociation in practice, even though it is not trauma-based.

The Plural community includes a broad spectrum of internet platforms. Cultural and religious groups that practiced dissociation have always gathered since ancient times as part of their practice. People with traumagenic dissociation gathered in hospitals, group therapy, or when connected to each other through therapists.[10] When the dawn of the internet in the 1990's, they found each other in Yahoo Groups and through the newsletter Many Voices, which has since been made available to the public for free online at manyvoices.org. The original dissociative disorder online support groups moved to Facebook in the 2000's, and then dissociation hashtags developed on Twitter after that - #DIDChat is a live meeting with specific questions and discussions each week. Discussion threads began on Reddit as well, and Plurals met together on Discord. Private servers were made available as well, including Criss Ittermann's *United Front* for peer support and group coaching classes, and *The Plural Association*, an international non-profit that hosts a dissociative disorder warmline for dissociation-specific issues that most hotlines are not prepared to handle.

YouTube channels came next, presenting as people with DID, and bringing controversy with it. Some clinicians felt that all of these videos were fake, because most people with dissociation are more covert than what was displayed. Others reported cases in their office where patients were clearly copying the videos, making the patients appear fake. Others expressed concern about things like exploitation or re-enactment or over-identification with alters, all of which could impede healing.

On the other hand, some clinicians felt this level of accessibility for the general population helped fight against stigma in support of those with dissociative disorders. Some felt having free psychoeducation available

---

[10] It is important to note that traumagenic dissociation is what Plurals call "disordered Plurality", in contrast to non-disordered Plurality, as discussed further below. Please see https://pluralpedia.org/w/Dissociative_Identity_Disorder for more information.

made the videos a useful tool that could be used with some discernment. Some felt it was beneficial in helping their patients understand and accept their own diagnosis, as long as they were cautious with online safety.

Mostly recently, podcasts have become available. *System Speak* began when the "system" began to study available research as a form of education to increase understanding to accept the diagnosis of DID. There were the DID videos on YouTube, but that was not accessible for this system. They discovered only a few ongoing podcasts as a source of support, and most of what was available was episodic and general in content. Recognizing this need for an ongoing DID-related podcast, appropriate boundaries were negotiated, and they began a new podcast as a way of educating themselves and others in effort to collaborate together on a project.

System Speak was also unique in setting boundaries around what was shared and how it was presented. The podcast was not about broadcasting private details, disclosing abuse history, or working out therapeutic issues publicly – though it could be very vulnerable at times. The podcast also was for specific practice: documenting one journey, educating many, and finding their own voice. It is served the purpose of finding a way to bridge the gap between survivor and clinician through clinical interviews shared regularly. The podcast was about advocacy, fighting stigma, and adding substance and quality to the online conversation regarding complex trauma in general, and Dissociative Identity Disorder specifically.

The explosion of the Plural community into what it is happened through community organization. The Plural community developed through shared experiences online and at conferences. The timing, after decades of virtual contact, coincided with shift from the abreaction-based therapy to phased-based approach. It was as if the community itself externally adopted the emphasis on communication, cooperation, and collaboration. Plurals took what they had been asked to do internally to develop safety and stability, and they implemented it externally to create a community in a way that had never before existed. This, collectively as a culture even with its own use of language, impacts how "trauma survivors hold multiple identities simultaneously that influence their conceptualizations of trauma, therapy, and the recovery process" (Brown in Bryant-Davis, 2019). Further, when one considers the decades of a lifetime from the original trauma, to seeking an accurate diagnosis, to finding appropriate treatment, the question becomes: "Who am I while I wait for correct treatment?" Plurality provides a whole-life encompassing identity with which one can identify and function, and with which ego states can agree, regardless of the wait.

Defining Plurality

Returning to the intersectionality of disability groups, the last decade included the linguistic movement toward "person-first language" in effort to emphasize the whole person rather than traits that might identify them, such as disability diagnosis (University of Kansas, 2013). It became a matter of respect from the clinician and dignity for the patient to shift from "DID client", for example, to "person with Dissociative Identity Disorder". Even more recently, an added push against even that stigma to provide a more non-pathologizing approach in dropping the “disorder” and simply using the phrase “person with Dissociated Identities” (Coy, 2020, Brown, 2021, and McMaugh, 2021). Along with this has come the use of simple “dissociated identities” or “DI” instead of “DID”, as well as the more casual term “multiple”.

This shift was noted by the Plural community in 2018, and great discussion ensued. Concerns regarding the DI term was that it still maintained a diagnostic-based orientation. For those with lived experience, it felt confining to the therapeutic setting – which is actually a minor part of Plural lives, especially considering the decades it takes to get diagnosed and find appropriate treatment, much less the length of treatment itself. Another concern was that DI indicates a level of privilege for those who have access to treatment. Finally, the pathologizing term added to stigma while also excluding those who are not yet diagnosed; those who consider themselves multiple but not disordered; and those who consider themselves multiple without any history of trauma.

For this reason, the broader and more person-centered term of “Plural” was formally adopted in 2018 through a very intentional process in the community. There was, for the first time, extensive collaboration among support groups online. Intense debate followed, regarding a variety of proposals submitted from Plurals themselves as to what term should be used. Then there was actual voting across the different support groups and a variety of online platforms, and more than 23,000 votes were cast. The winning vote was for the term "Plural".[11]

This combined effort was so successful, that Plurals worked together again to design a public survey. This was not research-approved by any internal review board, but designed by the community for the community, with consent including the publication and sharing of non-identifiable results. This is not uncommon in Plural culture, with online public opinion polls and annual surveys as an optional part of registration with the annual Healing Together Conference put on by An Infinite Mind.

Questions and tools used for the survey were decided by voting. The community submitted the survey questions, and then they voted to approve which questions were to be included. Once it was released, there were 866 respondents who completed the survey.

Results of this survey were shared at the first "Plural Positivity World Conference" (PPWC), a new annual virtual conference put on "by Plurals for Plurals", in 2019. The results were also presented as a Poster Session in the 2020 Annual Conference of the International Society for the Study of Trauma and Dissociation (ISSTD), and publicly posted on the System Speak Podcast website (Christensen, 2020).

It is interesting to note, that even after voting to adopt "Plural" as the term of choice:

- only 27% identified as Plural;

---

[11] I do not in any way mean that the term "Plural" was invented in 2018. The term was already in use by many for years, and in 2018 the term was formally adopted by the community generally through the voting process described.

- 35% of respondents instead identified as DID; and
- 22% still identified as Multiple

This indicates less than a third actually prefer the term "Plural" for themselves, despite the advantages agreed upon in voting to adopt the term for the community as a whole. It also drew lines between Plurality as a cultural group and those who link diagnosis to "identity":

- 34% Traumagenic (I am this way because of trauma.)[12]
- 2% Endogenic (I was this way before I was born, but not because of trauma.)
- 1% Exogenic (I was this way since I was born or grew up this way, but not because of trauma.)
- 38% Traumagenic-Adaptive (I am this way because of trauma, and still use dissociation adaptively to deal with life but not necessarily intentionally and not as part of my intentional cultural expression.)
- 13% Traumagenic-Cultural (I am this way because of trauma, feel mostly in control of my symptoms, and have intentionally adapted to it as a cultural lifestyle.)

This reflects 72% were traditional DID patients (traumagenic and traumagenic-adaptive), while 14% were the new Plural presentation, but not DID (exogenic and traumagenic-cultural).

---

[12] A history of the origin of the -genic terms for Plural experiences has already been written in a guest post on the Power to the Plurals blog. See https://powertotheplurals.com/origin-of-endogenic-and-traumagenic-system-terminology-guest-post-by-the-trashcan-collective/

During the 2019 PPWC conference, Plurals also voted on politically correct terms to be more inclusive of all experiences, as well as to reduce stigma for certain types of alters. Those who had been known as "animal alters" and "alien alters" are now called "non-human alters". They also identified "introject alters" (not psychodynamic introjects), such as alters developed from books, movies, or video games, and re-named them "fictives" (discussed further below).[13]

They also set goals as a community, such as increasing the safety of online support groups (which required a new level of cooperation between admins of different groups, which had never been done before) and the development of DID Awareness Day. They also organized ways to call out misrepresentation of dissociation and multiplicity in media and lack of institutional courage following therapist violations. They also issued a call for support groups to be more inclusive of those not yet diagnosed, as well as those who reported multiplicity but did not consider themselves "disordered".

Politics of Plurality

Politics played an early part in the development of the Plural community, and the political upheaval of 2020 only increased their passion. The community began to explore intersectionality more explicitly, noting several sub-groups with high populations in the Plural community:

[13] Please also see https://pluralpedia.org/w/Faitive and also https://plurality-dictionary.fandom.com/wiki/Special:Search?query=fictive&scope=internal&navigationSearch=true

individuals with disabilities, individuals who are autistic, and individuals of the LGBTQ+ community. It was from these historical rights movements that the Plural community formed its politics, and now they adapted language from the political climate and protests in 2020.

As Plural culture really began to organize since 2018, the understanding of Plurality began to expand and evolve, bringing with it both increased inclusivity and some divisiveness. One of the biggest controversies was that in effort to be more inclusive, many quickly invited and embraced *Tulpas* — a concept originally from Tibetan Theosophy and Buddhism that was then adapted by some online and gaming communities. Tulpa is a mystic or paranormal concept of an "other" (whether a being or an object) created purposefully through intentional dissociation, but is considered to be an actual other living and sentient being separate from Self. It is not a multiple personality, but two or more beings in one body.

This concerned traumagenic Plurals for two reasons: first, historically and collectively, traumagenic Plurals have already endured the impact of the memory wars and allegations of false memories, so adding Tulpas to the mix did not feel helpful in authenticating their stories; and two, "hard science" research was just now coming out with long-awaited evidence of DID being a distinct disorder and traumagenic in nature, so including non-trauma groups as part of the same community felt incongruent with that endeavor. On the other hand, the Tulpa community was equally concerned by the pathologizing of multiplicity, especially since their online community had been around since at least 2010, "upholding it as a non-disordered variant of human cognition" (Isler, 2017). In the end, the Plural community maintained "Plural" as an umbrella term, but by 2021 has split into two camps: traumagenic Plurals diagnosed with (or waiting for a diagnosis of a dissociative disorder due to trauma, and anthropological Plurals who may or may not have a trauma background at all.

Thus, tension increased between traumagenic Plurals who are now labeled as "disordered" by anthropological Plurals who are not[14], and whom some feel have appropriated their trauma for a cultural experience. The website "Plural Deep Dive" (2022) described this:

> "The logic behind this is that since the term emerged to communicate the experience of [dissociative disoders], using the term for something that is not a [dissociative disorder] is an appropriation of those mental disorders. According to OK2TALK (2019), the appropriation of mental disorders is when people use the language of mental disorders to describe their non-disordered experiences. In an article on the subject, they express, "When people begin to appropriate mental illnesses to describe their everyday life events, those who have no knowledge of mental health will take these descriptions as gospel, thus invalidating the struggles of those who are dealing with a potentially debilitating disorder." They go on to detail the struggles that people with mental disorders face, of not being taken

[14] Kinder and more accurate terms have also been used, such as "natural Plurals" for anthropological Plurals and "survivor Plurals" for those with traumagenic dissociation. Please see https://pluraldeepdive.weebly.com/syscourse-history.html for more information.

seriously and being unable to find help, when their language is erased."[15]

Another website clarifies the distinctions between traumagenic Plurals and anthropological Plurals this way (Lee, 2020a; Lee, 2020b):

> "Within the community, there is gatekeeping [and] exclusion over who exactly is plural. Some systems don't fit the diagnostic criteria, some don't like the implication of 'brokenness', and some with more unusual plurality are made to feel 'not plural enough'. One user wondered if 'plurality & dissociation are actually two different things' - trauma [and] PTSD is the disorder - not plurality itself. This is the idea of functional multiplicity: 'plurality is a functional [...] state of being: MPD is a nonfunctional disorder'. From this perspective, plurality could be considered a neurodivergence instead of an illness."

The more alarming point is the nature by which the online syscourse unfolds (ibid).

> "In 2017, a casual survey was conducted [online] to gauge the syscourse-related opinions of Tumblr's system community.[16] Of the 128 systems who responded, 119 identified with either DID or OSDD. Excluding all self-written answers, about 84% of respondents voted that they

[15] Please see https://pluraldeepdive.weebly.com/terminology-debates.html#2b for more information on this syscourse.

[16] See full results at https://firedrake.tumblr.com/post/159769236693/syscourse-survey-results.

did not think plurals without DID/OSDD should be included in DID/OSDD spaces, and about 64% voted that they did not think non-disordered plurals should use the terms systems, alter, and multiplicity. About 58% of respondents had an experience of being harassed, threatened, or otherwise harmed by 'a syscourser on the opposing side'. This survey shared a glimpse into the particularly volatile nature of syscourse on Tumblr, rife with verbal abuse, cyber-bullying, and the encouragement of suicide."

In contrast, the Lunastus Collective wrote (2019):

"It is vital to understand that all systems, regardless of their origins, are trying to survive and thrive in a world that often is hostile to the concept of plurality. Traumagenic systems, endogenic systems, and other types of systems, all have a valuable place within the plural community, and much of the infighting seems to stem from a lack of understanding of plural history and refusing to listen to one another. Thankfully, most systems support one another and are comfortable sharing spaces that are identified as inclusive. Many systems are making an effort to preserve community history, compile accurate information on plurality, and advocate acceptance regardless of labels.

"We ourselves hope that an accurate picture of what traumagenic and endogenic means can be part of that. It's our wish to see both terms lose the negative connotations they've gained; traumagenic systems aren't all antiendogenic gatekeepers who believe you can only be plural if you have a diagnosis, and endogenic systems aren't trying to appropriate a disorder or mock trauma survivors. It is truly a shame to see this sort of discourse after a long history of relative peace, and it is especially disappointing to see terms that we created– and intended to be inclusive and helpful—being used to hurt innocent people within the plural community. We do hope that someday, the community will learn to work together again so that we may focus on the hatred and discrimination that comes from outside of the community.

"'Traumagenic' and "endogenic' come from an endogenic system that loves their community. The terms were originally a product of community infighting, but became a way to help us explain our personal origins quickly and without potentially harmful phrasing. They were never meant to divide the community; the senseless backlash against systems that don't fit a specific mold isn't based in science, but anger and misinformation. It needs to stop. We hope the community can grow to a point where we embrace systems of all origins, and judge one another by our actions and character rather than how we believe our systems formed. We hope that people will be able to use whatever terminology is accurate for them without fear. After all, we are in this together."

Review of Literature

This brings up the question of distinguishing between the two and understanding both. Most traumatologists are familiar with dissociative disorders from a psychological perspective. They may be less familiar with, or even have no idea, actually, what to do with a more anthropological presentation of Plural that is not a traditional case of traumagenic dissociative disorder. Plurality has not yet been adequately addressed in the trauma field literature beyond a few breakthrough articles and the recent research on maladaptive daydreaming, which can overlap but has different origins and is a different process (and with which Tulpas would contend on the point of what is "maladaptive"). However, it has been researched extensively in anthropological studies, which gives some insight both for a compassionate understanding as well as context.

Firstly, the literature reports it is a misconception that plurality only occurs in a traumagenic setting, and a false assumption that it is always pathological (Isler, 2017). Beginning with DSM IV, the diagnostic manuals clarified this, removing both distress and impaired functioning as requirements for a DID diagnosis (Clayton, 2005). An example of this de-pathologizing is Vergani's reflection on Husserl's approach to the theme of the person: "[As] acts of the ego come into contact with other acts of the ego, constituting a *Personenverband*, a "community of persons" or a personal bond, which is governed by the fundamental law of motivation and organized around a key term, that of the person" (2019, p. 652).

Secondly, the only research thus far on non-traumagenic multiplicity was conducted by Professor Samuel Veissiere of McGill University in his landmark paper *Varieties of Tulpa Experiences* (2015). In this study, Veizziere completed a year of observational study, providing dating on the demographic profile of the community, as well as collecing socio-cultural information and reported experiences through surveys and interviews. Isler (2017 summarized:

> "Veissiere found that tulpas are perceived to be entities distinct from one's own thoughts, with over a third of hosts reporting that their tulpas felt as real as any physical person. This is achieved in part through tulpas seeming to be independent in their emotions, cognition, and opinions. They are experienced through a mix of auditory, visual, and somatic visualizations and hallucinations. Possession, a technique that allows a tulpa to temporarily command of the body, and switching, in which the host dissociates to have an out-of-body experience while the tulpa controls the body, are widely used. There are similarities between these advanced tulpamancy techniques and the experiences of DID diagnosed folk, namely having multiple identities and dissociating from the body's actions. However, the absence of amnesia, depersonalization, and other traumagenic symptoms in most tulpamancers make these techniques a reportedly positive and mutually enjoyable experience."

Interestingly, the results of Veizziere's assessments and testing indicated that more than 25% of the tulpa community were also diagnosed with an autism spectrum disorder. Things is consistent with anecdotal reports of the high degree of intersectionality between Plurality and autism.

There are also anecdotal reports of a high degree of intersectionality between Plurality and the GLBT community, notably the trans community specifically. The only published research on this thus far is by Baker (2020), who found that Plural selves was:

> "linked with mad pride movements to reclaim pathologizing psychiatric diagnosis [DID]. This is then linked to queer theoretical and activist perspectives by considering how de-pathologizing plurality follows similar endeavors in relation to (homo)sexuality, kink, and (trans)gender. Plurality of self is related to the wider queer endeavor of challenging stable, fixed identities and critiquing neoliberal capitalist individualistic ways of comprehending the self."

Isler followed this study up with his own observational and survey research in the Tulpa community. In his results, 56% of the Tulpa community reported a mental health diagnosis or an autism spectrum disorder (2017). Of these, 79% reported their diagnosis came prior to their experiences in tulpamancy, while the rest reported their diagnosis came later and was unrelated to their tulpamancy. Only one respondent out of fifty-seven reported that prior experience in tulpamancy helped them understand their DID diagnosis that came later. Isler concluded that "It is likely that the high frequency of disorders among tulpamancers is not caused by tulpamancy being pathological in nature, but rather, the practice being especially appealing towards those already diagnosed. The survey data supports this hypothesis: 66% of respondents diagnosed with a psychopathology report that their disorder either somewhat or significantly furthered their decision to make a tulpa" (ibid).

Differentiating Diagnoses

Isler's article emphasizes the tulpa community's goal of individuals creating tulpsas for companionship. This is distinct from traumagenic DID where alters may develop alongside each other in childhood and/or without awareness of the host. With tulpamancy, these Plurals develop alters intentionally, and the cultivate relationships with them. This leads to the study by Martin, Thompson, and Lancaster, which measured relationship satisfaction between hosts and their tuplas (2020):

> "During and after this creation process, hosts not only interact with their tulpa within the mind, but often also endeavor to allow their tulpa to have partial or full control of the body, a process is referred to as "fronting" or "possession" (r/Tulpas Glossary, 2018). Notably, the tulpa is considered an autonomous being with their own distinct personality and they are thus expected to be treated as such (Kiahdaj, 2017).

While traumagenic DID develops in response to trauma and attachment issues, non-traumagenic Plurals say they began the practice because they are lonely or struggle with social anxiety and reported that their conditions improved after the creation of their tulpa (Veissiere, 2015 & 2016; Isler, 2016; Martin, Thompson, and Lancaster; 2020). Interestingly,

Martin, Thompson, and Lancaster reported that they "also examined whether the relationship between the tulpa and host was related to relationship satisfaction non-linearly" and found that "the host's perception of relationship quality level increased when the host and tulpa both scored low for each domain of the PID-5-BF. However, when the host scored higher in disinhibition than the tulpa, this was correlated with higher relationship quality."

This brings up the question of distinguishing between the two and understanding both. Most traumatologists are familiar with dissociative disorders. They may be less familiar with, or even have no idea, actually, what to do with a political Plural - especially one who denies any trauma history. However, considering any patient has a right to ethical treatment and cultural humility from the clinician, it is helpful both to clinicians and patients to be aware of and understand what a "Plural" is presenting or aspects of Plural culture that could impact culture.

First, returning to Tulpas, it is helpful for the clinician to understand that Tulpas are a concept originally from Tibetan Theosophy and Buddhism that was then adapted by some online and gaming communities. Tulpa is a mystic or paranormal concept of an "other" (whether a being or an object) created purposefully through intentional dissociation, but is considered to be an actual other living and sentient being separate from Self. It is not a multiple personality, but two beings in one body. Thus, the astral or thought projections are considered to become alive and distinct from the one projecting them, making them "Other", which gives them "Personhood". While experienced as multiplicity and sharing many common themes, it is distinguished by these others being actual people rather than alters. Some Plurals then took this and adapted it to their alters, declaring that all alters are also people, and so they should also have personhood. Most peer-reviewed literature on these issues is anthropological rather than psychological, and Plurality has not yet been adequately addressed in the trauma field beyond maladaptive daydreaming, which can overlap but has different origins and is a different process. Having the historical context for the merge of these two cultures may be helpful for the clinician to understand what the patient is presenting.

Another common theme with Plurals, whether or not they have DID, is that their alters come with extensive backstories unrelated to the host. These may be fictives or tulpas, either of which can experience their own history apart from the host. This is different from traditional DID patients, where alters usually have different aspects of a shared history connected to early traumas.

Plurals often have very rich, vivid, and highly detailed inner worlds. Many of these intentionally develop their inner worlds further on apps, video games, or in computer games like "Sims". Alters may have relationships with each other, including holding cultural or religious ceremonies (externally) to marry each other (internally). Due to the rich inner worlds, alters may have homes, families, jobs, pets, friends, or even babies in the internal world, without any of it being related at all to any specific trauma in their history. Sometimes those families, friends, employers, or babies also become new alters, including non-human alters like pets. From the sharing of these inner worlds externally, the widespread use of fictives has emerged. An example of this would be sharing *faceclaims* on social media, where an alter finds or draws a picture close to what they look like internally and post it to share with external friends or alters in other systems.

Political Plurals are called such because they often view themselves as political activists and peer support specialists. They are often anti-*sysmed*,[17] which means "system of medicine" as a reference to the treatment establishment and is a play on words from "cis-gender". "SysMed" has become a derogatory slur used against the treatment establishment, and it is used against organizations, institutions, and publications that are viewed as oppressive – or who are considered to have betrayed the community, such as having supported "cancelled clinicians". It can also be used as a form of political polarity against traumagenic DID systems who consider themselves "disordered" or "distressed" by their symptoms and so want to actively participate in treatment. It is also used against traumagenic DID systems who do not use the Plural term as part of cultural humility, and against DID systems who are against including non-trauma multiples in the Plural community.

Most often, political Plurals view treatment as oppressive and outdated at best, and violating at worst. They view clinicians as having

[17] SysMed is a reference to systemic oppression through "system exclusion". See https://pluralpedia.org/w/System_Exclusionist for more information from a Plural perspective. They report that "the term "sysmed" is modeled after the term "transmed", as both follow a similar ideology: a certain phenomenon is only valid if they fit precise medical definitions and ideals. The latter is short for "transmedicalism", and when used as a personal identifier, "transmedicalist". Though, pluralphobia did not come from transmedicalism. "Sysmed" as a term originates from Twitter in late 2019, but no specific coiner exists for it." See also https://pluraldeepdive.weebly.com/terminology-debates.html#2b

their own "fragility" or lack of cultural humility that prevents them from changing or improving their work with Plurals. They view this lack of cultural humility as unethical. They also perceive the treatment establishment to be white, male, straight, and old – and thus not representative of the people who actually need treatment.

Interestingly, they also perceive there to have been no treatment or research development over the last twenty years. They reject structural dissociation theory because it denies multiplicity, because it is incongruent with lived experience, and because they consider the theory to be "ableist". They view treatment goals to be forced rather than collaborative. They perceive complicit silence and a lack of institutional courage when well-known public faces of the establishment lose their license or have charges brought against them for boundary violations, and organization and publications that continue to support them regardless.

The advocacy work of Plurals is extensive. They are quick to embrace newly diagnosed or newly identified Plurals to offer support and psychoeducation (discussed further below). They do social media blasts to fight against stigma and normalize the Plural experience. Leaders are communicating across platforms, calling out institutions and organizations when needed, and notify the community of reported therapist violations when those are made public. They have worked to create graphics to explain treatment models and have created a resource list by country and state based on lived-experience recommendation rather than membership or advertising.

The psychoeducation provided by Plurals most commonly focuses on the prevalence of Plurality and *functional multiplicity* as an alternative to integration. There are three ways this is done in the community. First, they offer support to those without access to treatment and those who may be lower functioning and in long-term treatment. Secondly, they attempt to improve quality of life for those who are waiting for treatment, waiting for DID specific treatment, and during the long course of treatment. Third, they organize politically to empower those who don't want treatment, those who are "done" with treatment (i.e., Trudy Chase declining integration), and those who want to reclaim power from oppression (be in charge of their own treatment and what that looks like for them, specifically).

This kind of peer support shows up in a variety of ways, from social media discussions publicly to private coaching and classes, from book groups to live weekly peer support groups, from topical presentations and webinars to their own conferences. Many of the peer support leaders are licensed in the states where they live as peer support specialists. Peer support specialists are also often likely than a therapist to provide cross-field support such as working with dieticians, occupational therapists, and anthropologists). They are collaborating with other conferences, such as those for trans folx and autism conferences. They have opened the international Plural Warmline, as mentioned above. These are significant developments and supportive resources, whether or not a person has access to therapy.

Treating Plurality

One of the hottest topics currently in the field is discerning between traditional cases of DID and self-identified Plurals in the treatment context, and then second, how to treat those identifying as Plural. This author wrote (2021):

> "When applying an ethical framework to these population, foundational principles still apply: doing no harm; promoting welfare; self-determination and autonomy; fidelity, faithfulness, and keeping promises; justice, equality, and fairness; and veracity and truthfulness (American Counseling Association, 2014). Doing no harm is non-maleficence, while avoiding the doing of harm by promoting welfare is beneficence. Autonomy references the client's right to choose their own course of action, which could be referenced developmentally as self-determination. Fidelity has to do with honoring commitments made to clients, which includes adhering to the other foundational principles as described above. Justice means providing equal treatment to all people, which includes the work of acknowledging our own bias and privilege in both the therapeutic relationship and the therapeutic process. Veracity refers to being truthful and acknowledging errors rather than deceiving or participating in the microaggressions of oppression, the misattunement of dismissing lived experience from the patient's perspective or failing to grasp the impact of the patient's cultural

perspectives and meaning. These values are common to all the helping professions (Corey et al., 2010).

> "While many patients may have little to no interaction with the online Plural community, an increasing number of them will, due to younger generations' organic fluency in the online world. Lacking awareness of the development of the online community as culture for trauma survivors, and Plurals specifically, at this point could be considered maleficence, while educating oneself on the dynamic of the online community becomes simple beneficence."

Ethical treatment requires cultural humility, so that regardless of how a clinician personally feels about these modern shifts in the field, one is present for the presenting patient in the treatment setting. This begins with exploring with the client what they are experiencing and what these experiences mean to them.

Traumatalogist clinicians are more familiar with traditional traumagenic Dissociative Identity Disorder. These systems are often covert, as the whole point of dissociation in these cases is to hide in plain sight as part of survival. These patients may not even be properly diagnosed without thorough assessment, and often do not present for assessment until the level of dissociation begins to interfere with adult functioning. This is often very distressing for these patients, and they present with significant phobia of "parts" or "alters" or others inside. These alters often have very limited internal interaction, though some may be more familiar with others inside. They often have very limited awareness of any "internal world", and most often these places connect to trauma settings of the past. There is usually a subtle sense of switching that can be witnessed by a trained clinician. These systems usually are hesitant to disclose names and roles of those in the system, and there are usually a limited number of alters in the system. Some non-human alters are possible, but this is not common.

Clinicians may be less familiar with the modern Plural presentation of the younger generation. These systems are often extremely overt in presentation, and they may even announce frequent switches between alters in mid-conversation without any externally obvious dissociation or disruption in cadence noted. Plural systems are neither bothered nor distressed by their multiplicity. They may be very proud of their systems, and they may identify with such Pride on several levels. They may identify as people rather than alters, and express unique personhood. Many of these alters or persons may themselves identify as hosting their own sub-system or world internally. They often have extensive internal communities with rich and detailed inner worlds. They may have done detailed mapping already, and they may already know their entire system and all their jobs or roles and all their names and ages. There may be hundreds or thousands of alters (or people), and each of these may have their own backstories, some of which come from fictive sources such as movies or video games. This gives Plurals a unique and distinct presentation, which is actually part of what they are presenting: their right to exist, their right to define meaning for themselves, their right to demand what treatment looks like for them.

Giving a patient voice in their own treatment is not without precedent. Gold (in Courtois and Ford, 2009) noted that "clients were allowed to guide staff to what was important to them..." He also emphasized that such experiences of "safety, and a sense of security... connection" were tasks being developed for the first time in the therapeutic setting, rather than reclaimed or re-established. "This is particularly salient in the treatment of patients with complex traumatic stress disorder[s], because the "injury" for which they seek treatment is essentially an interpersonal one..." (Jackson, Nissenson, and Cloitre, 2009).

This applies even to goals for treatment, such as whether to choose "integration" or not. "The role of the therapist in this enterprise is to guide the client through the process of thinking something through to a conclusion, while leaving the outcome or actual conclusion in the hands of the client" (Gold in Courtois and Ford, 2009). The exploring of such paths, both for functioning and for treatment, could be a useful season to utilize peer recovery coaches (PRC's) in the process. PRC's can be integrated into general medical settings, may support reduced acute care utilization and increased treatment engagement, and may be an impactful and potentially cost-effective addition to the care team (Magisdon, 2021). Consultations with clinicians who have lived experience may also be useful in similar ways.

At the annual conference for the International Society for the Study of Trauma and Dissociation (ISSTD) in 2021, this author proposed changes in the phase-based treatment model. This included recommendations to shifting from three-phases to four-phases. Just as the early 90's included abreactive work that did not adequately address safety and stabilization, current treatment models do not adequately provide time and space for functional multiplicity as a natural and supported part of an intentional process of healing. The *four-phase treatment model for plurality* moves the traditional phase three of treatment to phase four and inserts an additional phase as a new phase three, focusing on functional multiplicity.

This four-phase model takes a relational approach to phase one, including shame work as part of safety and stabilization. Somatic work is emphasized in phase two. Phrase three becomes about practice and rehearsal about holding both (object relations development), finding the grey, tolerating emotional responses, and building social connections. That leaves four to strengthen the emerging Self: this is who I am, this is what I know, this is what I think, this is how I feel, and this is what I choose in response. This four-phase model provides improved support for increased functioning while the patient develops skills of organizing Self internally and in context of the external world.

In this way, the model builds developmental tasks into the structure and process of therapy itself. Phase one becomes about "Your Presence" – with "your" being the therapist and safe support people, which helps develop health dependence, provides psychoeducation, rehearses pattern recognition, and builds the traditional skills for safety and stabilization. Phase two becomes "Their Presence" – which is about holding presence with selves (internally) and others (externally), and includes somatic integration, bilateral work, expressive work, peer support, and building external community. Phase three becomes about "Our Presence" – which includes a collective experience of Self (internally) and active rehearsal of Self-in-the-World as they practice presence, healthy independence, giving and receiving comfort, tolerating exposures to the past while in the present, and independent utilization of support system and coping skills. Finally, phase four becomes about "My Presence" – with an experience of Self that includes awareness of aspects, parts, or alters that previously were foreign, denied, or dissociated; maintaining functioning while also experiencing memories, emotions, and/or interactions; demonstrating healthy and flexible boundaries, self-protection without exclusive avoidance or phobias; and providing attuned responsiveness both internally and externally. These four phases of this treatment model for plurality provide a healing experience that integrate awareness, memories, emotions, and body in natural and responsive ways without having to be overly narrow or oppressive about how end-treatment goals are defined.

Even still, there are some Plurals who present as being asymptomatic. They report they are functioning well and are not distressed by their multiplicity. If they are functioning well and not distressed by their experience of multiplicity, then they are not "disordered" and treatment guidelines do not apply to them (Christensen, 2019; Barach, 2021). Because the treatment guidelines do not apply to them, their input is not needed for the development of treatment guidelines (Barach, 2020).

In addition, self-identified plurals reporting no trauma history have not been researched, and no standardized assessments have been developed for them. Therefore, they do not meet criteria for Dissociative Identity Disorder (Barach, 2021). Thus again, the treatment guidelines do not apply, nor do they need to be included in guideline development.

This still provides space, however, to identify and recognize the group in literature as part of cultural humility (Christensen, 2021). Further, such Plurals may still safely seek ethical and appropriate treatment for alternative conditions, such as depression or anxiety (Barach, 2020). This still supports the idea of Plurality as radical acceptance, where "to accept is not to be passively resigned or hopeless, but to be actively involved in understanding things as they are, rather than as one wishes or demands they should be" (Follette, Iverson, and Ford, in Courtois and Ford, 2009, p. 272).

Ultimately, the clinical discussion regarding Plurality comes back to understanding our own roles as clinicians, the lived experience of patients seeking help, the shared reality in the relationship we share within that sacred space between us, and their ongoing experience of everyday life outside our office setting. In personal communication with this author regarding these topics, John O'Neil summarized it beautifully through a philosophical framework in regards to what we know and how we know it (2022), laying out a six stage sequence:

1. Ontology, or what is really real, in that a given human being essentially is from a structure or system point of view (i.e., singleton; true DID with some amnesia for some switching; or plural as a singleton with 'subpersonalities', or plural with an ego-state disorder, or true plural without amnesia;
2. Etiology, or how that specific structure originated (i.e., congenitally, at birth, like right- or left-handedness; after birth, but as a 'voluntary' choice; Paul Dell's current theory of autohypnotic

capability as a necessary but insufficient cause; or trauma with or without deficit/attachment disorder as a necessary but insufficient cause such as described by the standard theory, structuralists, et al.);

3. Ontogeny, or how the structure evolves over time, such as through further trauma, attachment disorders, or other deficits, or through willful creative elaboration such as with everyday adaption, practice, or fictive development;
4. Epistemology, or what is supposed, assumed, believed, 'discovered', or 'known' about the structure and by whom (the host, alters, and the clinician), which then clarifies the first three understandings and involves an interplay with what is allowed to be supposed, 'discovered' or 'known' by whom;
5. Teleology, or the therapeutic goals of various system members and clinician toward which one might aspire, keeping in mind that the extent to which any system member speaks for all system members is variable, and something to continually wonder about; and
6. Ethics, objectively speaking, in that there is likely a "best outcome" for the system, and no clinician nor system member can be sure about what it may yet be as treatment unfolds.

That being clarified, there is also something to hope to progress towards, as part of the esthetic spectrum, that "feels" better to the system and can be encouraged by the clinician. In that context, "at one end of the spectrum, for non-traumagenic asymptomatic plurals, they are already there, and 'if it works, don't fix it'" (O'Neil, 2022). These plurals may simply need support in navigating life and other issues as much as any other patient who requests treatment in a clinical setting. "At the other end of the spectrum, there is DID with its multiplicity of ages, genders, functions, degrees of traumatization and symptoms, and somewhat miserable functioning in the 'real' world" (ibid) that may need significant treatment intervention to increase system access for all system members as needed, to reduce distressing complex trauma responses, and to improve quality of life in ways meaningful for each system as the treatment outcome. All systems, regardless of origin or structure development, have the right to seek treatment and to receive it with dignity, and all clinicians are ethically bound with the solemn responsibility to care well for them respectfully and compassionately.

REFERENCES

Alexander, J., Eyerman, R., Giesen, B., Smelser, N.J., Sztompka, P. 2004. Cultural Trauma and Collective Identity. University of California Press.

American Counseling Association. 2014. ACA Code of Ethics. Alexandria, VA.

American Psychological Association. 2017. Ethical principles of psychologists and code of conduct.

Bailey, T. D., & Brand, B. L. (2017). Traumatic dissociation: Theory, research, and treatment. Clinical Psychology: Science and Practice, 24(2), 170–185.

Barach, P. 2021. Personal Communication and Podcast Interviews. System Speak: A Podcast About Dissociative Identity Disorder.

Bentley, R (1860). Hungary, from 1848 to 1860.

Bigelsen, J., Lehrfeld, J.M., Jopp, D. S., Somer,E. 2016. Maladaptive daydreaming: Evidence for an under-researched mental health disorder, Consciousness and Cognition, Volume 42, Pages 254-266.

Boon, S., Steele, K., van der Hart, O. 2011. Coping with Trauma-Related Dissociation: Skills Training for Therapists and Patients. New York: W. W. Norton & Company.

Brand, B.L., Schielke, H.J., Putnam, K.T., Putnam, F.W., Loewenstein, R.J., Myrick, A., Jepsen, E.K.K., Langeland, W., Steele, K., Classen, C.C. and Lanius, R.A. (2019), An Online Educational Program for Individuals With Dissociative Disorders and Their Clinicians: 1-Year and 2-Year Follow-Up. Journal of Traumatic Stress, 32: 156-166.

Brown, L.S. 2008. Cultural competence in trauma therapy: Beyond the flashback. American Psychological Association.

Bryant-Davis T. 2019. The cultural context of trauma recovery: Considering the posttraumatic stress disorder practice guideline and intersectionality. Psychotherapy, 56(3):400-408.

Charlton, James I (1998). Nothing About Us Without Us. University of California Press.

Chiao, J.Y., Hariri, A.R., Harada, T., Mano, Y., Sadato, N., Parrish, T. B., and Iidaka, T. 2010. Theory and methods in cultural neuroscience, Social Cognitive and Affective Neuroscience, 5(2-3):356–361.

Christensen, 2021. The online community: DID and plurality. European Journal of Trauma & Dissociation, Volume 6, Issue 2.

Christensen, E. 2020. The Plural Positivity World Conference 2019 Survey Results Presented as Poster Session at the 2020 Annual Conference for the International Society for the Study of Trauma and Dissociation (ISSTD). San Francisco and Online. Retrieved 12 February 2021 online ISSTD CONFERENCE POSTER SESSION 2020: The 2019 PPWC Survey Results — System Speak.

Corey, G., Corey, M.S., Callahan, P. 2010. Issues and Ethics in The Helping Professions. New York: Brooks-Cole.

Courtois, C.A. and Brown, L.S. 2019. Guideline orthodoxy and resulting limitations of the American Psychological Association's Clinical Practice Guideline for the Treatment of PTSD in Adults. Psychotherapy, 56(3):329-339.

Coy, M. 2020. EMDR Training Class. International Society for the Study of Trauma and Dissociation. Online.

Davies, Norman (1984). Heart of Europe: The Past in Poland's Present. Oxford University Press.

ethics. 2021. In Dictionary.com. Retrieved 12 February 2021, from https://www.dictionary.com/ethics.

ethics. 2021. In Merriam-Webster.com. Retrieved 12 February 2021, from https://www.merriam-webster.com/dictionary/ethics.

Follette, V.M., Iverson, K. M., and Ford, J. D. 2009. Contextual Behavior Trauma Therapy (pp. 264-285) in Courtois, C.A. and Ford, J.D. (eds). Treating Complex Traumatic Stress Disorders. New York, New York: The Guilford Press.

Gold, S. 2009. Contextual Therapy (pp. 227-242) in Courtois, C.A and Ford, J.D. (eds). Treating Complex Traumatic Stress Disorders. New York, New York: The Guilford Press.

Harvey, M. R. & Tammala-Nara, P. 2007. Sources and expression of resilience in trauma survivors: Ecological theory, multicultural perspectives. Journal of Aggression, Maltreatment, & Trauma, 14(1-2), 1-7.

Henning, J.A. and Brand, B.L. 2019. Implications of the American Psychological Association's posttraumatic stress disorder treatment guideline for trauma education and training. Psychotherapy, 56(3):422-430.

Herman, J. 2015. Trauma and Recovery: The Aftermath of violence – from domestic abuse to political terror. New York: Basic Books.

Hicks, D. 2011. Dignity: The Essential Role it Plays in Resolving Conflict. New Haven and London: Yale University Press.

Hicks, D. 2015. A matter of dignity: Building human relationships. In Levine, S.S. (Ed.), Dignity Matters; Psychoanalytic and Psychosocial Perspectives (pp. 1-21). London:

Karnac. Jackson, C., Nissenson, K., and Cloitre, M. 2009. Cognitive-Behavioral Therapy (pp. 243-263) in Courtois, C.A. and Ford, J.D. (eds). Treating Complex Traumatic Stress Disorders. New York, New York: The Guilford Press.

Kezelman C.A. & Stavropoulos P.A. (2012) Practice Guidelines for Treatment of Complex Trauma and Trauma Informed Care and Service Delivery. Blue Knot Foundation.

Kezelman C.A. & Stavropoulos P.A. (2019) Practice Guidelines for Clinical Treatment of Complex Trauma. Blue Knot Foundation

Kezelman C.A. & Stavropoulos P.A. (2019) Complementary Guidelines to Practice Guidelines for Clinical Treatment of Complex Trauma. Blue Knot Foundation

Kitayama, S. and Cohen, D. 2007. Handbook of Cultural Psychology. New York, NY: Guilford Press.

Kluft, R. P. 2020. Podcast Interview. System Speak: A Podcast About Dissociative Identity Disorder. Fall 2021.

Kluft, R. P. 2021. Personal Communication, used with permission.

Lee, LB. 2020a (June 30). Quick'n'Dirty Plural History. Part 3: Usenet and its spin-offs and Soulbonders. Website. https://lb-lee.dreamwidth.org/1120824.html. Cited on https://polychordal.wixsite.com/bones/plural-history. Accessed 5 March 2022.

Lee, LB. 2020b (August 31) Quick'n'Dirty Plural History. Part 4 (LJ, the Genic Slapfight, and THE END!). Website. https://lb-lee.dreamwidth.org/1129216.html. Cited on https://polychordal.wixsite.com/bones/plural-history. Accessed 5 March 2022.

Lunastus Collective. 2019. Origin of Endogenic System and Traumagenic System Terminology. Blog: Power to the Plurals. https://powertotheplurals.com/origin-of-endogenic-and-traumagenic-system-terminology-guest-post-by-the-trashcan-collective/. Accessed 5 March 2022.

McMaugh, Kate. 2021. Personal Communication

Muller-Vahl, K. R., Pisarenko, A., Jakubovski, E., Fremer,C. August 2021. Stop that! It's not Tourette's but a new type of mass sociogenic illness, Brain.

Norenzayan, A. and Heine, S.J. 2005. Psychological universals: What are they and how can we know?, Psychological Bulletin, vol. 135 (pg. 763-84).

ok2talk. 2019. Stop Appropriating My Mental Disorders [Blog post]. Retrieved from ok2talk.org/post/183634210655/stop-appropriating-my-mental-disorders.

O'Neil, J. 2021. Personal Communication and Podcast Interview. System Speak: A Podcast About Dissociative Identity Disorder.

Olvera, C., Stebbins, G.T., Goetz, C.G. and Kompoliti, K. (2021), TikTok Tics: A Pandemic Within a Pandemic. Mov Disord Clin Pract, 8: 1200-1205.

Piekiewicz, I. J., Bańbura-Nowak, A., Tomalski, R., Boon, S. 2021. Revisiting False-Positive and Imitated Dissociative Identity Disorder. Frontiers in Psychology, volume 12.

Reinders, S. 2020. The Aetiology and Neurobiology of Dissociative Identity Disorder. Presented at International Society for the Study of Trauma and Dissociation Annual Conference. Online.

Reuben, K. E., Stanzione, C. M., Singleton, J. L. 2021. Interpersonal Trauma and Posttraumatic Stress in Autistic Adults. Autism in Adulthood, Vol. 3, No. 3

Salter, M. and Hall, H. 2021. Reducing Shame, Promoting Dignity: A Model for the Primary Prevention of Complex Post-Traumatic Stress Disorder, Trauma Violence Abuse, forthcoming.

Sándor, A., Bugán, A., Nagy, A. et al. 2021. Childhood traumatization and dissociative experiences among maladaptive and normal daydreamers in a Hungarian sample. Current Psychology.

Smogorzewski, Kazimierz (1938). "Poland's Foreign Relations". The Slavonic and East European Review. 16 (48): 558–571.

Soffer-Dudek, N. and Somer, Eli. 2018. Trapped in a Daydream: Daily Elevations in Maladaptive Daydreaming Are Associated With Daily Psychopathological Symptoms. Frontiers in Psychiatry, volume 9, p. 194.

Somer, E. (2002). Maladaptive daydreaming: A qualitative inquiry. Journal of Contemporary Psychotherapy, 32(2), 195-210.

Somer, E., Somer, L., & Jopp, D. S. (2016a). Parallel lives: A phenomenological study of people struggling with maladaptive daydreaming. Journal of Trauma and Dissociation, 17, 561-576.

Somer, E., Somer, L., & Jopp, D. S. (2016b). Childhood antecedents and maintaining factors in maladaptive daydreaming. Journal of Nervous and Mental Diseases, 24, 471-478.

Somer, E., Somer, L., Jopp, D. S. 2015. Parallel lives: A phenomenological study of the lived experience of maladaptive daydreaming. Journal of Trauma and Dissociation, pp. 561-576.

Steele, K. 20 February 2021. Calming the Inner Critic: Working with Punitive Introjects, Ego States, and Dissociative Parts. Envision Webinar. Online.

Steinberg, M. and Schnall, M. 2001. The Stranger in the Mirror: Dissociation – The Hidden Epidemic. New York: Harper.

Sunflower. Blog: Plural Deep Dive. https://pluraldeepdive.weebly.com/about.html. Accessed 5 March 2022.

The University of Kansas Research and Training Center on Independent Living. (2013). Guidelines: How to Write and Report About People with Disabilities (8th Edition). Kansas City: University of Kansas.

van der Hart, O. 2021. Trauma-related dissociation: An analysis of two conflicting models, European Journal of Trauma & Dissociation, Volume 5, Issue 4.

Vera, A. Z., Bruce, A., Garris, J., Tochen, L. Bhatia, P., Lehman, R. K., Lopez, W. Wu, S. W., Gilbert, D. L. Pre-Print, September 2021. The phenomenology of tics and tic-like behavior in TikTok. MedixIV BMJ Yale.

World Health Organization (2020). International statistical classification of diseases and related health problems (11th ed.).

Other Books from SYSTEM SPEAK

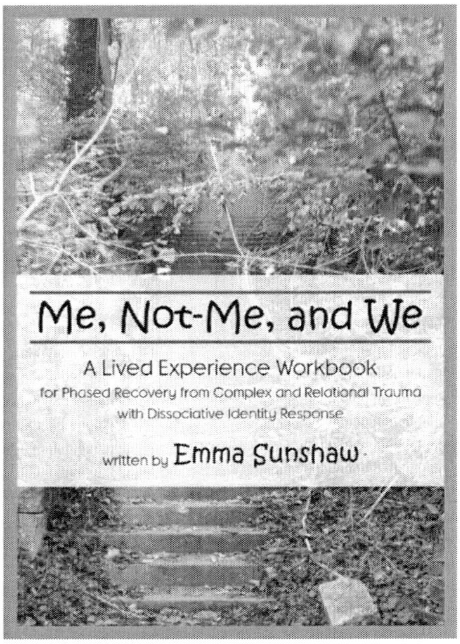

Me, Not-Me, and We
A Lived Experience Workbook
For Phased Recovery
from Complex and Relational Trauma
with Dissociative Identity Response

by Emma Sunshaw

if tears were prayers
a life with dissociative identity disorder

by Emma Sunshaw

SYSTEM SPEAK Podcast

Available on All Major Platforms

Made in United States
North Haven, CT
11 November 2026

22199106R00282